Inside the Social Studies Classroom

"... a much-needed addition to elementary social studies that will move the field ahead."

Keith C. Barton, University of Cincinnati

"This text fills a valuable niche and should quickly become a leading reference for teachers and teacher educators."

Linda S. Levstik, University of Kentucky

This book, resulting from a collaboration among an educational psychologist, a social studies educator, and a primary teacher, describes in rich detail and illustrates with excerpts from recorded lessons how primary teachers can engage their students in social studies lessons and activities that are structured around powerful ideas and have applications to their lives outside of school. The teaching portrayed connects concepts and skills emphasized in national and state standards, taught in ways that build on students' prior experiences in their local communities and connect with their family backgrounds and home cultures.

The analyses include rich descriptions of the teacher-student interactions that occur during lessons, detailed information about how and why the teacher adapted lesson plans to meet her students' background experiences and adjusted these plans to take advantage of teachable moments that emerged during lessons, and what all of this might imply concerning principles of practice. The principles are widely applicable in elementary schools across the country, as well as across the curriculum (not just in social studies) and across the elementary grades (not just the primary grades).

Jere Brophy is University Distinguished Professor of Teacher Education and Educational Psychology, Michigan State University.

Janet Alleman is Professor of Teacher Education, Michigan State University.

Barbara Knighton is an Early Elementary Educator, Waverly Community Schools, Michigan.

Inside the Social Studies Classroom

Jere Brophy
Janet Alleman
Barbara Knighton

Routledge
Taylor & Francis Group

NEW YORK AND LONDON

First published 2009
by Routledge
270 Madison Ave, New York, NY 10016

Simultaneously published in the UK
by Routledge
2 Park Square, Milton Park, Abingdon, Oxon OX14 4RN

Routledge is an imprint of the Taylor & Francis Group, an informa business

Typeset in Gill Sans and Sabon by
Keystroke, 28 High Street, Tettenhall, Wolverhampton
Printed and bound in the United States of America on acid-free paper by
Edwards Brothers, inc

Library of Congress Cataloging in Publication Data
Brophy, Jere E.
  Inside the social studies classroom/Jere Brophy, Janet Alleman,
  Barbara Knighton.
      p. cm.
  1. Social sciences—Study and teaching (Primary)
  I. Alleman, Janet.   II. Knighton, Barbara.   III. Title.
  LB1530.B764 2008
  372.83—dc22   2007052732

ISBN10: 0–8058–5571–8 (hbk)
ISBN10: 0–8058–5572–6 (pbk)
ISBN10: 0–203–92945–4 (ebk)

ISBN13: 978–0–8058–5571–5 (hbk)
ISBN13: 978–0–8058–5572–2 (pbk)
ISBN13: 978–0–203–92945–2 (ebk)

For all their support throughout the years,
we dedicate this book to Arlene Pintozzi Brophy,
George Trumbull, and Keith Knighton

Contents

Preface

This book is a product of years of collaborative research, development, and reflection on teaching conducted by a team consisting of a researcher on teaching, a social studies educator, and a primary teacher. It describes in rich detail and illustrates with excerpts from recorded lessons how primary teachers can engage their students in social studies lessons and activities that are structured around powerful ideas that have applications to their lives outside of school. The teaching features concepts and skills emphasized in national and state standards and in the guidelines published by organizations concerned with teaching of history, geography, and the social sciences. Yet it is planned and developed to build on students' prior experiences in the local community and connect with their family backgrounds and home cultures.

The team's collaboration culminated in the kind of research that produces findings of most interest and value to teachers and teacher educators: fine-grained analysis of exemplary teaching. The work began with development of instructional units that were suited to the developmental stages and prior knowledge levels of primary students, yet much more coherent and powerful than what is found in the major publishers' textbook series. The next step involved audiotaping and observing an exemplary primary teacher who adapted the units to her students' personal backgrounds and taught them in her classroom. The resulting sets of transcripts and supporting field notes, compiled over several years, then were analyzed by team members to discover what occurred in detail and induce principles of good practice.

These analyses were unusually penetrating, including not only rich description of the teacher–student interaction that occurred during lessons, but detailed information about how and why the teacher adapted the lesson plans to her students' needs and background experiences, how and why she adjusted these plans to take advantage of teachable moments or react to other events that developed during teaching, and what all of this might imply concerning principles of practice.

The teacher worked in a school serving primarily working-class and lower-middle-class students of mixed racial and ethnic backgrounds, so the principles of practice derived from research in her classroom are likely to be applicable in most elementary schools in the United States. In addition, as will be seen when reading the details, most of the principles developed from this work are applicable to teaching across the curriculum (not just in social studies) and across the elementary grades (not just the primary grades). They have special relevance for situations in which teachers are working to establish an initial knowledge base when students' relevant prior knowledge is limited and disconnected.

The book focuses on the planning and instructional decision making of an exemplary teacher. The supporting analyses ground her practice in principles from curriculum and instruction, educational psychology, and related sources of relevant theory and research. They are designed to develop coherent understanding and appreciation of the subtleties of her practice, synthesized in enough detail to allow preservice and inservice teacher-readers to understand it well enough to be able to apply it in their own teaching—not just by rote imitation, but adapting it to their own students and teaching circumstances.

Although not written as a textbook, the book should be useful as a text for courses in preschool and primary education or elementary social studies education. It also will be useful to elementary (especially primary) teachers who recognize that their social studies program is not as powerful as it might be and are looking for ways to improve it.

The book is rich with explanations and examples relating to both the content (structured around powerful ideas) and the processes (lessons and activities that connect to students' prior experiences and have application to their lives outside of school) involved in powerful social studies programs for young learners. To help readers understand the principles and adapt them for application to their particular teaching situations, it concludes with an Appendix that features reflection questions and application activities.

This is one of two books developed from the collaborative work described briefly here in the Preface and at greater length in the first chapter. It focuses on issues related directly to teaching social studies to young children. The second volume, currently in preparation, will focus on more general principles of teaching young learners effectively (establishing a learning community, managing the classroom, motivating students to learn, and so on).

Acknowledgments

We wish to thank the colleagues, students, and teachers who have collaborated with our work and enriched our understanding of classroom teaching and learning. This includes the faculty and staff of the College of Education at Michigan State University, an institution that exemplifies the concept of learning community and nurtures groundbreaking and collaborative work such as ours.

We also wish to express our appreciation to two individuals who provided vital text processing support to the project. June Benson was our secretary throughout most of the years of our collaboration. She consistently handled manuscript preparation and other normal secretarial tasks with efficiency and good humor, and, in addition, produced remarkably complete and accurate transcriptions of observational field notes and audiotapes of classroom lessons. Her successor, Amy Peebles, has continued to provide us with very high-quality text processing support, including preparation of the manuscript for this book.

We also wish to thank the administrative staff of the Waverly Community Schools for supporting our research and work together, especially Ruth Foster, the principal who first suggested and supported our collaboration. We also thank the families of Barbara's students over the years who agreed to allow their children to participate in our research.

Finally, Barbara would like to thank her husband, Keith, for being the one to say, "You should be a teacher if that's what makes you happy," and also for allowing his life to be an ongoing social studies lesson, complete with photos, vacations, and innumerable conversations devoted to developing big ideas with young learners.

Chapter 1

Introduction

This book is about teaching social studies in the primary grades (K–3). It offers a detailed analysis of both the curricular and the instructional aspects of primary social studies, illustrated with excerpts from audiotapes recorded in first- and second-grade classrooms. It demonstrates the feasibility of providing primary students with a much more substantive and coherent introduction to social education than they usually receive, and shows how a skilled teacher connects this content base to her students' prior knowledge and home cultures and develops it with emphasis on understanding, appreciation, and life application.

The Need to Improve Primary Social Studies

There is a need for this kind of resource because most elementary teachers are not well prepared to teach social studies by their preservice teacher education programs and do not receive much help from the instructional materials commonly supplied to them by their districts. Their preservice preparation usually focuses heavily on basic skills instruction in literacy and mathematics, reflecting the emphasis in most school districts' elementary curriculum guides, daily schedules, and testing programs. Future teachers typically take only one course in social studies education, often taught by a general elementary educator, a literacy educator, or someone else who is not a social studies specialist. This limited exposure usually is not enough to equip elementary teachers with a clear vision of social studies as a school subject with its own purposes, goals, and content base.

Some elementary teachers manage to develop expertise as social educators by enrolling in master's degree programs in social studies education or by systematically developing their knowledge of the subject. Most continue to focus on literacy and mathematics, however, so they lean heavily on the instructional materials provided by their districts as they plan their social studies programs. These materials include an adopted textbook series (typically purchased from one of four major publishers) supplemented by maps, globes, videos, or fictional and nonfictional children's literature selections that relate to the social studies topics taught at their grade level.

Limited exposure to social studies content in their preservice teacher education, combined with the low priority that school districts typically assign to inservice professional development in elementary social studies, leaves most elementary teachers poorly prepared to assess instructional resources, identify the most worthwhile ones, and use them in ways that support their students' progress toward major social studies goals. They think that familiarizing themselves with the content of the textbooks and following the guidelines they expect to find in the teachers' editions will enable them to provide good social studies lessons and activities.

This is not true, for two reasons. First, teachers tend to trust the textbook series because they assume that they are produced by experts who provide authoritative content and classroom-tested activity suggestions. However, the textbooks' content and activity suggestions leave much to be desired. The kindergarten and first-grade texts are mostly picture books with very little prose content. There is more prose in the second-grade texts, and its density increases at each subsequent grade. However, this content does not consist of networks of connected information structured around big ideas (which would make it both worth learning and relatively easy to learn). Instead, it consists of parades of disconnected facts that provide a "trivial pursuit" or "mile-wide but inch-deep" curriculum. Most of the suggested activities are similarly trivial—related to the topic but not designed to develop big ideas with an eye toward application to life outside of school. (The same is true of most videos and instructional resources accessible via the internet.)

Second, the teachers' manuals do not provide much help. They may highlight new vocabulary words or suggest topic-related activities or children's books, but they usually do not identify key ideas or guide teachers in systematically developing these ideas for understanding, appreciation, and life application.

The states provide curriculum standards in social studies, but their primary-grade guidelines usually are relatively limited and vague. School districts also establish standards, but these mostly reflect the states' standards. Consequently, relatively little is specifically mandated, and primary teachers show a great deal of variability in the amounts of time they allocate to social studies and in the content and activities they include in their social studies curricula.

Because the content base is so thin, it does not take teachers long to work through it, even if they use all of the activities suggested in the manual and any worksheets or other support material that may come with it. Faced with accountability pressures and testing programs that emphasize basic literacy and mathematics skills, some teachers teach social studies during only six or eight weeks of the school year. Most do more than that, typically by teaching about core democratic values and by supplementing the textbook content with the *holiday curriculum*—the civic socialization, historical re-creations, and other school activities traditionally associated with Columbus Day, Thanksgiving, the birthdays of George Washington, Abraham Lincoln, and Martin Luther King, Jr., and other special days that provide occasions for developing students' knowledge about American history and socializing their values as American citizens. Finally, many teachers supplement the text-based social studies curriculum through some of the literature selections and writing assignments they include in their literacy curriculum.

However, even a content base that includes the textbook, holiday activities, and social education-related children's literature selections will not lead to a coherent and powerful social studies curriculum, because these sources are long on trivia but short on meaningful development of connected big ideas. *Providing primary students with a more powerful introduction to social education will require both a content base that is structured around big ideas and teaching that emphasizes the connections among these ideas and their applications to life outside of school.* The authors have been working to develop curriculum and instruction that meet these criteria. We will present the theory and research that informs our work in the following chapter, but first we want to tell you about the collaboration that produced the work.

Our Partnership

This is one of two books developed through a unique collaboration between two university professors and a primary-grade teacher. Jere Brophy is a developmental and educational psychologist whose work prior to the collaboration focused on teachers' expectations and attitudes as they related to their patterns of interaction with their students, classroom management, student motivation, and generic aspects of effective teaching that cut across grade level and subject matter. Janet Alleman is a social studies educator whose previous work focused on curriculum, instruction, and assessment in elementary social studies and the teaching of undergraduate and graduate courses in social studies education. Barbara Knighton is a classroom teacher who has worked with primary students for fifteen years and enjoys a local reputation for doing so very successfully.

Collaborations between professors and teachers are likely to be productive in any subject, but they are especially needed in social studies because these two groups of educators often hold conflicting views about best practice. For one thing, teachers often are more satisfied with social studies textbooks than social studies education professors are (Brophy *et al.*, 1991b; Hinitz, 1992; Marker & Mehlinger, 1992). Many elementary teachers may not notice or be concerned by the texts' coherence problems and lack of focus on big ideas, because they are oriented more toward students than subject matter. They typically favor a traditional, "training" approach to citizenship education, which involves teaching a broad range of facts and inculcating traditional and locally favored values. In contrast, professors tend to emphasize concepts and generalizations drawn from the disciplines, teaching less content in greater depth and with more emphasis on application, and a critical stance toward values and traditions (but with acceptance of core democratic values such as justice, equality, responsibility, freedom, diversity, and privacy).

Professors tend to criticize teachers for relying too much on textbooks, teaching isolated facts and skills without enough emphasis on coherent structures and application opportunities, being overly accepting of textbook content as valid, teaching in ways that inculcate uncritically positive attitudes toward the nation and the status quo, and being unjustifiably pessimistic about what students are capable of learning. Teachers tend to criticize professors for being too academic and middle class in their orientation, overemphasizing generalizations from the disciplines while underemphasizing humanistic or value elements and content that is important in the students' lives or currently in the news, underemphasizing the need for direct teaching to develop a strong base of concepts and factual information before undertaking problem solving, and overemphasizing experimentation, inquiry/discovery, or other approaches to teaching that are either impractical for classroom use or not worth the time and trouble they require (Leming, 1989; Shaver, 1987; Stanley, 1985).

Our collaboration bridges these tensions in ways that address the concerns of both professors and teachers and lead to powerful social studies programs for young students. It had its origins in the 1980s, when Jere and Jan began working together on research relating to elementary social studies. Their initial research involved fine-grained analysis and critique of elementary social studies textbook series, looking comprehensively at their instructional goals, content selection and representation, questions and activities suggested as ways to develop the content, and assessment components. These studies confirmed and elaborated on previous findings that the textbook series are very limited as social studies instructional resources. Working inductively from their critiques, and paying attention to what was effective as well as what was ineffective, Jere and Jan developed a teacher education textbook (Brophy & Alleman, 1996, 2007) and articles on improving elementary social studies curriculum, instruction, and assessment (Alleman & Brophy, 1993, 1994a, b, 1998a, b, 1999a, b, 2000, 2002, 2003a, b, 2004, 2006; Alleman *et al.* 1999, 2003, 2007; Brophy & Alleman, 1991, 1993, 1998; Brophy *et al.*, 2000).

Textbooks and teachers' manuals are just resources, however; it is teachers who shape and implement the curricula that students actually experience in their classrooms (Thornton, 2005). Recognizing this, Jere and Jan shifted their focus from analyses of instructional materials to analyses of ongoing classroom instruction. They began observing in primary-grade classrooms during social studies lessons, recording detailed field notes on the spot and audiotaping to allow subsequent analysis of transcripts. Their intention was to identify classrooms in which powerful social studies teaching was occurring, analyze this teaching in detail, and then induce models or sets of principles that captured the essence of this teaching and could be incorporated into teacher education programs. This approach had been used successfully in research on literacy, mathematics, and science instruction, and was expected to be productive in research on social studies instruction as well.

Searching for a Feasible Method

However, implementing this idea proved to be a long and complicated process. First, Jere and Jan were unable to find primary teachers who provided powerful social studies instruction on a consistent basis. This was true even though the teachers they observed had very good local reputations and had been recommended by university colleagues, school administrators, fellow teachers, parents, or others who had direct familiarity with their work. And, in fact, these teachers generally were quite good—in everything but social studies. Their social studies programs tended to be weak for the reasons mentioned previously.

Some of them recognized this and confessed that they did not have a clear vision of social studies purposes and goals, so they tended to lean heavily on the textbook series, supplemented with activities they picked up from colleagues, teacher magazines, or other sources. Others were not even aware that their social studies instruction was not very powerful because it was not focused around a coherent set of major goals and big ideas. The importance of this had never been made clear to them, so they thought they were doing very good social studies teaching because they included a lot of hands-on activities. Many of those activities required a great deal of classroom time but delivered only limited conceptual payoff (such as using Popsicle sticks and construction paper to create tipis or log cabins, painting pictures or murals depicting historical events, constructing dioramas, or re-creating the First Thanksgiving). Programs that include such activities are viewed as better than programs that are limited to fill-in-the-blank worksheets, but they do not constitute powerful social studies if they are limited to the same relatively trivial content base.

Jere and Jan developed some useful information from these initial classroom studies, but recognized that they were not going to be able to study the kind of teaching they hoped to study unless the teacher had a good grasp of social studies purposes, goals, and big ideas. So, they turned to another approach that has been used with some success by investigators in the other subject areas: doing it yourself. They arranged to assume responsibility for teaching a social studies unit in a local classroom. During that unit, Jan provided the instruction and Jere observed and recorded field notes.

This approach also proved useful in some respects but lacking in others. Jan provided a coherent content base structured around big ideas, but the classroom was not set up as she would have preferred, so the physical settings for some of the activities were less than optimal. More importantly, as someone who came in to teach for just forty-five minutes a day for just a few weeks, Jan lacked the knowledge of the students and their families, the ability to shape the curriculum as a whole and the class as a learning community, and many of the other potentials open to regular classroom teachers. Both Jan and Jere felt that rather than pursue this approach further, they preferred to revert to their original plan of working with regular classroom teachers. This would allow them to observe instruction taking place under typical rather than special conditions, making it much more likely that most of what they learned in the classrooms under observation would be applicable to other classrooms as well.

Now, however, they decided that instead of just arranging to observe teachers do whatever they usually did in social studies, they would find teachers willing to collaborate with them in planning social studies units that would reflect guidelines for best practice. Specifically, Jan and Jere would provide a curriculum guide identifying the major goals and big ideas to develop in the unit, and the teachers would work from this guide to develop the specifics of lessons and activities.

Unfortunately, this approach did not work very well either. The teachers lacked both experience in developing curricula around big ideas and familiarity with potential social studies resources and activities, so our guidelines did not lead to the kind of instruction we hoped to see. The teachers did produce some very good lessons and activities, especially on topics related to their personal interests, but most drifted away from connected big ideas into parades of facts, overfocus on side issues, and activities that lacked connection to major goals.

These experiences led Jan and Jere to conclude that brief curriculum guides were not enough—that they would need to produce full-scale instructional units (with detailed resources) in which not only the goals and big ideas but the content to be developed and the associated learning and assessment activities would be elaborated at length. These units would focus on cultural universals, the same topics emphasized in the textbook series and in most states' elementary social studies guidelines. However, they would be much richer in content and much more clearly structured around big ideas than conventional social studies units.

Across the next several years, they eventually produced nine of these units, on food, clothing, shelter, communication, transportation, family living, childhood, money, and government. The units subsequently were published as a three-volume series designed for use by elementary teachers (Alleman & Brophy, 2001b, 2002, 2003c).

Barbara Joins the Team

While developing these units, Jan and Jere continued to search for collaborators who would be willing and able to teach them as we envisioned, allow us to observe and collect data in their classrooms, and provide useful feedback about the strengths and weaknesses of the unit plans. Gradually, our search focused on Barbara Knighton, who appealed to us for several reasons.

First, people familiar with her work led us to believe that she was an unusually good teacher, and our own early contacts with her and observations in her classroom reinforced this impression. She was warm, nurturant, and sensitive to the needs and interests of her students, but also concerned about developing their knowledge and skills, and systematic in her efforts to do so. The clarity and detail with which she was able to talk about her teaching suggested that she would provide unusually observant and detailed feedback if she became the teacher who initially field-tested our units.

Second, although she had never participated in a similar collaboration, Barbara felt ready and willing to do so because she viewed it as an opportunity to improve the weakest aspect of her teaching. As an experienced teacher who had received a lot of positive feedback, she had come to view herself as a skilled professional and was generally well satisfied with most aspects of her curriculum and instruction. However, she knew that she did not have a clear vision of social studies as a school subject and suspected that her social studies program could be strengthened considerably by the proposed collaboration.

Third, she taught in the public schools of a bedroom suburb of Lansing, Michigan, in a district that served a racially and ethnically diverse but socioeconomically midrange population. Most of her students lived in modest homes or apartments. Many came from traditional and intact families, but typically half or more lived with a single parent (divorced, separated, or never married), were members of reconstituted families, were being raised by grandparents or other relatives, or lived in adoptive or foster homes.

Within this district context, there was nothing special about the school in which Barbara taught (it was not a magnet school or a school that did anything special in social studies). Nor was there anything special about Barbara's assignment (she was a regular classroom teacher) or students (classes were not grouped by ability). If anything, she was likely to be assigned a few more of the most challenging students (e.g., autistic, behavior disordered) because of her reputation for good management. These classroom setting aspects appealed to us because they meant that what we observed in her classroom would have much broader generalizability than what we would observe in a school near the university, where many of the students were achievement-oriented children of unusually well-educated parents.

As it happened, over the next several years Barbara's teaching context shifted in ways that allowed us to observe the instructional units being taught under varying conditions. Barbara taught a self-contained first-grade class for several years, then collaborated with a second-grade teacher in a multiage teaming arrangement for two years (in which she taught social studies to the combined classes). For the next several years, she taught self-contained first- and second-grade classes within a looping arrangement (she taught a new first-grade group one year, retained these same students the next year for second grade, and then started with a new class of first graders the following year).

Finally, Barbara understood and found appealing our emphasis on structuring curricula around big ideas. She was familiar with the problems implied by terms such as emphasizing breadth at the expense of depth, trivial pursuit curriculum, and mile-wide but inch-deep, so she immediately recognized the potential power of structuring curricula around big ideas developed with emphasis on their connections and applications.

Negotiating Understandings and Inducing Principles

When we began working together, we focused on pilot-testing the units, with Jan and Jere acting as curriculum developers and Barbara as the teacher who first brought their units to life. Jan and Jere's instructional units supplied Barbara with a content base structured around major goals and big ideas, along with suggestions for activities and assessments. Barbara then applied her professional experience and her knowledge of pedagogy and her students to adapt and elaborate on these plans in preparation for teaching the units in her classroom.

Each unit required social studies to be taught for about forty-five minutes per day for about three weeks. Barbara typically piloted two of our units per year, one in the fall and one in the spring. At other times she taught previously piloted units or other social studies material (e.g., holiday units), or used the time slot for teaching health or science instead. Her schedule allowed for only twenty to twenty-five minutes per day for health or science and for social studies, if she taught two of these subjects per day throughout the year. This was not enough time to allow her to offer complete lessons or activities each day. Consequently, she alternated social studies with health or science by teaching a unit in one of these subjects for forty to fifty minutes each day for a few weeks, then shifting to a unit in the other subject.

Whenever Barbara piloted one of our units, and sometimes when she taught a previously piloted unit, Jan would come to her class to tape-record each day's instruction and take notes. Her notes described how the day's instruction went and identified where and how Barbara did anything more or different than what our unit plans called for. Jan also noted any other information that might be needed later to add context to the verbalizations that would appear in the transcripts (e.g., use of books, photos, timelines, or other instructional resources; involvement of special education teachers or other adults who were present in the room during any part of the social studies lesson). As soon as possible following the instruction, Jan also would get Barbara's impressions of the day's activities.

Once the tapes were transcribed, the three collaborators analyzed them in exhaustive detail. Prior to a half-day meeting each week, Jere, Jan, and Barbara independently studied and made notes on copies of the transcripts. Then, during the meetings, we worked our way slowly through the transcripts, raising questions, making observations, and offering interpretations.

These analyses included two levels: clarifying specifics and inducing generalities. *Clarifying specifics* involved filling in gaps or correcting any misinterpretations about what actually occurred during the lesson. This included such things as filling in missing words or making corrections in places where the transcriber was unable to make out what had been said (or transcribed a word incorrectly), noting that Barbara had been pointing to a photo in a book at a certain point in the transcript, or clarifying whether she had stayed with the previous respondent or had called on a new one when she asked a follow-up question. These clarifications of specifics ensured that all three of us shared a common understanding of what was happening at each point in the lesson.

Induction of generalizations occurred as we discussed the potential implications of these events: What had worked very well and what had been less successful, and why? What changes or additions might be made to improve the lesson plans? Which content explanations, question sequences, and activity segments were very well implemented, and which might have been improved (and how and why)? We did not always develop clear and confident answers to these questions, but frequently we did, and many of these conclusions about specific lessons provided a basis for inducing principles that have broader ranges of application.

Because our initial focus was on testing the units, most of the discussion in our early meetings was about where and why things had gone well or poorly, and what this implied about changing or elaborating the unit plans. However, as Jere and Jan became more familiar with Barbara's teaching, they increasingly began to make comments and raise questions about issues that went well beyond our unit plans, and sometimes even beyond social studies. These addressed more general aspects of Barbara's teaching (e.g., how she set up and maintained a productive interpersonal climate in her classroom, her routines for introducing and developing new content with students, her preferences for handling situations when students were unable to answer a question, and how she developed knowledge about her students and their families and then used this knowledge to personalize her curriculum).

Summaries of the understandings and generalizations that we negotiated in our meetings were preserved in meeting notes, and these were later revisited for potential alteration or elaboration. Over several years, we accumulated a volume and variety of notes (along with the transcripts they were based on) that went well beyond what we had envisioned when we started. Barbara had become a more complete partner in the collaboration, and we often were formulating models and principles of good teaching of primary-grade children in general, not just in social studies. We ended up with more than enough material to write not only this book on teaching powerful primary-grade social studies, but also a companion volume on building a learning community in the primary classroom, which deals with generic rather than subject-specific aspects of good primary teaching (Brophy, Alleman, & Knighton, in press).

Focus of the Book

This book focuses on principles of best practice in planning and implementing primary social studies. Its analyses are more fine-grained and extended than those found in social studies methods texts, because the material is drawn from thick description data collected over several years in the classroom of a talented teacher. Principles are elaborated within the context of existing theory and research on both generic and subject-specific aspects of best practice, including the guidelines put forth by the National Council for the Social Studies (1994). The instruction documented here reflects but goes well beyond these existing guidelines, both in the sense of elaborating what is involved in implementing them and in the sense of suggesting additional guidelines on aspects of teaching that have not yet been articulated in the scholarly literature. It exemplifies the subtleties involved in teaching at a very high level, and our collaborative analyses have brought to the surface many of these subtleties and developed guidelines for implementing them.

Our data did not include scores on formal tests of social studies knowledge and skills (no satisfactory standardized social studies tests exist for the primary grades). However, the data did include indicators such as students' responses to questions during lessons and work on follow-up assignments, and these indicators generally supported the feasibility and effectiveness of the curriculum and instruction that the students experienced.

We believe that Barbara's social studies teaching would be judged as highly effective according to just about any commonly accepted criterion, and that it is far more coherent and powerful than what is offered in most primary classrooms. We do not mean to suggest that it is the only or even necessarily the best way to introduce primary students to social studies, but we can say that it worked well with her students, and, given the diversity of the students she teaches, it should work well in most schools in the country.

Most of the material on Barbara's teaching that is presented and analyzed in later chapters can be traced either to the content and learning activities suggested in Jan and Jere's units or to the strategies and tactics that Barbara has developed for teaching her primary students. However, Barbara sometimes altered and frequently elaborated on Jan and Jere's unit plans, and Jan and Jere often raised questions or provided feedback that led Barbara to sharpen or elaborate her thinking about teaching strategies and tactics.

Rather than try to sort out what originated with whom, we offer a more coherent view of Barbara's teaching that reflects the consensus developed within our partnership over several years of frequent meetings. To simplify the presentation, we have personalized it around Barbara as the central actor (e.g., talking about Barbara's instructional goals, or how Barbara responds when students answer incorrectly). However, these passages also reflect Jan and Jere's ideas. Therefore, except in a very few instances where the text explicitly states otherwise, it should be assumed that Jan and Jere support Barbara's approaches to teaching and her underlying rationales as described in this book, and endorse them as models of exemplary teaching practice.

As we elaborate on Barbara's teaching, we identify its major features, place them into context by reviewing relevant theory and research, and illustrate them with examples drawn from the lesson transcripts. These examples are annotated to call attention to key features and elaborate on the principles we developed in our meetings.

The examples are drawn from Barbara's teaching of first or second graders. Many are paraphrased or embedded in the text as brief quotes, but some are edited transcript excerpts. Most of the editing was done to serve either of two purposes: (1) deleting or changing the names of students, teachers, or other individuals who appear in the transcripts (to protect their anonymity), and (2) deleting material that was tangential to the flow of the lesson around the points selected for highlighting in the excerpt (e.g., interruptions that occurred when the principal broadcast an announcement or a special education teacher came to pick up or return one of Barbara's students, or brief digressions that occurred when Barbara addressed management issues with individual students).

In this first chapter, we have explained the rationale for our work and described how our collaboration developed and functioned. In the next chapter, we situate the work with reference to previous research and scholarship on elementary social studies.

Chapter 2

Prior Research on Primary Social Studies

In most American elementary schools, the primary-grade social studies curriculum addresses three major goals: (1) socializing students concerning prosocial attitudes and behavior as members of the classroom community, (2) introducing them to map concepts and skills, and (3) introducing them to basic social knowledge drawn mostly from history, geography, and the social sciences. All three of these instructional goals and related content emphases are featured in state and district curriculum guides for elementary social studies, but they are not equally well addressed in the resource materials commonly made available to elementary teachers.

The Need for a Powerful Content Base in Early Social Studies

The major textbook series generally do an adequate job of providing appropriate content and learning activities for developing students' map concepts and skills. They are more variable in what they offer as a basis for socializing students as citizens of the classroom community (and subsequently, successively broader communities). However, many ancillary resources are available. These vary in quality, but many are useful as resources for planning experiences designed to help primary students learn to interact respectfully, collaborate in learning efforts, resolve conflicts productively, and, in general, display prosocial attitudes and democratic values in their behavior as members of the classroom community.

Unfortunately, good instructional resources are not readily available to support primary teachers' efforts to help their students develop basic knowledge about society and the human condition. There is widespread agreement among critics of the major elementary social studies series that the content presented in their primary texts is thin, trite, and otherwise inadequate as a foundation for developing basic social understandings. Even when the topics are worth addressing, the presented content is too simplistic to have significant application value for students, and often is already familiar to them (Alter, 1995; Beck & McKeown, 1988; Beck *et al.*, 1989; Brophy, 1992; Brophy & Alleman, 1992, 1993; Brophy *et al.*, 1991a; Egan, 1988; Larkins *et al.*, 1987; Ravitch, 1987; Woodward, 1987). The primary texts (especially the K–2 texts) are better described as picture books than textbooks. Their pages often contain rich collages of color photos relating to the unit topic, but these photos are accompanied by little or no text—

a sentence or two at most. The photos are potentially useful as instructional resources if students are induced to process them with reference to powerful ideas, but the texts typically do not convey such ideas to students. Nor do the accompanying manuals convey them to teachers or provide guidance concerning how the photos might be used as bases for powerful social studies teaching.

For example, a lesson on shelter might have several pages of photos showing a variety of past and present homes (tipis, longhouses, pueblos, yurts, igloos, jungle huts, stilt houses, log cabins, castles, mansions, high-rise apartment buildings, and several types of modern family homes). However, the text on these pages might say little or nothing more than "People all around the world live in many different kinds of homes." Students will not get much out of exposure to such collages unless they are helped to process what they are seeing with reference to powerful ideas that will help them to appreciate the reasons why the different kinds of homes were constructed by the people who built them. For example, students might learn that the Native Americans who built tipis did so because they packed up periodically to follow the buffalo and needed portable housing; that the eastern woodlands tribes had plentiful supplies of wood to use to build their longhouses whereas the southwestern desert tribes had to bake adobe bricks to build their pueblos; that rice farmers in many parts of the world have to build their homes high on poles because they live in marshes or floodplains that support rice farming; or that high-rise apartment buildings are found in large cities because a premium on centrally located space creates pressures to build up instead of out.

With exposure to ideas such as these, students can appreciate photo collages on homes as illustrations of human adaptability to time and place in meeting shelter needs. In contrast, students who are shown only the collages are likely to see nothing more than photos illustrating that some people build strange, exotic, or even bizarre homes for no apparent reason (reinforcing their already existing disposition toward presentism and chauvinism).

The Expanding Communities Sequence

The social studies curriculum for the elementary grades is usually organized within the expanding communities sequence that begins with a focus on the self in kindergarten and gradually expands to address families in Grade 1, neighborhoods in Grade 2, communities in Grade 3, states and geographic regions in Grade 4, the United States in Grade 5, and the world in Grade 6. The categories in the expanding communities sequence refer primarily to the levels of analysis at which content is addressed, not to the content itself. That is, although there is some material on families in first grade, on neighborhoods in second grade, and on communities in third grade, the topics of most instructional units are the human activities that are carried on within families, neighborhoods, and communities. These activities tend to be structured around cultural universals—basic human needs and social experiences found in all societies, past and present (food, clothing, shelter, communication, transportation, government, etc.).

Most social educators believe that, except for certain aspects of geography and economics, social studies content is not inherently hierarchical. Degree of difficulty resides more in the levels of depth and sophistication with which topics are addressed than in the topics themselves. Difficulty tends to increase as one moves from the concrete to the abstract, from easily observable and familiar situations to phenomena less rooted in experience, and from an emphasis on facts to an emphasis on concepts, generalizations, principles, and theories.

Concepts differ among themselves in level of difficulty. Those with straight-forward definitions or structures that are observable in clear illustrations are easier to learn than those with "if–then" or relational structures. Thus, goods, services, producers, and consumers are simpler economic concepts to learn than opportunity cost, scarcity, or comparative advantage.

Fair (1977) suggested the following generalizations about content difficulty:

1   The sheer quantity of things to be dealt with simultaneously makes for increased difficulty level (it is harder to compare or interpret three things than two).
2   Abstract content is more difficult than concrete content.
3   Fine distinctions are more difficult than gross ones.
4   Relying solely on print as the source for input makes for greater difficulty than using multimedia.
5   It is easier to develop skills in thinking about matters that students see as closely related to their own lives than about other matters.
6   Providing structure, cues, and props makes thinking easier.

Elementary social studies curricula usually reflect these ideas. The primary grades tend to concentrate on universal human experiences occurring within families and local communities, with content drawn heavily from psychology, sociology, and anthropology. In the middle grades, the focus shifts to geography, economics, civics, and history. Students begin to study states and nations of the past and present and to address some of the more conceptual and abstract aspects of the content.

In the past, the idea that social studies involves abstractions that are not well grasped until at least the fourth grade caused some to argue that social studies instruction should not begin until that time, and others to argue that history should not be taught until the secondary grades. However, subsequent debate and data collection led to the rejection of these arguments. It is now generally accepted that elementary students can understand general chronological sequences (e.g., that land transportation developed from walking to horse-drawn carriages to engine-powered vehicles) even though they may still be hazy about particular dates. They also can follow age-appropriate representations of people and events from the past (especially narratives built around central characters with whom they can identify, depicted as pursuing goals that they can under-stand), even though they might not be able to follow analytic treatments of abstract historical topics or themes (Booth, 1993; Brophy & Alleman, 2006; Crabtree, 1989; Downey & Levstik, 1991; Levstik & Pappas, 1992; Thornton & Vukelich, 1988; Willig, 1990).

Controversy continues over what content is suitable for elementary students to learn, but its focus has shifted. Arguments (based on skill hierarchies or

Piagetian stages) that they are not ready for certain topics have receded in favor of the idea that the difficulty level of content resides primarily in the manner and depth with which it is approached. Therefore, even the strange and abstract can be learned meaningfully if instruction emphasizes schemas that are concrete and familiar to the students (e.g., historical narratives built around the goals and motives of central characters; cultural comparisons focused on food, clothing, shelter, and other cultural universals). The focus is on content that is meaningful because it can be linked to students' social experiences, especially content that they find interesting because it engages their emotions or provides opportunity for identification with key persons in a narrative. Current arguments center less on what it is possible to teach children in the early grades than on what it is worthwhile to teach, why it is more worthwhile than alternatives, and how it can be taught effectively.

There is nothing inherently necessary about the scope and sequence of topics typically included within the expanding communities curriculum. Piaget cautioned against getting too far away from children's experience base to the point of trying to teach abstractions that will yield "merely verbal" learning. This warning is well taken. However, his ideas about what children are capable of learning at particular ages were too pessimistic and too focused on the learning of logical-mathematical structures through self-initiated exploration of the physical environment (Downey & Levstik, 1991). More recent neo-Vygotskian research on teaching in the zone of proximal development indicates that children can learn a great many things earlier and more thoroughly if guided by systematic instruction than they would learn on their own. Also, contemporary information processing and schema development research has shown that children can use situational schemas built up through prior knowledge and experience as templates for understanding information about how people in other times and places have responded to parallel situations (Bransford *et al.*, 1999).

Thus, there is no need to confine the primary grades to the here and now before moving linearly backwards in time and outwards in physical space and scope of community in subsequent grades. Children can understand historical episodes described in narrative form with emphasis on the motives and actions of key individuals, and they can understand aspects of customs, culture, economics, and politics that focus on universal human experiences or adaptation problems that are familiar to them and for which they have developed schemas or routines.

Cultural Universals as Unit Topics

Even though the elementary social studies curriculum is commonly identified with reference to its sequencing structure (expanding communities), the content of most lessons actually focuses on human activities involved in pursuing needs and wants related to cultural universals. This makes sense, because teaching students about how their own and other societies have addressed these human purposes provides a sound basis for developing fundamental understandings about the human condition, for several reasons. First, activities relating to cultural universals account for a considerable proportion of everyday living and are the focus of much of human social organization and communal activity. Until they understand the motivations and causal explanations that underlie these activities, children do not understand much of what is happening around them all the time.

Second, children from all social backgrounds begin accumulating direct personal experiences with most cultural universals right from birth, and they can draw on these experiences as they construct understandings of social education concepts and principles. Compared to curricula organized around the academic disciplines or around forms of cultural capital linked closely to socioeconomic status, content structured around human activities relating to cultural universals is easier to connect to all children's prior knowledge and develop in ways that stay close to their experience.

Third, because such content is about humans taking action to meet their basic needs and wants, it lends itself to presentation within narrative formats. Bruner (1990), Egan (1988), and others have noted that implicit understanding of the narrative structure is acquired early, and this structure is commonly used by children to encode and retain information. Narrative formats are well suited to conveying information about human actions related to cultural universals.

Fourth, in addition to providing frequent opportunities to introduce basic disciplinary concepts and principles, narratives focused on humans engaged in goal-oriented behavior provide frequent opportunities to explore causal relationships and make explicit some of the human intentions and economic or political processes that children usually do not recognize or appreciate. Stories about how key inventions made qualitative changes in people's lives or about what is involved in producing basic products and bringing them to our stores can incorporate process explanations (of how things are done) and cause–effect linkages (explaining why things are done the way they are and why they change in response to inventions).

In summary, structuring the curriculum around cultural universals helps keep its content close to the students' life experiences and thus meaningful to them, and representing the content within narrative structures makes it easier for them to follow and remember. It also "unveils the mysteries" that the social world presents (from the children's perspective), helping them to view the cultural practices under study as rational means of meeting needs and pursuing wants.

This approach also offers important bonuses for teachers. First, precisely because the stories focus on people taking actions to meet basic needs and pursue common wants, students are likely to view the content as interesting and relevant and to appreciate follow-up activities and assignments as authentic (because they will have applications to life outside of school). This facilitates teachers' efforts to motivate their students to learn, which can be a significant challenge in social studies (Zhao & Hoge, 2005).

Second, when the stories deal with life in the past or in other cultures, their focus on commonalities (people pursuing culturally universal and thus familiar needs and wants) highlights similarities rather than differences. This helps students to see the time, place, and situation through the eyes of the people under study, and thus to see their decisions and actions as understandable given the knowledge and resources available to them. Such promotion of empathy helps teachers to counteract the tendencies toward presentism and chauvinism which are common in young children's thinking about the past and about other cultures (Brophy & Alleman, 2006; Davis *et al.*, 2001).

Third, teachers can teach this content effectively without extensive preparation, because they already possess a great deal of relevant personal and professional knowledge. That is, their own schooling, and especially their personal experiences growing up within American culture, have equipped them with plenty of knowledge and experience to bring to bear when teaching about cultural universals, and it is easier for them to identify or construct instructional resources to use during lessons and learning activities.

If human activities relating to cultural universals are taught with appropriate focus on powerful ideas and their potential life applications, students should develop basic sets of connected understandings about how the social system works, how and why it got to be that way over time, how and why it varies across locations and cultures, and what all of this might mean for personal, social, and civic decision making. Such a content base is not provided in the major publishers' elementary social studies textbook series.

Teaching Cultural Universals for Understanding, Appreciation, and Life Application

Our development of instructional units on cultural universals was guided by several sets of principles. One set reflects an emerging consensus about what is involved in teaching school subjects for understanding, appreciation, and life application. Reviews of research on such teaching (e.g., Good & Brophy, 2007) suggest that it reflects the following ten principles:

1 The curriculum is designed to equip students with knowledge, skills, values, and dispositions that they will find useful both inside and outside of school.
2 Instructional goals emphasize developing student expertise within an application context and with emphasis on conceptual understanding of knowledge and self-regulated application of skills.
3 The curriculum balances breadth with depth by addressing limited content but developing this content sufficiently to foster conceptual understanding.
4 The content is organized around a limited set of powerful ideas (basic understandings and principles).
5 The teacher's role is not just to present information, but also to scaffold and respond to students' learning efforts.
6 The students' role is not just to absorb or copy input, but also to actively make sense and construct meaning.
7 Students' prior knowledge about the topic is elicited and used as a starting place for instruction, which builds on accurate prior knowledge but also stimulates conceptual change if necessary.
8 Activities and assignments feature tasks that call for critical thinking or problem solving, not just memory or reproduction.
9 Higher-order thinking skills are not taught as a separate skills curriculum. Instead, they are developed in the process of teaching subject-matter knowledge within application contexts that call for students to relate what they

are learning to their lives outside of school by thinking critically or creatively about it, or by using it to solve problems or make decisions.

10 The teacher creates a social environment in the classroom that could be described as a learning community featuring discourse or dialogue designed to promote understanding.

These principles emphasize focusing instruction on big ideas that are developed in depth and with attention to connections and applications.

Topical Organization of the Curriculum

Another set of principles is rooted in our thinking about topical units as appropriate vehicles for introducing young students to social studies. Like others who have focused on the primary grades, we believe that the curriculum should feature pandisciplinary treatments designed to develop "knowledge of limited validity" (Levstik, 1986) or "protodisciplinary knowledge" (Gardner & Boix Mansilla, 1994) about topics, rather than attempts to teach disciplinary knowledge organized as such. In identifying big ideas to focus on, we seek an appropriate balance among the three traditional sources of curriculum: knowledge of enduring value (including but not limited to disciplinary knowledge); the students (their needs, interests and current zones of proximal development); and the needs of society (the knowledge, skills, values, and dispositions that our society would like to see developed in future generations of its citizens) (Kliebard, 2004). Within this context, we believe that a pandisciplinary introduction to the social world (past and present, taught with emphasis on developing understanding, appreciation, and life application of big ideas) makes more sense for primary students than premature attempts to socialize them into the academic disciplines.

Teaching for Conceptual Change

Related principles come from research on teaching for conceptual change. Prior knowledge about topics sometimes includes naive ideas or even outright misconceptions that can cause students to ignore, distort, or miss the implications of new information that conflicts with their existing ideas. Teachers who are aware of common misconceptions can plan instruction to address them directly. This involves helping students to recognize differences between their current beliefs and the target understandings, and to see the need to shift from the former to the latter. Such instruction is often called conceptual change teaching.

Kathleen Roth (1996) developed an approach to conceptual change teaching of science and social studies. She embedded the conceptual change emphasis within a more comprehensive "learning community" model of teaching school subjects for understanding. This approach emphasizes eliciting valid prior knowledge that instruction can connect with and build on, not just identifying misconceptions that will need to be addressed. Our instructional units were designed accordingly.

Addressing Prior Knowledge and Misconceptions

Unit construction also was informed by a series of studies that we conducted on K–3 students' knowledge and thinking about cultural universals. These studies yielded a great deal of information about accurate prior knowledge that most students are likely to possess as they begin each unit, as well as commonly observed knowledge gaps and naive ideas or misconceptions that will need to be addressed during the instruction. The findings are noteworthy because some proponents of alternative curricula have claimed that there is no need to teach about cultural universals in the primary grades because children learn all they need to know about them through everyday experiences. This claim was made in the absence of research evidence. Our studies speak to it directly (Brophy & Alleman, 2006).

We found that the knowledge about cultural universals that children accumulate through everyday experiences is limited, disconnected, and mostly tacit rather than well articulated. Most of it is confined to knowledge about how things are here and now, without accompanying understandings of how and why they evolved over time, how and why they vary across cultures, or the mechanisms through which they accomplish human purposes. Also, children's knowledge frequently is distorted by naive ideas or outright misconceptions. We do not find this surprising, because their experiences relating to cultural universals usually are informal and do not include sustained discourse structured around key ideas. In any case, it is now clear that primary students stand to benefit from systematic instruction about these topics.

For example, our interviews on shelter indicated that K–3 students recognized differences in the size, construction material, durability, and general quality of the shelter provided by different forms of past and present housing, but they did not understand much about the historical, geographical, or cultural reasons for these contrasting housing styles. For example, they did not know much about why different forms were used by different Native American tribal groups. Most were not aware that certain tribes were nomadic societies that moved with the buffalo, so they did not appreciate that portability was a crucial quality of tipis. Many could not explain why certain tribes used tipis, and others suggested reasons such as that tipi dwellers were poor people who could not afford better homes, preferred a tipi because they could build a fire in it and the smoke would discharge through the hole in the top, or needed something to do with leftover animal skins that they didn't want to waste. Most were able to make sensible statements about differences (e.g., in size or construction materials) between longhouses and pueblos, but few understood that differences in climate and geography were factors contributing to the differences between these two forms of Native American housing (i.e., wood was plentiful in the Eastern woodlands but not in the desert Southwest).

Responses concerning log cabins and pioneer life were more accurate and less fanciful than responses concerning Native American homes and cultures. Even so, misconceptions were common (e.g., that the cabins could collapse easily because the logs were not nailed together). Furthermore, most of the students emphasized the deficiencies of these homes in comparisons with contemporary housing rather than appreciating them as inventive adaptations to their time and place (i.e., they displayed historical presentism).

In thinking about contemporary housing, the students focused on what is visible inside and outside the home but did not show much awareness of what is behind the walls or beneath the building. They knew that shelter is a basic and universal human need, but they were less appreciative of modern homes as controlled environments for comfortable living that cater to a great many of our wants as well as our more basic needs.

They usually understood that people have to pay for shelter and that most people prefer homes to apartments. However, they had difficulty explaining what is involved in renting apartments and why some people choose to do so. Only a few understood that renting is a profit-making business or that people can get mortgage loans to allow them to move into a home before they have accumulated its full purchase price. No student indicated knowledge of the buildup of equity, the appreciation of property value, or other concepts relating to investment or economic assets.

There was only limited awareness of the mechanisms through which modern houses are supplied with water, heat, light, and other conveniences. Almost all students understood that water is piped into the home, but many were vague or incorrect about the sources of this water, did not appreciate that the water is drawn from fresh- rather than saltwater sources and purified before being sent to homes, and did not realize that it arrives at the homes under pressure. Most understood that thermostats are used to adjust heating, but were vague about where the heat comes from or how the system works. Students' thinking appeared to progress from believing that a utility company supplies heat directly and the furnace is merely a storage place, to knowing that heat is generated in the furnace but not knowing how, to knowing that the furnace contains a fire that heats air (only 13 percent clearly understood that furnaces contain fires). A majority of the students knew that electricity is involved in creating light, because they knew that one must throw a switch to allow electricity to enter the bulb. However, they were unable to explain how the arrival of electricity causes the bulb to light up.

Most students understood that families pay for water that is piped into their homes, according to how much they use. However, most were unclear or incorrect about payment for heat and light. Few understood that "heat" bills are actually for natural gas consumed in fires that create heat in furnaces or that "light" bills are actually for electricity consumed when light bulbs are activated.

A list of the questions we asked and a summary of our key findings concerning children's thinking about each of the cultural universals is included in the introduction to its corresponding instructional unit (Alleman & Brophy, 2001b, 2002, 2003c), and a more complete presentation and discussion of the findings can be found in Brophy and Alleman (2006). We refer to many of these findings in this book in the context of discussing the teaching of particular topics.

NCSS Standards

Our unit development efforts also were informed by two definitive standards statements released by the National Council for the Social Studies (NCSS), one on curriculum standards and one on powerful teaching and learning. The curriculum standards are built around ten themes that form a framework for social studies (see Box 2.1). The publication that spells out these standards elaborates on each theme in separate chapters for the early grades, the middle grades, and the secondary grades, listing performance expectations and potential classroom activities that might be used to develop the theme (NCSS, 1994).

Box 2.1   Ten thematic strands for the social studies curriculum

Ten themes serve as organizing strands for the social studies curriculum at every school level (early, middle, and high school); they are interrelated and draw from all of the social science disciplines and other related disciplines and fields of scholarly study to build a framework for social studies curriculum.

I.   Culture

Human beings create, learn, and adapt culture. Human cultures are dynamic systems of beliefs, values, and traditions that exhibit both commonalities and differences. Understanding culture helps us understand ourselves and others.

II.   Time, Continuity, and Change

Human beings seek to understand their historic roots and to locate themselves in time. Such understanding involves knowing what things were like in the past and how things change and develop—allowing us to develop historic perspective and answer important questions about our current condition.

III. People, Places, and Environment

Technical advancements have ensured that students are aware of the world beyond their personal locations. As students study content related to this theme, they create their spatial views and geographical perspectives of the world; social, cultural, economic, and civic demands mean that students will need such knowledge, skills, and understandings to make informed and critical decisions about the relationship between human beings and their environment.

IV. Individual Development and Identity

Personal identity is shaped by one's culture, by groups, and by institutional influences. Examination of various forms of human behavior enhances understandings of the relationship between social norms and emerging personal identities, the social processes that influence identity formation, and the ethical principles underlying individual action.

V. Individuals, Groups, and Institutions

Institutions exert enormous influence over us. Institutions are organizational embodiments to further the core social values of those who comprise them. It is important for students to know how institutions are formed, what controls and influences them, how they control and influence individuals and culture, and how institutions can be maintained or changed.

VI. Power, Authority, and Governance

Understanding of the historic development of structures of power, authority, and governance and their evolving functions in contemporary society is essential for emergence of civic competence.

VII. Production, Distribution, and Consumption

Decisions about exchange, trade, and economic policy and well-being are global in scope, and the role of government in policy making varies over time and from place to place. The systematic study of an interdependent world economy and the role of technology in economic decision making is essential.

VIII. Science, Technology, and Society

Technology is as old as the first crude tool invented by prehistoric humans, and modern life as we know it would be impossible without technology and the science that supports it. Today's technology forms the basis for some of our most difficult social choices.

IX. Global Connections

The realities of global interdependence require understanding of the increasingly important and diverse global connections among world societies before there can be analysis leading to the development of possible solutions to persisting and emerging global issues.

X. Civic Ideals and Practices

All people have a stake in examining civic ideals and practices across time, in diverse societies, as well as in determining how to close the gap between present practices and the ideals upon which our democracy is based. An understanding of civic ideals and practices of citizenship is critical to full participation in society.

Source: National Council for the Social Studies (1994). *Curriculum standards for social studies: Expectations of excellence.* Bulletin No. 89. Washington, D.C.: Author.

Along with its curriculum standards, the NCSS released a position statement identifying five key features of powerful teaching and learning (see Box 2.2), framing them by stating that social studies teaching is viewed as powerful when it helps students develop social understanding and civic efficacy (NCSS, 1993). Social understanding is integrated knowledge of the social aspects of the human condition: how these aspects have evolved over time, the variations that occur in different physical environments and cultural settings, and emerging trends that appear likely to shape the future. Civic efficacy is readiness and willingness to assume citizenship responsibilities. It is rooted in social studies knowledge and skills, along with related values (such as concern for the common good) and dispositions (such as an orientation toward confident participation in civic affairs).

In developing our units, we did not begin with these NCSS standards. Instead, we began with lists of powerful ideas that might anchor networks of social knowledge about the cultural universal under study. As unit development proceeded, however, we used the NCSS content and teaching standards as guidelines for assessing the degree to which the unit was sufficiently complete and well balanced. No individual lesson was likely to include each of the ten content themes and the five features of powerful teaching, but all of these content and process standards would be well represented in the plans for the unit as a whole.

We have found that units planned to develop connected understandings of powerful ideas consistently meet the NCSS standards (as well as state standards), even though we used the standards as quality-checking criteria rather than as starting points for unit development. Units built around big ideas also include embedded strands that address history, geography, economics, culture, government, and decision making. However, our units were developed as

---

Box 2.2   Five key features of powerful social studies learning

Meaningful

The content selected for emphasis is worth learning because it promotes progress toward important social understanding and civic efficacy goals, and it is taught in ways that help students to see how it is related to these goals. As a result, students' learning efforts are motivated by appreciation and interest, not just by accountability and grading systems. Instruction emphasizes depth of development of important ideas within appropriate breadth of content coverage.

Integrative

Powerful social studies cuts across discipline boundaries, spans time and space, and integrates knowledge, beliefs, values, and dispositions to action. It also provides opportunities for students to connect to the arts and sciences through inquiry and reflection.

Value Based

Powerful social studies teaching considers the ethical dimensions of topics, so that it provides an arena for reflective development of concern for the common good and application of social values. The teacher includes diverse points of view, demonstrates respect for well supported positions, and shows sensitivity and commitment to social responsibility and action.

Challenging

Students are encouraged to function as a learning community, using reflective discussion to work collaboratively to deepen understandings of the meanings and implications of content. They also are expected to come to grips with controversial issues, to participate assertively but respectfully in group discussions, and to work productively with peers in cooperative learning activities.

Active

Powerful social studies is rewarding but demanding. It demands thoughtful preparation and instruction by the teacher, and sustained effort by the students to make sense of and apply what they are learning. Teachers do not mechanically follow rigid guidelines in planning, implementing, and assessing instruction. Instead, they work with the national standards and with state and local guidelines, adapting and supplementing these guidelines and their instructional materials in ways that support their students' social education needs.

The teacher uses a variety of instructional materials, plans field trips and visits by resource people, develops current or local examples to relate to students' lives, plans reflective discussions, and scaffolds students' work in ways that encourage them to gradually take on more responsibility for managing their own learning independently and with their peers. Accountability and grading systems are compatible with these goals and methods.

Students develop new understandings through a process of active construction. They develop a network of connections that link the new content to preexisting knowledge and beliefs anchored in their prior experience. The construction of meaning required to develop important social understanding takes time and is facilitated by interactive discourse. Clear explanations and modeling from the teacher are important, but so are opportunities to answer questions, discuss or debate the meaning and implications of content, or use the content in activities that call for tackling problems or making decisions.

Source: National Council for the Social Studies (1993). "A vision of powerful teaching and learning in the social studies: Building social understanding and civic efficacy. *Social Education*, 57, 213–23.

pandisciplinary (or perhaps we should say predisciplinary), integrated treatments of topics, not as collections of lessons organized around the academic disciplines treated separately.

Other Research

The need for an emphasis on understanding, appreciation, and life application is underscored by the research on social studies teaching. Most accounts have painted a dismal picture of overreliance on textbook-based reading and recitation followed by solitary work on fill-in-the blank assignments (Cuban, 1991; Goodlad, 1984; Thornton, 1991). Some have noted frequent absence of any social studies teaching (Houser, 1995; Howard, 2003; Parker, 1991; Pascopella, 2005; VanFossen, 2005). However, researchers have begun to describe social studies teaching that reflects research-based principles for teaching for understanding within classroom learning communities. For example, Stodolsky (1988) observed a wide range of instructional diversity occurring in thirty-nine fifth-grade classrooms. In addition to reading and answering questions, students also engaged in peer work groups, simulations, and projects including research using a range of resource materials. Higher-level thinking was stressed, along with social and problem-solving skills.

Perhaps the best-known and most influential work has been that of Fred Newmann and his colleagues on higher-order thinking and thoughtfulness in high school social studies classes (Newmann, 1990; Onosko, 1990; Stevenson, 1990). Newmann described teaching for higher-order thinking as challenging students to interpret, analyze, or manipulate information in response to a question or problem that cannot be resolved through routine application of previously acquired knowledge. He also argued that social studies instruction should both develop and reflect a set of student dispositions toward thoughtfulness: a persistent desire that claims be supported by reasons (and that the reasons themselves be scrutinized), a tendency to be reflective by taking time to think through problems rather than acting impulsively or accepting the views of others automatically, a curiosity to explore new questions, and a flexibility to entertain alternative and original solutions to problems.

Newmann and his colleagues identified six key indicators of thoughtfulness:

1   Classroom discourse focuses on sustained examination of a few topics rather than superficial coverage of many.
2   The discourse is characterized by substantive coherence and continuity.
3   Students are given sufficient time to think before being required to answer questions.
4   The teacher presses students to clarify or justify their assertions, rather than accepting and reinforcing them indiscriminately.
5   The teacher models the characteristics of a thoughtful person (showing interest in students' ideas and suggestions for solving problems, modeling problem-solving processes rather than just giving answers, and acknowledging the difficulties involved in gaining clear understandings of problematic topics).

6   Students generate original and unconventional ideas in the course of the interaction.

Thoughtfulness scores based on these indicators distinguish classrooms that feature sustained and thoughtful teacher–student discourse from two less desirable alternatives: (1) classrooms that feature lecture, recitation, and seatwork focused on low-level aspects of the content, and (2) classrooms that feature discussion and student participation but do not foster much thoughtfulness because the teachers skip from topic to topic too quickly or accept students' contributions uncritically.

Teachers whose classroom observation data yielded high thoughtfulness scores experienced content-coverage pressure primarily as external and tended to resist it by favoring depth over breadth. Other teachers experienced it primarily as internal and thus emphasized breadth of content coverage over depth of topic development. All teachers mentioned that their students tended to resist higher-order thinking tasks initially, but high-scoring teachers emphasized these tasks nevertheless. Their persistence paid off: the same students who initially resisted later described their classes as more difficult and challenging but also as more engaging and interesting.

Most of the ideas and methods observed by Newmann in high school classes also appear to be applicable in elementary classes. Thornton and Wenger (1990) reported observing lessons exhibiting many of the characteristics of thoughtfulness described by Newmann, and Stodolsky (1988) reported that the quality of students' task engagement was higher during more cognitively complex activities than during lower-level activities. In addition, several case studies have been reported in which teachers set up contexts and arranged tasks to allow students to construct meaning interactively instead of relying on a low-level textbook/recitation approach (Brophy & VanSledright, 1997; Levstik, 1993; White, 1993).

Similarly, many of the ideas and methods that we observed in Barbara's first- and second-grade classes also appear to be applicable in higher grades. Some of the school systems that have adopted our instructional units are using them in the middle grades as well as the primary grades, and many of Barbara's teaching strategies can contribute to powerful social studies instruction at any grade.

In the next chapter, we examine the structure and content of our instructional units more closely, to depict the curricular context in which Barbara planned her social studies teaching.

Chapter 3

Generic Aspects of Our Instructional Units

Jan and Jere's units on cultural universals provide the content base for Barbara's social studies teaching. The units differ by topic, but they all incorporate certain features that flow from the principles outlined in Chapter 2. They are designed to be far more powerful than the ostensibly similar units found in contemporary textbook series. Their content is basic and familiar in that they address fundamental aspects of the human condition and connect with experience-based tacit knowledge that students already possess. However, they do not merely reaffirm what students already know. Instead, they help students to construct articulated knowledge about aspects of the cultural universal that they have only vague and tacit knowledge about now. They also introduce students to a great deal of new information, develop connections to help them transform scattered items of information into a network of integrated knowledge, and stimulate them to apply this knowledge to their lives outside of school. Finally, the repeating components that are found in all of the units build students' awareness of templates and other big ideas that they can apply to all of the cultural universals. For example, timelines are used as learning resources during the historical components of all of the units, and decision-making skills are incorporated into the components dealing with personal choices and self-efficacy.

Our Approach Compared to Alternatives

We have noted that our response to the widely recognized content problem in primary-grade social studies is to retain cultural universals as the unit topics but develop these topics much more thoroughly than they are developed in the textbook series, and with better focus on big ideas. Others have suggested different responses. We briefly mention the major alternative suggestions here, both to explain why we do not endorse them and to elaborate our own position.

Cultural Literacy/Core Knowledge

E. D. Hirsch, Jr. (1987) proposed cultural literacy as the basis for curriculum development. He produced a list of over 5,000 items of knowledge that he believed should be acquired in elementary school as a way to equip students with a common base of cultural knowledge to inform their social and civic decision making. We agree with Hirsch that a shared common culture is needed, but we question the value of much of what he included on his list of ostensibly important knowledge (for example, knowing that Alexander's horse was named Bucephalus). Furthermore, because it is a long list of specifics, it leads to teaching that emphasizes breadth of coverage of disconnected details over depth of development of connected knowledge structured around powerful ideas.

Subsequently, educators inspired by Hirsch's book have used it as a basis for developing the CORE Curriculum, which encompasses science, social studies, and the arts (Core Knowledge Foundation, 1999). The social studies strands are built around chronologically organized historical studies, with accompanying geographical and cultural studies. First graders study ancient Egypt and the early American civilizations (the Mayas, Incas, Aztecs). Second graders study ancient India, China, and Greece, along with American history up to the Civil War. Third graders study ancient Rome and Byzantium, various Native American tribal groups, and the thirteen English colonies prior to the American Revolution. Because it is divided by grade levels and organized into World Civilization, American Civilization, and Geography strands, the CORE curriculum is an improvement over Hirsch's list of disconnected knowledge items as a basis for social studies curriculum in the primary grades. However, it focuses on the distant past, and on content that few elementary teachers are well prepared to teach.

We think that cultural universals have more to offer than ancient history as a basis for introducing students to the social world. An approach that begins with what is familiar to the students in their immediate environments and then moves to the past, to other cultures, and to consideration of the future constitutes a better rounded and more powerful social education than an exclusive focus on the past that is inherently limited in its applicability to today's students' lives. It also is more sustainable as an introduction to social education—more likely to be remembered and used in life outside of school.

History/Literature Focus

Kieran Egan (1988), Diane Ravitch (1987), and others have advocated replacing topical teaching about cultural universals with a heavy focus on history and related children's literature (not only fiction but myths and folktales). We agree with them that primary-grade students can and should learn certain aspects of history, but we also believe that these students need a balanced and integrated social studies curriculum that includes sufficient attention to powerful ideas drawn from geography and the social sciences. Furthermore, we see little social education value in replacing reality-based social studies with myths and folklore likely to create misconceptions, especially during the primary years when children are struggling to determine what is real (vs. false or fictional) and enduring (vs. transitory or accidental) in their physical and social worlds. Thus, although fanciful children's literature may be studied profitably as fiction within the language arts curriculum, it is no substitute for a reality-based social studies curriculum.

Similarly, we do not favor attempts to subsume the social studies curriculum within the literacy curriculum. It is advisable to include a lot of reading and writing about social studies-related topics within the literacy curriculum, because opportunities to read and write about informational texts are needed to support students' progress toward important literacy goals such as reading comprehension and strategy development (Duke & Bennett-Armistead, 2003). If well chosen, such texts can enrich the social studies curriculum.

They cannot replace it, however. Realization of social studies purposes and goals as depicted in the NCSS (1994) standards statement requires offering students a coherent social studies curriculum structured around big ideas linked to those purposes and goals. Disconnected readings, even if topic relevant, cannot supply the needed focus and coherence.

Issues Analysis

Many social educators believe that debating social and civic issues is the most direct way to develop dispositions toward critical thinking and reflective decision making in our citizens (Evans & Saxe, 1996). Some of them have suggested that even primary-grade social studies should deemphasize providing students with information and instead engage them in inquiry and debate about social policy issues. We agree that reflective discussion of social issues and related decision-making opportunities should be included in the teaching of social studies at all grade levels. However, we also believe that a heavy concentration on inquiry and debate about social policy issues is premature for primary-grade students, whose prior knowledge and experience relating to the issues are quite limited.

Developing the Unit Plans

In developing unit plans, Jan and Jere began by generating a list of big ideas about the cultural universal that might become the major understandings around which to structure the unit. The initial list was developed from three major sources: (1) social studies education textbooks written for teachers, standards statements from NCSS and other professional organizations, and the writings of opinion leaders and organizations concerned with education in history, geography, and the social sciences; (2) ideas conveyed about the cultural universal in elementary social studies texts and in literature sources written for children; and (3) our own ideas about which aspects of each cultural universal are basic understandings that students could use to make sense of their social lives. As Jan and Jere developed and discussed this basic list of key ideas, they revised it several times. In the process, they added some new ideas, rephrased existing ones, combined those that appeared to go together, and ordered them in a way that made sense as a sequence of lesson topics for the unit.

Once they were satisfied with the listing and sequencing of big ideas, Jan and Jere began drafting lesson plans. They elaborated the big ideas in considerable detail and considered ways in which they might be applied during in-class activities and follow-up home assignments. They also shared tentative plans with Barbara and other collaborating teachers. Barbara critiqued what was included, and contributed specific teaching suggestions, such as identifying places where she might bring in some personal possession to use as an instructional resource, incorporate a children's literature selection that Jan and Jere had not considered, or add a learning activity.

Sequencing the Lessons

Units begin with consideration of the cultural universal as it is experienced in the contemporary United States, and especially in the homes and neighborhoods of the students to be taught. Subsequent lessons bring in the historical dimension by considering how human response to the cultural universal has evolved through time. Later lessons bring in the geographical, cultural, and economic dimensions by considering how human response to the cultural universal has varied in the past and still varies today according to local resources and other aspects of location and culture. Still later lessons bring in the personal and civic efficacy dimensions by involving students in activities calling for them to consider their current and future decision making with respect to the cultural universal and to address some of the social and civic issues associated with it. Finally, a review and assessment lesson concludes the unit.

Looking across each unit as a whole, the sequence of instruction: (1) begins by building on students' existing knowledge, deepening it, and making it better articulated and connected (to solidify a common base of valid prior knowledge as a starting point); (2) broadens their knowledge about how the cultural universal is addressed in the context most familiar to them (contemporary U.S. society); (3) extends their knowledge to the past and to other cultures; (4) provides opportunities to apply what they are learning to present and future decision making as an individual and as a citizen; and (5) concludes with review and assessment.

Pilot Testing and Revisions

Early pilot studies suggested the need for a great deal of teacher structuring and scaffolding with primary-grade students who are both young and limited in prior knowledge, especially when introducing key ideas and when summarizing. (Less direct methods can be used at other times.) This was most obvious during a unit taught by a teacher who attempted to rely primarily on an inductive approach, seeking to elicit target concepts and explanations through questioning. Her attempts often failed, and even when they succeeded to a degree, the target idea usually ended up being phrased vaguely, incompletely, or only after several students had expressed various misconceptions. This reduced the salience and clarity of the key ideas that Jan and Jere wanted to emphasize. Consequently, most of our lesson plans call for an initial presentation of information, which is then followed by questions, rather than using questioning about prior knowledge to introduce the topic or relying heavily on Socratic teaching to develop it.

Another potential problem with Socratic teaching, especially with first graders, is what Piaget called egocentrism. Some younger students often use questions posed by their teacher as occasions for launching into stories that have little or nothing to do with the topic, in which case they distract from the focus of the lesson. In the case of lengthy anecdotes, they derail lesson momentum completely.

Pilot data on the teaching of particular topics provided guidance about which aspects were worth developing and which were not. Concerning home mortgages, for example, we found that students could understand the motivations of the parties involved (banks are businesses and make money by requiring families to pay interest; families agree to do this because it allows them to move into a house straightaway, without having to wait until they accumulate the full price). Instruction on these aspects of mortgage loans helps develop in students a sense of efficacy for future action (When I grow up, I will be able to borrow money to buy a house if I want to). Worthwhile social education goals are promoted by teaching these aspects of mortgage loans. However, attempts at more complete coverage (that might include loan structures, payment schedules, interest rates, and their interactions) would not be cost-effective with primary students and would shift the focus away from the purposes and goals of social studies.

Students' comments and questions in class sometimes indicated a need to broaden our approach to a topic or develop it further than we had intended. For example, in teaching about prototypical homes from the past and from other cultures, we intended to show different homes and explain the functional reasons why they assumed the forms that they did. Our shelter interview had made us aware that few students knew that the Native Americans who lived in tipis did so because they followed the buffalo and therefore required portable housing. Consequently, our plans for teaching about tipis included emphasizing their portability as a key feature. However, we found that although students could understand the explanation, they initially resisted it. They had never heard of nomadic societies and therefore had difficulty accepting the notion that some people move periodically without possessing a more permanent home base. Consequently, we added information about nomadic societies to our content relating to tipis.

Students' comments and questions about other forms of housing also indicated that they frequently understood that different forms of shelter exist, but not why they exist. For example, second graders typically know or easily learn that stilt houses are situated high on poles to keep them dry from the water below them, but they do not understand (or even appear to wonder) why people live in marshes or floodplains in the first place. These observations led us to elaborate our unit plans to say more about functions and cause–effect relationships that explain why different types of houses are constructed as they are and preferred over feasible alternatives.

In the case of portable shelters or stilt houses, these explanations include descriptions of the economies of the societies (periodic migration to accommodate animal grazing or hunting, cultivation of crops that grow in marshes or floodplains). Other explanations emphasize adaptations to local climate and geography. In the mountain valleys of Switzerland, steeply sloped roofs prevent dangerous accumulation of snow on the roof and cause the snow to pile up against the house, where it acts as insulation. Tropical huts and jungle homes not only capitalize on locally available construction materials (vines and leaves) but also incorporate ventilation and water run-off features that make them well suited to their climate (i.e., they are intelligent adaptations to local conditions, not just primitive shelters thrown together haphazardly).

Our classroom data also allowed us to assess the value of children's literature sources, both as content vehicles and as ways to connect with students' interests and emotions. Nonfictional children's literature is most useful in teaching about how and why things work as they do and how and why they vary across cultures. Fictional sources are more useful for reaching children's emotions, as in reading and discussing stories about homeless people or about the experiences of volunteers at a soup kitchen. Some children's literature that initially looked promising proved to be ineffective. For example, we originally intended to use a book entitled *A house is a house for me* (Hoberman, 1978) to introduce the shelter unit, because it offers cleverly written and illustrated material on the different forms of "houses" lived in by people, animals, or even inanimate objects. As the book progresses, however, the material moves away from the big ideas we wanted to stress. It also becomes more and more fanciful in applying the term "house," to the point that we became concerned about communicating misconceptions. Thus, this book was very relevant to our unit topic but not supportive of our instructional goals.

Some problems with children's literature selections were more subtle, so they were recognized only when the books were used during class (e.g., illustrations that were too dated or otherwise misleading, language that was too difficult or fanciful, and characteristics of the text or illustrations that tended to derail the class from key ideas to side issues). When such problems appeared in nonfictional selections, the books sometimes could still be used as content sources by incorporating their most useful parts and omitting the rest. However, fictional selections usually have to be either read all the way through or omitted entirely.

Sometimes our data produced information about how certain content can be developed effectively. For example, in our unit on shelter we wanted to develop students' consciousness of the problem of homelessness, empathy for homeless people, and sense of responsibility and efficacy concerning their potential for doing something about the problem. These themes are all addressed nicely in the children's book *Uncle Willie and the soup kitchen* (Disalvo-Ryan, 1991), which describes a child's experiences as he accompanies his uncle, who volunteers at a soup kitchen for the homeless.

Key Characteristics of the Units

The units emphasize teaching for understanding (and where necessary, conceptual change) by building on students' prior knowledge and developing key ideas in depth and with attention to their applications to life outside of school. They provide a basis for three to four weeks of instruction, depending on the topic and the degree to which the teacher includes optional extensions. All of the units feature six common components:

1   They begin with focus on the cultural universal as experienced in contemporary U.S. society, especially in the students' homes and neighborhoods (this includes eliciting students' prior knowledge and helping them to articulate this mostly tacit knowledge more clearly). Early lessons use

familiar examples to help students develop understanding of how and why the contemporary social system functions as it does with respect to the cultural universal being studied.

2   The units consider how the technology associated with the cultural universal has evolved over time. Lessons in this historical strand illustrate how human responses to the cultural universal have been influenced by inventions and other cultural advances.

3   The units address variation in today's world in the ways that the cultural universal is experienced in different places and societies. Along with the historical dimension, this geographical and cultural dimension of the unit extends students' concepts to include examples different from the familiar ones they view as prototypical. This helps them to place themselves and their social environments into perspective as parts of the larger human condition (as it has evolved through time and as it varies across cultures). In the language of anthropologists, these unit components "make the strange familiar" and "make the familiar strange" as a way to broaden students' perspectives.

4   The units include artifacts, classroom visitors, field trips, and, especially, children's literature selections (both fiction and nonfiction) as input sources.

5   The units include home assignments that call for students to interact with parents and other family members in ways that not only build curriculum-related insights, but engage the participants in enjoyable and affectively bonding activities.

6   The units engage students in thinking about the implications of all of this for personal, social, and civic decision making in the present and future, in ways that support their self-efficacy perceptions with respect to their handling of the cultural universal throughout their lives. Many lessons raise students' consciousness of the fact that they will be making choices (both as individuals and as citizens) relating to the cultural universal under study. Many of the home assignments engage students in decision-making dis-cussions with other family members. These discussions (and later ones that they often spawn) enable the students to see that they can affect others' thinking and have input into family decisions.

The repetition of these components across units builds students' conceptions of social studies as a coherent school subject with its own purposes, goals, and content. They learn that social studies is about how humans function in their environments and how human societies work.

Example Unit Outline: Shelter

Our units have been published in their entirety (Alleman and Brophy, 2001b, 2002, 2003c). To convey a sense of their organization and content, we reproduce here the titles and lists of main ideas to develop for the lessons in the unit on shelter.

Lesson 1: Functions of Shelter

- Shelter is a basic need.
- Throughout history, people have needed shelter for protection from the elements (sun in hot weather, cold in cold weather, precipitation, wind, etc.), places to keep their possessions, and places in which to carry out their daily activities.
- There are natural factors that affect the kinds of homes built in an area. These include climatic conditions, building materials found locally in large quantities, and physical features. Physical features refer to the terrain and include hills, mountains, valleys, plains, etc., as well as bodies of water such as lakes, rivers, etc.
- There are other human factors that people take into account in deciding the kind of home to build or buy. These include the availability of building materials, economic resources, cultural considerations, and personal preferences.

Lesson 2: Shelter Types in Our Community

- There is a range of shelter types in our local community, reflecting local climatic conditions, building materials, and physical features.
- Factors that contribute to a family's decisions about the type of shelter it will select include location in the community, cost, cultural influences, and personal preferences.

Lesson 3: Shelter Types around the World

- Geographic features, culture, economic resources, and personal preferences are among the factors that figure into people's choices about the type of shelter they will have.
- People all over the world adapt to their environment and, as a result, there are many types of shelters. Until recently, housing construction reflected the availability of local materials. This pattern still exists in some places, but in other places modern transportation has allowed choices to be expanded.

Lesson 4: Progress in Shelter Construction

- New construction techniques and technological improvements are invented and refined over time. Now, besides meeting our needs for protection from the elements, modern homes cater to our wants for a comfortable living space, hot and cold running water, electric lighting, comfortable beds and furniture, etc.

Lesson 5: Steps in Building a House

- Today's homes are planned to take advantage of advances in new designs, technologies, materials, etc. Many workers are involved to ensure that the plans are realized.

- Today, it takes a variety of workers to perform specific steps in building a house or apartment (explain main steps).

Lesson 6: Careers Associated with Shelter

- The home industry provides a range of opportunities for individuals to be creative and pursue careers.
- Many changes have occurred in the homebuilding industry over the past two hundred years (compare pioneer log cabins, nineteenth-century houses, today's houses).

Lesson 7: Costs Associated with Your Shelter

- You can buy a house without having the full purchase price, although you can lose it if you don't continue to make your payments.
- Some people choose to live in an apartment temporarily while they save enough money for a down payment. Others choose apartments as permanent residences for other reasons such as convenience, fewer maintenance responsibilities, etc.
- Banks (and sometimes private individuals) lend people the money to buy a house. The people have to pay back the amount of the loan plus interest. That's how banks make money.
- People have to pay to live in apartments. The rent money is kept by the owner of the building. Renting is a profit-making business.
- Whether you live in a house or an apartment, you pay utility companies for heat (fuel), water, and light (electricity).
- You pay money to the government (taxes) to maintain roads, provide police protection and fire protection, and operate schools. (If you are buying your home, you pay taxes directly to the government. If you are renting, some of the money you pay to the apartment building owner goes to the government for these services.)
- A large part of the family income goes for buying or renting and maintaining the property.

Lesson 8: Choice Making

- One of the choices people have to make is location—where they will live.
- Another choice is whether to rent or buy.
- Other choices concern issues such as the size of the place.

Lesson 9: Portable Shelters

- Portable shelters are built out of a variety of materials, take many forms, and are used for a variety of reasons.
- Especially in the past, portable shelters have been used by nomadic societies.
- Today, portable shelters range from being primarily recreational in our area to being a necessity in a few places.

Lesson 10: Design Your Ideal Future Home

- Location, climatic conditions, availability of materials, cost, and family size and composition are among the factors to consider when attempting to identify and "design" the ideal home.
- Individual tastes and preferences enter into the decision-making process.

Lesson 11: Homelessness

- Sometimes people cannot pay for shelter and utilities, owing to unemployment or underemployment, and some become homeless. Often these circumstances are due to illness, fire, flooding, loss of jobs, accumulation of bills, etc.
- People who are homeless can secure help from community organizations (e.g., the United Way, Rescue Mission, Salvation Army, religious organizations).
- As members of the community, we can contribute to organizations that assist people in need by donating time, food, money, clothing, etc.

Lesson 12: Review

- Revisits the main ideas from Lessons 1–11.

Incorporating the Units within the Larger Curriculum

Our nine units were developed for use within Grades K–3, and especially Grades 1 and 2. Depending on grade level and other factors, teachers need to adapt the content to their students by simplifying or elaborating as needed. If all nine units were used in a single grade level, they would constitute the social studies curriculum for the year. More typically, however, schools use fewer units each year but spread them across several grade levels.

Barbara follows this pattern. When teaching first grade, she begins with the food unit because it has the most connections with students' prior experience. It also lends itself well to introducing timelines, home assignments, and other components of her social studies program that will be included in future units. In addition to the food unit, she typically teaches the clothing, family, and money units to first graders but saves the units on shelter, communication, transportation, government, and childhood for second grade. She has found that although the latter units also can be taught to first graders, doing so requires more transmission of information and heavier scaffolding of students' responses. By waiting to allow her first graders to acquire another year of prior knowledge (including experience with some of the routines in her social studies lessons), she can teach the second-grade units with relatively less emphasis on information transmission and relatively more emphasis on co-construction of understandings.

Jan and Jere's units make up only part of Barbara's total social studies curriculum. Other components include map and globe work, historical and civic content taught around national holidays, and socialization concerning respectful interaction, collaborative learning, and other peer relationship aspects of life in learning communities. Starting with the next chapter, the rest of the book will explore her social studies teaching in detail.

Chapter 4

Using Narrative to Build a Content Base

The Special Challenges of Teaching Young Children

Teaching content-rich subjects (primarily science and social studies) is especially challenging in the early grades. Young students almost always have at least some experiential base to bring to bear, but their prior knowledge about topics addressed in these subjects is usually very limited. Furthermore, this limited knowledge base is mostly tacit (not organized or even verbally articulated, and perhaps never consciously considered), and it often includes many misconceptions. Consequently, unlike teachers in later grades, who usually can begin stimulating new knowledge construction by making connections to an already-established knowledge base, *primary teachers often are faced with the task of helping their students to develop and begin to integrate an initial knowledge base in the domain.* This requires taking little or nothing for granted, teaching (in some respects) as if the students know nothing at all about the topic.

In addition, primary teachers usually have to assume most of the burden of conveying new information to their students. They cannot rely on texts for this purpose, because kindergarten and first-grade students cannot yet read informational texts fluently, and even second- and third-grade students usually have not yet acquired a critical mass of reading fluency and study skills that would allow them to learn efficiently from reading. Thus, most of the content that primary teachers believe is important for their students to learn will have to be conveyed by themselves personally during lessons. They may use books, photos, physical artifacts, or other instructional resources in the process, but their students' initial exposures to new information mostly involve listening to what the teacher says during teacher-led classroom discourse.

Primary teachers need to work within certain constraints as they construct and manage this discourse. Their students' attention spans are limited, and they are not yet able to retain lengthy and complicated explanations, so extended lecturing is not a feasible teaching method. Also, their students do not yet possess a critical mass of cognitive development and domain-specific knowledge that would enable them to comprehend and use the disciplinary content structures and associated discourse genres that are used in teaching subjects at relatively abstract and advanced levels. For example, children have experiences with money and personal economic exchanges, but know nothing of macroeconomics; they can comprehend basic ideas about rules, laws, and authority, but not about comparative governmental structures or other advanced aspects of political science; and they can understand stories about everyday life and key events in the past, but not abstract analyses of macro-level historical trends.

Consequently, although it is just as important for young students as for older ones to offer curricula featuring networks of knowledge structured around big ideas, teachers cannot do this through lengthy explication of concepts, principles, logical arguments, or other advanced disciplinary structures that young students are not yet prepared to understand and use. Instead, they must stick to aspects of a domain that can be made meaningful to students because they can be connected to the students' existing knowledge, and especially to their personal experiences. In addition, it helps to convey this content using text structures and discourse genres with which the students already have some familiarity (and preferably, some fluency).

Narrative Structures as Teaching Tools

One particularly useful tool that meets these criteria is the narrative structure, because even the youngest students are already familiar with it through exposure to stories. Bruner (1990); Egan (1988, 1990); Downey and Levstik (1991), and others have noted that *even very young children are familiar with and adept at using narrative modes of thinking for describing and remembering things that are important to them. That is, they formulate and remember in story form.* The stories are built around one or a small group of central figures and include attention to their goals, the strategies they use to accomplish those goals (often involving solving problems or overcoming obstacles in the process), and the outcomes of their actions for both the central figures and others in the story. The narrative format provides a natural way to remember a great many of the details that fill out the story, organized within the goal–strategy–outcome "story grammar."

This makes the narrative format a powerful vehicle for teachers to use in helping young students bridge from the familiar to the less familiar. Children can understand information about the long ago and far away when the information is represented as stories of people pursuing goals that the students can understand, using strategies that involve doing things that the students have done themselves, can be shown, or can be helped to imagine. Just as children can understand fictional creatures (e.g., hobbits) and worlds (e.g., Harry Potter's) conveyed through narrative formats, they can understand stories about life in the past or in other cultures, so long as the depicted events lie within their own experiences or can be understood and imagined based on those experiences.

Many aspects of social studies are amenable to representation within narrative structures, especially those that involve human actions that occur in steps, stages, or series of events unfolding over time. History is the most obvious example. Although it has its abstract and analytic aspects, much of history involves reconstructing stories of specific events (e.g., the American Revolution) or changes over time (e.g., in modes of transportation). Studies of children's historical learning indicate that much of what they retain about history is organized within narrative structures, usually compressions of larger trends into stories that focus around goal-oriented activities or conflicts involving a few key figures (Barton

& Levstik, 2004; Brophy & VanSledright, 1997). They tend to think of the American Revolution, for example, as a fight between King George of England and George Washington and other Americans who resented his taxes and unfair treatment, not as a protracted and multifaceted conflict between a sovereign nation and a federation of colonies about to become a nation.

Primary-grade children may be limited in their ability to understand the geopolitical aspects of the past, but they can understand stories about wars as attempts to gain control over land or other resources, voyages of discovery as attempts to satisfy curiosity and acquire riches, immigration as attempts to escape oppression or exploit economic opportunities, and so on. Most historical events and trends involved people engaged in goal-oriented behavior, and thus can be conveyed using narrative formats.

Although it is less commonly recognized, narrative formats also are well suited to conveying information about many of the geographical and social science aspects of social studies, especially those involving human actions related to cultural universals. To teach about societies and cultures, whether past or present, teachers can construct narratives explaining how the people meet their basic needs for food, clothing, and shelter within the affordances and constraints of local climate and natural resources, how they communicate and travel locally and across longer distances, and how they act both individually (or as families) and collectively (through their governments) to meet needs and pursue agendas.

These stories provide frequent opportunities to introduce basic concepts and principles of geography, economics, political science, sociology, and anthropology. Also, because they focus on humans engaged in goal-oriented behavior, they provide frequent opportunities to explore causal relationships and make explicit the human intentions and economic or political processes that underlie and explain human behavior but often go unrecognized and thus unappreciated by children. Stories about how key inventions made qualitative changes in people's lives, about why Americans eat relatively more wheat and beef but the Chinese eat relatively more rice and chicken, or about the land-to-hand processes and occupations involved in producing common foods and fabrics and bringing them to our stores all incorporate process explanations (of how and why things are done as they are and how products are developed) and cause–effect linkages (explaining why things are done the way they are and why they change in response to inventions).

Barbara's Use of Narrative

Barbara uses narrative structures to introduce new topics. She typically begins with stories drawn from her own life, selected not just because they relate to the topic, but also because they offer opportunities to highlight big ideas or life applications. Next, she typically draws connections to her students' lives (e.g., family origins in or vacations taken to countries that will be featured in the lesson; jobs held by family members that connect to products or services to be discussed) or to local examples (farm products, stores, government offices, etc.). Then she begins developing a knowledge base structured around big ideas, typically rendered in an informal, storytelling style, often making additional personal or local connections in the process. Narrative structures are especially frequent in two situations: when she is building timelines or in other ways talking about the past, and when she is describing land-to-hand relationships or other processes that occur in steps or sequences.

Barbara's narratives are highly personalized. She frequently uses "I" and "you" language rather than impersonal third-person language. This gives her narrations a more authentic feel than traditional lecture explanations, and her frequent references to what "you" might do make students aware of potential life applications. They also subtly reinforce her efforts to develop her students' perceptions of efficacy (when she talks about things that they could do right now) or possible selves (when she talks about things they might do in the future).

Barbara's personalizations extend to family members. Her students learn the names and many of the significant events in the lives of her husband, parents, sister, and other relatives through their appearances in her stories. The same is true of the families of her students and of other teachers at the school, including adopted children, foster children, and others. Along with personalizing and localizing the curriculum, these references and connections lend intimacy to the learning communities she creates. *She often uses objects or photos as props,* especially if introducing something that she expects to be unfamiliar to many of her students. She routinely uses rich imagery and examples to build "word pictures" of what she is describing. For processes, she often adds hand choreography to supplement the verbal explanation. She also frequently inserts invented dialogue or mini-dramatizations. These are fictional but realistic conversations that might have taken place between people living at the time and place under study, or even thinking (self-talk) carried out by a single individual (such as an inventor).

These devices not only advance the storyline, but also provide opportunities to model (and thus make visible to students) the thinking and decision making that mediate people's problem-solving efforts and goal-oriented behaviors. She routinely depicts inventions, for example, as occurring because people became aware of a problem, brainstormed possible solutions, devised and tested prototypes until they found one that worked effectively, and added improvements later.

Although her narratives are engaging as well as informative, Barbara is careful to keep them focused around big ideas. She does not carry dramatization farther than it needs to go (she might don a hat to signify that she is temporarily personifying a character, but she does not use elaborate costumes); she does not use unnecessary props (ordinarily, there is no need to show apples, cars, or other familiar objects, unless she wants to stimulate her students to think about the objects in unusual ways); and she uses instructional resources only for as long as they are needed and for the purposes for which they were included (e.g., if she wants to show an illustration from a book, she shows and discusses the illustration with reference to the ongoing lesson, but then puts the book aside rather than interrupt the lesson to read the book at this time or look at other illustrations that are not as relevant). "Don't get lost in the props" is one of her rules of thumb for planning informational segments of lessons. This helps her to keep these segments brief and focused.

Barbara typically tries to get through her initial narratives without significant interruption, both to sustain their coherence and flow and to minimize students' exposure to misconceptions. However, she sometimes opens slots for student participation by asking questions or by making partial statements and then pausing to allow students to complete them (typically by supplying a key idea that she already has expressed or modeled two or three times previously). She concludes the initial presentation with a review or summary, highlighting big ideas and explicitly noting connections between successive steps in a process or linkages between causes and effects.

Then she goes back through the content again, but this time shifting from a narrative to a questioning mode. Gradually, as students become more familiar with the content, and to the extent that their responses to simpler questions are encouraging, she progresses from short-answer questions to questions that require extended explanations, and from questions that only require retrieval from memory to questions that require higher-order thinking. When students answer correctly, she often elaborates on their answers to reinforce big ideas or add information not brought out earlier. When they are unable to respond, or respond incorrectly, she ordinarily stays with them to try to elicit an improved response, using the techniques described in Chapter 14.

Although Barbara's narrative presentations can be described as teacher centered, they contrast with more typical modes of teacher-centered instruction, such as lectures, word webbing to develop concepts, rule and example methods of teaching principles, or drill-and-practice methods of teaching skills. Less obviously, they also differ in important ways from typical historical or literary storytelling.

Although they have an informal, spontaneous feel, her narratives are carefully planned to develop big ideas using purposefully chosen examples and illustrations. They offer simplified explanations that her students can follow and relate to their prior knowledge and experience. Her initial pass through the storyline sticks closely to the flow of main ideas; she is careful not to insert unnecessary information, teach unnecessary vocabulary, or in other ways make it difficult for students to follow the flow. She will add more details later when she goes through the material again, especially when she frames questions and elaborates on students' responses.

We will illustrate Barbara's narratives with two examples. The first, on clothing in the past, is representative of the majority of these narratives. The second, on the land-to-hand story of bananas, illustrates how she sometimes assigns roles to her students as a way to personalize the information and add cues that will help them to recall it in the future.

Clothing in the Past

This example is taken from Barbara's fifth day of teaching our clothing unit. The unit begins with lessons on clothing in the contemporary United States, focusing on its functions and on different kinds of clothes worn for different purposes or occasions. The next lesson looks at changes in clothing over time. Barbara decided to spread this lesson over two days because it includes several big ideas and a lot of information that would be new to most of her students. On the first day, she taught about clothing Long, Long Ago (in the cave days). On the second day, she taught about clothing Long Ago (in the Pilgrim and pioneer days) and in Modern Times. The excerpted material is from the first half of the second day, when Barbara reviewed material on Long, Long Ago from the previous day and introduced new material on clothing Long Ago.

The lesson is designed to develop four main ideas:

- Long Ago, clothing was used for protection, decoration, communication, and, later, modesty as well.
- Clothing has undergone a variety of changes over time. These changes have produced clothes that are more durable, water-repellent, lightweight, and convenient to use.
- Thread or yarn is spun from wool (or cotton, etc.).
- Cloth is woven from thread or yarn. It is a fabric, not a solid.

The first of these big ideas focused on the four functions of clothing that had been introduced in previous lessons. It would be reinforced in this lesson rather than introduced for the first time. The other three big ideas would be introduced and developed in this lesson. They focus on progress made over time in improving clothing and on helping children to understand the fundamental nature of cloth (i.e., it is a fabric woven from thread or yarn which in turn has been spun from raw material). Our interview studies had shown that most K–3 students either could not explain what cloth is or mistakenly viewed it as a solid akin to leather or plastic (Brophy & Alleman, 2006).

Barbara begins with a more extensive review than usual. Students' answers to her questions during the second part of the previous day's lesson were not as solid as she had hoped, and she wants to make sure that certain key information is in place. This involves "cementing" accurate information for students who need it, while at the same time adding a few new details to keep other students interested. It also involves repeatedly using key words (e.g., fiber) and describing or demonstrating key processes (e.g., stretching and spinning fibers, weaving them into fabrics).

As she speaks, she refers and sometimes points to objects and events depicted on the Long, Long Ago portion of a timeline that she began during the previous lesson and will complete today. Note that even though she is talking about prehistoric people, she sometimes refers to them as "we" (i.e., human beings), as a way to promote empathy.

T: Now, let me go ahead and remind you of some things that we said about Long, Long Ago. People were living in caves Long, Long Ago. When they first started living, they didn't need clothes because they lived in warmer places and they had more hair on their bodies. But as people started to move to places that were colder and we started to get shorter hair on our bodies, we needed ways to protect ourselves. One of the things that we were already doing for food was hunting—animals like buffalo and deer. So we took what we knew about those animals and we started using their skin to make clothing. One of the things that we were good at gathering was plants. Then people started noticing that they could use the plants that they had gathered to make parts of their clothing and to keep their bodies covered and protected. You can see: these fibers came from a plant. They picked the plant and they took it apart to get these long . . . they look like strings or fibers, and then somebody came up with the idea to weave those fibers together.

This review continues for a few more minutes until Barbara concludes it and makes the transition from Long, Long Ago to Long Ago as follows.

T: But the big idea was cloth, and people first started making cloth out of things—plant pieces or plant parts. One of the plants that they used was a plant that had little puffs on it. Those puffs turned out to be puffs of cotton. Have you ever had cotton balls? [Barbara "drops in" a mention of cotton puffs here, not only because it is an example that her students should be familiar with, but because later in the unit she will be teaching the land-to-hand story of cotton, and she knows that cotton plants are unfamiliar to her students.]

Ss: Yeah.

T: OK. What they would do with the cotton balls is they would take the cotton and they would stretch it and pull it and clean all the dirt out of it, and they would stretch it and make it long and they would twist it and pretty soon it would be a long fiber and then they would take the fibers and . . . [pauses to invite students to finish the sentence]

Ss: Scw it.

T: Weave them together. They would use that to make . . .

Ss: Cloth. [As she talks about cotton puffs and cotton fibers, she shows examples to the students, and she stretches and twists the fibers to demonstrate what she means as she describes these processes. Then she attaches the cotton puffs and fibers to the timeline for future reference.]

T: Cloth. But then they came up with another thing that they could weave or that they could pull into fibers and make into cloth. And this is going to surprise you. Are you ready? What did they start doing between Long, Long Ago and Long Ago to make having food easier? What did they do so they didn't have to go out and hunt and they didn't have to go looking for berries, they didn't have to go kill an animal? They started thinking, "I know what we'll do. We'll do . . . What? [In making this transition to the next point, she does not just stick to clothing but also ties back to the food unit, as part of her attempt to impart a general sense of the contrasts between life Long, Long Ago and life Long Ago. Then she models inventive thinking but leaves the sentence unfinished, hoping that one or more of the students would finish it for her. When no one does, she indicates more directly that she would like them to respond, and one of them supplies the answer she hoped to hear.]

S: They had a farm.

T: They had a farm, and what did they do on the farm?

S: They grew plants.

T: And

S: Vegetables.

T: What else did they do other than grow things on the farm?

S: Um . . .

T: What do you have on a farm other than plants? . . . Baaaaa. [Less direct efforts to elicit "animals" were not successful, so Barbara uses a "giveaway" clue here.]

S: Animals.

T: Animals on the farm. They figured out that if they cut the hair off of the sheep, they could . . .

S: Have wool.

T: They could (students repeat after teacher) pull it . . . and stretch it . . . and twist it into long fibers, so they could take the fibers and . . .

Ss: Weave them together.

T: Weave them together. [Barbara does not directly tell the students to repeat after her here, but the combination of her voice tone and modulation (accompanied by physical demonstrations) emphasizing each of these key steps, followed by a brief pause with an expectant look toward the students, communicates this invitation to them, and they respond accordingly. She then shifts to an informational book on the pioneer days, not to read it but to use some of its photos and provide her own commentary focusing on the big ideas she wants to develop. She first clarifies that although these are photos rather than drawings, they were not taken during the pioneer days. Instead, they depict modern people reenacting pioneer activities.] Let me show you some pictures I have.

S: Cool!

T: These folks are people who are pretending to be pioneers—people who lived Long Ago—one of the groups were pioneers. They are cutting the wool off of the sheep and they are going to make it into fabric. Sometimes they tied them to a tree or a post and then they would use scissors, because by Long Ago people had come up with ideas like making knives and scissors . . . and metal—they were using metal to make tools, so they would take the sheep and cut the wool off. They also did the same thing to goats and rabbits, and they would cut all of the fur off of them. Then they would take it and they had these great big combs. This was called combing because you had two combs and you would do like this with your combs. (Teacher illustrates.) I don't know if you've ever seen somebody's hair get combed, how it gets all straight and all going in the same direction. That's what they would do with these fibers from the sheep or the goat or the llama or the rabbit, and they would do like this with two brushes, and they would get all those fibers going . . .

Ss: Straight.

T: . . . nice and straight and in the same direction. [Here again, Barbara uses hand choreography along with the photos to help students visualize the processes described. She uncharacteristically includes unusual examples (goats, llamas, rabbits) along with sheep. After reading and reflecting on this transcript, she noted that she would not do this in the future. Except for those that students are likely to bring up themselves at this point, anomalies should be avoided in favor of focusing on prototypes (in this case, sheep) when introducing basic information.] They would make nice loooonnng fibers and they would spin them with a spinning wheel . . . there's a picture of a spinning wheel. See, it's got the wool right here, and it's spinning it around and around and getting it tight. If you take some yarn and you twist it and kind of pull, do you see how it twists up, and it gets longer and you can kind of stretch it out, and that's what they did. They would twist it and it would get tighter and tighter and longer and longer and it would twist up, and then what do they have to do with these big long fibers when they're done twisting them nice and firm and tight?

S: Make them into fabric.

T: Right, and how would they do that, Tim?

S: Weaving it.

T: That's right, they would weave it and they would do that with fibers.

S: I think I saw one of those kind of wheels before. [Barbara does not pursue this comment because doing so would not advance the lesson. In these situations, she shows acceptance of the comment with a brief nod or smile, but then resumes the intended flow. As this segment develops, she addresses several agendas simultaneously: repeatedly describing and illustrating processes involved in spinning and weaving; personalizing using the students' shirts; stimulating awe and wonder by emphasizing the large number of fibers needed to make a shirt and the fact that the pioneers had to do most of this work themselves and mostly by hand; reassuring the students that the shearing process did not harm the animals; and helping the students to understand the operations of the machines that were available during the pioneer days, appreciating them as advances even though they were not as advanced as today's machines.]

T: So they started to use wool and cotton.

S: And fibers.

T: And they would spin it to make a fiber and then they would weave the fiber into cloth. Then they could take the cloth and cut it out in shapes. People would sew things by hand. They would cut out the pieces and they would sew the pieces together until they had a whole piece of clothing. Imagine if everything you were wearing, somebody had to cut the hair off the sheep . . .

S: And weave it.

T: That's not even all of it. They had to cut the hair off the sheep; they had to comb it into long pieces; then they had to spin it into long fibers; then they had to weave it into cloth; then they had to cut it out with scissors; then they had to sew it with their hands; and I mean, if you look really closely at your clothes, one single string in Curtis's shirt is one fiber. Can you imagine how many fibers they had to have to make this shirt? I mean you can see all the fibers in it. Goodness gracious, can you imagine how long it must have taken just to make the cloth, let alone cut it out and sew it by hand?

S: And the buttons.

Cole: I wonder how long it was before they had machines?

T: They didn't have machines. They did all of this with their hands. Let me show you. She's sewing it by hand. This one's working to spin it, this one's sewing it, this one little girl is using yarn and she's knitting it into a sock. Everything they made was by hand.

Cole: Today we have machines. [Cole has now twice indicated that he wants to talk about machines. This is not exactly a "teachable moment," because the lesson plan already calls for teaching about machines involved in manufacturing clothing. In fact, Cole's second comment is something of an unwanted intrusion because responding to it directly would require Barbara to make the transition from Long Ago to Modern Times before she is ready to do so. So, she compromises by shifting to talk about machines, and in the process, drops in Cole's name to signal to him that she is responding to his question. However, rather than jump prematurely to modern machines, she talks about the machines of the time such as looms and spinning jennies.]

T: Here's the good news, Cole. Somebody came up with the idea to have a machine. Now the very first machine they had to help them—they still had to use their own arms and legs to make the machines go. Even the spinning wheel is a kind of machine to help them spin those fibers, but she's using the machine.

S: That they had to use their hands and feet.

T: Yeah, and she's weaving this by hand and then using the machine to make it nice and tight and strong. So the first machines were helpful, but they still had to do a lot of it with their hands, and it still did take them some time to get it made. Joellen?

S: How did they get it off the animal? Would they like put them to sleep or something?

T: It was just like a haircut. They didn't take the skin like they did when they got fur. They just cut all his hair off and used his hair. So that would be like if we were to take Laurel and we were to cut all her hair off. We would spin all of her hairs together into really long fibers, and we could weave. I mean, we wouldn't do that with a person. But that's what they did with the sheep and the goats and the animals . . . Soon somebody even came up with a machine that would do the sewing job with the needle, only look: She's pushing with her foot to make the machine go along. So she's like pushing with her foot and it's making the machine go around. It's not plugged into the wall. There was still no electricity here. So she's making it go by pushing it with her foot, and that's the first sewing machine that they had to use. So instead of sewing it up with their hand, they got to use a machine to sew the clothes together.

S: That would make some exercise.

T: It probably took a lot of strength. She probably got a lot of exercise by doing that.

At this point, Barbara diverges from the lesson flow for a couple of minutes in order to allow students to make comments and ask questions about the illustrations she has been showing. Then she makes a transition into the next part of the lesson, dealing with clothing in Modern Times.

The Story of Bananas

The story of bananas is the seventh lesson in the food unit, following lessons on the functions of food, food choices and snacks, changes in food over time, changes in farming over time, development of the food industry, and types of farming. It is one of four lessons on land-to-hand steps involved in bringing common foods to our tables (bananas, peanut butter, pasta, and apple pie). It is placed first in this sequence because it is the simplest story: bananas are grown, shipped, and eaten as is, whereas other foods undergo transformations before they reach the final form in which they are consumed (for example, the milling of wheat into flour, or combining with other ingredients). The lesson is developed around two main ideas:

- Bananas are an example of a food that is grown only in certain parts of the world due to climatic conditions but can be transported to other parts of the world. Bananas must be carefully preserved from the time they are picked until they reach the supermarket.
- We depend on many workers to bring this food to us.

As a series of successive steps, the land-to-hand story of bananas is well suited to the narrative format. In this case, Barbara incorporated student role assignments into the narrative, for both motivational reasons (engage them in the story more directly and help them identify with key characters) and learning reasons (provide supplementary cues—associations between particular students in the class and particular processes or jobs in bringing bananas to our tables—that help the students follow the story on this day and remember it in the future).

For the role assignments, one student was identified as the plantation owner, another as the operations manager, another as a worker who cut the banana stalks from the plants, etc. Although Barbara occasionally asked some of these students to briefly pantomime or act out a minor aspect of their role, this was not a full-scale dramatization requiring costumes, rehearsals, etc. Role assignments are relatively minor elaborations on her typical narrative approach, but she has found them worthwhile, especially when the story to be developed involves a relatively large cast of characters each playing a unique role (e.g., assembly lines, land-to-hand stories).

Prior to the lesson, Barbara read aloud and discussed with students their responses to the previous night's home assignment, which asked them to think about and discuss with their parents what kind of farm they might like to own. The students recorded their answers and brief explanations on provided forms. During this activity, Barbara noted that Tim had expressed interest in owning a fruit farm. When she asked him what kind of fruit he had in mind, he mentioned bananas. She replied that in that case, he was going to love today's lesson.

She then continued reading and discussing other homework responses. When she was ready to begin the story of bananas, she tied back to Tim's response as one basis for the transition. She also tied back to material in previous lessons on farms, which included the ideas that different kinds of soil and climate are suited to different crops. In addition, because the story would include a banana plantation in Honduras, she showed Honduras on the globe and referenced it both to the equator and to Michigan. She does this routinely when her instruction mentions other nations.

T: Tim, it's going to be a great day for you because indeed we are going to talk about a particular kind of farm, a farm where they grow bananas. Isn't that the one that you thought you would like? Today the farm that we are going to talk about needs special weather and it needs special land, just like the farms we talked about yesterday. We're going to talk about a banana farm. They have a special name for it. It's called a plantation. They don't call it a banana farm. You'll hear them say it's a plantation. That's just a fancy name for farm. You need to have nice warm weather for a banana farm or a banana plantation. See this line right in the middle of the earth? (points on globe). That's where it's warmest on the whole earth. So when you look at this globe, if you get closer to this line, you get . . .

Ss: Hotter.

T: Or warmer. If you go farther away, it gets . . .

Ss: Cooler.

T: Right. So look at Michigan. Here we are up here. Are we close to the line or far away from the line?

Ss: Far away.

T: So do you think this is a place where it's going to get hot enough for bananas to grow?

Ss: No.

T: So, Tim, the sad news for you is that if you really want to have a banana farm, a banana plantation, you can't live up here in Michigan. What are you going to have to do?

S: Move down to the line.

T: You'd move down closer to the line. You know what? He could decide that. That's what the people who wanted banana plantations did. They either lived there to begin with or they moved down there to be where it's warmer. Some of the countries that we have near us that grow bananas—they grow bananas in Honduras. They probably grow bananas . . .

S: In Mexico?

T: I don't know that they don't grow bananas in Mexico. They might. The place I was thinking of was Honduras and it's kind of next door to Mexico. So it makes sense that they might grow bananas there. [The idea that the climate is warmer near the equator is not stressed in the lesson plans and could have been omitted here, but Barbara includes it because she views it as a "building block idea" needed to make sense of some of the lesson's new information. She has found that each unit includes several of these building block ideas, especially in the early lessons. Working from analogies to a tower or pyramid of knowledge that has certain significant chunks missing, she uses the term as shorthand for her analysis of why students sometimes struggle with certain big ideas. The fact that climate tends to be warmer near the equator but cooler near the poles is fundamental and often assumed as background knowledge to much of what is taught in science and social studies, so Barbara takes pains to teach it explicitly when it first comes up and to reinforce it frequently when it appears subsequently (as here). In this situation, insertion of the building block idea also allows her to elaborate her personalization of the story around Tim as the plantation owner (explaining that he will need to move to a warmer climate). Note also that when a student suggests that bananas are grown in Mexico, Barbara is unable to respond definitively because she is unsure. Rather than pretend otherwise, she says that she is unsure but thinks that they probably do grow bananas in Mexico, and explains her reasoning. She values such opportunities because they allow her to demonstrate authentic applications of social studies knowledge and model the reasoning processes involved in bringing it to bear on questions of interest.

Issues of whether and when to introduce formal vocabulary can be problematic, especially in the early grades. In this case, Barbara does introduce the term "plantation," but uses the more familiar term "weather" instead of the less familiar term "climate," and does not use the term "equator" even though she teaches that the weather gets warmer as you move closer to "the line around the middle of the earth." Among both social studies educators and elementary teachers, some would agree and some would disagree with these decisions.]

S: Tim could grow bananas right there.

T: Right, he could move. He'd have to move when he was a grown-up. He'd have to take his family and move to Honduras if he wanted to have a banana farm.

S: He could fly there.

T: Look, it's way up here. That would take you lots of hours on an airplane to get there. Now, the reason Honduras works for bananas is because bananas need for it to be very warm . . .

S: Really hot.

T: Yup, really hot. They also need lots and lots of sunlight. As you get closer to that line, the sun shines more and more and more. So the banana plants, that's where they first started growing. That's where they grow the best, and so he would need a farm where it's very sunny, lots of warm weather, and the banana plants would grow there. Now, we're going to take you through what happens to the banana. What did you have for a snack, James? You've taken a banana from Tim's farm or the farm where it really came from all the way . . . Where's the banana now? It's in his belly. So, we're going to go from the land all the way to James's hand so he could eat it and get it into his body. The reason he ate that banana was because . . .

Ss: It's healthy.

T: It's healthy. It comes from the fruit group. It's got vitamins and minerals. It's going to help him grow. [Barbara now has connected to a second student, James, whom she observed eating a banana during snack time. So, the stage is set for a story of a banana grown on Tim's plantation in Honduras ending up in James's lunch box in Michigan. While she is at it, Barbara takes a brief excursion from this day's lesson flow to reinforce ideas about healthy snacks taught earlier in the unit.] The banana is going to start at the plantation. It's going to be on a tree. I actually have pictures that I want to show you. This is an encyclopedia. It has all kinds of facts in it. [Barbara shows and labels an encyclopedia here, and then proceeds to model its use as a learning tool. However, she uses just a few pictures that illustrate aspects of the story with which students are unfamiliar (banana flower, giant bunches on the plant), omitting pictures that do not seem necessary (bugs, crates, cutting down stalks with a machete). As she works through the story/role play, she consciously ties each step to the next to bring out the overall sequence and underscore cause–effect linkages.] This picture right here—can you see stuff that's kind of fluffy at the end of it?

Ss: Yeah.

T: Does it really look like the banana that you ate, James?

S: No.

T: It doesn't look very much like it—a little bit, the shape. It's long and skinny. Let me read to you what it says. "Each banana has a large bud at the end of a stem." So a stem is like a stick and a large bud is like a flower that's getting ready to bloom. OK? And as the stem grows, the leaves covering that part peel back and that's when that flower shows up. Then each of the flowers grows into a little tiny banana. Look at this picture. Those are little baby bananas. Look at how they're up in the tree. There are a whole bunch of them together. Look how many of them there are.

Ss: (Students are excited.)

T: You know what the workers on Tim's farm—on his plantation—will call those bananas? Fingers! Can you look at them and see why they're called fingers?

S: 'Cause they're so small.

T: They're small and do they look kind of like your fingers?

Ss: Yeah.

T: It kind of looks like a whole bunch of fingers stuck right there together, doesn't it?

S: Yeah.

S: There's a whole bunch of them.

S: I can see the bananas.

T: This is the first step. You have to grow the bananas. So we're going to make a card that says "grow bananas." [Barbara often writes key words on cards that will be posted and used in subsequent review and application activities. In this case, the cards will depict each of the major steps in the banana story.]

T: We'll write on them as we go. So the first thing you're going to do, the first thing that happened was they had to grow the banana! Grow the banana. Now, we have to take care of those bananas when they're growing. Somebody needs to make sure that those bananas grow. Do you know what sometimes happens to fruit and vegetables when you're growing them? Bugs come along.

Ss: Eeeeoooou!

T: Have you heard about that? Yup, bugs will come along and they want to eat the bananas or they want to eat the fruit and vegetables, so you either have to spray them or you have to get the bugs off the plants. So we'll say "Spray for bugs." Clean off the bugs. So, the workers that Tim hires will spray on the farm to keep the bugs off the bananas. Tim, who do you think you want to hire to spray the plants? Somebody responsible. Arden would be a good worker for your farm. Pick one other kid that you think would be a good farm worker.

S: A.J.

T: You know what A.J.'s job is going to be? Arden sprayed the bugs and he's taking care of them while they're growing. Good spraying, Arden. But now, the time has come when we're ready to get those bananas off the tree. Let me show you how they look now that they've grown bigger and they're ready.

Ss: Ooooo!

T: Can you see the tree? It looks a little palm-treeish because it's got those big leaves. What are those things?

Ss: Fingers.

T: They're bananas. They take great big knives called machetes, so you're going to have to be careful. I'm glad you picked A.J. because he's a careful guy. They come along to the tree and they WHACK!!! [Demonstrates] Gotta be strong. A nice big whack. And the big, huge knife cuts the whole thing off. Then he's going to carry that great big huge bunch of bananas. Kerchop!!!! The big bundle of bananas comes off. A.J. carries it to a storage house on Tim's farm. Now, while he's cutting the bananas off, Tim or someone that he hires needs to be talking with companies who might want to buy the bananas. Do you suppose that James's mom got the banana at Meijer, Kroger, Farmer Jack?

S: Meijer.

T: Tim's going to hire somebody to fly here to Michigan because Michigan is where the Meijer company is, and that person is going to say great things about Tim's banana plants, and he's going to talk them into buying bananas from Tim. Tim, who do you think would be great to come up to Michigan and talk to the people at Meijer about your bananas?

S: Gretchen.

T: You think Gretchen would? So meanwhile, he's gotta find somebody to buy the bananas. So [writes on card], a buyer. Is he going to send somebody to James's house? [Barbara often uses absurd questions like this one to set up or create salience for the point that she wants to emphasize (in this case, that several middlemen get involved between the

	growers and the buyers). She believes that this helps students to remember the point better, or, in some cases, to get the point in the first place.]
Ss:	No.
T:	He's going to send Gretchen to the Meijer company. He's going to sell all the bananas. Thousands and thousands and just crates and crates and crates. Remember the crates? We looked at the grapes in the crates [in a previous lesson].
Ss:	Yeah.
T:	Same thing. Crates and crates full of bananas. She's going to try and sell them to Meijer. So while she's finding a buyer, A.J is cutting down the bananas . . . We call that . . .
S:	Harvesting.
T:	Nice remembering! He's going to harvest the bananas. He's going to cut them down. [Writes on card.] Harvest the bananas. [Barbara was successful here in eliciting a key vocabulary term from one student, but she suspects that others had forgotten the term and some might even have forgotten what it means. Consequently, she repeats the term "harvest" twice here and in between provides its definition in simple words ("cut them down"). She frequently drops such vocabulary reinforcements into her ongoing narratives.] You know what? They don't have machines that could do that job yet. They have to cut the bananas out of the tree by hand just like people have done since Long, Long Ago. People first found bananas Long, Long Ago when they were foraging for food and they cut them out of the tree. We still do it the same way because bananas could get smushed or broken too easy. A.J.'s job—he took the bananas over to the warehouse and his job is done. You need to find somebody who's going to put them in boxes and big old crates. Who do you think could put them in crates?
S:	Alan.
T:	Alan, can you put all the bananas in the big, old crates? Are you a strong guy?
S:	Yeah.
T:	[Writes] Put the bananas in crates. You can't just put them in a bag because they're going to go a long way. Look how far those bananas are going to go! They're down here and they're going to go all the way up to Michigan.
S:	On a plane.
T:	If they're on a plane . . .
S:	Nine hours.
T:	Yeah, if they went on a plane. Now, you know what? Flying stuff on a plane is pretty expensive. So after they put the bananas in crates, they might not send them on a plane. They'll probably put them on a boat because it doesn't cost as much for a boat. But you know what? It takes a little bit longer. If we don't do anything to those bananas, will they last for months and months?
Ss:	No.
T:	No.

S: They would get black.

T: Right—they would get really brown and then get really black. So you know what they have to do? They have to pick the bananas while they're still pretty green because if they're going to be on the boat for a little while—a couple of days, even—getting to the United States, and if they picked the bananas when they were yellow, by the time they got to us, you're right, Mikey, they would be brown. Yeah, look at the picture that somebody painted—this banana picture. See. These are bananas that are already starting to get . . .

Ss: Brown.

T: Yellow's OK, a little bit of brown is OK. This is the way it looked when you ate it today, right, James?

S: Yeah.

T: Yup. So they have to pick it when it's green, so that by the time James's mom bought it at the store it was yellow, with maybe just a little teeny bit of green. They put those bananas in crates and they put them on a ship. [Writes on card] Put the crates on a ship . . . Tim doesn't own the boat. He pays somebody to let him put his bananas on the boat. So Tim doesn't need to hire anybody to go on the boat. But the people that own the boat do. As a matter of fact, Mariah is the captain of the boat, and Tim's going to pay her money to move the bananas to Michigan. Mariah, you probably need to hire somebody to help you out on your ship. [The school secretary announces on the PA system that Tim has to leave school with his mother for an appointment.] Tim, you know, you've still got those banana plants growing. Who can you hire to come to your farm and manage it while you're gone?

S: I pick Joellen.

T: OK, Joellen, you don't actually own the farm, but he's going to pay you to take care of it. Do you suppose you could do that?

S: Yup.

T: OK, so if you have to have decisions about the banana farm, you'll have to make those decisions, OK?

S: Yeah.

T: You know what? That happens in real life. People that own the farm might go away for a while, so the bananas are on the ship. Who are you going to hire to help take care of the bananas while they're on the ship? It can't be A.J. He's working on Tim's farm. In fact, Joellen's his boss right now.

S: Cole.

T: Cole, your job's going to be loading the bananas on and unloading them off. OK. Look. Here's the boat. It comes all the way around. It can't get to Michigan so it will probably go to New York City or maybe Philadelphia or maybe one of these cities along here. [Shows on globe.]

S: How come Philadelphia?

T: Because they're right there on the water. New York or maybe somewhere in New Jersey or Delaware—one of these cities along here. Then, Cole's going to unload the bananas off the ship, so [writes on card] off the ship.

	Then he'll put them into a truck—a semitrailer. Laurel, can you drive the semitrailer to Michigan with the bananas on it. [Writes on card] Semitrailer takes crates to Michigan. They go right to the Meijer warehouse. Guess who's working at the Meijer warehouse to unload the bananas?
Ss:	Who?
T:	A.J.'s dad [who actually does work at Meijer]. So he's got a whole bunch of his family working. So let's say it's dad's job. It's dad's job to unload Laurel's semitrailer full of bananas. So they have to unload the crates. After A.J.'s dad unloads the bananas at the Meijer warehouse, then they need to take the bananas to the store. They might do that in one of the Meijer trucks. Mikey, do you have a job yet?
S:	No.
T:	Your job—you're working right up at Meijer's. You're going to unload the bananas and put them in the banana section at the store. Have you seen the people that are in charge of the fruits and vegetables? Oh yeah, they're unloading boxes of bananas or boxes of lettuce or boxes of potatoes. So [writes on card], they're going to put the bananas on the shelf—bananas out to buy. They're probably still pretty green because they picked them before they turned yellow. It's been about two weeks since A.J. picked it, and now Mikey is putting it on the shelf at Meijer, and sure enough, here comes James's mom, pushing her cart. James says, "Mom, can I have . . .
Ss:	A banana!
T:	. . . for a snack tomorrow?"
T:	His mom says, "Sure," and she picks out a really nice-looking group of bananas and she puts it in her cart, and now she goes to . . . the cashier. [Barbara paused to open a slot for students to supply the term "cashier" here, but none did, so she supplied it herself and moved on.] Haley, do you have a job yet?
S:	No.
T:	Haley, you are the cashier, and James's mom can buy from the cashier.
S:	You have to be a good reader.
T:	Yeah, you do have to be a good reader to be a cashier, and you have to know numbers, too. All right. Are you ready to tell the whole story together? Oh, wait. I forgot James's part of the story. What was your job?
S:	Eat the banana!
T:	Eat it! That was the last job. Now I might have gotten them out of order a little bit so I have to make sure they're in the right order. All right. Here we go! Ready. Sitting up nice and straight and tall. Beginning again. Here we go! This is the story of how James's banana . . . [At this point, Barbara launches a review of the story, using the cards she has written to highlight the major steps in the right order. When she talks about the time elapsing between the harvesting of the bananas in Honduras and their delivery to a supermarket in Michigan, she uses the class calendar to point out the number of days involved (and in the process, model skills that connect to calendar work done in mathematics). Throughout the review, and

occasionally in the future when she makes reference back to this story, she includes the names of students assigned to key roles (Tim owns the plantation, A.J. cut down the bananas, etc.)]

Barbara concludes the day with a pair-share activity in which students talk with a partner about foods they like to eat that include bananas. This is preparation for a homework assignment calling for them to discuss the same thing with their parents and then write their responses. She omitted the manual's suggestion that the students be invited to draw pictures of workers doing different jobs in the story of bananas because she didn't think that her students could make accurate pictures of that kind of activity yet. However, she did have them record in their journals some of the important things that they had learned that day.

Barbara spent a lot of time on and included the role-playing feature in her story of bananas because it was the first of four land-to-hand lessons that all included attention to a common set of basic steps in crop farming (planting, nurturing and protecting the plants as they grow, harvesting, shipping, etc.). With this base firmly in place, she was able to move more quickly through the following three lessons, without including role assignments. However, she sometimes made use of the banana plantation role assignments by referring back to them to cue students to processes that she wanted to include in subsequent stories. For example, she cued the need to spray for bugs by asking about Arden's job on Tim's banana plantation.

During the transportation unit, Barbara included a similar role assignment feature in her lesson on automobile assembly lines. Rather than attempt to convey the hundreds of highly specific tasks that line workers carry out, however, she developed a simplified version structured around the major parts of cars that she knew would be familiar to her students (so one was assigned to be the person who would put in the seats, another would attach the fenders, another would put on the wheels, etc.).

Concluding Observations

Jan and Jere consider Barbara's narrative style to be particularly effective because it encourages minds-on learning. This is especially important in social studies, where hands-on learning is not always possible, and where many forms of hands-on learning are ineffectual because they distract attention from big ideas. In addition, *Barbara offers several reasons why she prefers her narrative style to more traditional lecture explanations*:

- It allows her to manipulate vocal qualities to hold students' attention and to include emotional components that engage them at deeper levels.
- It improves recall, both by increasing the percentage of information remembered and by focusing on the most meaningful and logically connected material rather than random discrete facts.
- It helps students see logic and connections.
- It creates a greater sense of intimacy between teacher and students and helps build personal relationships within the learning community.

- It removes much of the distance between the teacher as authority figure or expert and the students as learners, changing the tone from formal lecturing to a more intimate sharing of inside information about how the world works (to enhance this aspect of her storytelling, Barbara creates an intimate physical setting by sitting on a low chair and gathering her students close to her and to one another as they sit facing her on a thick rug).
- It makes it easier for Barbara to incorporate her own interests and specialized knowledge.
- It allows Barbara to control the vocabulary used to introduce and develop topics.
- It makes it easier for her to personalize the content to herself and her students.
- It allows her to begin with familiar content and many examples that build toward the big idea rather than stating it initially as an abstraction.
- It allows her to synthesize and make connections as she goes.
- It allows her to frame the current lesson within the larger picture of the unfolding curriculum by connecting it to previous lessons and foreshadowing future lessons.
- One partial drawback is that the conversational style encourages students to want to respond and give input, which sometimes derails the flow temporarily.

In regard to this aspect of her teaching, Barbara has an image of herself as a storyteller reflecting earlier oral traditions, and she describes herself as teaching in a "campfire" storytelling manner. However, she cautions against carrying it too far, drawing contrasts with language experience activities that overemphasize props at the expense of big ideas. She typically first lays a foundation by focusing students on the big picture, then builds part of it in detail, then reverts to the big picture again to help them get their bearings, then returns to building a little more on the foundation, then returns to the big picture again, and so on. The frequent consolidations help young learners keep track of where they are within the larger lesson or unit.

In order to teach effectively in this narrative format, Barbara believes that teachers must: (1) recognize that it often is necessary and appropriate to convey a significant body of mostly new information; (2) understand that students have sufficient capacity to understand the information; (3) possess a good grasp of the basic content; and (4) understand how it connects to content in past and future lessons (curricular articulation). The narrative format allows her to focus on explanations structured around big ideas, so she offers coherent content rather than disconnected lists of seemingly random facts. In the process, she routinely emphasizes the logic of developments, the motivations for people's decisions, and so on. The combination of simplification and coherence makes her explanations more meaningful to her students and easier for them to follow.

Sometimes she will incorporate role assignment (or occasionally, more elaborate role play) into content development when it is suited to the topic, because it engages the students, provides opportunities for them to participate actively, and appeals to multiple intelligences. However, it can become a problem if it becomes time-consuming, disrupts the idea flow, or elicits too many mis-conceptions. Whenever she does use this format, she makes sure to conclude the lesson with review or debriefing activities in which she stresses the big ideas, elaborates on important points that were skipped or poorly developed, and corrects any emergent misconceptions, to make sure that her students leave with correct information.

In summary, what appears to be spontaneous and informal storytelling is actually a carefully prepared narrative constructed to enable Barbara to establish a content base that consists of a network of information structured around big ideas. Having shown in this chapter how Barbara introduces these big ideas to her students, we shift attention in the next few chapters to the big ideas them-selves. Chapter 5 elaborates what is involved in structuring curricula around big ideas and illustrates how Barbara follows through in her teaching about several of the cultural universals. Subsequent chapters focus on big ideas drawn from history (Chapter 6), geography (Chapter 7), and the social sciences (Chapter 8).

Chapter 5

Structuring the Curriculum around Big Ideas

We noted in Chapter 2 that teaching school subjects for understanding, appreciation, and life application involves teaching networks of connected content structured around big ideas, developed with emphasis on their connections and applications. Jan and Jere's units are constructed accordingly, and when Barbara previews them to begin her instructional planning, she pays special attention to the big ideas highlighted for each lesson. Much of her planning involves devising ways to connect these big ideas to her students' prior experiences, to pave the way for her efforts to help them construct the intended understandings. She always plans explanations, questions, and activities to help them see (and in some cases, carry out) applications of these ideas to their lives outside of school. This is basic to making social studies meaningful, memorable, and otherwise powerful for her students. Chapters 5–8 illustrate how Barbara structures her teaching around big ideas.

Focus on Powerful Ideas

The importance of structuring content around powerful ideas has been recognized at least since Dewey (1902, 1938), who viewed them as the basis for connecting subject matter to students' prior knowledge in ways that make their learning experiences transformative. Transformative learning enables us to see some aspect of the world in a new way, such that we find new meaning in it and value the experience (Girod & Wong, 2002). When students explore in depth the concept of biological adaptation, for example, they begin to notice aspects of the appearance and behavior of animals that they did not notice before, and to appreciate the ways in which these observed traits have helped the animals to adapt to their environments (Pugh, 2002). They get more out of trips to the zoo, notice things about their pets that they never appreciated before, and so on.

Others who have addressed the classical curricular question of what is most worth teaching have reached similar conclusions. Whether they refer to powerful ideas, key ideas, generative ideas, or simply big ideas (Smith & Girod, 2003), they converge on the conclusion that certain aspects of school subjects have unusually rich potential for application to life outside of school—most notably, powerful ideas developed with focus on their connections and applications.

Powerful ideas have several distinctive characteristics. First, they are fundamental to the subject area in general and the major instructional goals in particular. They tend to cluster in the midrange between broad topics such as transportation and particular items of information such as the fact that the fuel used in airplanes is not the same as the fuel used in cars. Most are concepts, generalizations, principles, or causal explanations. Examples within transportation include the categories of land, sea, and air transportation; the progression from human-powered to animal-powered to engine-powered transportation; the importance of transporting goods and raw materials (not just people); the role of transportation in fostering economic and cultural exchange; and the development of infrastructure to support a given form of transportation once it gets established (e.g., roads, service stations, traffic control mechanisms).

Powerful ideas are embedded within networks of knowledge and connected to other powerful ideas. Teaching about an object, tool, or action principle, for example, ordinarily would include attention to propositional knowledge (what it is, why and how it was developed, etc.), procedural knowledge (how to use it), and conditional knowledge (when and why to use it).

Big ideas are more generative or transformative than other aspects of a topic, and they provide the basis for worthwhile lessons and learning activities. It is not possible to improve parade-of-facts curricula simply by replacing their worksheets with better activities; one must first replace the knowledge component by shifting from parades of miscellaneous facts to networks of connected content structured around big ideas that can provide a content base capable of supporting better activities. (If you doubt this, try designing worthwhile activities based on information about the states' flags, songs, birds, etc.) Big ideas lend themselves to authentic applications, of which many will be generative and even transformative; trivial facts do not.

Three Layers of Powerful Ideas for Teaching

Big ideas are multilayered. The most macro layer includes overarching cross-curricular and yearlong content. These ideas pop up frequently during planning and implementing of units and lessons. One such big idea that Barbara emphasizes throughout the year, for example, is "When you encounter something new or unusual, keeping an open mind without making value judgments allows you the opportunity to appreciate the realm of possibilities and fosters curiosity." Another example at this macro level is the idea that logic is a powerful tool for making sense of the world and how it works. Often big ideas at this level exist without teachers being aware of how they influence their teaching.

The next level of big ideas applies throughout a unit of instruction. These big ideas can affect the structure and planning of a unit. Their absence at this level can lead to disconnected sets of lessons that focus primarily on activities. Examples of big ideas at the unit level include the following: that geography affects how you meet your needs; that people are more alike than different; and that people make choices based on personal preferences, economic resources, local availability of potential options, climate, etc.

The final level of big ideas involves specific lessons. These ideas guide the teacher's decisions associated with discourse during lessons and related activities or assessments. Examples of lesson-specific big ideas include the following: that trade is one way to get the things you need or want; that it works best when each person has something the other wants; that families change and adapt to changes; and that the money people pay the government is called taxes.

It can be challenging for teachers to keep all three levels of big ideas in mind as they plan, implement, and assess lessons. However, doing so enhances meaningfulness, is cost-effective, and provides the most opportunities for powerful instruction in the time available ("If you don't know where you are going, how will you know when you get there?").

Barbara's Focus on Big Ideas

Through her collaboration with Jere and Jan, Barbara has become much more systematic in structuring her teaching around big ideas, both in her advance planning and in her decision making during lessons. From her experience, she believes that teachers go through four stages in developing expertise in structuring their teaching around big ideas. At first, they are "unconsciously unskilled" about big ideas, thinking that they already focus on them (often because they follow textbooks closely and assume that their content is structured around big ideas). However, if something causes them to assess their teaching critically in this regard, they become "consciously unskilled," recognizing that their instruction is more like a parade of facts than a network of content structured around big ideas. As they begin to work on the problem, they become "consciously skilled," being careful to maintain focus on big ideas when planning and teaching. Eventually, through repeated experiences teaching a given content network with emphasis on the same big ideas, they become "unconsciously skilled," highlighting and making connections among these ideas almost automatically, without much conscious thought.

Barbara was quickly sold on structuring content around big ideas once she heard the explanation for its importance and inspected lessons that had been designed accordingly. Consequently, she was highly motivated to implement this principle in her own teaching. She found it challenging to do so at first, however, and for a while she resorted to jotting down the day's big ideas on index cards that she kept handy for reference during lessons. As she gained experience in using this approach, she became less reliant on these lists and eventually phased them out. She also became less mechanical in moving through the big ideas, shifting from going through them one at a time in a fixed order (checking items off the checklist), to making connections back and forth routinely. She has noticed that her students bring up big ideas more frequently now, and she has generalized the approach to her teaching in other subjects.

Barbara has found that students in the early grades have difficulty handling more than one or two new big ideas per lesson, so if lesson plans call for introducing more than that, she will either pick one or two as primary and treat the others as secondary or else spread the lesson over two days. Also, some big ideas are not the focus of any single lesson but are developed across a sequence of lessons, so they need to be articulated at an appropriate time. Much of what she emphasizes in a given lesson depends on what her students have learned in recent lessons and how well they have mastered it. She gives extra emphasis to big ideas that they find difficult and extra review when it appears necessary.

A clear focus on the lesson's big ideas helps Barbara make confident decisions about what to include, how to make connections, and when to pull students back toward the big ideas if they begin to drift away from them. For example, when she first taught about developments in transportation, she often felt that she was floundering—just putting out a lot of facts and examples without clear big ideas around which to structure her narratives. When she teaches this content now, she is more comfortable and focused, because she emphasizes the big ideas that inventions made it easier for people to travel from one place to another and subsequent innovations improved on existing inventions once people became aware of their imperfections.

Barbara also uses big ideas as the basis for deciding which children's literature selections to include in a unit, and for planning how to present and use the books. A book about the eating habits of animals can be used as a vehicle for talking about the food groups, for example, and in reading the *Little red hen* story, she emphasizes that you have to grow, harvest, and grind wheat before you can use it to bake anything. In fact, Barbara uses this story for different purposes in different subjects. In language arts, the story is read and discussed as children's literature, with emphasis on its literary characteristics and social behavior moral. In social studies, she reviews the story as a setup for the land-to-hand story of apple pie and, in the process, inserts words such as harvest, dough, yeast, and mill that are not included in the book.

Barbara has several big ideas in mind as she and her students work together to create peanut butter during the food unit. She hopes that they will recall nutrition and food group information as well as understand the steps and careers related to growing peanuts and manufacturing peanut butter. She also helps them analyze the amount of processing that the peanuts go through to become peanut butter. Then, during the literacy portion of the school day, the class reads the fanciful book *Peanut butter and jelly* (Westcott, 1992) and compares the book to the actual steps learned in the social studies lesson.

Barbara taught a similar lesson in earlier years before teaching with big ideas. However, her goals then were simply to provide all the students with a shared experience and to sequence the steps in making peanut butter. Most of the lesson was spent shelling and cleaning the peanuts. Students were engaged and motivated, but they rarely carried any big ideas away from the lesson.

Barbara ordinarily includes four major elements in lesson segments that introduce big ideas: (1) using herself as an example; (2) using books, photos, or other instructional resources to provide examples; (3) making personal connections to her students' lives or experiences; and (4) making connections to the big idea and to previous lessons. She tries to weave these elements together, and she tends to come back to one of them if she hasn't included it for a while.

Both Jan and Jere in their development of units, and Barbara in her planning of instruction, struggle with the question of how far to develop a big idea, given limited time and the constraints on primary students' prior knowledge and learning capacities. All of us are comfortable with the notion of "knowledge of limited validity" (Levstik, 1986)—explanations that are comprehensible and accurate as far as they go but do not attempt to go beyond what is necessary to accomplish the lesson's goals.

For example, in teaching about developments in transportation, Barbara emphasized the invention of engine-powered vehicles as a quantum leap. To explain engines, she used the steam engine as an example, illustrating by drawing a fire under a pot of water, squiggly lines coming up from the water to represent steam, and a simple representation of a paddle wheel as something that the steam could turn. She was confident that this much of the idea would be clear to her students because of the drawings and an earlier lesson on hot air pushing up balloons. However, she was less confident of the cost-effectiveness of attempting to present more of the basic idea, such as by using examples of water-powered mills to communicate the idea that once you get something spinning, you can convert that motion into energy to move something else.

Explanations of complex phenomena to young students usually are partial, ending in some form of black box. However, the students usually will accept this. Barbara's steam engine explanation left off with "You need something that pushes it around and around and around. That's how you get your energy." At this point, a student asked how you would stop it, leading the discourse off into a different direction. Then another student wondered how boats could be steam powered because "Wouldn't the water put out the fire?" Barbara provided an explanation in response to this thoughtful question.

Cost/benefit issues arise in connection with questions about not only how much to explain, but also when to explain it. For example, when teaching about developments in transportation, Barbara identified Henry Ford as a key contributor and talked about his inventions and innovative ideas (assembly line, making cars affordable). In doing so, she explained "just enough" about assembly lines to enable her students to follow the flow at the time, but withheld a more thorough explanation because she knew that assembly lines were going to be the focus of a future lesson.

Maintaining Focus on Big Ideas without Getting Sidetracked

Barbara maintains focus on big ideas in deciding what content to include and how to develop that content. For example, one of the food lessons emphasizes that people sometimes use special meals to mark special occasions. As an example, she talked about how she and her husband went to an expensive restaurant to celebrate their anniversary. However, she did not add the name of the restaurant, the fact that it is located at the top of a well-known building, the fact that it revolves slowly to offer a panoramic view, or any of many other details that she might have inserted at this point, because none of them were relevant to the big idea of eating in expensive restaurants on special occasions.

Similarly, when teaching about breads around the world, she gave the name of each bread that she introduced and located the country that it came from on the globe. However, she did not emphasize remembering the names for each of the breads or the grains from which they were made. Nor did she introduce other geographical facts about each of the countries mentioned. Instead, she focused on the big idea that the three basic ingredients of flour, water, and yeast are used to make all of the different kinds of bread found in different parts of the world.

During a lesson on healthy foods, a student commented that an ad on television said that Life cereal is healthy. In response, Barbara could have foreshadowed a lesson in the communication unit by noting that ads are intended to get you to buy a product rather than to give you balanced and accurate information. However, even though this is a big idea of some importance, it was not relevant to the ongoing lesson and would have derailed the intended flow. Consequently, she acknowledged the comment but refocused attention on the point she wanted to make (that you can find out what is in foods by reading the ingredients information on the container).

Techniques for Focusing Students' Attention on Big Ideas

In addition to using big ideas to guide her own planning and teaching, Barbara uses several techniques to help her students recognize the importance of the big ideas, remember them, and to see their connections and applications. In the first place, when she is ready to state the big idea initially, she does so with particular emphasis (e.g., prefacing it with group-alerting statements such as "Look me in the eyes," or "Here's the scoop.").

Then she restates it several times, often rephrasing it. For example, as part of making the point that farms in the past were quite small but modern farms are quite large, she pointed to an illustration and said, "Look at those big fields full of wheat. Lots of space. Lots of land."

If a cause–effect linkage is involved, she often articulates the linkage both forward and backward ("What things do we have because there are wheat farms? . . . If we didn't have wheat farming, what wouldn't we have?"). These multiple repetitions and rephrasings in alternative formats help make sure that students both understand and remember the big ideas.

Barbara's responses to and elaborations on students' answers to her questions similarly reemphasize the big ideas. If the response does not include the big idea she was hoping to elicit, she may ask follow-up questions or elaborate on the response in ways that express the big idea. During reviews, she elicits restatements of the big idea from the students themselves through purposeful questioning, and concludes the segment with her own final restatement.

For variety, she also uses other techniques suited to the situation. She often builds up to the big idea by introducing some basic information and then asking questions designed to stimulate the students to articulate it themselves. For example, as she showed and led discussion about toys and games used by pioneer children, she noted or elicited that these children did not have a great many toys, that the toys they did have were simple, and that many of their playthings were found objects, or toys constructed from materials found near the house. Then she cued the shift to the big idea by asking, "What are you noticing about toys and games from long ago?"

On occasions when a student responds to a question or makes a comment that articulates the big idea nicely, she sometimes will ask the rest of the students if they agree with this statement, as a way to reinforce their attention to it. Other techniques that Barbara uses for maintaining each lesson's focus on its respective big ideas are identified and illustrated in Chapters 11–14. For now, however, we will focus on some of the big ideas themselves.

Cultural Universals

Jan and Jere's units provide for systematic instruction on food, clothing, shelter, communication, transportation, family living, childhood, money, and government. Each unit includes information about K–3 students' thinking about the topic, followed by lesson plans built around big ideas. We do not reproduce that curriculum material here, but instead relate some noteworthy observations about the way Barbara develops these topics with her students.

Food

An early lesson in the food unit is built around a food pyramid poster that reflects guidelines for healthful eating. The pyramid begins with a small "other" category at the top, then expands to larger meat and milk categories, then still larger fruit and vegetable categories, then ends with the largest category (grains) spread across the bottom. In combination, the pyramid shape and the placement of these categories provide a visual illustration of the guidelines for healthful eating (i.e., eat more servings per day of the foods in the larger categories toward the bottom of the pyramid).

When Barbara first started teaching with the food pyramid, she would invite her students to decide what groups to talk about first and to suggest examples of each food group. However, these lessons tended to get chaotic and also usually left the "other" category to the end. Now, she leads her students through the food pyramid in a top-to-bottom order and shows foods that she has brought from home as examples from each category. Beginning at the top allows her to start by showing examples of foods included in the "other" category (fat, oil, sweets). Then she moves to the next two categories (meat/protein and milk/dairy), which are more familiar to her students and easier for them to talk about. Here, she engages them in suggesting additional examples.

Going through the pyramid in a top-to-bottom order also means that the latter part of the lesson focuses on the foods that people should be eating most frequently, which facilitates transition into the follow-up activity that involves assessing potential meals to determine whether they are balanced and healthful. In the process, Barbara gets into complications such as that certain vegetable proteins are included in the meat group and some foods span two or more groups (ice cream includes sugar; hot dogs and bacon include a lot of fat and oil; pizza includes bread, vegetable, milk, and meat products). She includes spices even though they are not on the pyramid. She deliberately mentions calories but does not try to provide a scientific explanation of the term (this would not be cost-effective early in first grade). She notes that processed versions of foods often are less healthful than raw versions, either because the processing (e.g., cooking) has eliminated some of the nutrients or because less healthful ingredients are added (e.g., sugar).

All instructional planning involves making decisions about what content to include, but this question is especially challenging when teaching young students with limited prior knowledge of the topic. Ordinarily, lessons focus on the purposes and the goals of activities and the processes involved in carrying them out, without getting into extraneous details or trying to teach too much specialized vocabulary.

Barbara's decisions about whether to introduce a specific term are made mostly on the basis of her assessments of cultural literacy (i.e., the term will come up frequently in the future) and of the term's unit- or curriculum-specific centrality (i.e., it relates to a big idea). For example, the lesson on advances in farming does not include the term "harrow," and Barbara ordinarily would not introduce it. However, one year her teaching of this lesson included the following excerpt:

T: What do they do after they plow?
Ss: Plant.
T: They have to plant the seeds. Take a look [at an illustration in a book]. Here he is with the horse. And this back here, the seeds were in it, and the seeds would drop down into the . . .
S: (Inaudible) [Student asked something about the harrow.]
T: It's called a harrow. H A R R O W [spells the term]. That name isn't important, but the job was to get the seeds into the ground . . .

As can be seen in the way that Barbara was proceeding before the student asked the question, she was not intending to introduce the term "harrow" when explaining the process of dropping the seeds into the plowed furrows. Because the student asked, she did supply the term, but then quickly returned focus to the processes involved in planting.

Earlier in that same lesson, a student asked a very good question ("How would you get a plow if you didn't know how to make one?") that is difficult to answer in a way that a first grader could understand. A full explanation would get into concepts such as independent inventions, diffusion, and tool making as a specialization. However, Barbara provided a "just enough" explanation:

T: Somebody had to think of the idea. Somebody who was looking around and said, "You know, this would be much easier if I had a stick, or maybe if it had three sticks." And they did. Look, this has three sticks. [Pointing to an illustration of a primitive plow in a book.] And later someone said, "You know, I bet it would be easier if I put a big handle up here." And they put it together and tried it and it was better. And maybe they tried some things that didn't work. So somebody came up with the idea because they said, "How can I make this better?"

Even when they are not abstract, some things can be complicated to explain to young learners because doing so involves explaining several other things along the way. To explain about potting as an early method of food preservation, for example, Barbara had to explain the process of converting clay into pottery and also explain what lard is:

T: They also did something called potting. They would take meat and pound it until it was like a mushy paste and then put it into a pot that was made out of clay. Clay was down in the ground and they figured out that if they made a bowl out of it and put the bowl in the fire, it would get hard. So they would take this clay bowl and they would fill it with the mashed-up meat and fill the pot up and then they would cover the top of it with what we call lard. Lard is just the fat that comes out of an animal. The lard would keep the germs from getting to the meat. Let me show you a kind of picture. They would take the meat and they would pound it into a paste and they would put it in the pot and then they would cover it. If you've ever seen . . . like if mom's ever cooked with Crisco—big white goopy stuff. It looks almost like a glue stick—a mushy glue stick. So that lard, that mushy stuff, they would pack it down on top of the meat and that would keep the germs from getting in. And that was called potting. Then later on they would scoop all of the lard off the top and they could get to the meat. It would be all kind of mushed and dry so they would add water to it and they might make soup or stew out of it.

The need to provide these inserted explanations conflicts with the need to maintain the continuity of the "story." Yet it is important to include such explanations because if a text passage or teacher presentation contains too many unfamiliar terms, it will not be coherent enough for students to follow (Beck & McKeown, 1988).

Barbara's focus on the big ideas relating to the purposes of activities and the processes involved in completing them can be seen in the following excerpt, in which she recaps the land-to-hand story of pasta elaborated in the previous lesson. She emphasizes choices, repeats the term "pasteurized," reuses a prompt introduced earlier to elicit understanding of what pasteurizing does, and ties back to material on food preservation taught in a previous lesson. Mostly, however, she emphasizes motivations and cause–effect linkages in talking about why the different steps in the process of manufacturing pasta are performed.

T: I want to remind you of the story about pasta. First you grow the wheat, harvest the wheat, grind the wheat, take the flour to the pasta factory, then you mix the ingredients. All you need is flour, water, and eggs to make pasta. Sometimes you can choose to put other things in, like milk or tomatoes or spinach. You don't have to. You can. If you needed to make pasta, you could just use those three things to make pasta. Then to make the dough, you put all the ingredients in, you roll the dough, you pasteurize the dough—you get it really hot to kill the . . .?

Ss: Germs.

T: Then you cut the dough into strips for fettuccini or into corkscrews or into shells or into those funny little things we saw in the book called tortellini. So you cut the dough into whatever shape you're going to choose. Then, you can either have it fresh—nice and soft—or you could dry it. If you dry it, it will . . .?

Ss: Turn hard.

T: It gets hard. Why would you want to dry it? Who wants to eat crunchy pasta? Why would you dry it? Why would you do that, Arden?

S: So the germs won't get in it.

T: So the germs won't get back in there and the pasta will . . .?

S: Last longer.

T: Last longer. It's a way to preserve or save the food longer.

S: You don't want to eat it.

T: Yeah, I wouldn't want to eat it when it's hard and crunchy. You definitely need to boil it in water. Then you're going to put the pasta into a package, then put the packages into boxes so you have maybe ten or twenty packages all in one box. You load those boxes onto your semitruck. The semitruck takes it to the store and then someone will take those boxes off of the truck. They put the pasta on the shelf, and someone comes along and picks it out. There's lots to choose from. There's red ones that have tomato flavor and green ones that have spinach flavor, and long skinny ones and curlicue ones and ones that are called bow ties because they look just like bow ties, or ruffled ones. Maybe you want to make lasagna with it, so the choice of what kind of pasta to buy depends on what you like and what you're making.

Clothing

Our interviews with children about clothing indicated that most of them knew a lot about the nature and functions of business clothes, work clothes, and play clothes, but most did not know that cloth is a fabric woven from threads spun from the original raw material (they thought it was a solid, like plastic or leather). Consequently, the land-to-hand lessons near the beginning of the unit emphasize the processes of spinning threads or yarn and weaving fabrics. The first of these lessons tells the story of wool, because children can easily understand shearing sheep (using the haircut analogy) and can be shown the processes of spinning (twisting the fibers of combed wool into yarn) and weaving (the woolen yarn into a fabric).

It is relatively easy for children to follow this story because the wool used to spin yarn is transformed only minimally (cleaned, combed) from the raw wool sheared from the sheep, and because woolen yarn is coarse enough to allow the students to observe directly, or even participate in, the processes of spinning and weaving.

The next lesson provides the story of cotton. This is more challenging to explain to children because most of them are much less familiar with cotton plants than with sheep, and it is harder to demonstrate or scaffold participation in spinning and weaving processes because the fibers are much thinner. However, the students have already learned about these processes in the previous lesson, on wool. Teaching them about cotton requires detailed explanation of the processes involved in extracting fibers from cotton plants, but teaching subsequent material on spinning and weaving mostly involves tying back to familiar big ideas, not introducing these ideas for the first time.

The following excerpt illustrates Barbara's teaching of part of this lesson. Prior to the excerpt, she was reviewing responses to a home assignment calling for students to bring clothing items from home and talk about their functions. She saved a T-shirt for last, to facilitate the shift into the lesson on cotton.

T: I have a T-shirt. Who brought the T-shirt? . . . Tell us about it.

S: It communicates that I like rollerblading.

T: OK. What else is it good for?

S: Modesty.

T: Why is it good for modesty?

S: Covers your body.

T: Keeps your body covered. Is that made out of wool, do you think?

S: No.

T: I think not. He's feeling it and it's smooth. If you look at it closely, does it look like the wool we looked at?

Ss: No.

T: The wool looked kind of rough and scratchy. The fibers looked really different, didn't they? This is made from cotton, and I'm so glad you brought it today, because guess what we're talking about today?

S: Cotton?

T: Cotton. We're going to talk all about cotton and we're going to see if we can figure out how to go from the cotton to this shirt. Can I hold on to it while I talk?

S: Yeah.

T: All right. Thanks. What are you wondering, Mariah?

S: If you put cotton in a washer, it'll shrink.

T: Yeah. We'll talk about cotton and what to do with it and how to take care of it as we go. Wool comes from what?

Ss: Sheep.

Ss: Alpaca.

T: Sheep or alpacas or goats. Cotton, on the other hand . . . where does cotton come from, Darryl?

S: Trees.

T: Trees or plants. So cotton must not come from an animal. Cotton must come from . . .

S: Plants.

T: You can tell. You can see part of the plant right in there. So we're going to talk today about how cotton gets from a plant to a shirt. Does this shirt look like a tree?

Ss: No.

T: Does it look like a plant?

Ss: No.

T: Does it look like leaves?

Ss: No.

T: Does it look like something that's been growing?

Ss: No.

T: So we must have to do a lot of work to get from the plant to a shirt. More than likely most of you are wearing something cotton today. I know I have a cotton shirt on. If you're wearing blue jeans, blue jeans are made out of cotton. Mariah, I'm not sure if that's cotton. Can you feel A.J.'s shirt next to you instead?

S: Is mine cotton?

T: Yup. The way I'd know for sure, Mariah, would be if I checked the tag, because the tag tells us what it's made out of. This tag says 100 percent cotton.

TA: Ninety percent polyester, 10 percent spandex. [An undergraduate student teaching assistant reads the label in Mariah's shirt.]

T: So that's not made out of cotton. Mariah, we'll talk about how we got that on a different day, but I think everybody else should have been able to feel something that you were wearing to know that it's made out of cotton. Where'd we say cotton first started out, Curtis?

S: A plant.

T: It starts out as a plant, so I wanted to make this cotton shirt. The first thing I'm going to have to do is . . .?

Ss: Grow it.

T: I'm going to have to grow it. I'm going to have to put a . . . [pantomimes planting]

Ss: Seed.

T: A seed in the ground. What do we call the person who takes care of the plants?

Ss: Farmer.

T: A farmer. Sure. A farmer's going to have to put the seeds in the ground, grow the cotton plant, and he's going to have to take care of it. He might need a tractor. He might need people working with him. He might need to water it. He might need to feed it. Some people choose, instead of growing food on their farm, to grow cotton on their farm. What they do is they have plants that look like this [shows illustration from book] . . . It grows nice and tall and then a flower pops out, the flower changes color, and then you end up with this big boll right here. Then, on the inside of it, as it starts to die . . . you know how like right now our leaves are changing color because they're starting to die and the green that's in them is starting to go away so we can see the color? That's kind of what happens for the cotton boll too. The flower grows and everything's nice and green. And then it starts to die because the plant wants there to be more cotton plants, so inside here it makes seeds and it attaches those seeds to a white fluffy stuff. Now if I just left my cotton plant, eventually the seeds would float away with the white fluffy stuff and then the seed would land and then a . . .

S: A cotton plant.

T: A new cotton plant would grow, and that's how it used to be that they got a lot of cotton plants. Now we have farmers that get the seeds out of the cotton plant and put them in the ground themselves. That way they could make more plants than if that white fluffy stuff floats away. What do you think might make that go away?

Ss: Wind.

T: The wind would blow the cotton around.

S: Sometimes it moves a long way.

T: Yeah, if it was a nice hard wind. So, taking a peek at this cotton that's in here [shows raw cotton], you can see little bits of seed tucked in there. Where I'm looking on this side I can see. These are cotton bolls. What do you see?

Ss: Seeds.

T: Seeds. Look. I'm stretching it. Do you see the fibers? It's getting kind of stringy. Do you remember talking about fibers?

Ss: Yeah.

T: What do we do with the fibers?

S: Pull it.

T: Yeah, so do you have a guess already about what's going to happen down the road? This is a cotton ball [not a raw boll, but a manufactured cotton ball]. This is not really what grows in the plant. Do you see how it kind of looks a little different?

Ss: Yeah.

T: They've taken this [boll] and somebody in a factory has made this [ball]. This [raw boll] is real cotton and I can tell because it has little bits of plant and little bits of seed things in there. I bet if you take a look at this, you're going to be able to guess what our first job is going to be after we're done picking the cotton. So pass that around and give it a feel and take a peek at it. Does it feel like the cotton? What do you notice? It feels soft.

S: It feels like my shirt.

T: Kind of feels like your shirt?

S: It feels funny.

S: Where would you go to get cotton with seeds on it?

T: If I wanted cotton that had seeds, I would go to a place where cotton grows . . .

S: I mean how did you get that?

T: This is Dr. Alleman's. She must have gone to a cotton plant, broken off a piece of it and put it in her jar. Cotton needs to have a warm place to grow. Here in America, in the United States, cotton can grow down south in states like Mississippi, Alabama, Georgia, down closer to Florida where it's nice and warm. It can't be too wet. It needs to be warm and a little bit dry for cotton to grow. So, the first job was what?

Ss: Grow it.

T: To grow it. You've gotta grow the plant, plant the seed in the ground and grow it. Next, somebody has to get this cotton off. Look at that cotton field.

S: It's full.

S: That's a lot.

T: It looks like maybe even there's snow on there or somebody's glued cotton bolls to all those plants, but that's just the way it grows in the field. It looks just like that does in the jar. The farmer's next job is to get just the cotton off of the plant. Now, today we have machines that help pick the cotton, and those machines leave the cotton plant there and just get the cotton off of it, because you want the plants to grow for next year. [At this point, Barbara detours from the main storyline to talk about handpicking cotton and slavery, then resumes the land-to-hand story.] . . . OK, let's go on to what the steps are. The first thing you gotta do is . . .?

Ss: Grow it.

T: Grow the cotton. Then you have to . . .?

Ss: Pick the cotton.

T: Pick the cotton. Looking at that cotton, what do you suppose we need to do next to it? What do you think, A.J.?

S: Clean it.

T: Clean it. We've got to wash it clean, and what did we say was in that cotton?

Ss: Seeds.

T: Seeds, so we've got to get out the seeds, and there's dirt and twigs. What do you think, Mariah?

S: You have to weave it.

S: Stretch it.

T: You have to weave it, but before you weave it, like you said, you pull it, you stretch it . . . Now that I've got long fibers of cotton, what am I going to do?

S: Weave it.

T: You're going to weave it into . . .?

S: Yarn.

T: Fabric. After you weave it, it's called fabric. [From this point, Barbara leads the class twice more through the basic steps of growing the plants, removing the bolls, cleaning them, stretching the fibers, twisting them into threads, weaving the fabric, and then manufacturing the garment by dyeing, cutting out fabric parts, sewing them together, adding buttons, etc.].

The next lesson tells the story of silk. Barbara knew that her students were much less familiar with this fabric than with wool or cotton, so she began by talking about its look, feel, and other characteristics that motivate people to continue producing it even though it is time-consuming and expensive to do so. She talked about her wedding dress as one example and was prepared to cite others, but then noticed that Jan was wearing a silk blouse that day. Ordinarily, Barbara made no mention of the fact that Jan was sitting behind the students taking notes on the lesson, but on this day she seized the opportunity and asked Jan to circulate among the group and allow the students to feel her blouse. She then launched into the land-to-hand narrative, using a book on the topic that included good illustrations of each stage. The book was not a children's literature story but a book about fibers that was beyond her students' readiness, so Barbara told the story in her own words without reading from the text.

After her students had learned about three natural fibers (wool, cotton, and silk), Barbara was able to teach them "just enough" about synthetic fibers to support learning with understanding. The challenging part was teaching about the raw materials, which Barbara approached by regaling her students with stories about how scientists had figured out ways of processing and combining surprising raw materials such as oil into fibers that could be spun into thread. After that, the rest of the story was familiar (thread is spun from raw material, fabric is woven from thread).

Transportation

Barbara's teaching about transportation includes some content that ordinarily would be classified as science rather than social studies, including basic concepts about engines, transmission systems, and other key components of cars (she studied automotive engineering before deciding to become a teacher). For the most part, however, she focuses on teaching about transportation as a cultural universal. That is, individuals, families, and small communities rely on transportation not only to enable people to go where they want to go, but also to bring necessities to their homes, raw materials to factories, and finished products to stores. Increasingly, they have relied on long-distance transportation to broaden their worlds through economic and cultural exchange (exporting their products and importing products that are not available locally).

In developing this material, Barbara emphasizes the needs, goals, and logical thinking involved in developing and improving on new forms of transportation. She depicts people Long, Long Ago as noting that many animals were large enough to load material on or to pull loads piled on travois, sleds, carts, or wagons. This led to attempts to domesticate large animals for this purpose (teach them to be calm and cooperative around people and train them to carry things). Similarly, rivers were major barriers to land transportation. Time and energy devoted to this problem led first to the development of wide, flat boats used to ferry people and their belongings across rivers, and later to the development of bridges.

She also emphasizes logical explanations for variations in transportation used across time or geographical locations. People who lived on islands or along coasts led the way in developing and perfecting water transportation; rivers are the major "highways" in relatively undeveloped areas (and, in the past, in the United States); sleds pulled by huskies were very well suited to transportation in the Arctic regions; bicycles and small motorcycles are very well suited to densely populated cities in Asia and elsewhere; and so on.

Communication

Barbara finds that the communication unit is the most difficult of our cultural universals units for her students. Compared to a topic like clothing, it is much larger and more multifaceted. There are many types of communication to address, each requiring term definitions, and it is harder to see connections across lessons. At first there did not seem to be any single big idea to hang things on, although eventually she settled on the giving and getting of messages as the key idea.

She also noted that timeline activities for this unit are more challenging because rather than developing relatively linearly over a long time period, communication technologies evolved relatively slowly prior to electronics but then exploded. Furthermore, many inventions allowed people to do something completely new that could not be done before, rather than being mere improvements over existing technologies.

The timeline itself is more complicated than the others because it requires more photos and illustrations obtained elsewhere (relative to Barbara's own drawings). She feared that reference to so many inventions occurring within a relatively small timeframe could cause her students to lose sight of where things are "placed" on the timeline. Consequently, for the communication unit, she treats the twentieth century as its own timeline segment, to allow room for adding all of the important recent communication inventions.

The process aspects of electronic communications are also challenging to teach because they are not tangible or even showable through photos or illustrations. The following excerpt comes from a lesson in which Barbara provided basic explanations about radio and television broadcasting and reception. Starting from the idea that voices and other sounds come to us as waves traveling through the air, she explained that microphones at the originating site pick up sound waves from the people we hear on the radio; these are converted to pulses and sent electronically to the broadcasting tower; they are sent out as sound waves through the air from the tower; and they are received by our radios and converted back into their original form, enabling us to hear the speech as if it had been spoken right in the same room.

T: We talked yesterday about radio and I want to show you something. Do you remember that man yesterday whose name was Marconi? He's the one who first figured out a way to use radio waves to send a word message. He invented this machine to do it. You can see that the first radio was about 1900 [on the timeline], so it was about 100 years ago when he first figured out how to make it work, and he sent messages a long way and he could do that with both a radio and sound. If you take a look, the first radios looked a lot different than our radios do now [shows illustration from a book].

S: Wow!

T: Some of the things were the same . . . they had dials and we have dials on radios sometimes, like in your car, the dial is the knob you turn. It had a speaker, which is where the sound comes out, so those were some things that were the same. You can see—this is actually the picture of a radio tower. Radio and television work a lot the same. They both have antennas and they send out a signal, and the signal waves through the air—like when you drop the pebble in the water and the wave goes away from the pebble. The same thing happens with a TV transmitter and a radio transmitter. It sends the wave until it gets to your house. Here's the microphone at the radio station and it goes through this thing that's called a transmitter, and that just means that it sends it. It takes the man's voice and it sends it through here and it takes it to the tower and sends it through the tower. They've gotten smarter and better at sending radio signals, and now do you know what? Mr. K. [Barbara's husband] loves to listen to hockey games from where I used to go to school where we met. It's so far away that our radio can't pick up the radio waves from there. It's too far away. It's like 500 miles away and our radio doesn't work that far away. But you know what they do now? They take the radio waves and they send them through the computer so he can pick a spot on the computer and if he dials up the right place on the computer on the web, the radio station comes right over our computer. Do you know what? A couple of years ago, nobody thought of that idea. But somebody figured out that it would be a cool way to do it.

S: Mrs. K., the radio waves don't have very far to get to the school because they're not very far from the telephone line. [This accidental detail in the illustration has prompted the misconception that the radio waves travel through the telephone lines. Barbara addresses it by pointing out that no wires are hooked to the tower sending out signals, and by giving more information about wave transmission and reception.]

T: Oh, you know what? The telephone wires don't have anything to do with the radio. The radio waves go right through the air. Take a look at that tower. There are no wires hooked to that tower. Those red lights that you see, those are things moving through the air that you can't see. They are around us all the time. There are radio waves here in the room right now. If I was to take a radio and turn it on, the music would come out on the radio because there are radio waves right in here, but you just can't see them.

S: Mrs. K., the radio waves are invisible, just like the air.

T: Yeah. They're moving through the air. There are pieces inside the radio and their job is to catch those waves and turn it back into the sound that the person was making at the station. This morning as I was driving in, the woman was telling all the news and what the weather was going to be, what the temperature would be today. It took her voice and sent it through. My car with its antenna caught the waves and then made them come out. When I change the knob in my car, that tells my radio which waves to catch because each station sends out different waves. There's also a radio station called WITL, there's a radio station called WFMK here in town, there's a radio station called Q106, there's a radio station called 95FM. That dial in my car with the numbers tells my radio which station—which waves—to catch.

S: Sometimes people have a ball on top.

T: Some people choose to put a ball on top of their antenna, but you know what? The radio waves go right through that, just like they come right through the glass in our windows or the walls. So radio waves can go right on through stuff. [She moves on to talk about uses of radio.]

Barbara provided just enough information to support basic understandings, without getting into complications such as AM versus FM wavelengths. She made references to "jobs" that various components of broadcasters and receivers perform, as a way to provide partial explanations for some of the functions. Then, to tie back to her students' lives, she questioned them about what kinds of things they could hear on the radio (news, music, ads, weather, etc.) and mentioned some of the local stations and radio personalities.

She then went on to television, building on the prior segment by noting that not only speech and sounds but also pictures and continuous video can be broadcast through the air to receivers in our television sets. Because it was of more interest and relevance to her students' lives, she provided more information about television production and careers, taking them through various steps and associated job roles in television broadcasting (actor, announcer, director, camera operator, etc.). She likened the editing of video to the editing of newspaper copy, explaining that both involve getting rid of mistakes and fixing it so it looks best. This built on a newspaper simulation done previously, which also emphasized key responsibilities and job roles (reporter, editor, editor-in-chief, person who lays out the page, printer, etc.).

During the communication unit Barbara introduces her students to a selection of world languages as well as to sign language and Braille. Her lesson on world languages is built around a poster that shows eight languages and the countries in which they are spoken, as well as examples including common greetings equivalent to "hello" or "good morning." As usual, she enriches the lesson with a lot of personalizing and local connections.

For example, one year she noted that she had taken French and Spanish and counted to ten for her students in each language; she included tiebacks to what the students had learned about words as symbols and about Columbus mistakenly thinking he had reached India; and she showed a Frosted Flakes box that a fellow teacher had brought to her from Cancún, so she could show her students what the name of the cereal and the other information on the box looked like in Spanish.

She also included a lot of additional geographic and cultural information along with what she was teaching about languages (her students could take some of these languages when they got to high school; words that have the same meaning often also have a similar sound when they come from countries that are close to each other; some languages are spoken in many different countries, either because they are neighbors in the same world region or because they originated in countries that sent ships around the world and colonized the places they discovered; the people of Quebec speak French rather than English like the rest of Canada; China has more people than any other country in the world; and Asian languages are read top to bottom rather than left to right). When she introduced each country, she located it on the globe (pointing out Cancún in Mexico).

When teaching sign language, Barbara includes references to illustrations in a book, but mostly provides her own demonstrations. She goes beyond teaching just enough about sign language to create a basic understanding, because she wants her students to recognize certain signs that allow her to communicate classroom management messages nonverbally. She uses these signs in addition to or instead of verbal language, either to communicate with the class as a whole (e.g., stop and think . . . now respond) or to communicate with individuals without interrupting a lesson (e.g., to direct their attention or give them permission to go to the lavatory).

She relies more on a book when teaching about Braille, conveying the basic idea by drawing comparisons between reading words rendered in printed letters and reading words rendered in Braille dots. She helps her students to understand that Braille readers discern patterns in the dots that they can associate with words, just as ordinary readers discern patterns in letter combinations that spell words. Her students were fascinated with Braille and eager to inspect and feel the Braille dots in the book. Barbara concluded the lesson by noting that all languages are based on symbols, whether alphabet symbols, picture-like symbols, hand symbols used in sign language, or the dot symbols of Braille. (See Morin and Bernheim (2005) for resources for teaching about sign language and Braille in the context of the Helen Keller story. This resource includes illustrations of the sign language and Braille alphabets.)

In this chapter, we have explained the importance of structuring curricula around big ideas and have given examples relating to several cultural universals. In the next three chapters, we consider big ideas drawn from history (Chapter 6), geography (Chapter 7), and the social sciences (Chapter 8).

Chapter 6

Developing Big Ideas about History

Elementary social studies features a lot of historical content. The primary grades typically include the holiday curriculum and units on the history of the students' families and the local community and on Native American and pioneer life. Each of our units on cultural universals includes a historical strand tracing significant developments in the human condition related to the cultural universal under study.

Teaching about history in the early grades does not involve attempts at systematic coverage of the chronology, with attention to a lot of names, dates, and other specifics. Instead, it focuses on noteworthy advances in the human condition in general and in our country in particular.

The thematic strand on Time, Continuity, and Change that appears in the National Council for the Social Studies' (1994) curriculum standards offers guidelines for teaching about history. In the early grades, it calls for experiences that allow students to:

- demonstrate an understanding that different people may describe the same event or situation in diverse ways, citing reasons for the differences in views
- demonstrate an ability to use correctly vocabulary associated with time, such as past, present, future, and long ago
- read and construct simple timelines
- identify examples of change
- recognize examples of cause-and-effect relationships
- compare and contrast different stories or accounts about past events, people, places, or situations, identifying how they contribute to our understanding of the past
- identify and use various sources for reconstructing the past, such as documents, letters, diaries, maps, textbooks, photos, and others
- demonstrate an understanding that people in different times and places view the world differently
- use knowledge of facts and concepts drawn from history, along with elements of historical inquiry, to inform decision making about and action taking on public issues.

Teaching History for Understanding, Appreciation, and Life Application

Theory and research on the teaching of history for understanding suggest several principles that are particularly relevant to elementary teachers (Brophy & Alleman, 2007). First, *focus instruction on the study of particular individuals and groups of people rather than on impersonal abstractions*; study these people with emphasis on developing understanding of and empathy for their contexts and points of view; and focus on general trends in the evolution of social systems rather than on particular dates or detailed chronologies (Knight, 1993; Levstik & Barton, 2005; Willig, 1990). Children in the primary grades are interested in and can understand accounts of life in the past that are focused on particular individuals or groups (cave dwellers, Native American tribes, the Pilgrims, life on a plantation or on the frontier in the eighteenth century), but not impersonal, analytic expositions of formal historical themes.

Represent historical material to students in the form of narratives that depict people with whom they can identify, pursuing goals that they can understand. For example, primary-grade children can easily understand that the "Pilgrims" were persecuted for their religious beliefs and left England because they wanted to be free to practice their religion as they saw fit. However, they may not able to follow an abstract analysis of the theological differences between the "separatists" and the Church of England. Incorporating history teaching within strong narrative storylines is helpful for elementary students generally (relative to older students), but especially for students with attention deficits or other learning disabilities (Ferretti *et al.*, 2001).

Foster empathy with the people being studied. Children often believe that people in the past were not as smart as we are today, because they did not have all of the social and technical inventions that ease our contemporary lives. Teachers can foster their students' development of empathy by helping them to appreciate such things as bow-and-arrow hunting, horse-drawn carriages, or butter churns as ingenious inventions that represented significant advances for their times, not just as tools that seem primitive when compared with today's technology. They also can help their students to understand that people in the past were just as intelligent and resourceful as people today, but did not have the benefit of all of the inventions that have accumulated since their historical era. Consequently, they had to make the best decisions they could given the options they had.

Expose students to varied data sources and provide opportunities to conduct historical inquiry, to synthesize and communicate their findings, and to learn from listening to or reading biography and historical fiction selections as well as conventional textbooks (Fertig, 2005; Harms & Lettow, 1994; Lamme, 1994; Levstik & Barton, 2005; Sunal & Haas, 1993). It is important, however, for the teacher to *guide students in their use of these varied data sources.*

Barbara's History Teaching

The historical strands of Jan and Jere's units all include periods designated as Long, Long, Ago (cave days), Long Ago (Pilgrim and pioneer days), and Today (or Modern Times). Barbara's timeline lessons establish these terms and the images and information packages that accompany them. Certain units also call for sustained attention to events that occurred in between these anchoring periods, such as developments in farming that made it possible to establish stable communities between Long, Long, Ago and Long Ago (Food Unit), and developments in engine-driven transportation (trains, ships) that occurred between Long Ago and Today (Transportation Unit).

When she introduces these developments, Barbara places appropriate words and symbols on the developing timeline for the unit, but she does not assign specific names or dates to these in-between periods. Instead, she maintains focus on the basic storyline of gradual improvements in people's capacities to meet their needs and wants with respect to the cultural universal under study (i.e., she maintains focus on the forest without getting lost in the trees).

As she narrates the basic storyline, Barbara strives to make it believable to her students—stressing that these were real people and actual events in human history, not just stories like those encountered in the literacy curriculum. She draws rich word pictures, encourages her students to visualize, and frequently models the thinking of key historical figures ("I'll bet he thought that . . .").

By providing her own narrative rather than relying on texts, and by developing images primarily through her own image-rich depictions, her drawings, and her use of carefully selected illustrations, *Barbara makes sure that her students' initial exposures to the historical strands are focused on the main storylines that she wants to develop.* Elaborations are withheld until the storyline itself is in place, and details not essential to it are omitted. For example, when first introducing the storyline about food during the Pilgrim and pioneer days, she omits mention of the first Thanksgiving (this is addressed in detail in a brief Thanksgiving unit). Nor does she attempt to introduce and use terms such as "hoecakes" or "johnnycakes," because she wants to stick with the main story that European settlers learned to grow corn and use it, among other purposes, to make cornbread.

Barbara also tries to keep her students abreast of the historical authenticity of artifacts or representations from the past. In showing photos taken at the reconstructed Plymouth Plantation, for example, she clarified that these were photos of people reenacting the past, not actual photos taken at the time (because cameras had not been invented yet). Similarly, in showing a book on historical developments in transportation that was illustrated with artwork, she noted that the bridges shown in the illustrations were artistic interpretations, not photos of actual bridges.

Countering Presentism

An initial focus on a simple storyline is essential to establish a common information base from which students can construct additional understandings. However, Barbara needs to proceed carefully to avoid undesired side effects. The images and information packages that she uses to "put meat on the bones" of the three main time designations (Long, Long, Ago; Long Ago; and Modern Times) are prototypes that could become stereotypes. Also, if not handled carefully, her emphasis on how life was relatively primitive and difficult prior to key inventions can reinforce students' already existing dispositions toward presentism.

In fact, sometimes Barbara even deliberately underscores the contrasts as a way to capture her students' imagination and interest. Early in the communication unit, for example, she says, "This will surprise you" and then goes on to explain that Long, Long, Ago people used animal blood to paint on the walls of their caves. Later, she introduces the "shocking" fact that, prior to the printing press, only rich people learned to read because they were the only ones who had enough money to afford books. However, in elaborating on these points, she emphasizes that the behaviors were understandable and rational because people had to use what was available at their time and place (the blood painters were not bizarre or sick, and the rich people with the books were not mean). In developing the latter point, she also builds appreciation for both books and schools, depicting them as enabling resources formerly available only to the rich but now available to all.

To counter tendencies toward presentism, Barbara consistently uses "we" language when talking about people of the past, especially when talking about how "we" (i.e., humans) figured out how to do something better (e.g., once we learned how to farm, we no longer had to depend on hunting for food, so we no longer had to follow wild animal migrations). *She also consistently emphasizes that people's behavior was rational and "made sense."* For example, early in the transportation unit, she talks about how the first roads were built along paths that developed because people traveling from place to place on foot had figured out the shortest or most convenient routes (avoiding mountains, marshes, etc.). She concludes by noting that "it just made sense" that footpaths would develop along the easiest routes and later roads would follow these footpaths.

Barbara used both of these techniques in talking about the invention of air transportation: "It took lots of learning and thinking to figure out how to transport things through the air. So it wasn't until a couple hundred years ago that we started moving things through the air, using things like hot air balloons. Then we figured out how to make planes . . ." She attributed the relative recency of air travel inventions to the difficulty of the task, not to any limitations on the intelligence of people from earlier times.

Similarly, after talking about the invention of the wheel and simple wheeled vehicles, Barbara noted that "I'm so glad that somebody Long, Long, Ago was thinking and figuring out a way to move things more easily and that they came up with this idea of a cart and that a cart might have two wheels on it." She then synthesized by saying that in order to move things on land, people began with just walking, then carrying things, then dragging things, then rolling them on wheels. She represented these stages on the timeline and asked, "Doesn't that kind of make sense to you?"

Barbara also takes advantage of opportunities to attack stereotyping and presentism directly, especially in situations where they commonly appear. In teaching about cave people, for example, she explains that they hunted animals with spears and then ate their meat raw and used sharp rocks to scrape their hides clean to make clothing, but they did not coexist with dinosaurs or use the kinds of stone vehicles depicted in Flintstones cartoons. In teaching about Native Americans, she emphasizes that tribes living in different locales had very different lifestyles (e.g., only the Plains tribes lived in tipis and followed the buffalo; most Native Americans relied primarily on farming and fishing, not hunting and gathering). She also goes out of her way to inject realism when she is aware that Disney movies or other media have communicated historical stereotypes or distortions to children.

She emphasizes that things from the past usually continue into the present (we continue to eat most of the foods eaten in the past, as well as to practice crafts such as pottery and dressmaking; furthermore, handmade pottery or dresses may offer finer quality, unique designs, or other features that make them more prized than mass-produced items). She also notes that not all inventions are improvements (e.g., clothing in the days of multiple petticoats, hoop skirts, and high button shoes was less comfortable and too complicated not only compared to today's clothing, but compared to the simpler clothing of earlier times).

Co-Constructing Timelines

Timelines are useful devices for helping students learn and remember landmark events in history. We recommend that at least one timeline be kept on permanent display. Teachers can purchase commercially produced timelines, but for the primary grades we think it is better for them to develop their own, preferably in collaboration with their students. We have seen the value of these "interactive" timelines when observing Barbara teach her first and second graders.

She introduces her students to timelines by creating a timeline of her own life. She brings to class a collection of artifacts (trophies and keepsakes from childhood, graduation and wedding photos, etc.), sequenced by age. Then she displays each of these artifacts (and adds some simple drawings made quickly on the spot) during a lesson that highlights her life to date. Subsequently, she affixes these illustrations to a timeline that extends for several feet and is posted on a wall. As a follow-up, she assigns her students to develop their own personal timelines, working in collaboration with family members. At this point, they clearly understand that a timeline depicts significant events in the order in which they occurred.

Subsequently, when teaching the historical strands of her social studies units on cultural universals, Barbara develops additional timelines depicting key advances in each of these aspects of the human condition. Her timeline for the transportation unit, for example, depicts people walking and carrying or dragging things in the Long, Long Ago (cave days) section; people riding horses, carrying things in horse-drawn wagons, or using canoes or sailboats in the Long Ago (pioneer days) section; and trains, cars, trucks, and airplanes in the Modern Times section.

Barbara's homemade timelines are not drawn to scale and do not usually include specific dates, but they are well suited to the content taught at the grade level. Furthermore, they are used as teaching and learning resources, not just displayed as decorations. Each artifact or drawing is used to illustrate a big idea emphasized in teaching about historical developments, and the completed timeline stands as a resource to which Barbara can refer in her subsequent teaching and her students can refer as they work on assignments.

Preservice and most inservice teachers tend to view timelines and timeline lessons as problematic, because they associate them with memorizing a lot of dates rather than with learning about progressions over time in a domain, or because they do not view them as appropriate for primary students. However, Barbara's students always seem to be excited about them. One reason is that Barbara enjoys teaching about history, constructing timelines, and using them as instructional resources. Other reasons include the following: timeline lessons involve opening big packages of new information; the information subsumes "mysteries of the past," rendered in Barbara's engaging narrative style; much of the content is interesting or exotic (hunting, gathering, animal-skin clothing, etc.); and her students feel efficacious as they collaborate with her in adding new material to the timeline.

Once the initial structure is in place, Barbara brainstorms with her students about what kinds of drawings would be good to symbolize the time periods and eventually assigns each student the responsibility for producing a particular drawing. These drawings (or key elements cut out from them) are then attached to the timeline or posted below it to provide additional detail.

An Example

Before constructing timelines for particular units, Barbara engages each new class in developing the permanent timeline that will be displayed for the rest of the year. This activity is spread over two days and is designed not only to accomplish construction of the timeline itself, but also to introduce and "cement" a cluster of big ideas and associated images and vocabulary that will be used to frame the historical segments of each unit.

Barbara develops the initial framework for the timeline by assigning labels to each of the major time periods and adding symbols chosen because they are easy to draw and recognizable as icons standing for events that are representative of the time period and will be emphasized in the lessons. Rather than just select these on her own, however, she solicits suggestions from her students. She wants them to be involved in co-constructing this instructional resource and to feel ownership of it. In the following excerpt, Barbara is introducing the permanent timeline.

She had intended to divide it into three segments (Long, Long, Ago; Long Ago; and Today), but she added a fourth segment (the Future) at the suggestion of a student. The flexibility of this format (creating her own instructional resources) allows her to make these kinds of adjustments. To help students notice and stay aware of the segmentation, she used a different-colored marker when writing or drawing material related to each of these four time periods.

She began by drawing and calling attention to the line itself, then eliciting suggestions about icons that would be suitable as symbols for each of the time periods.

T: What thing will I put up there first to let you know that I'm making a timeline? What do you think would go there?

S: Stuff from Long, Long Ago. [This is a good answer, but Barbara wants to call attention to making the line itself, to emphasize that timelines are constructed resources.]

T: Yes, I'm going to add those on, but before I put those on, what will I put first?

S: A line.

T: A line, because it's a timeline and it's showing us that these things happened in order. Now, tell me, Gretchen [this is the student who had just given this response], which one do I put up first? What words do I have first?

S: Long, Long Ago.

T: Long, Long Ago. [Writes on timeline] Wait for just a second . . .

S: Long Ago. [Another student calls this out. Barbara accepts it and adds it to the timeline.]

T: What would we put up last, Gretchen?

S: Today.

T: Today.

S: And the future. [Barbara did not include the future on previous timelines, but she accepts this suggestion.]

T: And we're even going to add Future . . . [writes on timeline] This we're going to call the Future. These are the things that will happen when you guys are . . .

Ss: Grown-ups.

T: Grown-ups. You're right. That's what we'll call this right here—the Future. So: Long, Long Ago; Long Ago; Today; and the Future. Let's put some things on here that'll help us remember each of the different parts. I want you to think for just a minute, so don't say anything, but just use your thinking and remembering. [Cues students to think back to earlier lessons that dealt with the past.] What did we call the people that lived Long, Long Ago? Think for just a minute. It helps to remember where they lived. Think about that and it'll help you figure out the name. Cole, what do you call the folks that lived Long, Long Ago?

S: Cavemen.

T: We called them cavemen. Renee, does that mean that there were just men around Long, Long Ago?

S: No.

T: No. We use the word "men" sometimes to mean people. [Renee is likely to raise this issue, so Barbara preempts a potential flow disruption by acknowledging it and then moving on quickly.] Think for just a minute about the two groups of people that we talk about sometimes when we talk about Long Ago. Both of those words start with the letter P. That's a clue that I give myself. Those aren't the only people who lived Long Ago, but those are the two groups that we talk about. Think about it for just a minute and then I want somebody that'll just tell me one of them. I don't want you to tell me both. [Barbara wants to broaden participation and also deal separately with Pilgrims and pioneers, because she will introduce separate symbols for them (the *Mayflower*, a log cabin).] Every kid in here should know this, because we've talked about this three different times. [This was the first year in which

Barbara led construction of a generic timeline that would include key terms and symbols from all of the social studies units, and she was introducing it late in the school year. Since then, she has introduced it early and then left it displayed throughout the year.] What do we call those folks? Derek, what's one of the groups?

S: Pioneers.

T: Pioneers. Pioneers is one of the groups.

S: What's a pioneer?

T: Those are one of the groups that lived Long Ago. They did some hunting. They got around in wagons. They built log cabins or log houses. [This response focuses on the images that Barbara wants her students to associate with the term "pioneers."] We've talked about them a little bit before. What's the other group called, Krista? We talk about this group a lot at Thanksgiving time. Those are the folks who were on the boat called . . .

S: Pilgrims.

T: Yes, Pilgrims . . . they came on the boat called the *Mayflower*. Pilgrims also lived Long Ago. What do you suppose we should call the folks that live Today? That's us. You've heard me give a name to the people that live today. Do you remember, Mikey?

S: M . . .

T: You know it. It starts with an "m." I heard you start it. [Encourages student who lacks confidence] Mmmm . . .

S: Modern.

T: Modern people. Yeah, we call those folks modern people. I don't have a great name for what we could call the people that will live in the Future. I know that's when you guys will be grown-ups, so could I write something like that on here that tells that you guys are grown up, that it's when you are adults?

Ss: Yeah.

T: So I'll write down Fantastic Farm Family Adults. [This is a reference to the name for this year's learning community—The Fantastic Farm Family—selected in part because the students would be learning about farms during the food unit.]

T: Let's put a couple of pictures—one picture at each one of these spots that will help us remember those words that we just added up there. When we're talking about cavemen and people that lived Long, Long Ago, what would be one good picture that I could add on here that always reminds us of people that lived Long, Long Ago? What would make sense to have as a picture that will always remind us of folks that lived in caves? What do you think, Carter?

S: A cave with people in it.

T: That makes sense. Let me add that right here. There's a cave, and we'll just put quick pictures. There's a person in here, and here's the cave that they lived in, so that'll help me to remember that when I'm looking at this timeline, I'm thinking about people that lived Long, Long Ago, and that would be folks that had a cave. What would be a picture that would help me remember what I'm talking about when I talk about pioneers or Pilgrims? What do you think we should draw, Mikey?

S: You should draw kind of like a house.

T: What kind of house do you think?

S: A house kind of like our houses.

T: Did they have houses like ours Long Ago?

S: No.

T: So what kind of house would make sense for a pioneer or a Pilgrim?

S: Logs.

T: Houses made out of logs would be good. We could do that. That would help us remember. Do you have a little bit different idea, Tim?

S: Tipis.

T: Tipis we could put there because people Long Ago did live in tipis. ["Tipis" was a good answer and Barbara will return to it later, but now she wants to sustain focus on the Pilgrims.] I'm trying to think—what would be a picture of something that when I saw it, I would automatically think "Pilgrims." What would make sense, Krista?

S: The *Mayflower*.

T: Do you think if I draw a picture of the *Mayflower* that every time you saw it you would say, "Ah, Pilgrims. That's something that happened Long Ago"? [Models use of symbol as memory cue.]

Ss: Yeah.

T: So we can start to get those two things stuck together in our head. Let me do that. Let me see if I can do that . . . [draws ship]

S: The Sunflower.

T: Not the *Sunflower*—the *Mayflower*.

S: You could put a big flower on it.

T: It didn't have a big flower on it. [Many teachers would have taken this suggestion, but Barbara wants to be historically accurate. Also, she prefers the *Mayflower* to other possible symbols for Pilgrims, such as tall hats with buckles, because the latter are stereotypes.] It did have a great big mast with some sails on it. Those are to catch the wind, and it uses the wind to make it move . . . So, I'm making this picture and when you see that, your job is to say, "Oh, Pilgrims, Long Ago." All right, this picture's going to mean cavemen. This picture's going to mean Pilgrims. What would be something that is just for today—it won't be something from Long Ago and it wouldn't be something from Long, Long Ago, but when I see it, I can go, "modern people." What are you suggesting, A.J.?

S: Somebody bike riding.

T: What were you thinking, Carl?

S: Somebody on their feet.

T: What were you thinking, Laurel?

S: Houses like there are today.

T: One more idea, Arden, and then we're going to talk about it.

S: Climbing trees.

T: Let's think about this for a minute. Biking. Actually, bicycles were made Long Ago, so people could ride on a bike Long Ago. So would it make sense for us to use a bike for our Today?

Ss: No.

T: Climbing trees. Could people climb trees Long Ago and Long, Long Ago, Cole?

S: Yeah.

T: So would it make sense to put a picture of someone climbing a tree to help remind us about modern people?

Ss: No.

S: A house.

T: Well, Laurel suggested a house or buildings.

S: [Student in the background says] Maybe a car.

T: The buildings that we have now, are those buildings that they had Long Ago?

Ss: Yeah.

T: Are they buildings that they had Long, Long Ago?

Ss: No.

T: So that wouldn't make sense. What was your suggestion, Arden?

S: A car.

T: A car. You know, a car is going to be kind of interesting because it's not from Long Ago and we didn't just invent them Today. It was kind of between the two of them. So it might be a good thing to do, but I think, probably though, Arden, maybe the picture that would make the most sense would be a tall building in a city. Let me see if you've seen cities like this [draws skyscrapers].

Ss: Yeah, um hum.

T: With windows and doors to go in them, and more windows in the building. Does that kind of remind you of a modern city?

Ss: Yeah.

T: So if you saw this picture, you'd think, "Oh, modern people. They live Today." What do you suppose I could put for the future? What's something that's not around yet but may be in the Future and it would be a way to think about what might life be like in the Future? What are you thinking, Cole?

S: Robots.

T: Robots. Alan, what were you thinking?

S: Flying cars.

T: Flying cars. That's kind of strange, but we don't know for sure, so his answer is just as possible as anybody else's. Let me just stick with those two ideas. What I think I can do is draw a little flying car next to a robot. [Barbara draws a human-like robot, because that is the image most familiar to the students. In this context, she does not want to get into complications such as the fact that industrial robots do not look like people.] Let's see if I can come up with something that works . . . [draws on timeline, then shifts to review]. We're going to go back through. Remind me again what we decided we would remember to help us sort out Long, Long Ago; Long Ago; Today; and in the Future. When we think of Long, Long Ago we'll say, "Oh, caves. That's when cavemen lived. That's when people lived in caves." So when I say, "Long, Long Ago," Renee, you'll say, "That's when people lived in caves." What will you say, Cole, about Long, Long Ago?

S: Cavemen . . . people lived in caves.

T: Long, Long, Ago, people lived in caves. Tell me again.

S: Long, Long Ago, people lived in caves.

T: Tell me about Long, Long Ago, Sam?

S: People lived in caves.

T: Tell me about Long, Long Ago, Krista.

S: People lived in caves.

T: When I think about Long Ago, I say, "Oh, Long Ago, Pilgrims came on the *Mayflower*." Alan [drops in name of inattentive student to cue his attention], Long Ago, people came on the *Mayflower*. Houston, tell me about Long Ago.

S: The Pilgrims came on the *Mayflower*.

T: What would you say about Long Ago, Tim?

S: Pilgrims came on the *Mayflower*.

T: What could we say about Today? Modern people live in . . .

Ss: Cities.

T: Cities. What could we say about Today, Curtis?

S: People live in cities.

T: What could we say, Mikey?

S: Modern people live in cities.

T: What could we say about the Future? When you grow up, you might have flying cars and robots. What could you say about the Future, Arden?

S: When I grow up, I might have flying cars and robots.

T: A.J., what could we say about the Future?

S: When I grow up, they will have . . .

T: . . . They *might* have. [Barbara wants to underscore that this is informed speculation but not established fact.]

S: They might have flying cars and robots.

T: Do we know for sure there will be flying cars?

S: No.

T: Do we know for sure there will be robots?

Ss: No.

T: Nope. We don't know these things for sure. Those are just our guesses. Tomorrow, let's be ready to add what we've learned about clothing and what we've learned about food and what we've learned about families, and then on Monday, I'll tell you about transportation and how that's been different over those times.

Note that in the latter part of the first day of this timeline lesson, Barbara spent a lot of time pointing out and reviewing the meanings of the symbols and their connections to the packages of key information she wanted her students to remember about the time periods. The next day, she conducted further review and added some new symbols, particularly for the Long Ago section (bison-like animal, bow and arrow, etc.).

Adapting Timelines to the Content

Jere, Jan, and Barbara have had many discussions, without always reaching firm conclusions, about what kinds of content would be most useful for inclusion in timelines and what symbols would best represent that content. We also discussed the potential usefulness of three-column charts that would illustrate progress from Long, Long Ago, through Long Ago, to Modern Times along key dimensions (e.g., farmer pushing hand plow, farmer using horse-drawn plow, farmer using modern tractor; cave people hand-crafting primitive clothing, pioneers using early spinning jennies and looms, modern people making clothes using sewing machines). Well-conceived and illustrated charts like this could be powerful learning resources for young students, if kept simple and developed through good narrative and discussion.

Certain units lend themselves to inclusion of key developments that occurred between the cave days and the pioneer days or between the pioneer days and Modern Times (e.g., the domestication of animals, leading to a shift from hunting and gathering to farming for food, and the commercialization of society, leading to purchasing many things in stores rather than making them at home). In talking about the period between Long, Long, Ago and Long Ago, Barbara emphasizes that once people learned how to farm, it became possible for more of them to focus on activities other than finding food. This in turn enabled them to form larger communities (villages, then towns, then cities), and led to occupational specialization. In talking about the period between Long Ago and Modern Times during the transportation unit, she emphasizes that once people learned to use animals to pull carts, they developed numerous improvements in this basic form of transportation (shifting from two wheels to four wheels, adding harnessing equipment, building roads, etc.).

When teaching the timeline segments of particular units, she adapts the symbols accordingly. In the transportation unit, for example, to illustrate the point that cave people had to walk, she drew a stick figure showing a caveman walking and included a spear to help the students remember what the figure was supposed to represent. During the communication unit, the Modern Times section of the timeline relies more on reproductions of commercial illustrations than on Barbara's own drawings because the time period included many communication inventions that are difficult and time-consuming to draw.

Barbara wants to be able to focus on the storyline rather than on construction of drawings during this segment, because, relative to other cultural universals, communication evolved slowly prior to electronics, but then exploded. Furthermore, many of the inventions allowed people to do something new that could not be done before, rather than just being improvements on existing inventions. Having the illustrations prepared in advance and ready to add to the developing timeline at the appropriate moment helps Barbara to ensure that inventions are added in the right order and discussed with emphasis on how they "changed the world."

Barbara's co-constructed timelines and the carefully chosen vocabulary and imagery that she develops in conjunction with them provide needed learning and memory supports that enable her young students to understand historical material that they are hearing for the first time. In combination with her informal narrative style, these elements make her history lessons similar in format to the storytelling and reading activities that her students experience during literacy lessons, but their content is carefully planned to address social studies goals.

Having illustrated here in Chapter 6 how Barbara teaches historical material, we will shift attention in Chapter 7 to her teaching of geographical material.

Chapter 7

Developing Big Ideas about Geography

Geography is the study of people, places, and environments from a spatial and ecological perspective. The spatial aspect refers to where different places in the world are located, both precisely (at a particular intersection of latitude and longitude, within a particular nation and region) and relative to one another (in terms of direction and distance), as well as the patterns of distribution of human activities occurring at different places (land use, settlement, industry and other economic activities). The ecological aspect looks at characteristics of the physical environment, such as climate, landforms, and vegetation, which provide affordances and constraints for human habitation and in turn are affected by human activities.

Geographers bring a spatial point of view to bear on the topics they study. Historians approach issues or events as developments in time and ask what happened, why it happened at that time, what preceded and perhaps caused it, what else was happening at the same time, and what the consequences were for the future. In contrast, geographers approach the issues or events as developments in space and focus on where the event happened, why it happened where it did, how things at that place and perhaps at other places helped to cause it, and what the consequences were for the place and for other places. Both historians and geographers seek to understand and explain why phenomena occur, not just to locate them on timelines or maps (Libbee and Stoltman, 1988).

Geography pervades the elementary social studies curriculum. Texts for each grade typically include a unit on map and globe studies, placed at the beginning or end of the book. These units focus on building basic knowledge and skills and are not integrated with the content of the other chapters. However, the characteristics of places influence local human activities relating to food, clothing, shelter, transportation, and most of the other cultural universals, so instruction on these topics should include significant geographic strands (looking at how and why places in the world differ in their crops and food consumption patterns, types of homes constructed, and so on).

Studies of communities, states, nations, and regions are by nature studies of places, so units on these topics should include use of maps and globes as well as the study of ways in which the local geography provides affordances and constraints to human activities. Historical studies also should include geographical elements, routinely to note the locations at which significant events occurred, and frequently to identify geographical factors that help explain why the events developed as they did.

The Five Fundamental Themes of Geography

Professional associations have cooperated to help teachers understand geography as a discipline and to suggest powerful ideas to emphasize in teaching it. The *Guidelines for geographic education: Elementary and secondary schools* (Joint Committee on Geographic Education, 1984) provide a clear content and skills framework that is structured around five fundamental themes that we shall shortly outline (Petersen *et al.*, 1994). Key resources for elementary teachers include *K–6 geography: Themes, key ideas, and learning outcomes* (GENIP/NGS, 1987), a book on how teachers can connect their theme-based geography teaching to the social understanding and civic efficacy goals of social studies (Stoltman, 1990), a map of the United States that demonstrates the five fundamental themes (GENIP/NGS, 1986), and a teacher's handbook based on the themes (Ludwig *et al.*, 1991).

Boehm and Petersen (1994) developed an elaboration of the five fundamental themes based on experience in using them with teachers. They noted that the themes provide a convenient and adaptable format for organizing geographical content and avoiding the practice of teaching geography through rote memorization. The five themes are as follows.

1 *Location: position on the earth's surface.* Absolute and relative location are two ways of describing the positions of people and places. Location is the most basic of the fundamental themes. Every geographic feature has a unique location or global address, both in absolute terms and in reference to other locations.

Absolute location. We can identify locations as precise points on the earth's surface using reference grid systems, such as the system of latitude and longitude. Maps of smaller segments of the earth (such as cities or states) often use alphanumeric grids that allow us to measure distances and find directions between places. Different types of maps show locations of population centers, climate zones, political entities, or topographic features. Projections are needed to transfer information from a spherical earth to a two-dimensional map. This process often leads to distortions in distance (size), direction, or shape.

Relative location. Relative location is a way of expressing a location in relation to another site (Peoria is 125 miles southwest of Chicago, Australia is in the southern hemisphere, etc.). Both absolute and relative locations have geographical explanations (e.g., of why places are located where they are or why they have certain economic or social characteristics). Over time, certain aspects of relative location may change even though absolute location does not (e.g., as transportation routes in North America shifted from inland waterways to railroads to highways, cities at various locations saw shifts in their relative importance in the transportation system and in the nature of their links to other cities).

2 *Place: physical and human characteristics.* Location tells us where, and place tells us what is there (in particular, what makes the place special). All places have distinctive characteristics that give them meaning and character and distinguish them from other places.

Physical characteristics. These include the place's landforms (mountains, plains, natural harbors, etc.) and the processes that shape them, its climate (the reasons for it and implications for human and animal life), its soils, its vegetation and animal life, and the nature and distribution of its freshwater sources. These physical characteristics are studied with emphasis on how they affect one another and support or challenge human occupation of the place.

Human characteristics. These include the racial and ethnic characteristics of the people who live in the place, their settlement patterns and population factors, and their religions, languages, economic activities, and other cultural characteristics. Also included are the perceived characteristics of places, which may vary across individuals or time periods (Central America might be viewed as a place of political turmoil, an attractive vacation site, or an interesting blend of Hispanic and Indian cultures).

3 *Human–environment relations (relationships within places).* All environments offer geographical advantages and disadvantages as habitats for humans. For example, high population densities tend to accumulate on floodplains, and low densities in deserts. Yet some floodplains periodically undergo severe damage, and some desert areas, such as those around Tel Aviv or Phoenix, have been modified to support large populations. People continually modify or adapt to natural settings in ways that reveal their cultural values, economic and political circumstances, and technological abilities. Centuries ago, the Pueblo tribes developed agricultural villages that still endure in the desert Southwest. Later, Hispanic and Anglo settlers established mines and mineral industries, cattle ranches, and farms in these deserts, relying on manipulation of water resources. Today, contemporary Americans look to the desert Southwest for resort and retirement developments, military training and research, and high-technology industries.

Geography focuses on understanding how such human–environment relationships develop and what their consequences are for people and the environment. Subthemes include the role of technology in modifying environments (with attention to pollution and other costs as well as to benefits), environmental hazards (earthquakes, floods, etc., as well as human-induced disasters), the availability of land and natural resources and the limits this places on human possibilities, the purposes pursued and methods used by people to adapt to environments, and the ethical values and cultural attitudes that affect their behavior.

4 *Movement: humans interacting on the earth (relationships between places).* Places and regions are connected by movement. Over time, humans have increased their levels of interaction through communication, travel, and foreign exchange. Technology has shrunk space and distance. People travel out of curiosity, and they migrate because of economic or social need, environmental change, or other reasons.

Several subthemes surround the reasons for movement and the forms that it takes: transportation modes, everyday travel, historical developments, and economic reasons for movements. Other subthemes surround global interdependence: the movement of goods, services, and ideas across national and regional borders; the development of trade and common markets. Still other subthemes surround models of human interaction: the reasons why people move (e.g., from rural areas to cities) and issues relating to the size and spacing of urban areas and the relationships between cities and their surrounding regions.

5 *Regions: how they form and change.* The basic unit of geographic study is the region, an area that displays unity in terms of selected criteria (types of agriculture, climate, landforms, vegetation, political boundaries, soils, religions, languages, cultures, or economic characteristics). Regions may be larger than a continent or smaller than a neighborhood. They may have well-defined boundaries, such as a state or city, or indistinct boundaries, such as the Great Plains or the Kalahari Desert.

Subthemes include uniform regions, functional regions, and cultural diversity. Uniform regions are defined by a common cultural or physical characteristic (the wheat belt, Latin America, the Bible Belt). Functional regions are organized around a focal point (the San Francisco Bay area, a local school district). Understanding regions sharpens appreciation of the diversity that exists in human activities and cultures, and of the ways in which different groups of people interact with one another within regional contexts.

NCSS Standards Relating to Geography

The National Council for the Social Studies' (1994) curriculum standards include a strand on People, Places, and Environments. In the early grades, it calls for experiences that allow students to:

- construct and use mental maps of locales, regions, and the world that demonstrate understanding of relative location, direction, size, and shape
- interpret, use, and distinguish various representations of the earth, such as maps, globes, and photographs
- use appropriate resources, data sources, and geographic tools such as atlases, databases, grid systems, charts, graphs, and maps to generate, manipulate, and interpret information
- estimate distance and calculate scale
- locate and distinguish among varying landforms and geographic features such as mountains, plateaus, islands, and oceans
- describe and speculate about physical system changes, such as seasons, climate and weather, and the water cycle
- describe how people create places that reflect ideas, personality, culture, and wants and needs as they design homes, playgrounds, classrooms, and the like
- examine the interaction of human beings and their physical environment, the use of land, building of cities, and ecosystem changes in selected locales and regions
- explore ways that the earth's physical features have changed over time in the local region and beyond, and how these changes may be connected to one another

- observe and speculate about social and economic effects of environmental changes and crises resulting from phenomena such as floods, storms, and drought
- consider existing uses and propose and evaluate alternative uses of resources and land in home, school, community, the region, and beyond.

In teaching about cultural universals, opportunities to incorporate big ideas from the five themes and the NCSS standards occur frequently. Characteristics of locations, for example, create affordances for and constraints on their potentials for growing different crops and raising different animals (sources of food and clothing), supplying materials for use in constructing houses, and supporting different types of recreation and occupations. Such geographical affordances and constraints should be noted routinely, often supported by references to maps or globes (to identify places in the world where different kinds of houses are needed or different crops are grown, or to identify regional recreation destinations such as lakes or ski hills).

Teaching Geography for Understanding, Appreciation, and Life Application

Preparation for powerful geography teaching includes thoughtful previewing of the curriculum as a whole (not just social studies) to *identify lessons that feature particular places and thus offer opportunities for infusing geographical understandings.* This might include locating these places on a map or globe and emphasizing some of their salient geographic features, especially those most relevant to the topic of the lesson. For example, to build background knowledge for appreciating a story about an Inuit family living in a remote area of Alaska, a teacher might present or elicit key information about the far northern location, the very cold climate, the need to depend on hunting and fishing for food, and so on. Table 7.1 shows examples of such geographic references observed in some of Barbara's lessons.

Frequent reference to maps and globes in the context of the five fundamental themes of geography will help children construct a network of basic generalizations to anchor their understandings of the social world. They should understand, for example, that the climate becomes cooler and eventually colder as one moves away from the equator toward the poles or upward from sea level toward mountaintops; that shipping and fishing are important industries in coastal and island communities; that farming is a major activity in parts of the world that feature rich soil and mild climates; that extraction industries are emphasized in areas that are rich in coal, copper, oil, or other underground resources; that populations tend to be dense in greenbelts but sparse in deserts or polar areas; and so on. They also should develop a sense of ways that humans have overcome or compensated for geographical constraints by altering landforms (building canals, tunneling through mountains, constructing dams) or developing specialized technology (irrigation in dry areas) or knowledge-based industries (Swiss watch making, Japanese electronics) (Brophy & Alleman, 2007).

Early *map work* with children should include opportunities for them to construct maps, not just answer questions about or color in portions of supplied

Table 7.1 Examples of geographical insertions into lessons on cultural universals

Unit	Example
Food	Uses globe to show places in Central America where bananas are grown, and to show how far these places are from Michigan. Also, reinforces recognition that Michigan is easy to locate because its lower peninsula can be viewed as a mitten surrounded by several of the Great Lakes.
Food	Repeatedly uses globe to point out locations of countries of origin of different breads discussed in the "Breads Around the World" lesson.
Clothing	Uses map to point out places in the country where cotton is grown.
Food	Uses globe to underscore that Japan is an island, which is the main reason why fishing is important there.
Transportation	In response to a question about Antarctica, notes that it is cold and snowy there, so it must be located far away from the middle of the globe (shows on globe).
Transportation	As an observation about an illustration in a book, says that the picture looks like it was taken in a desert country, "Maybe like Kenya that we talked about yesterday."
Transportation	Commenting on an illustration from Nepal, notes that Nepal has high mountains where it is cold at the top, even though the country is located close to the equator.

maps. Developing a schematic map of a small surface such as a table or desktop (on which a few items have been strategically placed) will help them to understand that maps offer a bird's-eye perspective from above and that symbols or geometric shapes are used to represent salient features. Subsequent construction of maps of their rooms at home, of the classroom or school, of the playground, etc. will help them to acquire other basic understandings such as that maps are representations constructed with particular purposes in mind; that they are constructed to scale, so that the relative sizes of the included features and the distances between them correspond to those in the real world; and that map makers help readers to interpret the maps by including a compass rose (typically but not always indicating that the map is oriented with north at the top) and a legend that explains the meanings of symbols.

Maps and globes vary in level of detail, beginning with simple, often schematic, versions that show and label only the continents and oceans and progressing to the most detailed versions that include information on national boundaries, major cities, rivers, mountains, latitude and longitude lines, etc. Simple, uncluttered versions are ideal for the introductory map and globe lessons taught in the primary grades.

Barbara's Geography Teaching

Rather than teach about maps in isolation from the rest of the curriculum, Barbara prefers to insert map lessons into situations that provide a sense of purpose and authenticity for what her students are learning. The following lesson was included in the communication unit, following a lesson on signs and symbols.

A Map Lesson

To begin, Barbara noted that on the next day (Saturday) she had to go to Western Michigan University, and asked her students to help her make decisions about resources she could use to find her way. She began by first suggesting, and then eliciting from students, ideas about potentially helpful signs and symbols she might see along the highways (e.g., signs mentioning Kalamazoo or symbols such as the big brown W or the bronco mascot associated with the university). Eventually, however, she suggested that wandering around the roads and looking for such signs or symbols probably was not the best way to proceed, and asked if there was something she could do before she even left home that would help her know where to go.

Several students suggested looking at a map. Barbara agreed that this was a good idea and then announced that she was going to pass out maps and let each table group look at the maps to see what they could find on them. Her students were excited to do so, and as they settled into the task, she circulated, pointing things out (such as the cardinal directions) and asking questions about the maps that each table group was using. This was the first time that she had used maps with this class (she had used the globe), and whenever she introduces a new instructional resource that she knows will elicit curiosity and interest, she gives her students time to explore it before using it in her teaching. After several minutes, she continued the lesson as follows.

T: OK, we're going to take some paper and make a list of all of the things that we found on those maps [to display as a poster]. Anybody find where I'm going tomorrow?

Ss: No.

Ss: Yes.

T: You guys did, right? Where am I going tomorrow?

S: Kalamazoo.

T: A city called Kalamazoo, and it was on some of those maps. I'm going there tomorrow. Cory, what did you find on the map?

S: Michigan.

T: Michigan is a what?

S: Um . . . city?

T: Michigan is not a city. Michigan is a ssss . . .?

S: State.

T: Look me in the eyes, folks. Michigan is a state. [Here and below, Barbara stresses this basic fact.] That's the state that you live in. Trudy, what state do you live in?

S: Michigan.

T: Yes. What state do you live in, Amanda?

S: Michigan.

T: What state do you live in, Isabel?

S: Michigan.

T: What state do you live in, Cameron?

S: Michigan.

T: What city do you live in? What do you think, Cory?

S: Um . . . Lansing.

T: Lansing is the city that we live in. Some people would ask, "Where do you live?" You answer Lansing, Michigan. So you tell people both the city and the state. Tomorrow I'm going where again, Trudy?

S: To Kalamazoo.

T: Kalamazoo is in Michigan. It's just a different . . .?

S: City.

T: David, where did you used to live?

S: Detroit.

T: Kids, is Detroit a different state or a different city?

Ss: City.

T: Detroit is just a different city. It's here in Michigan. [Shows a map.] OK. Take a look. Do you see this yellow part? This yellow mitten is the lower peninsula and this yellow piece is the upper peninsula. Look. Lansing is a city in there. Detroit is a city in there. Kalamazoo is right over here under my finger. That's another city. Grand Rapids is another city. All of those are inside Michigan. They're inside the state. What other things did you find on your map? What did you find on your map, Beth?

S: I found Fairbanks.

T: Yes, Fairbanks. That's a city in Alaska. That's where my sister lives. What'd you guys find on your map?

S: Rapid.

T: That's Rapid City, but what other things did you find on your map?

S: Water.

T: Kids, what color was the water on your map? [Asks one table group.]

Ss: Blue.

T: What was the color of the water on your map? [Asks another table group.]

S: Blue.

T: [Repeats this question three more times.] So, do you think it's pretty safe for me to write down that water is always blue on a map?

Ss: Yes.

Ss: No.

T: How about if I write it down and if we find out that we're wrong, I'll change it. Do we have a map where the water is not blue? . . . We don't have one yet, do we? So we'll keep an eye out and as long as the water's always blue, we'll leave that part right there. What else can you find on your map? Danny?

S: New York City.

T: That's another city. What other than cities and states did you find on your maps? Cory?

S: Mexico.

T: Mexico. That's a whole other . . .?

S: Country.

T: Mexico is one country. What's this country right here . . . this big huge one?

S: Canada.

T: Canada is right up here across the top in pink. Mexico is down here in brown. What else did you find?

S: Texas.
T: Texas is another state. What else did you find?
S: Rivers.
T: Rivers. Good thinking. What color are rivers, kids?
Ss: Blue.
T: So, on the maps, the rivers were all . . .?
Ss: Blue.
T: The kids at this table found a symbol that they found on their map. What symbol, Gary?
S: An X.
T: What do we call that X? It's a . . .?
S: Treasure. [This student is thinking about pirate treasure maps. Barbara does not want to get sidetracked here, so she moves on quickly.]
T: It's not a treasure; it's a com . . .
S: Compass.
T: Yes, it was a compass. It tells directions. What are the four directions, kids? Can you tell me?
Ss: North, south, east, west.
T: It told what direction to go. If I had a map, and it didn't tell me what directions there were, and I started heading off in the wrong direction, would that map do me any good?
Ss: No.
T: Would it, Jerry?
S: No, you would get lost. It wouldn't be the right place.
T: No, it wouldn't be the right place. Some kids also found some dots. Can anybody tell me what the dots were? What were they, Sharon?
S: Every time there was a dot, there was a city.
T: Was that really a picture of the city?
S: No.
T: So what was that dot? Does that great big M—is that really the restaurant? [Ties back to previous lesson on symbols.]
S: No.
T: No, that's just a symbol for McDonald's. That little Sparty guy—is that really Michigan State?
S: No.
T: No, it's just a symbol for Michigan State [referring to the university's "Sparty the Spartan" mascot.] That dot—is it really the city?
S: No.
T: No, it's just a sssss . . .?
S: Symbol.
T: It's just a symbol for a city, isn't it?

At this point, Barbara moved from the front of the class to her chair in the social studies corner and gathered the students close to her on the carpet so she could begin reading and showing illustrations from *The map book* (Cutting & Cutting, 1996). This book teaches about maps by following a child from his house, through his neighborhood, to school, and so on. Barbara alternated between reading brief parts of the book, elaborating on its content, and showing the accompanying maps. In the process, she taught several basic ideas about maps, taken not only from Jan and Jere's communication unit, but also from her district's guidelines: maps are representations showing what an area looks like from above; symbols are used to represent the things they stand for; only permanent, nonmoving things are included—no people, cars, etc.

She emphasized that map conventions often follow logic (little drawings of bridges to symbolize bridges, green for parks or forests, etc.) and that maps need to be updated periodically. Gradually, the discourse evolved into a co-construction or discussion mode in which Barbara sometimes responded to student comments or questions and sometimes asked questions to cause them to think about the issues raised and perhaps reason out answers to their own questions.

T: This is called *The map book* [starts reading]. "This is my house. It is number 4. Every morning I say 'Goodbye, Mom,' and I walk to school, and I always go the same way. This map shows how I go to school." Is this map really actually his house?

S: No.

S: No, it's just a symbol.

T: Is this really his house? [Picture of house in book]

S: Yes.

T: He lives on that piece of paper inside that little flat house? It's not really, it's just a . . .

S: Symbol.

S: Picture.

T: It's just a picture of his house and that picture is a symbol for his house and there it is. Is that really a street?

S: No.

T: Is that really the river?

S: No.

T: No. Those are just pictures that someone has drawn to make it look just like his house, so that we can see all the things that he goes by on the way to his house. "I walk down Little Street. This is Little Street and what it looks like." Here's Little Street on the map.

S: Little Street?

T: It's just a name. It's not important. "I go over the East River on a big bridge. This is a picture of the river and the bridge." Here's the picture. Here it is on the map. When you look at the picture of it, does it kind of make sense, the way it looks on the map?

S: Yeah.

S: No.

T: I see these parts right here [on the map] are these parts of the bridge right there [on the picture]. The water's going under the bridge, the river's going under the bridge. When you see this [map], does it remind you of this [picture]?

S: Yeah.

T: It does for me. Now for some of you, it might not remind you very much, and that's because you need to see a lot of maps before you start to remember what all the pictures mean, what all the symbols are. "I walk down Big Street past Green Park. This is a picture of the park." This is the actual picture of the park. On the map, it looks like that. Does this kind of remind you of the way this looks?

Ss: Yeah.

S: No.

T: It's these buildings right here behind the kids. You're right, they didn't make a very good picture of it [acknowledges student who said "No."]. Now, this picture of the school on the map, does it have any kids there?

Ss: No.

T: Does it have any cars or buses there?

S: No.

T: Do you know why?

S: Because it's just a picture and they can't fit all those things.

T: The only things they put on a map are the things that don't move. If I get this map out tomorrow when it's Saturday, there won't be any kids at school. The school would be empty. Would there be any buses at the school?

Ss: No.

T: No, because the buses drove away and the kids all went . . .?

Ss: Home.

T: Home. So should they be on the map tomorrow? No, because they've all moved. They've all gone. So they only put things on maps that stay there, because what if I went and I'm looking for something, and I get to the school and I can't tell it's a school because there's no buses and no kids and my map says there should be buses and kids there? So the things that they put on the map are things that stay.

S: Stay put.

T: Stay still. Like the bridge—does the bridge ever get up and move?

Ss: No.

S: What if they tore the building down?

T: Then what would they need to make?

S: A map with the building not there.

T: Right. And sometimes you get out an old map and you think, "Well, there's no road there" and they've put a road in. So you have to be careful to know that your map is pretty . . .?

Ss: New.

T: New. Yeah, that's pretty important. So, yeah, if they were to take down one of these things, they'd need to change their map. Like the bridge—is the bridge going to get up and move?

Ss: No.

T: Is the park going to move?

S: No.

S: What about trees?

T: Did any of the maps that you had have just one tree on them?

S: No.

S: They didn't have any trees.

T: No, because trees are something that can die or fall down so people usually don't put trees on there. Who was at the "U" table? . . . What was that green stuff?

S: Forest.

T: Forests they like to put on maps sometimes because that's usually a whole bunch of trees and if one tree dies or gets cut down, there's usually another tree. So forests they'll sometimes put on a map, but trees they don't usually, because trees can come and go. Here they have a few trees to kind of show you forests, but I don't think that that means that there is exactly that many trees there. Down Big Street, past Green Park, there he is going home. Over the bridge, over the East River, down Little Street, and home again. I'll leave this book right here in case you want to take a closer look at him and his maps. [Having introduced key concepts using contemporary maps and *The map book*, Barbara now shifts to the topic of maps in the past.] I want to show you some of the maps here. Some of these are really early maps from Long, Long Ago, some are maps from Long Ago. Long, Long Ago, people started going places, and the way that they got someplace is that they would go with somebody that had already been and then they would just remember it. That got to be hard because, if I wanted to go someplace that I hadn't been before, I had to go find somebody who . . .

S: Who knew where it is.

T: Who knew where it was, and that might not be easy to find, and so that's when they first started deciding to make maps. Only, the first maps weren't written down. They were like stories that people would tell. So I still had to find somebody that knew a story of how to get from one place to another. When they started writing things down, they would put them on stone or maybe papyrus—that thin paper that was from plants.

S: Made from the animal skin.

T: Not animals—that's parchment. I'm coming to animal skins in a second, but they put it on papyrus that was made from plants that they weaved together. Or maybe they would draw it on animal skins and they would put that story of how to get someplace on a map. The oldest maps are about two thousand years old. That's just a few years older than me!

S: Yeah, right!

T: Maybe more than a few years. The first map they would write and try to give directions, but they found that an easier way to make a map was to put some pictures on there that all meant the same thing. Taking a look at this map right here, and right above my finger there's a little picture. Do you have a guess in your head as to what that little picture was?

S: Yeah.

T: What's that stand for, do you think—a McDonald's?

Ss: No.

T: They didn't have McDonald's back then so it couldn't be McDonald's. What do you think it was? If I looked at the map and I got to that spot, what do you think would be there?

S: Two buildings?

T: Maybe a house or a building. Sometimes, because this is kind of a big space, they couldn't fit all the houses that were there, that's probably a little bitty city or a little bitty village. Tell me, I've got two fingers there. Which one do you think is the big city?

S: The one with the big dot.

T: Why?

S: It looks a little bigger than that one.

T: That's it exactly. The picture looks a little bigger. What did we use to mean cities on the maps that you all just looked at? We don't draw these little pictures anymore. What do they draw instead? Jerry?

S: Numbers.

T: Not numbers for the cities. There were numbers on the roads. What did they have for the cities? Do you remember?

S: Dots.

T: Dots, and if they wanted a big city, they would put a . . .

Ss: Big dot.

T: And for a smaller city, it had a . . .?

Ss: Little dot.

T: Little dot. So the symbols have even changed over time, haven't they? It used to be these little houses and now they're little dots—easier to figure out. The Greeks were really good with maps. They knew a lot about the world. They were really good about writing down the things that they figured out. There was one guy called Ptolemy and he would make make-believe lines in between the countries so that people would know who owned what stuff, and also he made some lines that are really kind of complicated but they're called latitude and longitude and they help us find places when you look at a great big map of the whole world, and they let you know exactly where you are. If I said that Jerry's seat was at the end of the A table, you all would know exactly where I meant, right?

S: Yeah.

T: Where would he be sitting? Point to it. What if I said that Jerry was sitting at the I table, the chair closest to Mrs. K.'s desk, where would you think he was sitting? Well, there are ways for people to do that, only they use numbers, and what they might say is that Lansing is at spot 42, 135, and people that know maps would be able to get out their map and find exactly where that spot is on the map. Just like I described to you where a spot was, they have a spot so they can find anywhere in the world. If you tell them the numbers, they can find that spot just like that on their map.

Barbara continued this historical overview for a while, talking about how monks made maps and how explorers like Columbus both used existing maps to find their way and made new maps when they reached unexplored territory. Then she concluded the lesson by returning to the question she had raised to start it: how she would find her way the next day.

T: . . . So they finally figured out that the earth wasn't flat—it was . . .?

Ss: Round.

T: So does it make sense to make a flat map?

Ss: No.

T: So what did they do?

S: Made a globe.

T: They made a globe. Guys, doesn't it make sense that if the earth is round, to make your map round?

Ss: Yeah.

T: So when I'm ready to go on a trip, I can just pop this [the globe] into my pocket and take it with me?

Ss: No.

S: No, it's too big.

T: It is too big. It doesn't work too well. What if I made it just a really small globe? Can I put that in my pocket?

Ss: Yeah.

T: Would it be comfortable to walk around with a little bitty globe in my pocket?

S: No.

T: It really wouldn't, would it? So, what they did, is they figured out a way to take a map and kind of cut it into pieces so it laid flat. Take a look at this map. All right. Here's Michigan. Does this have any roads on it?

Ss: Yes.

S: No.

S: Black lines.

T: Those little black lines are not roads. Those little black lines are rivers. You're looking from so far away that cities don't show up very much, and roads don't show up at all. Is this going to help me get to Kalamazoo tomorrow?

Ss: No.

T: I need to get a close-up map of where?

S: Kalamazoo.

T: I can't get just Kalamazoo because what else has to be on the map? Where am I starting from?

S: Your house.

T: Where's my house?

S: Lansing.

T: My house is not in Lansing. Anybody know?

S: America.

T: Fowlerville is where my house is.

S: Is that in Michigan?

T: That is in Michigan. It's a different city in Michigan. So my map has to have Fowlerville and it has to have Kalamazoo on it. Both. Take a look at this map of Michigan . . . Take a look right here. The U table found one of these on their map. It's a compass. It tells me that straight up is north, which means that straight down is south, this way is west, and this way is east. That helps me because I know . . . take a look. I'm right here and Kalamazoo is over here, so I have to go a little to the south and a little bit to the west.

S: That's the mitten. [Lower Michigan is shaped like a mitten.]

T: That is the mitten. That's Michigan. There are numbers on the big roads and that tells me which road to take to get to where I'm going. There's also a box on here. Let me see if I can find it. It's right here. This is a box of all the symbols that are on this map. It tells me what kinds of roads are what lines, it tells me if I see a blue sign with an H, that means it's a hospital. It tells me if I see a little bitty picture of an airplane, that means that's where I'll find . . .

Ss: An airport.

T: An airport. It tells me that if there's a little bitty picture of a tree, this is going to surprise you . . .

Ss: A forest.

T: Nope. That's where I'll find a park. Those are symbols. If it has a little bitty picture of a tree, that's a park. So they are symbols. This thing with the symbols in it is called a key. It gives me clues to help figure out the map. There's an H right there. That's Sparrow Hospital. There's a little red airplane right there. Gary: Do you know what that little red airplane is?

S: An airport.

T: Where . . .?

S: My dad works.

T: Yeah, that's where your dad works, right where that little red airplane is. Cool! . . . Oh, see these numbers? There's numbers on the top and there's letters down the side. Numbers here, letters here. So if I want to find Lansing . . . we'll learn more about this next year as second graders. Lansing is right there. You come over here and say "L" and go down to the numbers at the bottom, straight down to the numbers at the bottom—11. So if somebody wanted to find Lansing, I'd say "Look at L-11." . . . Do you remember those lines I told you about that the Greek man Ptolemy came up with? Those are kind of like those lines.

S: This is like the inside of it. [Inset map]

T: That's just a great big close-up map of Detroit. If I was going somewhere in Detroit—that's got more roads on it and more cities and more places and hospitals and schools and stuff.

S: There's an airport.

T: There's Battle Creek, there's Lansing. So they're just closer maps.

The lesson continued in this vein, with students asking questions and making comments, and Barbara responding. At the end, she showed them how she would use the map to determine the route from Fowlerville to Kalamazoo.

Incorporating Geographic Context into Other Lessons

Barbara inserted another, briefer, map and globe lesson on the day before Jan left for a special teaching assignment in Vietnam. This occurred as she was teaching the transportation unit, so she also took the opportunity to talk about the different forms of transportation that Jan would be using during her trip. She used the globe to locate Vietnam with reference to the "mitten" of Michigan, then noted that air travel would be required because Vietnam was located halfway around the world and across a large ocean.

In the process, she also used some maps. Noting that Jan's flight would carry her beyond the edge of the U.S. map, she asked if the edge of the map means that the world stops right there (a "no" question, which elicited the desired "no" answer). She elaborated by saying that the world is more like the globe than the map, and that the places in the world shown at the edges of maps connect with other places at the edges of other maps showing the next parts of the world.

She also reinforced some of the basic ideas about map and globe representations that she had taught earlier. The need for this was evident when a student pointed to dots representing some of the smaller Indonesian islands and asked, "Is that a place where people can live on the water?" Barbara explained that these were small islands, so small that only dots were used to represent them on the globe, yet large enough for hundreds or even thousands of people to live on.

Barbara routinely reinforces basic geographical concepts when opportunities arise, especially concepts associated with common confusions or misconceptions. For example, students commonly mix up cities, states, and nations. Consequently, whenever Barbara uses the word "state," she gives some examples, especially states that are salient to the students (California, Florida, Texas, and immediate neighbors such as Indiana or Ohio). Similarly, whenever she mentions countries, she gives prototypical examples (France, China, Mexico, Canada).

She also uses maps and especially the globe frequently, especially when doing so provides an opportunity to tie geographical concepts into lessons on cultural universals. For example, using the globe in connection with the land-to-hand story of bananas allowed her not only to point out the location of Central American nations where bananas are grown, but also to note that these nations have warm climates because they are located near the equator. The land-to-hand story of silk clothing did not afford the same opportunity, because although she could show China, there is nothing that can be shown on a globe that provides part of the explanation why silkworms are raised there. However, the globe can be used to show how far China is from the United States, and thus how far silk garments must be shipped to get here (thus adding to their cost).

Recent chapters have focused on teaching of big ideas about cultural universals (Chapter 5), history (Chapter 6), and geography (Chapter 7). This series of chapters will conclude with Chapter 8, which focuses on big ideas from the social sciences.

Chapter 8

Developing Big Ideas about the Social Sciences

Most of the discipline-based content taught in the early grades is drawn from history and geography. However, social studies also includes content drawn from the social science disciplines of anthropology, economics, political science, psychology, and sociology. Secondary social studies features discipline-based courses in these subjects. In the elementary grades, content from these subjects is included in the history and geography strands and in lessons on cultural universals, communities, and nations.

Anthropology (Cultural Studies)

Anthropology is the study of cultures. The discipline is not taught as such in the early grades, but a good deal of material on cultures is included in units on history (most notably, studies of contrasting Native American tribes) and geography.

Preschool and early elementary children's knowledge of other nations and cultures is limited. They tend to identify with their own country but to be aware of at least some other countries, although they usually do not possess much specific knowledge unless they have traveled abroad. Their beliefs combine accurate information with stereotypes and misconceptions. Their ideas about Africa, for example, may feature images of jungles, wild animals, witch doctors, and people starving, living in huts, and living primitive lives generally (Palmer, 1994; Wiegand, 1993). Early positive attitudes toward the home country are sometimes accompanied by at least temporary negative stereotypes of other countries or world regions (Barrett, 2005).

Primary students are familiar with human actions relating to cultural universals that they can observe in their homes and neighborhoods, but they usually know little or nothing about how and why these practices vary across locations and cultures. Their impressions of other countries tend to be limited to famous landmarks (e.g., the Eiffel Tower) and whatever they have gleaned about their cultures (e.g., they may associate tofu and fish eating, chopsticks, pagodas, samurai, and martial arts with Japan) (Brophy & Alleman, 2006).

Children's tendencies toward chauvinism and noticing the bizarre or exotic show why it is important to help students see each culture through the eyes of its own people rather than through outsiders' stereotypes. It also helps to emphasize universalities in people's purposes and motives and to point out that what at first may seem exotic or bizarre upon closer inspection usually can be see as sensible adaptation to the time and place, and often as parallel to certain features of Americans' own culture. For example, teaching about Native Americans might focus on a few well-selected tribes studied in depth (e.g., an eastern woodlands tribe, a plains tribe, a southwestern pueblo tribe, a Pacific Northwest tribe, and a tribe from the local area). The teaching might emphasize that, depending in part on local geography, climate, and resources, different tribes used different forms of shelter (long houses, tipis, pueblo apartments), clothing (animal skins, woven cloth), food (meat from hunting and trapping, vegetables from farming, seafood from fishing), and transportation (dugouts, canoes, travois pulled by dogs and later by horses). Some tribes were nomadic, moving with the seasons to follow the animals they hunted, but most lived continuously in the same place and emphasized farming supplemented with hunting and fishing (Brophy & Alleman, 2007).

Barbara's Teaching about Culture

Each of Jan and Jere's units include a cultural strand that looks at how human actions relating to the cultural universal under study vary across locations and cultures. Initially, Barbara was somewhat uncomfortable teaching this cultural content, so she relied more than usual on books instead of instructional resources that she had developed herself or co-constructed with her students. She knew a lot about history and felt confident teaching about the past, but she knew less about geography and anthropology. An additional source of discomfort was the problem of teaching about cultures in relatively undeveloped parts of the world, especially those featuring subsistence economies. She knew that this material would have to be taught carefully to avoid engendering chauvinistic attitudes, but she was not sure about how to do so.

As Barbara broadened her knowledge about cultures and developed effective ways of teaching about disparities in economic development and resources, she became much more confident in teaching the cultural strands of the units. She finds that these lessons are valuable and her students are very interested in learning about practices that are unfamiliar to them.

Economic Development

Explaining economic disparities in regional development is difficult, both because the very idea can upset children (most of whom still believe that this is a just world in which people get what they deserve) and because primary students cannot understand macroeconomic explanations. However, it is possible to develop initial understandings of these disparities based on local differences in geographic and natural resources that create job opportunities. This puts local situations into a broader context and develops a few big ideas to help students understand.

One such idea is the development and diffusion of inventions (until something is invented, it is not an available resource to anyone, and even after it is invented, only those people who live in areas that the invention has reached can benefit from it). Another basic idea is ability to afford the costs (some technologies or processes are expensive and thus available only to people who have enough money to pay for them, including transportation from elsewhere if necessary). A third basic idea is geographical location, especially the uneven distribution of people across different places around the earth. People tend to cluster in temperate rather than extreme climates, and they tend to leave the hinterlands for the cities because that is where the money (capital) and jobs (factories, etc.) are concentrated. In areas of sparse population and few well-paying jobs, individuals and families cannot afford expensive modern houses, cars, etc., and communities cannot afford expensive schools, roads, etc.

During the childhood unit, for example, Barbara used books showing illustrations of children in third-world countries and pointed out some of their experiences (dirt roads, long walks to school, seeing monkeys along the way, water pumps rather than drinking fountains at school, walking barefoot, and using homemade toys). However, she did so in a matter-of-fact tone and without much comment. She focused on promoting understanding and acceptance without judgment.

She emphasized that different sets of choices are available in different places: some have few factories, stores, businesses, or jobs, so most activity involves farming and gathering food. Some do not have electricity or the machines that depend on it, so people cook over an open fire rather than on a stove. The same cultural universal and the same basic processes are involved (e.g., using fire/heat to cook food), but the particular method used depends on local availability of choices. More choices are available in economically advanced countries, but even here we sometimes choose to cook over an open fire (barbecuing, camping).

After developing this basic information, Barbara had the students look at pictures of places to get a general sense of their degree of economic development, then predict whether or not the people use stoves to cook on, whether the houses have running water, whether the communities have school buildings, and whether the children could buy or would have to make their own toys. Although she was uncomfortable teaching such content at first, she does so more confidently now that she has learned to explain economic-related differences in people's behavior at a level that her students can understand. Her basic approach is to start with the logical reasons for the behavior (e.g., burning buffalo chips for fuel), then push for empathy based on this understanding, then summarize in a matter-of-fact way.

A basic principle is that people act rationally given their options relative to their needs, and we can promote empathy and explain decision making by citing this principle and playing up similarities to ourselves. This tactic is easily and mostly legitimately applicable in talking about how customs and cultural differences reflect adaptation to time and place, but it is somewhat misleading when applied to issues related to economic development. If a student should ask why people in a third-world country do not use more cars or build more brick houses, there is no simple answer. Nations go through several stages in developing from subsistence agriculture to modern industrial economies. In the process, a great many things have to happen along many different dimensions, some of which are difficult to explain to young children. Timelines may be of some help here, along with references to the number or percentage of high paying jobs available.

Cultural Differences

Our focus on cultural universals makes it easier to teach about culture without promoting stereotypes or confusing it with level of economic development or social class. Lessons about human actions relating to cultural universals are lessons about human similarities: people in different locations and cultures pursue the same basic purposes and goals, even though they may use different methods to do so. The essential and universal elements are the functions of the behavior and the needs that it meets, not the particulars of the technologies involved (which usually can be explained either scientifically or with reference to artistic preferences).

Barbara emphasizes these points routinely when teaching about cultural practices. For example, she depicts rickshaws in Asian cities as parallel to taxis in our cities (i.e., visitors to the city or locals without their own personal transportation often need transportation within the city; along with mass transportation systems, options usually include services such as taxis or rickshaws that will pick you up where you are and take you where you want to go; passengers pay for these rides, enabling taxi drivers or rickshaw pullers to earn a living).

Where feasible, Barbara depicts unfamiliar cultural practices not only as parallel to some of our own practices and reflective of local climate and resources, but also as things that the students might want to do themselves. For example, she introduced a lesson on birthdays around the world by stating that she would share some of the celebrations held in other cultures, adding that "Maybe by the time I'm done, you will have an idea of something you want to do on your next birthday that comes from a different place in the world." This introduction depicted variety as positive and created a potential purpose for the information.

Sampling from ten countries, she selected a mixture of celebration customs that included familiar and unfamiliar, food and nonfood examples. As she introduced each new country, she located it on the globe and showed artifacts associated with birthday celebrations. She began with Mexico and piñatas, the variation most familiar to her students. In some cases, she demonstrated how to say "Happy birthday" in the country's language. When she got to Ghana, she distributed fried bananas, ate one herself, and suggested that her students try one too. Although her focus was on birthday celebrations, she also added other information about each country (its location, its language, the ingredients used and methods of preparing special birthday foods, and so on), to broaden horizons, add intrigue, and build interest and appreciation.

She concluded the lesson with a homework assignment calling for the students to tell their parents about some of the things learned in the lesson and to discuss customs from other parts of the world that might be included in the child's next birthday celebration. She read from and discussed responses to this assignment the next day, then followed up by having students write in their journals about what they would like to do for their next birthday. Later she collected these journal entries and compiled them into a class book to circulate to the families.

Barbara still must rely to some degree on commercially available resources, especially books, for teaching about cultures. In teaching about schools, for example, she first questioned her students to elicit key ideas about their own school, then led compare-and-contrast discussion of three other schools depicted in books (a one-room school in rural Michigan and schools in Japan and Tanzania). These schools were selected for their contrasts both to Barbara's own school and to one another. All three books contained very useful illustrations, but the books on schools in Japan and Tanzania were relatively negative and focused on differences. Consequently, she used them mostly for their illustrations, without reading significantly from the texts.

Another complicating factor is that culture is often conflated with other things, particularly the general economic development of the region and the urban/suburban/rural location of the depicted community. For example, the book on Japan depicted students taking trains to their school. To put this into context, Barbara noted that these students lived in a large city with a well-developed train and subway system, and that Japanese students who lived in suburban or rural areas usually would not ride trains to school.

In teaching about clothing in different parts of the world, Barbara explains that differences in the thickness and extent of typical clothing are related primarily to climate, but differences in styles and colors are related more to culture. Culture is an abstract concept that can be difficult to explain to children, so she uses her wedding dress as a prototypical example. She shows her wedding picture and notes that her dress reflects American expectations about wedding dresses (i.e., white, relatively ornate), but that in Japan, brides typically wear red because white is associated with misfortune. She then adds other examples, such as the fact that in the United States people wear dark clothing to funerals, but in some other countries they wear white, because in each case the clothing color reflects cultural expectations concerning somber occasions.

In her rites-of-passage lesson, Barbara frequently draws parallels between her own personal timeline or her students' experiences and some of the rites of passage discussed in the books that she uses as resources. She includes quite a range of examples, but avoids sexual practices, body mutilations, and so on. She emphasizes the similarities more than the differences and treats the differences as variations on the same big themes represented by universal life stages and experiences: children everywhere sleep, get up, eat breakfast, and go to school, even though the sleeping arrangements, breakfast foods, and schools may be different.

The following excerpt illustrates Barbara's treatment of cultural and religious practices as reflecting personal choices that ought to be respected. She was in the process of showing and giving information about breads around the world.

T: This bread is called matzo bread. It's from a country called Israel. They make it at a special time of year. According to people who are Jewish, there's a time of year when they say nobody should be able to eat yeast, and by not eating yeast, it helps them to think about what happens for their religion. This bread helps them to celebrate holidays.

S: It tastes like a cracker.

T: It does, doesn't it? Sometimes those are called matzo crackers.

S: This tastes nasty!

T: If you don't like the way it tastes, you say, "Hmm, this isn't one that I enjoy very much." But you know what, there are other folks that enjoy it. How do you think they would feel if they heard you say something like that?

S: I don't know.

T: Oh, you know, you're a smart guy.

S: I don't know.

T: What if somebody said your favorite food tasted really awful and they said really mean things, how would you feel?

S: Yucky.

T: Yucky. So you know what? It's ok to say, "Hmm, that's kind of different. I don't think I like it." But it's not ok to say mean things about how something tastes. Somebody else might enjoy it. [Goes on to next bread example]

In this brief excerpt, Barbara employs three strategies for socializing her students' thinking about cultural differences: (1) she depicts a religion-based practice (avoiding yeast during part of the year) as a rational decision (it helps them to think about what happens for their religion . . . helps them to celebrate); (2) provides language for expressing distaste respectfully rather than chauvinistically; and (3) points to the golden rule as the rationale for doing so (helps the student to realize that he would feel "yucky" if someone harshly rejected his preferences, so he should avoid harshly rejecting theirs). She picks her spots for such socialization, however, not wanting to make too much of the issue.

Later in the food unit, for example, one student noted that her family looks for chicken restaurants because they do not eat beef. The student did not connect this practice with her family's religious beliefs, so Barbara did not make this connection either, focusing instead on the point being developed at the moment (economic aspects of food decisions). Similarly, during the family unit a Hindu student mentioned that his family did not celebrate Easter. Barbara acknowledged his comment but did not pursue it.

All of her cultural content is taught within the context of promoting understanding and appreciation. Her students learn the big idea that people all over the world have the same basic needs and do the same basic things, although the specifics differ. An associated big idea is that we need to appreciate the parallels and understand unusual practices for what they are, without displaying chauvinism.

Economics

Economics is the study of the production, distribution, and consumption of goods and services. It addresses decision making about obtaining and using all kinds of resources (not just money, but others such as time, energy, or raw materials). Elementary students are not yet ready for macro-level economics (gross national product, banking systems, etc.), but they can learn basic economic concepts and principles. Many of these (needs and wants, scarcity, supply and demand, opportunity cost) lend themselves to experiential learning through activities calling for students to make decisions about how to spend their time or money.

Children's economic understandings are limited and often distorted. Many believe in a benevolent world in which people get whatever money they need from banks simply by asking for it and shopkeepers sell items for the same price at which they were bought (Berti & Bombi, 1988). They may know that money is printed by the government but not that the amounts of money in circulation are carefully regulated; they may know that banks are places to keep money safely but not know about other banking operations; or they may think that the value of an item depends only on the resources that go into producing it (without considering supply and demand).

Primary students usually are vague about the differences between renting or buying housing and the motives for doing one rather than the other. Many describe banks simply as places where people put extra money for safekeeping (each person's money is kept in a separate box). Others speak of using banks to pay bills or cash checks, but do not know anything about checking accounts, loans, or other financial services. Most know when and where credit cards are used, but only a minority of primary students understand that using them reduces one's bank account (Brophy & Alleman, 2006).

The curriculum materials developed by Jan and Jere include a unit on money that addresses these knowledge gaps and misconceptions (Alleman & Brophy, 2003c). In addition, most other units include economic content, especially in the land-to-hand lessons on food and clothing. Barbara finds these land-to-hand lessons particularly valuable and would like to see them extended to other topics such as money, transportation, and the products made in the community or state.

Barbara's Teaching about Economics

Barbara uses specific details within, and especially commonalities across, the land-to-hand lessons to teach basic economic understandings. For example, she emphasizes that to bring most foods to our tables, the raw materials have to be grown and harvested on farms, then transported to factories for processing, then transported to storage warehouses, then transported to stores, then put out for customers to purchase. Farms, factories, trucking companies, and supermarkets all produce products or offer services and employ many workers who perform many roles.

Each step along the way raises the price of the product, because each organization needs to pay its employees and also make a profit from its operations. For example, a jar containing a pound of peanut butter costs much more than a bag containing a pound of raw peanuts, because the manufacturer must charge the higher price and sell millions of jars of peanut butter to cover all of the employee salaries and company profits involved in supplying peanut butter to our food stores. Barbara develops similar ideas in talking about why air transportation is expensive and why buying a house costs a great deal of money.

She also models the thinking processes involved in conducting cost/benefit analyses during decision-making activities that focus on economic issues. One such activity involved choosing between eating at home or eating at a restaurant. In developing the problem with her students, she helped them to understand that it embodies a trade-off of time and money. That is, eating at home requires you not only to spend the money needed to buy the ingredients at a supermarket, but also to put in the time and work involved in preparing the meal, serving it, and cleaning up afterwards. These services are performed for you at the restaurant, but the costs of paying for them are reflected in the price of the meal, which is much more expensive than eating the same meal at home would be.

She cited opportunity costs as well, noting that people who could afford the restaurant meal might choose it over making the same meal at home, but they had to keep in mind that the extra money they spent on this meal would no longer be available for other purposes. She concluded by explaining her personal choice: she and her husband often eat out because they both have demanding jobs and busy work schedules, so saving time is often a priority for them.

Note that Barbara did not attempt a formal definition of cost/benefit analysis (or even use the term) during this lesson. Her goal was to develop in her students the disposition to take both cost and benefit considerations into account when making decisions about expending limited resources (primarily by modeling the thinking processes involved in doing so). Because opportunity cost was featured in the state's curricular guidelines for her grade, she included similar modeling (and scaffolding of students' economic thinking) in other lessons on issues such as deciding whether to buy a new or used bike or whether to spend part of money being saved for a bike to buy a new video game (and thus delay access to the bike).

Barbara also exploits opportunities to develop economic understandings that arise as teachable moments. For example, during a segment on economic trade-offs embedded in clothing purchase choices, a student mentioned that his shirt had been purchased at a flea market. In responding, Barbara explained what flea markets are (many of her students did not know) and added that their prices tend to be cheaper because flea markets are held outside and the vendors do not have to pay for upkeep of a building.

During the transportation unit, students' questions and comments indicated that they were not very aware of the expenses involved in maintaining cars. Barbara helped them to see that besides having to buy the car in the first place, there are ongoing expenses for gas, maintenance, and insurance. She noted that auto liability insurance is mandatory in Michigan and defined it briefly as "paying somebody who promises to help you if there is an accident." She gave this "just enough" definition because the concept came up in passing. If insurance had been included as a basic concept in the lesson, she would have defined it more completely, for example by saying that you pay a small amount in exchange for the right to get a big amount if there is an accident; the company agrees to do this because they make a profit by collecting small amounts from so many people.

Political Science (Civics and Government)

Elementary social studies programs typically do not attempt to teach political science as such. However, they do emphasize teaching children basic ideas about government and socializing them to develop desired civic values. Many states require instruction in core democratic values, typically defined to include life, liberty, the pursuit of happiness, justice, the common good, equality, truth, diversity, popular sovereignty, patriotism, the rule of law, and individual rights. These core values can be defined at varying levels of sophistication for students at different grade levels. For example, justice can be defined for younger students as taking turns and being fair to others but explained to older students in terms of treating people fairly in the eyes of the law without favoring particular individuals or groups.

Primary students are not interested in or ready for instruction in the macro aspects of political science or in some of its drier content, such as lessons on how a bill becomes a law. However, they are very interested in issues of fairness and justice (as will be seen when they learn about slavery or past restrictions on women's rights). We also find them to be responsive to lessons on the basic reasons for and functions of government.

For example, children can understand that people need governments to provide essentials that are too big, complicated, or expensive for them to provide for themselves, such as keeping us safe (military, police, fire, hospitals) and enabling us to function in the modern world (schools, roads, traffic regulation). They also are interested to learn other basic ideas about government: governments collect taxes to pay for their activities; there is not always consensus on what governments should be doing, which is why we have political parties and elections; and the United States vests power in the people and elects its leaders, but some other countries are ruled by monarchs who inherit the throne or despots who forcibly seize power and maintain it through repression.

Ideas about how representative government works can be conveyed by incorporating basic economic concepts. Just like individuals and families, governments face prioritizing and budgeting decisions because their potential expenditures (needs and wants) exceed their resources. Assigning available funds to the highest-priority projects means that lower-priority projects will have to be postponed or rejected (opportunity cost). People lobby their representatives to push for priorities of most importance to them, which leads to debates, coalitions, bargaining, and other processes that result in compromises. In theory, these political processes will please the greatest number of people to the greatest extent possible (pleasing everyone completely is not possible).

Jan and Jere's unit on government includes these and other big ideas. Information about the content we emphasize in teaching civics and government to primary children, and about learning activities we recommend for developing this content, can be found in the lesson plans for that unit (Alleman & Brophy, 2003c).

Barbara's Teaching about Civics and Government

A highlight of the unit on government is a lesson in which Barbara uses a photo essay to "walk through" a day in the life of one of her students. The student is shown waking up in a house or apartment that has passed government safety inspections. She is wearing non-flammable pajamas. She brushes her teeth using safe water provided by her local government and a toothbrush and toothpaste certified by the federal government. The foods she eats for breakfast and the clothes she wears for school also must conform to government safety regulations.

Her lunch money was minted by the federal government. Her school bus is provided by the local government, and its driver is licensed by the state. The roads that the bus travels on, the stoplights and other traffic regulation signs encountered on the way, and the police who enforce traffic safety laws are all provided by governments, using money raised through taxes. So are the school and the teachers, including Barbara herself. And so on.

By leading discussion of these photos, Barbara helps her students to see personal connections between themselves and the governments that affect their lives. Her students learn that governments provide infrastructure, resources, and regulatory functions that are needed to support everyday life in our society. Rules and laws are not just restrictions but mechanisms through which governments help people get along, keep things fair, protect property, and keep people safe.

Barbara's development of civic values and dispositions is rooted in her approach to classroom management. Beginning on the first day and continuing throughout the rest of the school year, she molds her class into a learning community. She socializes her students to identify with one another and the community as a whole, to feel a sense of belonging, and to display concern, respect, readiness to collaborate, and other prosocial dispositions in their social interactions (Brophy *et al.*, in press).

In establishing and maintaining the learning community, Barbara frequently makes reference to the Golden Rule (treat others as you would like them to treat you) and related principles of respect, fairness, justice, and helping those in need. She builds on this base when teaching about government, connecting to core democratic values and to the idea that local communities, states, and nations establish governments in part to ensure that their citizens are treated fairly and get help when they need it. In addition to developing these ideas systematically when talking about learning community and government, Barbara incorporates them into lessons on other topics when opportunities arise.

For example, the childhood unit includes a lesson on how children can help others and contribute their communities. As usual, she began with a personal example, telling how her husband helped a neighbor whose car was stuck in heavy snowdrifts. She summarized the big ideas as follows:

> "So, we help each other at school, we help each other at home, and we help each other in the neighborhood. You are part of a family at home, you are part of a family here at school, and the folks that are living nearby you, they are kind of like your family, too. They are part of your neighborhood."

Then she brought in the larger community, asking about ways that students might be able to help in that realm. She began by tying back to a drive held earlier in the year, when students had been asked to bring toothbrushes, shampoos, and other personal care items for donation to needy people. Then she began eliciting ideas for ways that her students could help others. Initially most of their ideas involved helping at home or at school, but Barbara gradually cued them toward examples in the neighborhood and community.

To conclude, she related stories about two children who "helped others in a big way" (a boy who began repairing bicycles and donating them to an orphanage, and a boy who successfully lobbied his town council to build a safe place for him and his friends to play baseball). In developing these stories, she developed efficacy perceptions by exposing her students to models that they could identify with, then emphasizing that they might be able to do similar things themselves.

Barbara also teaches about generosity and helping those in need during the food unit, which includes a lesson built around *Uncle Willie and the soup kitchen* (DiSalvo-Ryan, 1991). This book relates a boy's experiences when he accompanies his uncle to a soup kitchen where the uncle volunteers. Barbara notes that the food distributed at the soup kitchen was donated by individuals and businesses, and she depicts these donors as kind and generous people who are doing good for people in need. She adds that her own parents give food baskets to the Red Cross for distribution at Thanksgiving.

Upon finishing the story, she notes that Uncle Willie and most of the other people distributing food at the soup kitchen were volunteers working without pay. She asks why the volunteers "feel great about themselves," then elicits responses centering on the idea that helping other people is an admirable thing to do and makes you feel good about yourself. In addition to socializing these civic values, she takes the opportunity to teach a little about government (in this case, its provision of safety nets for the needy). She explains that in addition to going to soup kitchens and other operations run by churches and charitable organizations, poor people can obtain government-provided food stamps that they can exchange for food at supermarkets.

Chapters 5–8 have focused on the conceptual bases for Barbara's social studies program—big ideas drawn from history, geography, and the social sciences, synthesized in lessons on cultural universals. In Chapter 9, we will consider the instructional resources she uses as tools for developing her students' understanding of those ideas.

Chapter 9

Using Instructional Resources

We have noted that Barbara frequently uses instructional resources, both as sources of input (objects, photos, illustrated books, globes, and maps) and as tools for scaffolding learning (timelines, lists, charts and other graphics). She selects and uses these resources purposefully, limiting herself to those that she believes are useful for developing big ideas and will add significant value to the lesson. She prefers to use resources that she has constructed herself whenever possible, because she finds that commercially available resources are too "busy" or otherwise not ideally suited to her purposes. If she feels that a resource is necessary but also likely to distract her students from lesson purposes, she will allow them time to inspect and ask questions about the resource before she begins to use it to develop big ideas (as in the map lesson excerpted in Chapter 7).

Barbara's construction and use of timelines was described in Chapter 6, and her use of maps and globes was described in detail in Chapter 7. Other chapters note in passing her use of other instructional resources, particularly the objects and photos she brings from home when introducing new content and the children's literature selections and illustrated texts she uses in many lessons. In this chapter, we look more systematically at her uses of instructional resources other than globes, maps, and timelines.

Teaching with Visuals

In writing about visuals and other instructional resources, Jere and Jan have emphasized using them in ways that enhance opportunities for students to thoughtfully process, integrate, and apply curriculum content that is structured in goal-oriented ways and accompanied by a great deal of teacher–student discourse. Resources should be large enough for the whole class to see (if not, use multiple copies); up to date and timely; simple rather than complicated; likely to promote depth of understanding rather than emphasizing minutiae or the exotic; gender and culturally sensitive; and free of stereotypes, misconceptions, and fanciful representations.

For introducing new content, teachers might select objects or visuals such as photographs or other illustrations to stimulate interest, foster speculation and hypothesis formation, establish an anticipatory learning set, or link the new learning to prior learning (such as by providing students with opportunities to compare and contrast or to make predictions from the familiar to the new).

Visuals might be used to promote curiosity (e.g., a montage of photos that illustrates changes in communication over time); illustrate sequences or connections (e.g., photos that illustrate the land-to-hand relationship of wool to cloth or the methods that pioneers used to make their own clothing); broaden the meaning and subsume the familiar within a global and multicultural perspective (e.g., photos that depict a range of shelter types and construction materials to underscore the idea that climate, culture, and the availability of resources influence the types of shelters that people build; photos to illustrate that children in various parts of the world dress more alike than differently); or connect content to students and their families (e.g., photos showing parallels between family life in America and in other parts of the world) (Brophy & Alleman, 2007).

Barbara uses objects, photos, and other instructional resources for these purposes, but only when and for as long as they are needed. She does not automatically use commercially available illustrations or even instructional resources marketed directly to teachers and developed for use in instruction, because she finds that these materials often violate some of the principles outlined above. *A particularly common problem with commercially available resources is that they contain visual details that are interesting to students (provoking questions and comments) but unrelated to the big ideas she wants to develop. This is why she prefers to develop her own instructional resources whenever possible.*

Another problem with instructional resources is that they "get in between" teachers and their students, or "take the teacher a step away from the students." Instead of attending fully and directly to their teacher, students are splitting their attention between what the teacher is saying and the visual input supplied by the instructional resource. This may cause them to miss part of the teacher's verbal message even if they are attending visually to those aspects of the instructional resource that the teacher wants them to pay attention to, and they are likely to miss the point altogether if they are attending to other aspects. Thus, Barbara views instructional resources as double-edged swords that may bring costs as well as benefits.

She uses objects or illustrations mostly to show things that are either unfamiliar to most of her students (e.g., pieces of beef jerky) or familiar in some respects but not as they relate to the lesson's big idea (e.g., cotton balls are familiar as swabs but not as examples of the raw material from which to spin threads and weave cloth to make cotton garments). Occasionally she will display a very familiar object that the lesson will cause students to view in a new or expanded way, as when she identified a banana in a student's lunch box as having been picked three weeks previously in Honduras and transported to the Lansing area via a series of transportation modes.

Barbara often considers potential instructional resources but ultimately decides not to use them because their anticipated benefits do not justify their probable costs. For example, she owns a small tractor equipped with a plow, a harrow, and other attachments, which she could bring to her school to use during the lesson on farming. However, she would have to go to a lot of trouble to do so, and even if she did, she fears that her students would be so fascinated with the machinery that they would become distracted from the big ideas she wants to develop. So, she uses illustrations from a book on farming instead.

Some items found in homes that it is not possible or cost-effective to bring to the classroom can still be used as instructional resources if they are included in the home assignments. Through this mechanism, Barbara's students experience learning activities such as inspecting the furnace and heating system, identifying the countries of origin of clothing items, and identifying the ingredients in processed foods.

There are some lessons for which instructional resources would be desirable but are not readily available. Barbara has no access to authentic objects from Long, Long Ago, for example, and many of the visual illustrations supposedly depicting this time period are overly fanciful or otherwise likely to induce misconceptions. Also, when lesson segments are about processes rather than objects, the potential value of instructional resources is limited. For example, a picture or even an example of potted meat would not convey much to students who observed it, unless they also had seen a demonstration, or at least an imagery-rich description, of the steps involved in potting as a method of preserving foods. In situations like these, Barbara relies more on building imagery through rich word pictures and demonstrating or pantomiming of processes than on showing objects or photos.

When she does find instructional resources well suited to her purposes, she does not hesitate to use them. Occasionally she even builds a lesson around them, as with the food groups chart or the poster on world languages. The latter poster shows samples of writing and phonetic guides to speaking of common phrases in eight world languages, along with visual imagery associated with the countries in which those languages are spoken. This poster is well suited to the lesson's purposes and actually preferable to Barbara's own constructed illustrations because it is large enough for all of her students to see it easily, and it includes pictures of things that her students have not seen before (mostly well-selected ones that Barbara would have wanted to show in any case). Nevertheless, the overall poster is relatively simple—not too cluttered; Barbara could not draw many of these things very easily; the poster is appealing to students but not too gaudy; and it has information on it that Barbara herself did not possess (such as some of the phrases used in other languages).

Barbara often brings in objects that are featured in lessons but unfamiliar to many of her students, such as bouillon cubes, pieces of raw wool and cotton, and artifacts from birthday celebrations in other cultures. She also distributes examples of objects that represent unfamiliar forms of products that most students have experienced only in their more familiar forms (e.g., homemade jam, freeze-dried potatoes, unusual forms of pasta). To illustrate that food containers include information on nutrition and to socialize her students to pay attention to this information, she brought in containers from cereals, snacks, and other foods popular with children and led the class in reading and discussing the nutritional information printed on them.

She brought items of wool clothing for the lesson on wool but did not bring items of cotton clothing for the lesson on cotton, because she knew that most of her students would be wearing cotton clothing that day. She also brought in an actual stalk of wheat to show students the seed part that we eat (usually after it is processed into flour). To explain how flour is made, she used an illustrated book and showed a bag of flour at the end. The first time she taught the story of apple pie, she followed through on the lesson by including the baking and eating of a pie. She did not repeat this demonstration in subsequent years, however, because it was not cost-effective. Baking and eating the pie involved a lot of time, trouble, and mess, and the students already were familiar with apple pie anyway.

Books

Barbara often uses books as instructional resources. Many are books written for children (both fiction and nonfiction), in which case she will read all, or at least some of, the text (but framing it beforehand and elaborating as she reads in order to focus attention on the big ideas she wants to develop). Other books are written for more general audiences and used mostly for their illustrations. When teaching with these books, she displays the relevant illustrations but does not read much if any of the text.

Both types of books require thoughtful preparation and decision making about optimal use. With nonfiction books, Barbara restricts her students' exposure to the sections most relevant to lesson goals. Even within these sections, rather than read the text to her students, she typically develops the content using her own narratives. She then puts the book aside, although she often will leave it out for students to inspect later in the day or the week.

She usually cannot use the same approach with children's literature selections, however; if storybooks are included, they usually must be read from beginning to end. If only parts of the story are relevant to social studies or if the story is too fanciful to serve as a primary resource for a social studies lesson, she may finesse the problem by reading the story and scaffolding discussion of it as literature during literacy teaching, then referring to the relevant parts of it during a subsequent social studies lesson. If the story as a whole is well suited to the social studies lesson (as with the book *Uncle Willy and the soup kitchen*), she will incorporate reading of the entire story into that lesson.

Sometimes it is difficult to decide whether or not to use a book in this manner. For example, the book *How to make an apple pie and see the world* (Priceman, 1994) is used as a major instructional resource for the lesson on apple pie. It is a fanciful story in which a baker flies all around the world to pick up the ingredients needed to make an apple pie, then comes home to make it. The story and its illustrations contain a lot of details that predictably distract students from the main ideas developed in the lesson. Yet its content relating to the ingredients for an apple pie and what is involved in making one is accurate, and Barbara finds that using the book helps her to "carry" information about multiple ingredients, the global origins of these ingredients, the steps in making the pie, and so on, without losing track. Consequently, she believes that the book is worth using for the apple pie lesson, although she emphasizes that it is important to keep the lesson's major goals and big ideas in mind in order to use it effectively. She would be less willing to use the book if it also were fanciful instead of factual about the ingredients that go into apple pie and the steps involved in assembling and baking them, or if her students had difficulty distinguishing which parts of the story are fanciful and which are realistic. However, she finds that the fanciful parts of the book do not engender misconceptions about the realities emphasized in the lesson.

Elsewhere in the food unit, Barbara uses an illustrated book on pasta making to develop the story of pasta; a book that describes and illustrates the basic ingredients and processes involved in making bread; a book showing illustrations of different kinds of breads made around the world; and the book *Uncle Willy and the soup kitchen*. In the communication unit, she uses a book about a television station as a resource when talking about the steps and associated job roles involved in producing and broadcasting television programs, and books on sign language and Braille to provide illustrations of these forms of communication. In the childhood unit, she reads and paraphrases parts from a book entitled *How kids grow* (Marzollo, 1998). This book is well suited to the lesson because it presents vignettes of children representing different age levels and talks about the new things they can do now that they have reached their respective ages.

Later in that same unit she uses books that illustrate rites of passage for children and adolescents in several cultures. She selects these books carefully, including certain practices that are exotic to Americans (e.g., a Kenyan ceremony for adolescent boys that involves shaving their heads and developing mud caps), but avoiding practices such as genital mutilation that would be inappropriate for discussion with primary students. Furthermore, she takes pains to frame and scaffold her students' thinking about the Kenyan ceremony to focus attention on its similarities to familiar rites of passage, not its exotic aspects.

The Kenyan example appeared toward the end of a lesson in which Barbara first introduced the concept of rites of passage, gave examples from her own life, and elicited examples from her students. Initially, most examples focused on markers of increasing autonomy or responsibility (staying home alone, baby-sitting neighbors' children, going on dates, getting a car, etc.). Next she introduced some religion-related rites, such as Catholic first communions and confirmations and Jewish bar mitzvahs. Then she continued as follows.

T: Here is one I hadn't heard about until I read about it just the other day. Kenya is right here [shows on globe], so it's on the same continent but just a little ways from Ghana, where we read about before. In Kenya, they have a special ceremony called safana. I'll write this for you here [writes word]. This is really going to surprise you. This is really different from mine [her own rites of passage described earlier]. You're going to be surprised at what they do. Are you ready? . . . They take the boys who are the right age to have their rites of passage—to start becoming considered adults—and they take them and cut off all their hair. That was a lot different from mine, right?

Ss: Yeah.

T: Then they take mud and make it into a kind of hat or a cap—almost like a ball cap. Now, remember what we said the other day about discrimination—things that seem different or strange to you. What you might say is, "Wow, that's kind of a surprise. That's really different. I hadn't expected to hear that." But you're not going to do this: "Eeuooo!" or "Gross!" or "Yuck!" That's discrimination. So what you will say in your head is, "Wow, that would be really strange."

S: Horrible.

T: Not horrible—you don't know—but they're pretty excited. They're probably looking forward to it because it means they're going to be looked on as an adult. Don't you look forward to when you're an adult and you get to be the boss of yourself?

Ss: Yeah.

T: Well, that's what they think. I'm sure they think the same thing. Every kid I've ever known thought that same way. So they take the mud and they make a cap out of it, and because it's so hot there, the cap will eventually dry. After it's dry, they take it off very carefully and they save it and they paint it. That's part of their ceremony. Sound different?

Ss: Yeah.

T: Different from any of these [points to terms and illustrations associated with more familiar rites of passage]?

Ss: Yeah.

T: But the point is still the same. He's starting to become . . .

Ss: A grown-up.

T: An adult [goes on to talk about the Kenyan ceremony for adolescent girls, then a ceremony from New Guinea involving body painting. She closes the lesson with a summary reemphasizing that although the particulars differ, cultures around the world often have rites of passage that signify transitions from lower to higher status, culminating with being considered an adult and expected to participate as such in the society's activities].

The fanciful aspects of storybooks for children often complicate Barbara's attempts to maintain focus on big ideas. For example, she introduced the book *Charlie needs a cloak* (dePaola, 1973) near the end of her lesson on wool. This is a fanciful story about a shepherd named Charlie who fleeces his own sheep to get the wool needed to make a cloak. The story contains a lot of fanciful elements, but it also includes the basic steps in moving from raw wool to a finished garment. Barbara would not use it to introduce these steps, but she thought that it would be an enjoyable way to review the steps after they had been introduced and developed using realistic resources. The book worked reasonably well for this purpose, but Barbara had to break lesson flow several times in order to address some of its fanciful elements. For example, a student interrupted her description of Charlie carding the wool to make a comment about an illustration in the book. This led to the following detour:

T: The sheep wants its fleece back. That's just pretend. Would a sheep really do that?

Ss: No.

T: No, these sheep are kind of pretend. They wouldn't really play in the house, either. That's just part of what's making the story fun [continues with story].

Later, a student noted that Charlie's red cloak looked like Little Red Riding Hood's cloak. Barbara replied, "It kind of looks like Little Red Riding Hood's cloak, doesn't it? Little Red Riding Hood had a cloak and the Charlie from this story had a cloak," then returned to the flow. Still later, because time was running out and she wanted to run through the steps one more time, she found herself pointing to some illustrations and saying, "Ignore this part. That's just the author being silly with the pictures."

Photos and Illustrations

Barbara frequently uses photos or artwork to provide visual images of objects or processes mentioned in lessons, especially if these are both central to the lesson's big ideas and unfamiliar to many of her students. She made frequent reference to the illustrations in the book *Uncle Willy and the soup kitchen*, for example, because she knew that her students were unfamiliar with soup kitchens and because the term is misleading (the area where the people come to eat looks more like the school's cafeteria than the kitchens in her students' homes). In pointing things out, she focused on the parts of the illustrations that were central to the story and likely to be unfamiliar, without dwelling on irrelevant details (such as the colors of the walls or tables, the particulars of the meal being served, and so on). Similarly, in telling the land-to-hand story of bananas, she showed illustrations of unfamiliar story elements (a close-up of a banana flower and an illustration of large bunches of bananas growing on the plants), but not familiar story elements (e.g., insects, crates).

In talking about clothing worn by the Pilgrims, Barbara frequently made reference to photos in a book on Plymouth Plantation, pointing out and elaborating on unfamiliar picture details such as garters, suspenders, and petticoats. Concerned about accuracy of representation even with photos, she explained to her students that although the photos showed authentic representations of Pilgrim homes, clothing, and daily activities, they had been taken in recent years and showed modern people playing the roles of Pilgrims at a recreation of Plymouth Plantation (i.e., they were not taken back in the time of the *Mayflower*, when there were no cameras). She also noted that the clothing shown in many of the photos was finery worn on special occasions, not the plainer clothing worn the rest of the time.

Beside showing photos and illustrations to provide images of the unfamiliar, Barbara uses them as resources when scaffolding her students' information processing and reasoning, especially when reviewing steps or processes that she has just introduced through her own narrative. For example, after introducing and showing examples of each group on the food pyramid, she shifted into an activity involving matching food items to their appropriate groups. She demonstrated the process by showing actual food items, determining the appropriate group, and explaining why it was the right choice. As she got further into the activity, she shifted from actual foods to food illustrations and from primarily explaining to primarily questioning her students. Similarly, after using the illustrations in a book on farming to supplement her verbal explanations of the basic processes involved, she led her students in a review of the story by showing the pictures in sequence and asking them to explain what the farmer was doing.

In a parallel example, after explaining about considerations that people may take into account in determining what kinds of clothes to wear, she showed pictures of people in different places wearing different kinds of clothing and asked them to talk about whether the people used the weather, what they could afford, their culture, or their gender to make clothing decisions. She made sure to include examples showing how people in different cultures may respond differently to the same motive or goal (e.g., hats versus turbans as forms of protection from the sun).

Barbara also makes frequent use of photos or illustrations to respond to her students' questions. For example, during the transportation unit, one of her students asked about the difference between a boat and a ship. She provided a short answer on the spot (emphasizing that the main difference is size), but deferred a more extensive answer until later when she was going to be using a book that contained illustrations that would help her respond to the question at greater length. More generally, whenever she knows she will be using a good illustration of some particular point she wishes to make, she will defer introducing that point (or address it only briefly if it comes up) until she can include the illustration.

Photos and illustrations are not always as effective as Barbara hopes they will be. Sometimes this is because the illustration itself is ambiguous (e.g., when she showed an illustration of an open can of tuna, the student she called on to talk about it thought the tuna was mashed potatoes). More frequently, there is something about the illustration that distracts students from the point she wants to bring out. Usually this is some detail in a picture that is "busier" than she would like. However, sometimes even the focal point of the illustration is not ideal. For example, she wanted a photo of a snowmobiler to illustrate the kinds of clothing used for sustained protection against cold, but the only picture she could find showed the snowmobiler flying through the air after an accident.

Video and Other Technology

Barbara occasionally uses video clips or commercially available video tapes or CD Roms (e.g., a video showing work on the assembly line in an auto manufacturing plant). In general, however, she does not view videos as ideal learning resources for her young students because they are fleeting, so after showing them, you have to rely on memory. She prefers objects or illustrations that can be kept in view as she talks about them, then kept available for subsequent inspection and use by her students.

When she does use video, she tries to structure and scaffold her students' viewings to enhance their value as learning experiences. She prepared them for viewing the auto manufacturing video, for example, by developing initial understandings of the principles of mass production (including drawing an analogy to the belts that push food to the checkers at supermarkets when describing assembly lines). During the viewing, she occasionally pointed to things that she wanted her students to notice, especially if they were not featured in the tape's narration.

Illustrative of Barbara's experiences with video was her experimentation with using clips from children's television shows for an activity on advertising. After showing each clip, she asked her students to decide whether the clip was from a show or a commercial, and if the latter, what persuasion techniques were being used. The activity did not go well, however, because her students often could not remember key aspects of the clip they had just seen, even though Barbara was prompting them with questions that included certain key words (e.g., "persuade") and phrases (e.g., "Are they saying bad things about other roller coasters?" "Are they using somebody famous?" "Are they telling you that everybody does it?").

Barbara is not sure that she will repeat this activity because she is not sure that the video clips were cost-effective. However, she has decided that if she does repeat it, she will show each clip three times: the first time just to expose her students to it and allow them to assuage their initial curiosity and desires to talk about what they see, then a heavily scaffolded viewing to make the points that she wants to develop, and then a third viewing for review. This would virtually insure that the activity would be more effective, but it would require scheduling an extra day to complete the lesson (thus once again raising cost/benefit issues).

She also has experienced cost-effectiveness problems with other forms of technology, such as audiotapes or PowerPoint. The technology itself often is unreliable to use or time-consuming to set up; the key content may be hard to see or hear (or otherwise lacking in immediacy for her young learners); and, as with video, the exposure is fleeting.

Constructed Learning Resources

Barbara often finds that commercially available teaching resources are too narrow in scope, too busy, or likely to create misconceptions. She prefers to construct resources that will help her students to stay focused on big ideas and learn without distraction or confusion. Along with timelines, they include charts, graphs, lists, word webs, and other visual/spatial learning and memory supports.

These resources typically are co-constructed with her students and incorporate a lot of their own language, which encourages feelings of identification and ownership. Co-constructed materials have the handmade look of children's projects, yet their logic and construction reveal the involvement of an adult (Alleman *et al.*, 2003). They feature representations of the big ideas that Barbara wants to develop, along with the key vocabulary she will emphasize when doing so. Besides familiar language, she uses color, spacing, and other visual techniques to make it easier for her students to access and use the materials. She views these constructions as learning resources, not merely teaching resources, because she uses them to scaffold development and review of content during lessons, then posts them for subsequent reference during activities. Sometimes she also sends copies home for use with parents in home assignments.

Barbara's use of charts and other graphics varies according to her assessment of each class's ability to follow them. She minimized complicated charts with one class because it had difficulty handling a lot of text in that format. She is especially likely to use a graphic that she intends to use later in her review or in a future lesson.

When teachers and students co-construct a resource during a lesson, it benefits both parties in several ways. Students feel energized and involved (as opposed to feeling passive or forced); they participate in the lesson and engage with the content (because they are drawing on their existing knowledge to create something new); and they render the content in their own words, which makes it easier for them to understand, remember, and work with later. The teacher relates to the students as a member of the learning community, rather than an authority figure who stands apart. Finally, both teacher and students have a visual display that they can use in the future for reference, review, and examples.

Barbara listens carefully for cues from her students that enable her to get ideas for lists or posters that might be helpful to them as they try to make sense of each lesson's big ideas. Sometimes students' comments will cause her to shift plans by making up a resource on the spot or dropping one that is not working well (even one that looks attractive or has worked well in the past). Where necessary, she tailors resources to areas that her students need to make extra connections with or review more thoroughly. She always keeps paper and marking pens handy in case she decides midway through a lesson that she wants to preserve something for later use.

Charts

Charts are frequently useful as social studies learning resources because they facilitate comparison and contrast (e.g., across time periods or cultures) along common dimensions (e.g., food, clothing, or shelter). Well-conceived and well-designed charts can highlight big ideas effectively because they compress a lot of key information into a single graphic and make use of spatial design elements to help readers keep track of dimensions and relationships. Good secondary social studies textbooks include many tables and charts to support learning of the material elaborated in the paragraphs.

Charts can be valuable learning resources in the primary grades as well, if their construction takes into account young learners' limited capacities for reading and information processing. This can be done by simplifying the charts (reducing the number of dimensions included, as well as the number and vocabulary level of the words used in the entries) and using spacing, lines, color, highlighting, and other visual/spatial design components to help students see the chart's structure as they process its information. Barbara prefers to use charts that have limited text, because her young learners cannot read much connected text but can keep track of single words or short phrases. She often develops simplified versions of the charts included in Jan and Jere's lesson plans, or else begins by using separate parts of the chart, combining the parts only after her students have become familiar with them.

For example, the childhood unit includes a chart showing advances in three domains (physical qualities, communication of emotions and attitudes, and behaviors) across seven age/stage levels. On the day that Barbara began working with this chart in class, she showed only the first two rows (for infants and toddlers). In later lessons, she developed the full 3 × 7 chart. However, she felt that this was more detail than was cost-effective, so she decided that in the future she would just use the seven ages/stages and list noteworthy advances under each of the seven headings, without trying to classify them separately as physical qualities, emotions/attitudes, or behaviors.

Later in the childhood unit, she led her students in co-constructing a chart comparing features of their school with parallel features of schools in Japan and Tanzania. She started preparation for this construction the previous day, when she presented information about schools in Japan and Tanzania, then asked her students to pair-share their responses to a series of questions ("How do kids get to school? What do they see on the way? What is it like inside? What do they learn about?"). Then, during the actual chart construction, she stimulated thinking about comparison and contrast by asking even more specific questions (e.g., "What kind of furniture do you see?", rather than "What is inside the school?") She also stimulated thinking with questions about what American students who moved to Japan or Tanzania (or students from those countries who moved to the United States) would find similar and what they would find different in their new schools. With Barbara's help in focusing on productive dimensions for comparison and contrast, her students were able to make many good suggestions about information to include on the chart.

Lists

It is easier for students to process lists than charts, because lists do not require attending to multiple dimensions simultaneously. Consequently, Barbara uses lists quite often. Some of these are ordered lists that show steps in a progression (e.g., time periods, life stages, steps involved in the land-to-hand story of a loaf of bread or a wool sweater). Others are simply lists of her students' responses to a question (e.g., about different forms of transportation), displayed to help the students keep track of what potential response alternatives have been mentioned already.

In the childhood unit, for example, Barbara elicited suggestions for entries on a list entitled "Kids and Their Jobs" by asking her students to identify chores that they are expected to perform at home or responsibilities they bear at school or in other aspects of their lives. As she elicited suggestions, she added them to the list, sometimes expanding or lifting the language to get to the right level of generality (e.g., when a child identified listening to the teacher as one of his responsibilities, she converted his idea to "going to school to think and learn"). When the list began to get lengthy, she paused to review the items included on it already, then sought to elicit new additions. Once her students began to run out of new ideas, she added a few entries of her own (items that she wanted included because she would refer to them later in the lesson).

The final review lesson for the childhood unit also involved construction of a list. This time, Barbara asked her students to identify important things they had learned about childhood. The students did a good job of identifying big ideas, so she mostly added their responses to the list without significant modification. Sometimes, however, she adapted or lifted their language to include preferred terminology. For example, when one student said that she had learned that Barbara had been noisy as a baby but got quieter as she got older, Barbara said, "Yes, I was more in charge of my body and my choices." When another student said that he had learned that children in the past had games so they could learn, Barbara rephrased his response as "Games were for learning." As the students' response rate slowed, Barbara began to cue them toward big ideas that they had not generated on their own. She also included frequent tiebacks to other big ideas and to learning resources constructed during the unit, such as the timeline showing major developmental markers in her own life.

Barbara views constructed lists like these as group products that reinforce her efforts to socialize ideas such as "we are all responsible for our learning" and "classmates have worthwhile things to say". This encourages her students to attend to all of the ideas, not just the ones they suggest personally. The requirement that each student contribute a new idea avoids repetition of the same few salient ones. It also facilitates follow-up activities for which the lists provide input. In this case, for example, the follow-up activity called for students to draw a picture on a small fabric square representing something they learned about childhood. Barbara later sewed these squares together into a quilt that served as a remembrance of the unit.

An example of a sequenced list occurred during the transportation unit in a lesson segment built around a children's book describing and illustrating the manufacture of school buses. Rather than simply read the book to her students, Barbara used her typical narrative approach as she explained the main steps involved and showed illustrations from the book. As she did so, she added words or brief phrases to a poster she was developing on the chart stand. By the time she had completed the book, she also had completed a poster showing the sequence of steps in bus construction, which then served as a resource for immediate review and later follow-up activities.

An Example

One of Barbara's most extensive list-making activities occurred early in the transportation unit. Following the first lesson, the homework assignment called for students to talk with their parents and list forms of transportation that family members had used. The next day, she called on her students individually to draw on their home assignment responses to contribute items to a list of forms of transportation. This list and an accompanying word web would be preserved and used as a learning resource in subsequent lessons.

She had each student come up and stand next to her as he or she suggested additions to the list, temporarily acting as co-teacher. These "*co-teacher moments*" provide brief opportunities for students to take the teacher role by explaining or describing something (in this case, telling the story of how the student's family happened to use a particular form of transportation). They are brief, informal, and structured through Barbara's questioning, not extended presentations prepared in advance.

Given that the students themselves suggested the items after meeting with their parents, Barbara could be confident that the items on the list were both in their minds and in their vocabularies. She began by recapping the definition of transportation and some associated big ideas that were introduced during the first lesson, then set up expectations for the development of the list.

T: We started talking about transportation on Friday. Transportation is just a great big word that means . . .

Ss: Moving from one place to another.

T: Moving from one place to another or going from one place to another. It always involves from one place to another, even if it's far away or if it's just close by. Sometimes it means moving people and sometimes it means moving things. But transportation is moving from one place to another. Your job over the weekend was to list different kinds of transportation that you or your family have used in the past, so we could start to get a great big list full of different kinds of transportation. A.J., I'm going to pass your list right back to you [Barbara had collected and scanned the home assignment responses], and you will read for me the things on your list and I will add them to mine [to get the list started, Barbara already had entered items from her own list. This is another example of her modeling the importance of the homework assignments by doing them herself, bringing the response form to class, and sharing its contents with her students.]

S: Car.

T: Do we have "car" yet?

Ss: No.

T: Well, we've got it now. Next?

S: Bus.

T: Do we have "bus" yet?

Barbara continues in this vein, calling on students individually and adding to the list anything that hasn't been added already. Because the list will be lengthy, she uses three different colors to record the entries to make it easier for students to identify and maintain focus on each separate word. Occasionally she elaborates or qualifies responses by providing definitions or descriptions, clarifying that some things (certain animals such as elephants and certain motorized vehicles such as riding lawn mowers) can be used for transportation but usually are not, and foreshadowing a later lesson on developments from people-powered to animal-powered to engine-powered transportation by occasionally asking, "Who does the work?" when we use a particular form of transportation (e.g., bicycle, camel, van). Mostly, however, she focuses on compiling the list.

In calling on individuals to come up and take their turn to add to the list, Barbara begins with students whose homework responses were limited to the most popularly mentioned forms of transportation and ends with those whose responses contained at least one unique item (thus making it possible for each student to contribute something). This segment generally goes smoothly, although confusions arise because Barbara occasionally is looking for general classes of transportation (e.g., trucks, airplanes) whereas students sometimes suggest particular examples or subclasses (e.g., garbage trucks, jet planes). As she elicits the different forms of transportation, she lists them in three separate columns to provide visual evidence of the fact that there are many more forms of land transportation than sea or air transportation.

Eventually the list grows to encompass forty-two items, including car, bus, train, delivery van, camels, horses, elephants, snowmobile, skateboard, boat, motor home, monorail, bicycle, airplane, your feet, pogo stick, motorcycle, covered wagon, parachute, hot air balloon, garbage truck, helicopter, rocket ship, wagon, scooter, tram, subway, tractor, submarine, go-kart, and golf cart. Upon concluding the list, Barbara transitions into a word web activity, linking back to a similar activity done in a recent health lesson.

T: Wow, here's the list that you all came up with. Let's count them up and see how many ways we already know of to transport something. Here we go. Count with me. 1, 2, 3, 4, 5, 6, 7, 8, 9, 10, 11, 12, 13, 14, 15, 16, 17, 18, 19, 20, 21, 22, 23, 24, 25, 26, 27, 28. Take a breath. Here we go. 29, 30, 31, 32, 33, 34, 35, 36, 37, 38, 39, 40, 41, 42. Forty-two different ways that we've already talked about—ways that people or things get transported—moved from one place to another. I'm going to start talking about a way to sort some of those, and I'll bet you'll start recognizing some of those already from us talking and making our list. I've done some sorting already, as we started to talk about them. You might recognize a picture like this. Transportation. If you remember, we made one of these kind of pictures not too long ago, in health . . . what do we call this kind of picture? What do we call it, Laurel?

S: A web.

T: A web, because all different kinds of ideas are going to come sticking out the sides just like there are all different kinds of ideas that go along with transportation—kind of like a spider would make pieces of the web in all different directions, we're going to make our ideas go in all different directions with this web. Transportation—tell me again what it means? Tell me, let's see . . . Sam, tell me what transportation is?

S: Moving stuff to a different place.

T: Moving things from one place to another. I'll put moving things right there because that way we'll remember what transportation is about. This first piece that's going to stick out the side of our web—we're going to talk about things on land. You're already thinking that there are a whole bunch of things that you could say. You guys had a chance to come up with some things first. Now it's my turn. Ready to go? Land. Some things that you find on land. What are some things that you notice about those things? A train, a car, a bicycle, a scooter. What do you notice about all of those things?

The lesson continued in this vein, with Barbara going through the list and asking her students to identify whether the entry should be classified as land, water, or air transportation; negotiating agreement if necessary; and then adding it to the word web accordingly. In a few cases, she noted that an item (e.g., a seaplane) could be classified in two or even all three of the categories. After completing the word web, she concluded the day's lesson by distributing labeled illustrations of forms of transportation and then calling on students to give the name of the form of transportation shown on their illustrations (i.e., read the labels) and then say whether that form of transportation was land, water, or air transportation.

Word Webs

When the content consists of major classifications that subsume subtypes or examples, Barbara may construct a word web to provide a visual illustration of these relationships. One example was the just-described word web showing forms of land, water, and air transportation. Other examples included a web built around the main idea of four functions of shelter (protection from the elements, providing a place to keep possessions, providing a place to carry out daily personal and family activities, and, in the case of people who work out of their homes, providing a place to carry out one's occupation) and a web illustrating classification of clothing-related occupations according to whether the work is done before the clothes are made (e.g., farmer), during the process (e.g., sewer), or afterwards (e.g., cashier in a clothing store).

Barbara occasionally also uses Venn diagrams, although usually only with second graders and only after they have been exposed to them in math lessons. For most purposes, she prefers simpler formats that support her young learners' basic information processing by using spacing, lines, and so on to help them "keep separate things separate" (and do not require them to attend to more than one relationship simultaneously). Also, social studies features overlapping concepts with fuzzy boundaries, and examples often can be classified within two or more categories instead of just one. The graphic features of Venn diagrams suggest unintended absolutes or false dichotomies, and often distract attention away from the main points toward arguments about how to classify anomalous examples. (See Chapter 10 for more about anomalies.)

Graphs

Barbara also uses simple tallies or more formal graphs to illustrate numerical information in visual form. She does this in part because these data representation formats are introduced in the mathematics curriculum, and using them in social studies provides opportunities for authentic applications. Also, *many of her graphs display information about her students or their families, so the information is personalized and meaningful to them.*

One such graph, for example, illustrated the numbers of foods from each of the major food groups that her students had consumed the previous day. Another graph showed the numbers of students in the class who represented each of six family types identified in the family unit (nuclear, extended, adoptive, single-parent, blended, and foster). Another illustrated her students' main reasons for cereal purchases, classified under six headings developed in a food unit lesson (ingredients/taste, healthy, reasonable cost, packaging or supermarket displays that make the food appear appealing, trinket in box or premium offer, or endorsement by famous people). In each case, she constructed the graph based on information supplied by students, scaffolded interpretation of what it indicated about trends among her students and their families, and used it as a resource for underscoring big ideas emphasized in the lesson plans.

Barbara's Nine Principles

Jan and Jere encouraged Barbara to articulate the *principles that underlie her development and use of constructed learning resources*. In response to this challenge, Barbara generated the following nine principles:

1   *Focus on big ideas.* The resource should feature the big ideas that will be developed in the lesson and used in subsequent activities.

2   *Accessible language.* Barbara ordinarily does not begin co-construction of learning resources until after she has made an initial presentation on the topic. This enables her students to participate in the construction more readily and leads to learning resources that are written mostly in their own words (and thus familiar and meaningful to them).

3   *Repeated information.* To make the language even more accessible, the constructed resources feature key words that Barbara takes care to introduce and repeat frequently during instruction.

4   *Connections to other lessons.* The featured big ideas and key words are included not only because they are central to the current lesson, but also because they will be used again later, in subsequent lessons.

5   *Resource information.* Barbara will pose questions early, then develop constructions to be used as resources for addressing them. Much of what she posts in her room are usable resources that her students can keep referring to, not merely topic-relevant images. Eventually she accumulates more of these constructed resources to post than she has space available to post them, so taken-down materials are kept available in a class library where students can access them to revisit across the year. At the end of the year, she gives each student several of these items to add to his or her memory box, and keeps a few for herself to provide a record of the class in the future.

6   *Being visually accessible.* Barbara makes sure that her co-constructed resources are easily accessible and meaningful to her students by using familiar language, short words or phrases, and color coding, lines, and other spatial supports.

7   *Being acceptably manageable.* Barbara emphasizes resources that are relatively quick and easy to construct. Her purpose is to help each particular class of students learn, remember, and use big ideas, not to produce materials that have a slick, professional appearance.

8   *Doesn't become the focal point.* These resources are tools, not ends in themselves. If you get caught up in procedural issues (e.g., where to put something on a Venn diagram, trying to use too many colors), you can lose focus on the big ideas of the lesson.

9   *Organizes information.* Where relevant, the learning resource should not only feature big ideas, but organize them in ways that facilitate applications.

We have shown how Barbara develops plans for teaching each lesson's big ideas, using appropriate instructional resources. Before shifting focus to the interactive aspects of her teaching, we will address two additional aspects of her planning in Chapter 10: how she plans foreshadowings, tiebacks, and other connections that help integrate the curriculum for her students, and how she tries to minimize her students' exposure to confusing, inaccurate, or otherwise undesired information.

Chapter 10

Making Connections and Avoiding Undesired Content

Making Connections

Helping students to see connections (both across the curriculum and between the curriculum and life outside of school) is one of the most powerful ways for teachers to insure that their students learn with understanding, appreciation, and life application. Barbara is well aware of this, and often says, "I'm all about connections" when describing her teaching.

In today's schools, it is more important than ever for teachers to help their students see connections. The textbook series are not helpful in this regard, being notably incoherent and disconnected. Creeping departmentalization has left even many elementary teachers working with their homeroom students for only part of the day. Unless they take steps to inform themselves, they will not even know much about what their students are learning in subjects that they do not teach, let alone how to draw connections to it. Also, the current stress on testing has led to an emphasis on subject-specific test preparation, not integrated learning.

Barbara emphasizes helping her students to see connections, both across the curriculum and between the curriculum and their lives outside of school. Those curricular connections help to keep her students' learning integrated, which fosters coherent and connected understandings. She frequently makes connections within the social studies curriculum by foreshadowing upcoming content or tying back to content taught earlier. She also builds connections across the curriculum by integrating content or skills from other subjects into her social studies teaching or by noting connections between something taught in social studies and something taught in one of the other subjects. Finally, she routinely notes connections between curricular content and life outside the classroom (bringing up key ideas about healthy eating, for example, as they relate to lunch choices in the school cafeteria and breakfast, dinner, and snack choices at home and in the supermarket).

As she develops basic content, Barbara brings out connections that she wants her students to remember in particular contexts. She describes this as helping students not only to remember information, but also to know where to "file" and retrieve it. For example, whenever either the topic of slavery or the topic of cotton farming arises, she notes that at the time, cotton farming was an unusually labor-intensive enterprise—a great many hands were needed to pick the crop—and this provided an economic incentive for slavery. She emphasizes this point consistently because it is important to understanding why slavery developed primarily in the South. She also helps students to organize and "file" what they are learning by consistently repeating (or asking questions to elicit) big ideas, categories, sequences, steps in a process, and other pegs around which to structure and remember information.

Barbara routinely makes other kinds of connections as well. When reacting to students' responses to homework assignments or questions asked in class, for example, she often adds to what the students say by tying back to previous lessons, foreshadowing upcoming lessons, or drawing connections to students' lives outside of school. In the following example, Barbara is reading aloud and reacting to home assignment responses to a question about communication in the past. In the process, she exploits connections with previously taught material and with students' personal experiences. In addition, she takes the opportunity to emphasize that dinosaurs already were extinct long before humans appeared, and she reemphasizes the point after finding out that the mistaken idea came from a parent.

T: Daniel says that Long Ago, American Indians or Native Americans wrote picture stories on animal skins. We didn't talk about that, but he's absolutely right. They used pictures too, just like Long, Long Ago with the people that we talked about in caves.

S: We talked about people writing pictures on caves. I mean on skin.

T: You mean the monks on the parchment.

S: Yeah.

T: Good remembering. Brenda said that Long, Long Ago, people might have used their finger to write with.

S: Ow!

T: You've finger-painted before and it didn't hurt, did it?

S: No.

T: So they might have used the blood and their fingers to make the pictures on the wall. That was a great idea. We hadn't thought to mention that. She mentioned that Long, Long Ago, people might have used smoke or drums to communicate. Bradley said Long, Long Ago they didn't have any pencils. Long Ago the monks wrote the stories and today we have printers. Carlton said cavemen wrote with blood. There were dinosaurs just dying out. There were cavemen. Let me tell you something interesting because lots of kids think this, that when there were dinosaurs, there were cavemen. Look me right in the eyes, friends. [Barbara sometimes pauses and says this as a way to cue her students that she is about to say something important.] Dinosaurs were gone a long, long, long time ago, way before there were any people. Never ever were there dinosaurs and people at the same time. Did you know that?

Ss: Yeah.

Ss: No.

T: A lot of kids didn't know that. And you know what? It wasn't until I was like in high school and starting to grow up that I figured out that dinosaurs and people were never there at the same time [implies that she is "letting them in on a secret" here].

S: Weren't there cavemen there when there were dinosaurs? [Barbara has already addressed this question, but for this student—and probably others— the misconception is well entrenched and thus not easily dislodged.]

T: No, no cavemen even. No people at all. Dinosaurs died—they all died way before there was ever the first person.

S: That wasn't my idea. That was my dad's.

T: Was that your dad's? You can go home and share that with him. Not even cavemen did we have at the same time with dinosaurs. Now, there were some strange-looking animals that we don't have nowadays, like great big furry elephant things called wooly mammoths and saber-tooth tigers, but no dinosaurs. Will you mention that to him?

Questionable or even clearly mistaken ideas sometimes appear in responses to home assignments, and, as in this case, the student sometimes reports that the idea came from a parent. Barbara tries to avoid rejecting such statements out of hand, partly because she has discovered that students' questionable statements often represent misunderstanding or inaccurate reporting of what the parent actually said. Consequently, she often responds with temporizing statements such as "I don't think that's right, but maybe your mother was thinking about something that I am not thinking about. Why don't you talk to her about it tonight at home?"

For example, in reaction to content about family conflict, a student declared that her family never fights. What she knew about this student's home situation led Barbara to interpret her statement as wishful thinking, so she responded, "I bet it would be great if nobody ever fought, but I bet sometimes there are arguments, right? . . . That's part of being a family . . ." She often uses this "I bet it would be great if . . ." strategy when students say things that are questionable but not easily verifiable (and especially when attempting to verify them might take her into dangerous territory). Her response acknowledges the possibility of the ideal state claimed by the student, but also notes that reality is usually different. In this case, she took advantage of the teachable moment presented by the comment and went on to talk at some length about how conflicts are normal and problem solving is a normal and effective response to such conflicts (which was one of the big ideas developed in the day's lesson).

Barbara will not let a clearly wrong statement stand, however, especially one that connects with the curriculum. The misconception that humans and dinosaurs coexisted is very common among children because of *The Flintstones* and other cartoons, so Barbara makes a point of addressing it directly and forcefully whenever it comes up, until the correct information is cemented in her students' minds. This takes some doing, because strongly held and widely reinforced misconceptions are difficult to overcome and because any new students who join her class during the school year are likely to bring such misconceptions with them. A case in point arose later that same year when such a student made a reference to riding dinosaurs. By that time, Barbara had explained about dinosaurs several times with the class as a whole and with certain individuals, especially Cory. So, instead of explaining it yet again to the class as a whole, she told the student to talk to Cory about whether people and dinosaurs coexisted.

When teaching about other cultures, Barbara consistently helps her students to connect the unfamiliar with the familiar, in ways that encourage them to empathize with the people being studied and view their customs as understandable rather than bizarre, stupid, or disgusting. For example, here is how she taught about breads made in other countries, using material from an illustrated book:

T: Let me show you some pictures I have and tell you about bread that comes from some other places. We'll see if we can find some things that are the same. This kind of bread is called roti, and it comes from a country called India. As we view it, see if there's something that seems familiar with bread that you've tried. Here's India right here [on the globe]. Let's take a look. It says take flour and add oil and water, mix together and form the dough, knead the dough until it's smooth. Do these things sound familiar?

Ss: Yeah.

T: Yeah, we seem to be kneading breads a lot, mixing in water. They add something to make it smoother. They take off a small chunk of it and roll it. And look, she's rolling that piece flat. She adds a little bit of flour on each side and then she fries it. A.J., it looks a lot like a what?

S: Tortilla.

T: It does, doesn't it! And then they cook it on the oven or the stove and it puffs up and then they flatten it back out.

S: It's bread.

T: And then they put toppings on the inside. So even though this comes from India, which is over here, and Mexico is over here—look at how far away those two places are!

S: They're real far from Michigan.

T: Their bread—tortillas, bread and roti are a lot alike, and you know what? They didn't teach it to each other. Each place came up with the idea on their own. Take flour and water and make it into bread. A lot alike in lots of places.

Foreshadowing

Barbara frequently foreshadows upcoming content by mentioning briefly a topic that will be developed more fully in a subsequent lesson. Sometimes she does this as a way to put off dealing with something that a student has raised or that she knows is likely to come up. More typically, however, she does it as a way to highlight connections and establish groundwork for productive tiebacks when she takes up the topic again in the future.

In the food unit, for example, when leading the class in analyzing the food groups represented in a potential Mexican meal, she elicited that this particular meal contained no fruit and suggested adding a banana for dessert. Part of the reason for this suggestion was the desire to foreshadow an upcoming lesson on the land-to-hand story of bananas. Also, Mexico borders on a major banana-producing region, so bananas likely would be available there.

Later, when teaching about food in the pioneer days, Barbara noted that the pioneers did not have refrigerators or freezers, so food preservation was a problem for them. This foreshadowed an upcoming lesson on developments in food preservation methods. She also included samples of beef jerky as instructional resources for this lesson, providing another opportunity to make reference to food preservation methods. Many other examples of foreshadowing are noted in the lesson excerpts presented throughout the book.

Tiebacks

Although she frequently foreshadows upcoming content, even more often Barbara ties back to content taught previously. *These tiebacks call attention to connections and frequently cue background knowledge that will help students to learn the new content with understanding.* They reflect Barbara's recognition that curriculum is holistic and flowing; students should keep encountering and using what they have learned in previous lessons, not stop thinking about it.

Another reason for tying back is Barbara's focus on developing limited content in depth (and thus avoiding the mile-wide, inch-deep problem). In teaching about job roles and occupations involved in producing, packaging, advertising, and distributing products, for example, she could have used any of a great many different products as the basis for her examples. However, she chose to use peanut butter, a product that had already been studied with focus on the steps involved in producing it. When feasible, she takes advantages of opportunities like this to bring back familiar content but use it in a different way. She refers to this as connecting to what her students already have from earlier lessons, thinking of it as adding more bricks to an established foundation.

A similar idea, calling for multiple juxtapositions of content, is featured in an approach to instructional design called Cognitive Flexibility Theory. The underlying principle is that revisiting the same material at different times, in rearranged contexts, for different purposes, and from different conceptual perspectives facilitates not just mastery, but the ability to access and apply learning in life outside of school (Spiro *et al.*, 2003).

When teaching about food in Mexico, Barbara noted that corn was a basic staple used to make tortillas, muffins, and pancakes. She then tied back to the recently taught lesson on the food pyramid by reminding her students that healthful eating involves many choices from the bread (grain) group. Later, when teaching about pizza as a form of bread made from dough, she tied back not only to the nutritional aspects of bread, but also to earlier experiences making bread and reading *The little red hen.*

When teaching the clothing unit, Barbara frequently tied back to the previously taught food unit, not only to make connections between particular specifics, but also to build a general paradigm for analyzing topics (start with the here and now, then look at developments over time, then look at variations across cultures, then consider applications that call for decision making). In the process, she revisited big ideas about food that also applied to clothing (e.g., the domestication of animals and the development of farming led to reliable supplies for basic needs; this made possible the proliferation and specialization of occupations; machines were invented to accomplish production steps that formerly had to be done laboriously by hand; eventually this led to mass production of products sold in stores).

At two separate places during a lesson on mass communication, Barbara inserted examples that referred consecutively to the local area, the state, the nation, and the world. These examples were chosen not only to include some geographical connections, but also to help her students keep track of the hierarchical relationships among these geographical terms. Students in the early grades often forget or become confused about these relationships, so Barbara ties back to them frequently until she thinks that her students' understanding of them has solidified.

Sometimes Barbara even ties back across years. In teaching about early rafts during the transportation unit, for example, she tied back to a sink/float activity that most of her students had experienced in kindergarten (she makes it her business to know about her students' learning experiences in the previous and subsequent grades). For a time, she taught second graders every other year as part of a looping arrangement that assigned a cohort of students to the same teacher for two consecutive years. When teaching second graders, she often reminded them of relevant experiences they had shared the previous year in first grade.

Integrating Across Subjects

Jan and Jere are wary of notions about integrating across subjects. Curricular integration sounds good in theory, but assessments of attempts to implement it usually find either that the purposes and goals of one of the subjects are advanced at the expense of those of the other subject or that the resulting lessons and activities trivialize both subjects (Alleman & Brophy, 1993). Barbara has made the same observation, noting that reading a book about saving money to buy a bicycle, or even setting up a classroom store, are not equivalent to mastering the content in an economics lesson. Similarly, a major project involving writing and assembling a class newspaper may teach a lot of worthwhile content and skills, but it is no substitute for a complete communication unit.

Consequently, we caution against attempts at wholesale curricular integration and, especially, integrated curriculum models that subsume social studies within the literacy curriculum. In these models, social studies loses its coherence and power as a school subject with its own unique and worthwhile purposes, goals, content, and activities.

We do, however, recommend highlighting tie-ins across subjects that will help students to see connections and experience the curriculum more holistically. Barbara makes these kinds of connections routinely, particularly connections with the literacy curriculum. For example, many of the books or other texts that she uses during literacy instruction are selected because they tie in with content taught in social studies or science. We have noted her dual use of the book *The little red hen.*

As another example, her class read the book *Froggy gets dressed* (London, 1992) during a literacy lesson conducted at about the same time that she was teaching the clothing unit in social studies. This book contains many scenes of dressing and undressing that connect well with the clothing unit (and in particular, with the lesson on developments in clothing that emphasizes that, at one point, clothing got so complicated that dressing and undressing were lengthy processes). Many other examples of Barbara's use of texts for literacy instruction that tie in with the content being taught in social studies are highlighted in the excerpts that appear throughout the book.

Barbara also provides her students with opportunities to use processes or skills taught in the literacy curriculum as tools for mediating their learning in social studies. For example, when she was teaching beginning sounds in literacy lessons, she frequently gave beginning sound cues when students could not think of the name of something in a social studies lesson (e.g., making "L" sounds when the student was trying to think of the word "lettuce").

Several such tie-ins with the literacy curriculum were noted in her teaching of the transportation unit. In connection with a poem read to the class, her students then were asked to "find" vehicles and write, "I found _____ because _____." Another assignment called for students to illustrate a form of transportation and then write something about it. Also, the class as a whole developed a simile book on transportation, composing and illustrating similes such as "brave as a bulldozer." In all of her social studies units, her students keep journals and do a lot of additional writing as a way to express and preserve what they have been learning.

Barbara also used a poem about riding the subway as an instructional resource for a literacy lesson taught shortly before the social studies lesson on mass transportation systems. Then, as she introduced subways as a form of mass transportation, she couched the topic within the group's common experience ("You already know about this because of our poem about the subway").

Tie-ins with literacy occur routinely, but Barbara also highlights tie-ins with other subjects when opportunities arise. When introducing timelines in social studies, for example, she makes reference to the concept of the number line previously taught in mathematics. She frequently constructs and uses graphs in her social studies teaching, not only because they often are useful instructional resources for social studies purposes, but also because graphing is a data presentation skill taught in mathematics. A home assignment calling for the tallying of foods eaten each day from each food group was suggested in Barbara's mathematics program as a way to generate data to use when teaching about graphs in that subject. However, she then used the graph in social studies to analyze and make recommendations about food intake habits, which made both the graph and her social studies lesson more applicable to life outside of school.

Barbara also frequently includes counting or other mathematical skills in social studies lessons as a way to provide opportunities for authentic applications of those skills (e.g., holding up a calendar and leading the class in counting out the number of days that would elapse between loading of a bunch of bananas onto a truck for transportation from a plantation in Guatemala, through transportation to a Guatemalan port, through shipping to a U.S. port, to arrival at that port city).

Social studies lessons on cultural universals provide frequent opportunities for tie-ins with science, especially in their historical strands (e.g., inventions) and land-to-hand lessons. Many such examples can be seen in the excerpts from Barbara's teaching included in the book. Other examples follow.

When narrating basic information about food, Barbara included a fact that she described as surprising: eating food helps your body to stay warm. She did so not only for motivational purposes (i.e., surprising information piques curiosity), but also because it provided a vehicle for connecting to big ideas about calories, energy, and fuel taught in science.

During the transportation unit, she led the class in analyzing different forms of transportation with respect to whether the power was supplied by humans, animals, or engines. When a student mentioned sleds and snowboards, Barbara immediately recognized these as anomalies because although the riders can steer in desired directions, the power that provides impetus is neither humans nor animals nor engines, but gravity (when going downhill). This led her to insert a brief ("just enough") explanation of gravity, by describing it as a force that pulls things down toward the earth. She demonstrated by dropping a marker and using motion and voice tones to connote the idea of pulling objects down.

Many of Barbara's tie-ins with science involve reinforcing or using skills being taught in science to process data in social studies. For example, early science lessons focus on the skills of observing, describing, and comparing. During a lesson on clothing, she passed around clothing items representing different types of fabric and encouraged her students to feel the fabrics, then describe and compare them (she referred to this as directing her students' thinking while they were experiencing). Similarly, during the food unit, she passed out examples of different kinds of pasta and encouraged students to draw comparisons after observing and handling them. She later included a similar activity calling for the describing and comparing of forms of bread made in different parts of the world, this time scaffolding by asking her students to first state whether the examples being compared were the same or different, and then, if different, to explain how they were different.

Other skills emphasized in science include using data to make decisions and then justifying these decisions with appropriate explanations. Barbara's social studies teaching often includes activities that call for students to use these skills. Following the introduction of the food pyramid, for example, she included activities calling for students to consider an example or illustration of a particular food, identify the food group in which it belongs, and explain why they think so. She scaffolded her students' thinking in these activities by repeatedly using key questions (e.g., "How did you know?") and phrases (e.g., "It comes from milk, so . . .").

Finally, Barbara's social studies teaching often includes tie-ins with the health and safety content included in the Michigan Model curriculum. For example, a poster illustrating the food pyramid and another illustrating healthy snacks were used as instructional resources for lessons taught in the food unit. In these instances, Barbara not only integrated across the curriculum, but also eliminated the need for separate social studies lessons and Michigan Model lessons on healthful eating. Similarly, her teaching about modesty during the clothing unit incorporated several definitions and euphemisms from the Michigan Model lesson on private parts.

Controlling Students' Exposure to Anomalies and Misconceptions

We have shown how Barbara in some respects expands on lesson-specific content in order to foreshadow, tie back, or make connections with students' experiences. In certain other respects, however, she tries to retain tight control over the content to which her students are exposed, so as to avoid events that may disrupt lesson flow or in other ways threaten students' attainment of the learning goals. These events include exposure to anomalies, misconceptions, or other content-related ideas that may confuse students, as well as exposure to content that may excite, upset, or otherwise engage students emotionally in counterproductive ways.

Our instructional units emphasize prototypical examples of concepts and principles, without getting into qualifications, exceptions, or other complications unless there is a good reason to do so. The basic approach is to establish a big idea by defining it carefully and exploring several of its prototypical examples or applications, maintaining sufficient lesson coherence to sustain forward momentum without getting sidetracked. Only after this content is cemented in students' minds does Barbara introduce complications such as anomalies or common misconceptions. She wants to make sure that her students have enough information to enable them to "handle" or "file" these complications productively.

Anomalies

Barbara's example sets sometimes include anomalies, although she does not introduce these until she has established an initial structure using prototypical examples. *The following principles govern her decisions about what anomalies to include*: (1) include those that her students are likely to notice and bring up on their own (e.g., a jacket described as Mr. Knighton's has the name "Taylor" on the label); (2) include those that are common or will come up in future lessons (e.g., tomato as a vegetable; the fact that although clothing made from animal skins is a prototypical example of life Long, Long, Ago, leather and fur coats are made in modern times as well); and (3) omit those that do not need to be taught and are unlikely to come up (e.g., flying squirrels).

Barbara sometimes will bring up an anomaly as preemptive measure, especially if the anomaly is likely to be salient and memorable for her students. She finds that it is better to inject the anomaly herself and thus control the way it is discussed than to have one of her students bring it up and perhaps implant a misconception that will stick in the minds of the listeners. More generally, she tries to minimize her students' exposures to misinformation or other content that conflicts with intended learning outcomes, as insurance against the danger that some students will remember the undesired version rather than the desired version.

A similar concern led her to stop using daily oral language (DOL) exercises that deliberately expose students to incorrect phrasings (such as "Me and Fred went . . ."). She found that when she exposed her students to these incorrect phrasings through DOL teaching, the same incorrect phrasings started to appear in their written journals.

If Barbara believes that a particular anomaly needs to be addressed, she will omit it from her initial concept development (saving it for a review segment or the next day's warm-up) unless she has reason to believe that one of her students might bring it up first. Some examples are as follows: when first talking about milk and dairy products, she focused exclusively on cows (only later noting that other animals such as goats and sheep give milk); when talking about wool, she initially focused exclusively on sheep (only later mentioning that fibers from other animals such as goats, llamas, or alpacas also are used to weave cloth that looks like and often is referred to as wool); she defined personal (as opposed to mass) transportation as vehicles that individuals and families own for their exclusive personal use and gave some of her own vehicles as examples (only much later noting that people other than herself or her husband sometimes borrow and use these vehicles); she delayed introducing roller blades as an example of personal transportation because although high school and college students (among others) sometimes use roller blades for transportation, her students usually do not.

By planning her content carefully and incorporating adjustments based on prior experiences with the units, Barbara is able to deal proactively with much troublesome content by either avoiding it or preempting potential problems with it. Still, comments and questions from her students frequently introduce anomalies that force at least minor departures from her lesson plans. Some examples follow.

When Barbara was teaching about the four functions of clothing (protection, communication, decoration, and modesty), a student brought in a camouflage hat. Although it could be classified as a form of protection from the elements, its primary function was a highly specific and unusual one (camouflage during hunting or warfare) that she would not have mentioned otherwise.

When Barbara asked her students for examples of motorized vehicles, one of them mentioned her camper. This required her to get into the distinction between campers and motor homes. She clarified that motor homes include their own engine and qualify as vehicles in their own right, whereas campers do not because they must be pulled.

Finally, when Barbara asked for examples of animals used for transportation purposes, her students mentioned taking elephant rides at the circus and camel rides at the zoo. This required her to clarify that both of these animals can be used for transportation (and are, in some parts of the world), but the rides taken at the circus and the zoo were for recreational rather than transportation purposes.

Misconceptions

Barbara's approach to dealing with potential misconceptions is similar to her approach to teaching anomalies: save them until an initial conceptual structure is in place, preemptively address those that are common and important enough to require attention, and avoid the rest unless they are brought up by students. When a misconception does get articulated, she may attempt to bury it rather than address it directly if she has reason to believe that this tactic will be successful (typically, in situations where the misconception was verbalized only briefly and in passing).

For example, one day Barbara initially referred mistakenly to a farmer "making" food. She recognized the problem instantly but also decided that it was not worth stopping to correct the term and lose lesson flow, so instead she went out of her way to depict farmers as "growing" food repeatedly over the next several minutes. This tactic appeared to work successfully, because no reference to farmers "making" food appeared throughout the rest of the lesson. Sure enough, however, during a review the next day, one of her students answered a question by speaking of farmers "making" food, and Barbara had to correct to "growing."

Barbara's experience in teaching the lesson based on the story *Uncle Willy and the soup kitchen* has led her to include two preemptive moves in the elaborations that she adds as she reads through the book. First, in defining a soup kitchen, she emphasizes that it serves many different kinds of food besides soup. Second, she emphasizes that not all of the people who eat in soup kitchens are homeless; some live in homes (or, more typically, rented rooms) but do not have enough money to buy much food.

In teaching about tanker trucks, Barbara mentions explicitly that these trucks carry not only gasoline but water and other liquids such as milk, as well as flour and other powders. In talking about television programs, she emphasizes that many of the things depicted in cartoons could not happen in real life (e.g., people or animals getting smashed flat and then jumping up again), and that this even applies to some of the content of dramatic shows (e.g., the Highlander as a person who lives forever). After talking about these and other fantastic elements of television shows, she identifies *Home Improvement* as an example of a more realistic show (selected because it is suitable for viewing by children and because it is set in Michigan).

As with anomalies, Barbara frequently has to deal with misconceptions that she would prefer to avoid, because her students bring them up. For example, when she included farming among examples of occupations, one of her students declared that being a farmer is not a job because you do not leave the farm to go somewhere else and work. During the clothing unit, another student verbalized the commonly held misconception that the clothes sold at a department store are made at the store (i.e., rather than made at clothing factories and then shipped to the store). For detailed information about commonly held misconceptions in children's thinking about cultural universals, see Brophy and Alleman (2006).

Controlling Students' Exposure to Undesired Content

Barbara often takes actions to limit or control her students' exposure to undesired content. Usually this content is undesired simply because it is not relevant to her intended flow of big ideas. However, certain kinds of content are especially threatening because they are not merely off-topic but likely to steer the discourse down paths that Barbara wants to avoid. When students raise these topics, she is quick to jump in and take over, either by cutting them off and moving on quickly or by presenting information or explanations that allow her to structure the way the topic is addressed (so as to avoid anticipated danger).

Potential danger situations arise when students' answers, questions, or comments touch on topics that (1) connect with district guidelines or administrative pressures to either include or avoid certain material; (2) could lead to problems with parents, such as by leading them to believe that Barbara is criticizing their religious or moral beliefs or advocating something they find objectionable (we say "leading them to believe" because Barbara needs to be concerned not only about what she says but about how it might be misinterpreted in her students' reports to their parents); (3) introduce content that may upset students or cause some of them to become flooded with negative emotions (e.g., death, family dissolution); (4) introduce taboo content that may lead to snickering or childish overreactions; or (5) begin to elicit personal and family stories that may go on for some time and derail the lesson. *Some of the tactics that Barbara uses to navigate these dangers include*:

- Preempting the problem by omitting dangerous content from lessons and moving away from it quickly if students bring it up. This is most easily done when the troublesome content is not central to the lesson (e.g., bloody details of slaughterhouse operations, or rites of passage in hunting and gathering societies).
- Modeling and socializing realistic orientations toward potentially provocative content, and using matter-of-fact language when talking about it. This both inoculates students against overreactions and provides them with tools for addressing the content rationally.
- Developing euphemisms and sanitized language for talking about touchy subjects.
- In general, talking about potentially threatening content in ways that infuse rationality and preempt excessive emotionality (e.g., describing the shearing of sheep as a painless procedure akin to getting a haircut; talking about parental separation or placement of children in foster homes as temporary solutions that serve everyone's best interests).
- Helping her students distinguish between answering her questions and telling stories, and reminding them of the difference when necessary. Barbara is especially likely to make this preemptive move when a student says something (e.g., "my grandpa likes to fish) that sounds like the beginning of what could become a lengthy personal or family story. In addition to reminding the student that "we are not telling stories now," she often resumes the flow by directing a question to that same student. Student-initiated storytelling is especially threatening to the flow because it raises the danger of contagion to other students.

Occasionally Barbara encounters teaching guidelines that could place her in conflict with her students' families if she fulfilled the guidelines to the letter. For example, the guidelines for some health lessons include unrealistically rigid proscriptions against alcohol, tobacco, and junk foods. She tempers those proscriptions because she does not want her students going home and condemning their parents out of hand. In place of rigid, always/never guidelines, she acknowledges that people often like to do things that are not good for them and calls for making sensible lifestyle choices (cookies are OK in moderation, but eat healthily in general).

Barbara skirted the potential for a different kind of problem with a parent that also arose during her teaching about healthy foods. One of her students identified raisins as a healthy snack, adding that her mother had told her that if you eat raisins, they will give you "protein and stuff." Barbara recognized that the mention of protein was incorrect, but she merely replied, "Oh, because they come from fruits, and fruits have vitamins and minerals to help keep you healthy." It was not cost-effective to address the student's mistaken mention of protein here. First, Barbara hesitates to correct directly something that a parent supposedly told a child, especially when the child's report might have confused what the parent actually said. She had reason to believe that this was one of those times. Also, given the big ideas that she wanted to emphasize, it made more sense to "bury" the reference to protein here in order to stick with the big idea (choose healthy foods most of the time).

Certain topics call for very careful treatment (i.e., avoiding some aspects altogether, using politically correct language or euphemisms for the rest). These include anything having to do with religion, socioeconomic status, family composition, sex and modesty issues, gender issues, and handicapping conditions. Barbara wants to teach her students about some of life's realities and the reasons for them, but she controls content to exclude unnecessarily emotional material and uses matter-of-fact language and other rational teaching strategies to manage the ones that are included (or injected by students).

To optimize attitudes related to family or cultural differences in economic resources, she promotes empathy by playing up similarities to ourselves and explains decision making by emphasizing that people act rationally given the options available to them. Early in the year, she has everyone formally sign a pledge that they will not laugh at or make fun of things that are different or unusual, and she reminds her students of this pledge when necessary.

Economic Disparities

Issues relating to differences in families' economic resources are raised in lessons about community "safety net" services, a book about repairing bicycles and donating them to an orphanage, and references to activities such as school drives for people in need. She tries to avoid dehumanizing these people by referring to them as "the poor" or "the homeless." Instead, she portrays them as people who need assistance, adding that some of her own students might at some point find themselves in this situation. When collecting for these drives, Barbara just states that the collections are intended to benefit children who do not have food, shelter, or other basic resources because their parents do not have the money to pay for them. She usually leaves it at that, although if students raise questions about why the family lacks funds, she will talk about how people sometimes lose their jobs and need help until they can get back on their feet again.

Taboo Topics

"Taboo" topics that could derail a lesson include anything having to do with sex, private parts, bathroom functions, obscene words, or undergarments. Barbara is willing to bring these up where they connect to the curriculum, but she treads carefully. For example, during the communication unit she initiated a discussion of television programs that her students were not allowed to watch, and why. This required her to make reference to *Beavis and Butt-head* (some teachers would never use any word that included "butt"), violence, swearing, and so on.

She described swearing as words that make people uncomfortable and thus should not be used for that reason, even though they are not against the law. Then she got into some of the shows that involve violence, monsters, and other things that might scare children or give them nightmares. She told her students that they would be more prepared to watch these shows when they were older, because "You're growing up and in your head you're able to figure out what's scary and what's not scary better."

During her review of the communication unit, she asked about ways that communication can hurt people. A student made reference to bad words, and Barbara acknowledged that they had talked about profanity and swearing like on *Beavis and Butt-head*. Then another student mentioned hostile gestures. This led Barbara to say

> "There are some gestures, and I'm not even going to show them to you because they are rude and it wouldn't be OK for me to do that, but some-times like when people are driving and they get really angry and they can't shout at you, they do nonverbal communication by doing really naughty gestures with their hands or body."

This led another student to add, "or with their fingers." Barbara replied mildly, "Yes, so that can be a way that communication hurts." Then she went on to talk about teasing.

The clothing unit features modesty as one of four basic functions of clothing. Introducing this idea is challenging because notions about modesty vary and are essentially arbitrary and because introducing the topic requires mention of body parts and underclothes. Barbara's approach incorporates definitions and euphemisms borrowed from the Michigan Model's health lesson on private parts. In developing this content, she takes a matter-of-fact approach and makes it clear that she expects her students to do the same.

T: The question we're going to work on today is why do people wear clothes. Why do people wear clothes? The very first answer that we're going to come up with is an answer that . . . it just kind of makes sense. Why do you all have clothes on here at school today?

S: So people don't see all your body parts.

T: Right. There's a rule at school that says everybody has to wear clothes so that nobody sees your body parts. There's a word for that—it's called modesty. Modesty just means that you're not going to show other folks your body parts. The rule that we have here at our school and in our community is that people at work or people at school need to wear a shirt to cover the top of their body and they need to wear pants or shorts to cover the bottom part of their body. The reason we do that is because we don't want anyone to see the parts of our body that are under our clothes. That's kind of a rule that we've all agreed to. Your moms and dads have agreed to it . . . that's just the way it is. Now, at home, maybe your family has decided a little bit differently and maybe at home it's OK for you to have your pants not on or maybe it's OK for you to be in the house without your shirt on. That's something that your family decides together. Here at school, the rule is that kids need to have a shirt on and to have pants on . . . we don't show our underclothes. Underneath my clothes, I have stuff on. Underneath your clothes, you have stuff on. It's the same for every person around here at this school. Our rule is that not only does nobody see your body under your clothes, but nobody sees your underclothes, and that will be like your undershirt, your underwear, your underpants, a bra, a slip. These are all clothes that you wear underneath your clothes. You know they exist. Everybody wears clothes underneath, and part of keeping yourself modest is not showing the clothes that you are wearing underneath. So modesty means you're wearing clothes to cover up your body. [Goes on to other functions of clothing.]

Barbara introduced recognition of family variations in modesty rules to preempt a student from saying something like "At home, I don't have to put on a robe when I come out of the shower." In doing so, however, she stuck with safe examples (i.e., she did not suggest that walking around nude might be acceptable in some households). Later she deliberately introduced terms such as underpants and bra in a matter-of-fact manner. Her students responded accordingly (no one giggled or made remarks about "bad words").

When sex or modesty issues arise that are not connected to the big ideas she wants to develop, Barbara will preempt or move quickly past them rather than address them. For example, she omitted mention of garters in talking about wedding clothing, having discovered in previous years that some students may overreact to this term. Similarly, in a lesson on childhood games and pastimes, one of her students mentioned spin the bottle. Barbara did not acknowledge or react to this comment, wanting to "dodge this bullet" and move on.

Negative Emotions

Preemptive or flow restoration strategies also may be needed whenever the content requires references to topics that elicit strong emotions from her students or elicit off-topic comments, questions, and attempts at storytelling. Topics that may set off negative emotions and disturb some students include death, divorce or separation, children being sent to foster homes or orphanages, hunting and killing of animals, guns, slavery, famous people who were assassinated, or abuse of people or animals.

Any mention of death or killing may excite certain students (disturb some but cause others to want to tell stories), so Barbara limits attention to this topic in the curriculum and usually moves away from it quickly when it is brought up by students. For example, in the clothing unit, she describes and shows illustrations of sheep shearing in detail and makes a point of noting that the process is akin to a haircut and does not harm the sheep. However, when she describes how early people made clothing from animal skins, she talks about how they scraped the skins clean and cut them to the desired shapes, but does not dwell on the fact that they first had to kill the animals. In talking about the development of silk, she includes the step of stifling (killing) the silkworms, but she does not dwell on the process itself. Instead, she explains the reason for it (if silkworms are allowed to break out of their cocoons, they will chew the silk fibers into small pieces, but longer pieces are desired as fibers for silk clothing).

Here and elsewhere, whenever the content requires mention of killing animals to get food or other products from them, she talks about this matter-of-factly. She wants her students to understand some of life's realities and the reasons for them, but without getting into gory details.

Incidents of physical injury or death frequently come up in current events discussions, especially relating to the war in Iraq. Teachers at Barbara's school have been forbidden to talk about this war's political aspects, but they can focus on the human side of it. In recent years, Barbara has arranged for each of her classes to correspond with at least one soldier stationed in Iraq or elsewhere in the Middle East, mostly soldiers with familial links to children at the school. She recognizes the potential for problems if one of these soldiers should become a casualty, but she points out that the school already has seen four deaths of family members (two of them murders) in recent years.

What can happen when the topic of death is introduced is illustrated in the following excerpt. Barbara was introducing the timeline. She usually divides it into only three major sections (Long, Long Ago; Long Ago; and Modern Times), but on this day she extended it to include the future (at the suggestion of one of her students). Elaborating a bit about the future, she decided to "dance with death" in the process of teaching about time as a continuum.

T: (Extending the timeline on the board) This will be when you guys are adults, and then the time will keep on going along that line until even after I'm gone and I'm not alive anymore and after you guys are not alive anymore . . . but time will keep going this way. After awhile, all of you guys will not be around anymore but maybe your kids will be alive or your grandkids, but there will be a time when all of us are gone and none of us are alive anymore, and that will be way far in the future.

Howell: What does that mean?

T: You mean "gone"?

Howell: Yes.

T: It means that some day all of us will not be living anymore.

Howell: We'll all die?

T: Yes, because that's what happens for people. In fact, the people that all lived Long, Long Ago . . .

Ss:	They died.
T:	And the people that lived Long Ago . . .
Ss:	They died.
T:	But these were all the people who came before us—our ancestors.
S:	Will there be dinosaurs again someday?
T:	We don't know for sure what will happen in the future. We can make some guesses, but we don't know that there will be dinosaurs again.
S:	We can all be scientists and make guesses, too.
T:	Yes, that's how we think about things that happened way back when.
Howell:	Will scientists die?
T:	Everyone does eventually, but we have scientists that are thinking now about the future. Now let's take a look at some pictures . . . [At this point, she shifts back to the flow by showing pictures and asking students where they would be placed on the timeline.]

As soon as Barbara mentioned that time would continue after all of us are gone, the student most obsessed with death (Howell) asked for an explanation and then for more clarification (his questions suggested that he may not have fully realized yet that he and everyone else was going to die). Then, just as that point appeared to be cleared up and Barbara might have been able to get back to the flow, another student asked about dinosaurs (another "magic" word).

Barbara made the best of this situation by modeling rational thinking and talking about making some educated guesses. She was briefly pleased when another of her students made a connection to what she had been teaching the class about their own current and future efficacy ("We can all be scientists and make guesses, too"). However, Howell immediately shifted focus back to the topic of death ("Will the scientists die?"). At this point, Barbara made a brief response and then took coordinated actions designed to leave this topic behind and get back to the flow (not only signaling verbally that the activity was now moving into a new phase, but showing illustrations likely to attract the students' attention).

The topic of families can foster questions or comments that threaten the flow in two very different ways. First, the topic can be upsetting to certain students who come from strife-ridden or otherwise difficult family backgrounds. This danger is especially acute in lessons on family structures and functions. The second, and more widespread, way in which references to families can disrupt lessons is their tendency to stimulate students to begin to tell stories about their family experiences. These episodes often begin with a brief reactive observation (mention of fishing elicits "I go fishing with my uncle," or mention of making jam elicits "My grandma makes strawberry jam"). Barbara often intervenes quickly in these situations to remind the students that right now they need to focus on the lesson, not tell stories.

Most of the disturbance potential in content about families is diffused early in the year when Barbara takes pains to get to know her students individually and encourage them to identify and bond with one another as a classroom "family" (Brophy *et al.*, in press). In the early weeks, she allocates about forty-five minutes each day for relationship building. This includes publicly interviewing each student in depth, noting connections to other students as they appear (e.g., Laurel has a stepmother, too). She also hangs posters showing information about each student's family, including family photos. Typically, several students have complicated family compositions that do not fit the prototypes.

For example, one year one of her students lived with her natural father and mother but had half-siblings living in the home as well; one's father had died the previous year; one was currently a foster child but might be adopted by the foster parents; one had nieces older than she was; and several spent a lot of time at the homes of both separated/divorced parents (so they had two families). Her class was aware of most of this before she even began the unit, so the students took it in stride when reminded of it during her teaching about six types of families (nuclear, extended, single parent, blended, adoptive, and foster).

Rather than focus from the beginning on examples of each type that may exist in the class, Barbara uses a book that illustrates the six types (but mostly providing her own commentary rather than reading from the text). She uses careful and occasionally sanitized language that avoids references to blood or genes and casts decisions to separate, get divorced, or give up children for adoption or temporary placement in foster homes as problem solving in everyone's best interest when things are not going well. She skirts or minimizes issues of parental conflict and child abuse or neglect.

In talking about the single-parent family illustrated in the book, she said that "Her dad decided that it just wasn't working for the two of them [him and his wife] so he moved away." She was deliberately vague here because she wanted to focus on the separation itself and not the parental conflict that led to it, and she omitted the term "divorce" because she had at least one student whose parents may not ever have gotten married in the first place (she wasn't sure). However, she did address divorce more directly in a later lesson, focusing on the legal and court aspects but again minimizing attention to parental conflict.

As she went through the six types of families, she asked her students to identify which type was like their own family. Then the homework assignment that night called for talking with family members to identify some things that were special about their family. Several potentially troublesome questions and comments came up in the wonders segment that introduced the unit (Can families get married, so there's a new stepdad? Do all families die? Why do families fight?), in reactions to the content on the six types of families (some families don't live together, "My dad lives way out in a different country"), and during the in-class review of responses to the homework assignment (my family doesn't celebrate Easter, my family is special because I have a stepmother). Barbara responded to these questions and comments in her usual matter-of-fact manner as shown in the following excerpt:

T: (Reading from Lionel's homework assignment) Lionel says, "My family is special because when I was a baby, my dad wasn't happy and my mom wasn't happy together." So in Lionel's family, his mom and dad chose not to be together and have two different houses. Do you sometimes get to be at mom's house?

Lionel: Yes, I live with my mom.

T: And sometimes with dad?

Lionel: Yes.

T: So you have two houses to be in. That's what has to happen for some parents. They make decisions about the family. Sometimes families don't work out and things change, and it's up to the family to settle those problems when they come up, and that's what Lionel's family did. They had a problem and they solved it. [Goes on to next student.]

Later, Barbara had each student stand up and show his or her family poster to the class, then say which type of family it represented. When she got to one of the foster children, she first had him name everyone shown in his poster, then asked which type of family he represented.

S: A foster family.

T: A foster family, because they're going to take care of you for a little while. [She previously had defined a foster family as a family that you go to live with, not for all the time, not for your whole life, but for a while, while your mom or dad is working to get ready to take care of you again.] Now, I've heard that you all are thinking about becoming a different kind of family. You've talked about changing your name, right—maybe someday being adopted. That would change your family, wouldn't it? Because you guys would still be together, right?

S: Yes.

T: That would be pretty cool. So, when we come to the graph, what are you going to put yourself down for?

S: Foster family.

Magic Words

High-interest topics likely to provoke side discussion or storytelling include anything connected with Disney; *SpongeBob* or other cartoons; the Harry Potter series and other popular children's books and movies; vacations (e.g., Florida); or popular toys. Most of these "magic words" are predictable and avoidable when not desired, although some are unique to each new class. One year, for example, any mention of trains would stimulate several students to want to begin telling stories of personal experiences. Another time, Barbara was taken aback when mention of motorcycles stimulated one student to begin making vroom noises and several others to want to tell stories about their fathers' motorcycles.

Any mention of gender role differentiation is likely to produce comments from girls. Consequently, Barbara discusses the topic at length early in the year and refers back to this discussion later when necessary. One year, one of her girls had a special interest in this topic and tended to comment on it whenever it arose. During one of her lessons, a question elicited reference to the term "cavemen." Barbara quickly jumped in to preempt a potential sidetrack and yet also honor the student's special interest by turning to her and asking if the term meant that there were just men around long, long ago. Her question elicited the expected "no" answer and allowed her to remind all of her students that sometimes the word "men" is used to refer to people in general (although she refers to "cave people" in her lessons). In another lesson on early factories, Barbara noted that at the time, only men worked in factories. She did so as a preemptive move because this point had been discussed previously and she was pretty sure that one of her students would bring it up if she did not.

Developing Big Ideas

Chapters 5–8 focused on the big ideas that Barbara teaches about cultural universals, history, geography, and the social sciences. Chapter 9 described her use of visuals and other instructional resources. Chapter 10 has described how she elaborates on some aspects of lesson topics (to bring out connections to other parts of the curriculum or to her students' experiences), but controls exposure to other aspects so as to minimize flow disruptions and threats to students learning.

In Chapters 11–14, we will describe and illustrate the ways that Barbara introduces and develops big ideas as she interacts with her students during lessons. We characterized the major features of her informal, narrative style in Chapter 4. In Chapters 11–14, we will unpack her teaching to show how she establishes an initial knowledge base through a narrative presentation, then gradually shifts from primarily presenting information to primarily questioning and responding to students. In the process, she broadens and deepens her development of the day's big ideas, makes several kinds of connections, and addresses the needs and interests of individual students.

Chapter 11

Introducing New Knowledge Bases

In Chapter 4, we described and gave examples of Barbara's narrative approach to social studies lessons. Starting with this chapter, we will analyze her lessons more closely, to highlight the planning and instruction involved in teaching for understanding by focusing on connected networks of knowledge structured around big ideas. *In this chapter, we focus on the planning and teaching strategies involved in establishing an initial knowledge base with learners who not only are young, but possess very limited prior knowledge of the topics being taught.* In the following chapters, we examine the ways that Barbara transitions from establishing a knowledge base to extending and applying it by asking her students questions and then following up on their responses.

Jan and Jere's instructional units provide Barbara with content bases to develop as well as plans for follow-up activities and home assignments. The lesson plans begin with digests of basic information about a key aspect of the cultural universal under study. The digests consist of connected information developed around featured big ideas. The lessons develop these big ideas in ways that allow students not only to understand them, but to use them for making sense of the social world and in other ways apply them to their lives outside of school.

Early lessons focus on concepts and principles needed to understand how the cultural universal is addressed in contemporary American society, especially the students' homes and neighborhoods. Subsequent lessons focus on inventions and other significant developments through time, then on the nature of and reasons for current variations across locations and cultures. The lessons that come near the ends of the units typically present less new information and instead focus on the implications of what has been learned for personal, social, and civic decision making.

In contrast to "trivial pursuit" or "mile-wide but inch-deep" curricula that feature disorganized breadth and little or no depth, our units feature limited but focused content. Lessons were developed around what we believe to be basic understandings that will allow children to make sense of those aspects of the social world that relate to the cultural universal under study. Consequently, instead of parades of miscellaneous facts, the lessons feature networks of connected content structured around big ideas. These big ideas, and the information digests that accompany them, provide most of the content base for Barbara's social studies program. This program includes her district's social studies guidelines, which in turn reflect the state's guidelines.

Adapting and Elaborating Lesson Plans

As she studies our units to adapt them to her teaching context, Barbara draws on her professional knowledge and experience and on her knowledge of her students and their families. Her social studies program is subsumed within her overall approach to teaching. For example, as part of her emphasis on helping students to see connections, she searches for ways to exploit connections between the lesson being planned and other lessons in social studies or other subjects, as well as connections between lesson content and the experiences of her students and their families.

Barbara has found that her six- and seven-year-olds learn and retain big ideas better when she builds toward them by using examples drawn from her own life and their lives, instead of beginning by stating the big idea as an abstract generalization and only then moving to examples. Consequently, as she thinks about teaching each big idea, she identifies anecdotes from her own life and examples from her students' lives that she can use to lay groundwork for building toward the big idea.

Choosing Physical Settings

Planning includes consideration of the appropriate physical setting for each of the day's activities. If a lesson segment involves primarily verbal interactions, and especially if it involves showing illustrations in a book or other resource, Barbara sits in a low chair in a corner of the room and has her students sit on a rug in front of her, gathered closely in a semicircle so that all can see the illustrations clearly when she displays them. Frequently used resources such as the globe and drawing supplies are close at hand, where she can reach them without leaving her chair.

In contrast, if a lesson segment calls for students to engage in writing or to refer to the timeline or another large illustration posted at the front of the room, Barbara will teach from that location and seat the students at tables, arranged so that all are facing the front. If more extended writing or interaction with peers is involved, she will reseat them in order to facilitate interaction between partners or members of small groups.

She has socialized her students to make transitions quickly and quietly, and she sustains lesson momentum during these times by continuing to talk about lesson-related content. Alternatively, she may give her students a brief thinking task to do while they make the shift (e.g., generate a response to a question or an example from their own lives of a principle under discussion).

Choosing Instructional Resources

Barbara shares Jan and Jere's concern about limiting the breadth of content in order to focus on developing big ideas in depth, so *her primary consideration in deciding whether to use anecdotes, examples, books, illustrations, activities, or other instructional resources is her assessment of their potential value in helping her students understand and apply the lesson's big ideas.* Other criteria (e.g., whether the resources are easy to obtain and use, whether the students are likely to find them interesting) are relevant as secondary considerations, but her primary focus is on adapting the lesson plans to ensure that the big ideas are developed effectively.

Most of her adaptations focus on the big ideas themselves. If the terminology used in defining concepts and explaining principles is not well suited to her students, Barbara will substitute for or elaborate on certain aspects of Jan and Jere's version of the content base. Also, if the content includes reference to objects or processes likely to be unfamiliar to her students, she will plan ways to supplement verbal descriptions or explanations with physical examples, photos, or other illustrations. She wants to make sure that her students can understand and visualize the processes they are learning about—not just memorize a definition or generalization that might not mean much to them.

However, she typically omits the adding of such instructional resources in the case of content that is already familiar to her students, to avoid making the lesson any more cluttered or complicated than it needs to be. For example, she brought woolen fleece and three pieces of wool clothing to the lesson on the land-to-hand story of wool, allowing students to feel them and gain visual and tactile sensations of wool to supplement the understandings developed through her verbal explanations. She also brought some fluffy cotton to the subsequent lesson on cotton, but she did not bring items of cotton clothing because she knew that most of her students would be wearing cotton clothing that day.

When she sees the need for an instructional resource, Barbara prefers to make or assemble her own version so that she can tailor it to the lesson's big ideas and her students' experiences. She finds that illustrations in books and even maps, posters, or other materials specifically marketed to teachers as instructional resources often contain language that is confusing or unfamiliar to her students, details that distract attention from the big idea, or other features that detract from their usability.

Where unfamiliar or difficult language is a problem, Barbara may teach her students the language used in the resource and help them make it their own, adapt the language on the spot to fit what is familiar to the students, or repeat key questions or phrases to simplify the learning task. In any case, she uses commercially manufactured instructional resources the same way as she uses the ones she co-constructs with her students: as bases for extended discourse, not just as series of questions to answer or outlines to fill in.

Most of the instructional resources Barbara uses are relatively simple and traditional, and many are made by Barbara herself. She uses props mostly when introducing new topics, partly to engage students' interest. Later she uses them sparingly, to support a big idea or perhaps a transition to a new topic or aspect. She is careful to ensure that the props do not "take over" her lessons (i.e., distract attention from big ideas).

Developing Skills

Although much of the content of the lessons focuses on big ideas and related propositional knowledge, Barbara always looks for opportunities to teach skills, strategies, and other procedural knowledge within natural application contexts.

For example, after developing a base of knowledge about food groups, she asked her students to look at pictures of different foods and say which groups the foods came from. In the process, she made a point of asking the students to explain the rationales for their choices, because the state's benchmarks for social studies, science, and health included teaching skills for using data to make decisions and justifying these decisions with explanations. To help bring out the connections, both for the students giving responses and for the classmates listening to them, she repeatedly posed key questions ("How did you know?") and scaffolded reasoning ("It comes from milk, so . . .?").

Starting by Eliciting "Wonders"

Barbara typically introduces units, and often new topics within units, by eliciting "wonders" (topic-related questions about which her students are curious). She finds that the questions she elicits come right out of her students' personal experiences and thus provide important clues to their current interests and prior knowledge. When she asked students what they wondered about clothing, for example, most of their questions focused on how clothes are made. No one asked about historical developments or cultural differences in clothing or about criteria to consider in shopping for clothes.

Barbara's students sometimes generate artificial answers if she asks them what they would like to learn about a topic, whereas questions reflecting what they are wondering about the topic come more naturally to them, and one idea often suggests another. She frequently models some of her own wonders to get the ball rolling. She also structures wonders segments to foreshadow the major strands of the unit, to begin building this structure in the minds of her students as well. Concerning food, for example, she models wonders about where foods come from, about foods in the past and in other cultures, and about why we cook some foods and refrigerate others. As she collects and lists the students' wonders, she groups them in ways that foreshadow upcoming lessons.

Having collected and previewed a list of wonders when she introduced a topic, Barbara returns to the list periodically as the topic is developed over the next days or weeks. One purpose for this is to reinforce the expectations and dispositions that she works to instill as part of establishing her classroom as a learning community. Reviewing the list to see which wonders have been addressed and which have yet to be addressed underscores the expectation that her students' learning interests are taken seriously. These occasions also provide opportunities to foreshadow upcoming lessons and review or make connections to big ideas from earlier lessons.

Although she frequently collects wonders, she usually does not use KWL (Ogle, 1986) or other techniques that involve eliciting and posting statements of what the students think they already know about the topic. These techniques are best used when most of the elicited statements are likely to be accurate. Unfortunately, asking primary students what they think they already know often produces more fanciful or distorted statements than accurate ones, and writing these down so that they can be revisited later provides repeated exposure to them and risks instilling misconceptions.

Barbara also has found that it is harder to shift to eliciting wonders if she first begins by inventorying prior knowledge. Students who know something about the topic will tend to hog the time and inhibit their peers from wondering aloud. Perfectionistic students may hesitate to communicate a "fact" for fear of being wrong, but they tend to be willing to ask a question. Barbara often asks inhibited students what they have heard about the topic from their parents, because this reduces their fear of making a mistake and makes it easier for them to focus on something specific rather than trying to think about the topic in its entirety.

For these reasons, Barbara usually does not attempt to inventory prior knowledge and instead begins with anecdotes and examples selected to build toward the big idea. When she is ready to introduce this idea more formally, she does so by using the terminology she has selected, often cueing its importance by announcing, "OK, here's the scoop" (or the big news, the big idea, etc.). Subsequent discourse features planned redundancy using this terminology. In this way, she introduces and reinforces accurate representations of the big ideas, but using vocabulary and examples that connect with students' prior experiences and help them construct accurate understandings.

Establishing the Initial Knowledge Base

Barbara emphasizes that when introducing content that is almost completely new to students, it is important to securely establish an initial base of information and then build on it, rather than confront students with too much too quickly before they have such a base in place. For example, her students' knowledge about the distant past is very limited, and many of the ideas and images they do possess are misconceptions developed through exposure to media such as Alley Oop or Flintstones cartoons. So, when she gets to the historical segment of the first social studies unit she teaches in a given year, she takes pains to develop coherent sets of ideas and images of daily life and technological development Long, Long Ago (cave days) and Long Ago (Native Americans, Pilgrims, pioneers).

To begin, she spends a lot of time building images of life Long, Long Ago by developing a cave days story that is sufficiently detailed to provide meaningful context for material taught about Long, Long Ago in this and future units. She supports this story with illustrations (some of which are attached to the timeline that she begins to co-construct with the students), and corrects common misconceptions (such as that cave people coexisted with dinosaurs or used stone-wheeled vehicles like those shown in cartoons), as well as any other misconceptions that students might articulate. She continues with an exclusive focus on Long, Long Ago until she believes that the basic story and associated images that she wants to emphasize have become cemented in her students' minds and attached to the term "Long, Long Ago" in ways that will make them easy to access in the future. Only then does she move on to Long Ago.

In introducing Long Ago, Barbara similarly sticks to the big picture that she wants to outline, without getting into complications such as that in some places in the world today, people still do things the way they did Long Ago in America. Also, because at this point she is developing an advance organizer or overview, she avoids going into unnecessary detail about major components of the big picture. Concerning food Long Ago, for example, her introductory content omits mention of anything having to do with the First Thanksgiving (this will be covered in depth during a brief Thanksgiving unit), and she limits vocabulary to terms needed to make the points she wants to make.

Starting with the Prototypical

As part of limiting and focusing lesson content, Jan and Jere's units emphasize prototypical examples of concepts and principles, without getting into anomalies unless there is good reason to do so. Similarly, although they address misconceptions that are both known to be common and likely to distort understanding of big ideas, they omit reference to misconceptions that are not as directly relevant or frequently observed. Barbara follows these same principles, so the anecdotes or illustrations that she includes are prototypical examples of big ideas or their applications. Once the big idea itself and several of its prototypical examples or applications have been established and "cemented" in her students' minds, she will introduce anomalies or complications, at least to the extent of making students aware that they exist (for example, that some people still make clothes the way they were made in the past).

Building on Prior Knowledge

Barbara also sequences her information and examples so as to connect with and build on students' prior knowledge and experiences. Where necessary, she will begin with concrete objects, then move to photos or other pictorial illustrations, and then to discussion of more abstract aspects of the topic. In teaching about the categories in the food pyramid, for example, she begins with actual examples of foods on the first day but then shifts to pictures of foods on the second day. If she is going to be relying primarily on verbal discourse to develop aspects of a topic, she wants to be sure that her students possess sufficient prior experiences and accessible images to enable them to follow the discussion without difficulty.

She also tries to sequence from the more familiar to the less familiar. In a lesson calling for using the food pyramid categories to analyze the content of prototypical meals from three countries, she began with the American meal because that was most familiar to her students. In teaching about types of farms, she began with dairy farms because, first, they are frequent in Michigan, where her students live; second they produce a clear, single product (milk) that also is familiar; and third her students typically already know that milk comes from cows and have readily accessible images of cows. When introducing transportation as a cultural universal (something that "you find all over the world") and emphasizing its fundamental contributions to aspects of everyday living that we take for granted, she began by calling attention to objects in the classroom and using questions to lead her students to the recognition that everything in the classroom had been transported there from somewhere else, including even the materials used to construct the classroom itself.

An Example

Barbara's handling of early lessons in the childhood unit typifies both the techniques she uses to introduce topics and the way she builds connections as she develops the topics. She began the unit by showing pictures of the new baby that the teacher from the classroom next door had delivered just ten days previously. This arrival was of great interest to Barbara's students and had been discussed in class several times during the previous week. After a period of circulation and discussion of the photos, Barbara told her students that she was circulating them because their next social studies unit was about childhood—looking at developments in the lives of children beginning when they are babies and continuing through young adulthood. Next she elicited wonders from her students, beginning by modeling a few of her own and then calling on the students for theirs. Finally, she used her own life as an example of the developments she would be teaching about.

She displayed, distributed, and led discussion of items from her memory box (photos and memorabilia from birth through young adulthood). She chose these items and scaffolded the discussion to build toward the main idea of the day: that children grow and change with age, and in the process have new experiences and acquire new freedoms and responsibilities. However, she did not begin to articulate this main idea until well into the lesson, when she asked her students to compare two pictures of her taken at different ages. From that point onward, she increasingly made statements or phrased questions focusing on the idea that increases in age are accompanied by increases in physical size and capabilities, broadened experiences, increases in freedoms and responsibilities, and involvement in rites of passage.

Barbara refers to this as her "set the hook, then reel them in" approach. She prefers it to a more linear advanced organizer approach because she believes that it makes her lessons more interesting to her students. Also, it builds a better experiential base of readiness or context within which to understand the big idea being developed.

Over the next several lessons of the childhood unit, Barbara built on the foundation laid in the first lesson. She continued to make connections to scaffold her students' learning by building on the familiar or applying newly taught concepts or principles to familiar experiences. For example, one lesson focuses on psychological and behavioral developments across the early years of life. As Barbara taught this lesson, she consistently incorporated four things that the children were familiar with at that point: her own early development as elaborated in a previous lesson illustrated with objects from her memory box; a book that she had read to them about the characteristics of different infants and toddlers; what they had seen or heard about Julie, the baby delivered recently by Mrs. H., who taught the classroom next door; and parallel developments in their own lives.

T: I want to start out by filling in on my chart today. We're going to start out with me as a baby. How many of you think I'm the cutest baby you've ever seen?

Ss: (a few raise their hands)

T: All of you get extra recess, the rest of you . . . no, no, no. All right. We're going to talk about four different things with babies. Physical qualities talks about the body. The second part talks about communication of emotion: that is, how you let folks know what you're thinking and feeling. Attitudes—the way you act or behave toward other folks. The last one is behaviors—things that you do. So think about either you or me as an infant. Here I was. What were some things about me or my body or you or your body when you were an infant? Take a look at these pictures in the book I have here. The one with all the cute little kids. Do you remember Jody?

Ss: Yeah.

T: What is special or unique about his body?

S: He sleeps a lot.

T: What about Brittany and her body? What can you tell me? Give me a hands up. What did you think of, Chad?

S: She rolls a lot.

T: She could roll over. That's a pretty special thing for an infant—they learn to roll over. Tisha?

S: Learning to crawl.

T: Yeah, learning to crawl. What else about the baby's body, Alan?

S: She has earrings.

T: Oh, that's that baby. We're talking about all babies. All babies wouldn't have earrings. What about hair? What about teeth? Do they have teeth?

S: Yeah.

T: When they're born?

S: No.

T: What happens to your body as an infant?

S: You grow teeth.

T: You grow teeth. Remember? That was one of the things that my mom kept track of for me. On June 10, there was my first tooth. Anything else about the baby's body, Marty?

S: They sleep.

T: They do. They need lots of sleep! Sleep, sleep, sleep, sleep, sleep. How do babies let you know what they're thinking or feeling?

S: They cry.

T: Just like Julia yesterday. She wanted her diaper changed. Annie, how do babies communicate?

S: Cry.

T: She does! Fortunately she hasn't cried really loud when I'm there, but Mrs. H. said when she's really frustrated she cries, and when I was hungry, you know what I used to do?

Ss: Cry.

T: And when I was mad, I . . .

Ss: Cried loud.

T: And when I was tired, I . . .

Ss: Cried.

T: And when I wanted to get up, I . . .

Ss: Cried.

T: There's one other thing I know that Julia does that I'm guessing I did when I was an infant: she kind of makes cooey, gurgly sounds. Sometimes little babies can even smile. In fact, that's one of the pretty exciting things for moms and dads. Julia can't smile right now. She's only a week and a half old. But as she gets older, that'll be one of the exciting things for Mr. and Mrs. H.—when she first smiles. What are some of the other things they do to let you know what they're thinking?

S: My little brother started crawling to my mom and then he pointed at something.

T: Like making gestures like this when they want you to pick them up, or pointing. So it's something we call gestures. In fact, that's probably even true for toddlers, too. They do some of those same things. What about attitudes for babies? Attitudes tell you how they act toward different people. What do you think, Jared?

S: Some babies could have bad attitudes.

T: So they could have grumpy days and happy days. Let me ask you a question. If it took me a long time to get the baby's bottle ready today, do you think tomorrow the baby would remember?

Ss: No.

T: So you know how sometimes us—school kids or teachers or adults—sometimes when you get angry at somebody you can fuss at them for a couple of days. Do babies do that?

Ss: No.

T: They forget easily, don't they?

Ss: Yeah.

T: They forget stuff easily. How do babies behave? What things do babies do? What do they do, Sean?

S: Cute things to make you treat them nicely.

T: Do babies do that—do they think "Oh, if I do some nice things, Sean will treat me nice?"

S: No.

T: What things do babies do?

S: Act cute.

T: Oh. Are they doing it on purpose or is that just the way babies are?

S: It's just the way they are.

T: So they don't put a lot thinking into it. Behavior means things that we choose to do. So we find babies to be cute, but really, babies don't do much.

S: Sleep and play around.

T: They do a little play, then sleep. What, Christie?

S: Eat.

T: What else, Devon?

S: Crawl.

T: Crawl, cry. Let's think about toddlers. Toddler, that's me right here. Think about my body. What are some changes in my body? . . .

Similarly, in a later lesson on rites of passage, Barbara began with a very familiar example important to her students: being promoted from first grade to second grade. Next she revisited the timeline they had constructed of her own early life, inviting them to identify events that signified that she had acquired new privileges or responsibilities or had attained a new status. Then she invited them to identify rites of passage in their own lives, occasionally cueing events that she knew applied to specific families (confirmations, bar mitzvahs). This scaffolding was effective, because her students began to generate good examples of rites of passage in their own past or future lives (joining the safety patrol at school, being allowed to stay home by themselves for increasingly lengthy periods, dating, getting a bicycle or car).

Alternative Topic Introductions

When introducing a new topic, Barbara usually begins by conveying a lot of information, using the narrative mode illustrated in Chapter 4. However, sometimes her students already possess a base of prior knowledge that she can connect with and build on. In these situations, she uses less telling and more eliciting through questions. For example, she teaches the food unit before the clothing unit, so when she introduces the historical strand of the clothing unit, she does not need to start from scratch. Her students already have learned something about life Long, Long Ago (cave days), Long Ago (Pilgrim and pioneer days), and Today (Modern Times) through the co-construction and discussion of a timeline during the food unit.

There is less need for elaborate buildup when Barbara teaches lessons that extend or apply big ideas already introduced in earlier lessons. To introduce the lesson on the story of cotton, for example, she began by asking her students where cotton comes from, in order to establish that it comes from a plant rather than an animal. With that understanding in place, she then noted that otherwise, the story of development from raw cotton through finished cotton clothing is similar to the story of development from fleece to woolen clothing (the subject of the previous lesson). In many of the lessons that occur toward the ends of units and call for students to apply what they have learned during decision-making or citizenship activities, a brief review of relevant big ideas is sufficient.

Building on Previous Lessons

To introduce the historical strand of the clothing unit, Barbara uses the timeline from the food unit as a resource for helping students to retrieve some of what they learned about life in the past. She begins in a questioning mode. In addition, instead of asking for group responses or volunteers, she directs her initial questions to three students who are slow to warm up, as a way to get them involved in the lesson immediately.

T: Cory, we have three spots on our timeline. What are they?
S: Long, Long Ago, Long Ago, Today, and the Future. [Barbara has forgotten that they added a "Future" segment, at the suggestion of a student, when they made this timeline.]
T: And the future we even added on. We know for sure that Long, Long Ago, Long Ago and Today . . .

S: But you don't know what's going to happen in the future.

T: We can make some guesses, we can say some things that we think. What can you tell me about Long, Long Ago, Arden?

S: People hunted for animals.

T: People hunted for animals. For what?

S: For food.

T: That's what they had to do, they hunted for animals. People hunt for animals now, but they don't have to. They could choose to go to a store. Arden, could they have picked to go to a store Long, Long Ago?

S: No.

T: Nope. There were no stores Long, Long Ago, so people hunted for food. What else can you tell me, Dabney, about Long, Long Ago?

S: We had to ride in wagons.

T: Riding in wagons was something that happened Long Ago. We're talking even before that. How did people get from place to place?

S: Walking.

T: Yeah, people had to walk everywhere. So if I wanted to go somewhere, I had to walk from place to place. What else can you tell me? What did we call those folks? Where did they live? What did they eat? How did they get their food? What things do you already know about them? [Provides cues for possible responses] Mariah?

S: They had to get their food and water.

T: Where would they get water from?

S: The lakes.

T: So they couldn't turn on a faucet?

S: No.

T: So if they wanted water, they had to get it from a lake.

S: They couldn't get water from a faucet or go to a store.

T: So all of those things are from?

S: Today.

T: Today. Yup. Tim, tell me one more thing about Long, Long Ago. Where did those folks live?

S: In caves, and they had a boat . . . was it the *Sunflower*?

T: You're thinking about the *Mayflower* and you're thinking about . . . [As part of her larger agenda of helping students "file" their learning in ways that help them retrieve it in relevant contexts in the future, Barbara often interprets their incorrect answers as answers that are correct for some other question but not this one.]

S: Long Ago.

T: Did they have boats Long, Long Ago? No. Because these people lived in caves. Mikey, what did we call them?

S: I don't know.

T: They lived in caves so we called them . . .?

S: (answers incorrectly)

T: Cave people is the name that we've used for these folks. [Barbara has twice tried and failed to elicit the answer from Mikey, so she supplies it.] Folks lived in caves Long, Long Ago, and they lived right up alongside the dinosaurs and hunted and ate dinosaurs. [Barbara has made a point of explaining that dinosaurs were extinct long before humans appeared. She injects this misconception here as a way to confront it once again if need be, but her students remember the accurate information.]

Ss: No!

Ss: There were no dinosaurs!

T: So if I was going to make a timeline long enough for dinosaurs, I'd have to make my timeline go way, way, way, way, way back 65 million years ago, because dinosaurs were way back there and people didn't start until just Long, Long Ago, which wasn't even a half a million years ago. So these cave people would not have had anything to do with dinosaurs. They had two ways of getting food. You told me hunting. That's one way. Let me tell you the other way and see if you can tell me what it means. The other way was gathering. We talked last year about how they got their food by hunting or gathering. Think about what gathering means. What did they do to get their food, Alan?

S: They got it by spearing animals.

T: That's hunting. What does gathering mean? Spearing an animal is hunting. What would gathering be?

S: People would keep the animals.

T: You're remembering that people here started the idea of keeping the animals but this gathering was something different. Gathering is when you can go out and find the stuff that you need to eat. Do you remember some of the stuff that they found?

S: Sheep.

T: That's what they hunted for. What did they go out and find for food that's not an animal? Remember, we looked at it. I put some in your hand. Some kids decided to eat it and some kids didn't. Do you remember the rice that we had? [After all these cues fail to elicit an acceptable answer, Barbara gives one herself and moves on.] We had wild rice. Wild rice just growing on grass out in the wild and they would go out and just pick it up. What else could they gather, Mariah?

S: Berries, fish.

T: Berries, fish, rice. What else, Laurel?

S: They had nuts.

T: Nuts. Alan, what else did you mention?

S: Seeds.

T: You're right, but you mentioned something else. Did you ask about an apple tree? [earlier—not heard by transcriber] Did they gather apples?

S: Yeah.

T: Sure, they could gather and find foods. [At this point, Barbara shifts to conveying new information, as she relates the basics of how people made clothing in the cave days.] The people that lived Long, Long Ago—when there were first starting to be people Long, Long Ago, they had much more hair than we do and much longer hair than we do now. Let me show you a picture that I have and you can see that what we think . . . remember how we talked about dinosaurs? The only way they could tell what they looked like was by using their bones to make a good guess? That's what they did for these people because there were no cameras Long, Long Ago. They found some bones and they're making a really good guess by looking at the bones, just like they did with dinosaurs. This is their guess about what people must have looked like Long, Long Ago. [Barbara clarifies that the illustrations are science-based re-creations, not actual photos.] You can see that they started out by having lots of hair on their body and that hair protected them and kept them warm and dry, but slowly people started to change a little bit and they didn't have as much hair on their body. Because, you know, you have hair on your body. Check your arm out. Do you have little hairs there? Yeah, people changed. Those hairs that you have all over your body? They used to be really long hairs and kept you warm. But then those hairs started getting smaller, and now what did people need to figure out? A way to . . .

S: Keep warm.

T: Keep warm and protect themselves. [Expands answer to add second big idea.] So if the people that lived in the cave started to get cold, they jumped in the car and drove all the way over to Meijer . . . [Here again, she injects an absurdity to add motivation and keep students alert.]

Ss: Nooooo!!!!!

Ss: They didn't have cars.

T: No cars? Let me show you a picture of what they really did. What did they have around them that they could use? Mariah?

S: They could kill a bear or something like that and cut off the hair.

T: They could find an animal and when they killed the animal, they would scrape, with rocks, they would scrape the meat off of the fur and they would turn it into clothes. So the first clothes that people had were made from fur. Some people even today choose to use skins from animals to make their clothes. Do we have to do that now?

Ss: No.

T: Is it a choice now?

Ss: Yeah.

T: The strange thing is that before, everybody wore fur because that's all there was. Nowadays people can choose to wear fur, but there's not as many animals around, so if you want fur it's hard to find, and most people have to pay lots of money for it. So I'll put fur over here [in the "Long, Long, Ago" section of the timeline] because fur was the first thing that people used to make clothes out of. Tell me what you know about clothes. Howell, what do clothes do for you when you're cold?

S: They keep you warm.

T: Do you think the fur from a bear would keep you warm?

S: Yeah.

T: And that's why they used the fur to make clothes from. Now, that's how they made clothes Long, Long Ago. Here's the problem, though. Some people lived in places that were warm. Do you think you'd want to have a bear fur on today?

Ss: No.

T: No. Look at me—I'm already sweating. Can you imagine if I had fur for my clothes? I'd be way too . . .

Ss: Hot.

S: Some people die from getting too hot. [Barbara ignores this comment, to avoid derailing the flow into the topic of death.]

T: So sometimes when people made their clothes from fur, they would just use small pieces to cover just parts of their body for . . .

Ss: Modesty. [Successfully elicits key term.]

T: Modesty. [Goes on with story of clothing Long, Long Ago, shifting from animal to plant sources.]

Starting with a Question

Sometimes Barbara begins with a question that calls for students to offer opinions or make predictions. For example, she introduced a segment on transportation around the world by asking the students to vote on whether they thought it would be similar to or different from transportation in the United States. In overseeing the vote, she pushed her students to think independently and thoughtfully, but indicated that the class would revisit the issue later in light of the evidence explored. She used "we" language in announcing the result: "It looks like most of us are thinking that it will be different than it is here."

Barbara believes that beginning with such questions helps make the subsequent presentation of information seem more authentic or meaningful to her students, because it provides evidence that can be used in answering the question. She also finds that organizing lessons around such questions help her to keep track of the lesson's big ideas and to make good choices about instructional resources and examples to use in developing the content (in this case, which nations to consider and which children's books to include). She frequently uses a similar approach to teaching mathematics, where a common lesson structure involves beginning with a question, then gathering relevant data, then negotiating an answer to the question.

Addressing Strong Interests First

Sometimes when Barbara communicates an idea or shows a learning resource to her students, they respond with a flurry of comments and questions indicative of high interest and curiosity. However, these reactions often focus on aspects of the content that are tangential to the big ideas she wants to develop. When this occurs, she will give the students time to work through these curiosity and interest issues before attempting to move forward with the lesson flow.

For example, Barbara began a lesson on pasta by showing a variety of pasta types, including raw lasagna noodles and other examples of uncooked pasta. She did this because she knew that most of her students' ideas about pasta were limited to the prototype of cooked spaghetti noodles. Sure enough, most of her students were unfamiliar with some of the pasta varieties shown and were eager to handle them and talk about them. Several were surprised to find that uncooked dried pasta is hard, and one suggested that the examples were not real (i.e., that they were akin to decorative apples made of plastic).

Similarly, Barbara split a lesson on types and functions of families across two class sessions because she knew that after exposure to different types of families (depicted as engaged in various activities) via a children's book on the topic, her students would be eager to talk about things that families do, giving examples and telling stories from their own family experiences. Consequently, the first class session and a follow-up home assignment focused on family functions (what families do for children, things that families do together), which allowed the students time to absorb and discuss aspects of the topic that were personally important to them. After experiencing these activities, her students were ready to explore less familiar and more analytic aspects of the topic, so she shifted focus to definitions and depictions of different family structures and a home assignment calling for students to characterize their own families as one of the types described.

Purposeful Sets of Examples

Deciding how to define key concepts and what to include as examples can be challenging. For one thing, many concepts emphasized in social studies are "fuzzy sets" that overlap with related concepts. Needs and wants, for example, often are not cleanly distinct. We need calcium, but not necessarily milk. People meet common motivational needs in a variety of ways. There are only fuzzy distinctions between meat and fish, fruit and vegetables (e.g., tomatoes), and so on. Many anomalies or other complications can be avoided because they are not in the students' prior knowledge or common experience and are not centrally related to big ideas emphasized in the unit (e.g., peanuts as a vegetable that grows underground). However, others must be addressed because they will come up (e.g., tomato, chocolate milk) or it is important to bring them up (e.g, common misconceptions relating to big ideas emphasized in the lesson).

Another complicating factor is that *teachers often wish to address multiple agendas when deciding what to include in sets of examples.* For one thing, although it usually is wise to begin with familiar and prototypical examples when introducing a concept, it also is wise to include less prototypical examples to give students an idea of the range of referents to which the concept applies. For example, Barbara showed her students photos and illustrations of a variety of clothing worn by the Pilgrims and the pioneers, to make sure that they were not left with overly narrow "First Thanksgiving" and "Davy Crockett" stereotypes.

Teachers also might want to include examples that serve multiple purposes because they have some special connection to the class or the local community, have been used or will be used elsewhere in the curriculum, or in some other way promote curricular personalization or integration. For example, Barbara used both a set of actual examples of foods and a set of photos and illustrations of foods as resources when introducing the food unit and teaching about the food pyramid. She identified the following as *principles that guided her choices in deciding what items to include in those example sets*:

- They are easy for the teacher to access.
- The examples within given categories are, or at least look, quite different (to represent the full range, or at least most of it).
- Some examples are easy and within the students' experience (apples), but others are not (dried cranberries).

- Some will be used later in the unit or at some future time (dried fruit later would be discussed both in the Long Ago lesson and in the lesson on food preservation).
- They are items of interest to the students (e.g., a doughnut).
- They are foods that represent combinations of more than one food group (pizza).
- There are not too many examples from each group or anything that would be unnecessarily confusing or exceptional (e.g., tomatoes).

Discussion of these principles led to additional suggestions that examples might be chosen to reflect culture (collard greens), geography (macadamia nuts and pineapples if teaching in Hawaii), or even religion (matzo).

Barbara deliberately included a picture of chocolate milk because her school allows this as a choice during lunchtime. This prompts parental concerns about whether chocolate milk offers comparable nutrition to white milk (or is more fattening). Consequently, as she talks about chocolate milk, she gives information relating to these questions and encourages her students to convey it to their parents.

Barbara has found that a given example might work well for certain purposes but not others. Pizza is an effective example when used in social studies to illustrate a compound food composed of multiple ingredients. However, it leads to trouble if used in mathematics to represent a circular object to be divided. Her students have difficulty maintaining focus on pizza as a representation of geographic concepts (circle, cylinder) because they are preoccupied with details of what they know about pizza as a food (leading to comments that one 10-inch pizza might be bigger or smaller than another because it comes from a different store, be thinner or thicker in the crust, be a rectangle instead of a circle, have different ingredients on top, etc.). Consequently, another criterion to use in thinking about potential examples is whether they include nonrelevant features that may interfere with the intended instruction.

In the food unit, Barbara assembled a collection of snacks for her lesson on healthy snacks. Her criteria for inclusion in the set were (1) easy accessibility, (2) all food groups represented, (3) non-prototypical examples included, (4) both healthful and less healthful examples, (5) examples that seem similar but differ in health value (cucumber and pickle), (6) snacks that students often bring from their homes, and (7) peanuts—both to feature them as a desired snack and to foreshadow a later lesson on peanut butter.

In assembling examples of different forms of bread found in different parts of the world, her selection criteria included the following: (1) breads that would be new or unfamiliar to her students, (2) many different countries of origin, (3) different grains or other ingredients, (4) specialty/holiday/cultural breads, and (5) breads designed for special functions (e.g., hot dog buns).

In choosing examples of birthday celebrations around the world, she included familiar examples that her students could understand and might have experienced themselves, activities meant for participation by both boys and girls, and examples that would be unfamiliar to most if not all of her students, yet within their capacities to understand.

In teaching about sign language, she began by signing each of the letters for her students, then combining them to sign a few students' names (promising to resume this during lunch or recess for others who wanted to see what their name looks like in sign language). Then she signed words (such as "baby," "car," and "cat") that are signed using motions that have logical connections to their meaning, are familiar to her students, are likely to be of interest, and are easy to sign and interpret. She explained the rationale for the sign if it was not obvious to her students (e.g., the sign for learning pantomimes scooping something up from the environment and putting it into your head). She also included signs that she intended to use as management tools with her students (e.g., signs for "sit down," "stand up," and "time for recess/play").

In teaching about milk and dairy products, she included Swiss cheese because some of her students might not be familiar with it. She also included yogurt, both for the same reason and because many of her students would be unsure about how to classify it (she made sure to use plain yogurt, so the classification task was not complicated by fruit contents).

In teaching about types of farms, she made sure to include both dairy farms and ranches, because even though both involve cattle, they have different purposes and generate different products. When she introduced truck farms (farms that produce vegetables that are trucked to local markets), she gave the definition and several examples before eliciting her students' ideas, because she knew that the term would be either unknown or confusing to them. Her initial examples emphasized products grown locally, but then she expanded to examples from elsewhere (oranges from Florida, pineapples from Hawaii).

In showing examples of specialized clothing associated with particular occupations, she included an illustration of a chef because one of her students' grandfathers was a chef. When the illustration came up, she called on that student to talk about it.

Introducing and Controlling Vocabulary

Barbara is careful about the terminology she uses with her students, especially terms or phrases that communicate big ideas or are connected with them in some important way. Specifically, she makes a point of teaching a word's meaning and expecting students to remember and use it when (1) it is a big idea or a key part of one, (2) it is cost-effective to teach it now (i.e., it is connected to one of today's big ideas and the lesson has progressed to the point at which it is needed), (3) students are likely to encounter the word again, either in the curriculum or in life outside of school, and (4) the term provides concise shorthand for what would require a much longer statement in order to convey the same meaning.

Her typical procedure unfolds in four steps: (1) present the term; (2) present its definition; (3) use the term and then ask questions that require respondents to provide its definition or show that they know it; and (4) ask questions that incorporate the definition and require respondents to supply the term. Through this purposeful elaboration approach, she defines, elaborates, and subsequently uses key words or phrases in ways that support the teaching of big ideas and provide her students with "a place to organize the information" in their minds. Examples of some of her terminology decisions and the rationales for them follow.

Deciding Which Terms and Distinctions to Teach

Barbara uses her knowledge of the curriculum to determine which terms to emphasize as key words and how to tailor their definitions to the ways they will be used in the lessons. For example, the historical strands of the lesson plans call for teaching about Long, Long Ago; Long Ago; and Today. In defining and using these terms, Barbara often substitutes "Modern Times" for "Today," because she wants to use the term to refer to the past fifty to one hundred years, and the term "Today" would be confusing when used with this connotation.

She also uses her knowledge of students to guide her vocabulary choices (e.g., to avoid probable confusions or substitute a more familiar alternative for a less familiar one). For example, she has found that her students easily understand the meanings associated with the term "weather" but not those associated with the term "climate." Consequently, she believes that it is not cost-effective to try to introduce and maintain distinctions between the two terms at these grade levels, so she uses the terms synonymously (as in explaining that banana plants thrive in countries where the "weather" is warm and sunny).

Her terminology decisions sometimes are influenced by special definitions used in the disciplines, political correctness concerns, or other considerations beyond what is likely to be understandable to her students. For example, our lesson plans refer to Native Americans as Indians because we found in our interview studies that K–3 students were familiar with the term "Indians" but often either unfamiliar with the term "Native Americans" or mistaken about its meaning. However, Barbara's district mandates using the term "Native Americans." She has found that if she introduces it carefully the first time and then uses it consistently thereafter, her students do not have trouble learning and remembering it.

On the other hand, Barbara also consistently uses the term "man-made" because she feels it is more natural and widely used in society than suggested alternatives such as "people-made" or "human-made." However, this choice requires her to consistently remind her students that the term includes women, as well as to deal with occasional concerns expressed by budding feminists in her classes.

The terms "motor home," "camper," and "RV" have overlapping but not identical meanings. Barbara sees no need to teach the distinctions, so she uses "motor home" and "camper" more or less interchangeably. However, she does not use "RV" because she has found that her students never use that term and often do not know what it means.

Tailoring Definitions to Instructional Goals

Barbara's definitions often are tailored to promote understanding of big ideas or use of terminology in subsequent activities. For example, she defines a farm as a place where people grow food or keep animals that become food, because she wants to move her students beyond their tendency to define a farm as "where a farmer lives." Emphasizing the connotation of food production helps students connect the term "farm" to the big ideas about food production taught in the lessons on farming.

For related reasons, Barbara introduces and consistently uses the term "harvest" as a verb, defining it as removing the desired parts (foods, fibers) from the plants when the crop is ready. She takes pains to establish this term and its meaning because harvesting is one of a common set of steps that occur in all kinds of crop farming (and thus are featured consistently in our land-to-hand lessons).

In a lesson on developments in transportation, Barbara defined paving as putting something on top of the dirt to make the road easier to use, thus emphasizing its function and tying it directly to the big idea that inventions gradually made transportation faster and easier. Once she has introduced a term in a way that focuses on its function, she often will remind students of this connection or attempt to elicit it from the students during reviews. For example, the following exchange occurred during a review of the story of *The little red hen* (which was being studied in literacy):

T: Who made the dough from the flour and the milk and the eggs?
Ss: The red hen.
T: And she added yeast to make it . . .
Ss: Bubbly and puffy. [These were not the same terms that Barbara had used
    when originally describing the function of yeast, but she accepted them and
    moved on because they indicated that the students understood its function.]

Whenever Barbara wants to establish a term or get her students to use it consistently, she remains conscious of this goal not only when conveying the information originally, but also when responding to students' answers to her subsequent questions. For example, she asked a student about the combing of fleece and elicited the response that combing was needed to untangle the fibers. Barbara nodded and said, "Untangle it, or unravel it." She wanted the students to remember "unravel" rather than "untangle," both because it is more accurate and because the word is used in the home assignment for that lesson.

Sometimes she needs to work persistently to establish a term. For example, one of the transportation lessons involves distinguishing between personal and mass transportation. In the following exchange, Barbara leads her students through a list of examples to establish the term "personal transportation":

T: Renee, do you have any personal transportation?
S: I have two cars and I have a motorcycle, and I have a scooter.
T: A scooter. Whose scooter is it?
S: Mine and my brother's.
T: So that means it is your personal . . . [Barbara tries to elicit term, but fails]
S: Scooter.
T: Transportation. [So she gives the term and tries again.] So tell me about that
    scooter. It is your . . .
S: Brother's and . . .

T: Personal transportation. [She fails again, so now gives the answer. This time Renee repeats it.]

S: Personal transportation.

T: It sure is. What have you got, Krista?

S: A bike.

T: You have a bike. Who does it belong to?

S: Me.

T: It belongs to you personally. Who rides it?

S: Me.

T: So that bike is your . . .

S: Personal transportation. [This time elicits successfully.]

T: It is. That bike is your personal transportation. Now, listen closely to my question, because I want to make sure that you think before you say anything. Here's what's on the list so far. Truck, car, van, snowmobile, quad, motorcycle, tractor or lawn mower, rollerblades, bike, wagon, and scooter. Do any of you have a personal transportation at your house that is different from the ones on this list? Alan, what do you have?

S: Me and my grandma have a little train and it has little houses and things.

T: Listen to this. I am so glad that you brought this up. A train is a kind of transportation, but personal transportation transports you personally. Does that little toy train transport you?

S: No.

T: No, so even though the train belongs to you and you use it to transport things and have fun with, personal transportation transports you personally. You, person, you. So could I put "toy train" on this list?

S: No.

In analyzing this transcript, Barbara noted that whereas she usually gives the word and then a definition and then some examples, in this case she gave examples of personal transportation before introducing the word. She thinks that this is because the term is more abstract than most terms used in the lessons, so it could not be introduced in a simple way. As an additional complication, the term had to be developed in a way that facilitated its contrast with mass transportation.

Enriching Understandings

If a term refers to an object or process unfamiliar to her students, Barbara will provide a physical example, show a photo or illustration, or draw a "word picture" using richly descriptive language that supports students' development of accurate images. When talking about her own pickup truck, she described it in some detail and drew a sketch of it because previous exchanges in class had shown that some students were not clear about what a pickup truck was and how it differed from other trucks. She similarly described and sketched a seaplane because she did not have a photo of one.

Sometimes Barbara will expand a basic definition using image-rich content because she wants to be able to use the term in the future as a trigger to cue students' recall of not only its definition but a network of content connected to it. In introducing the pioneers, for example, she repeatedly emphasized their travel in wagons, both to help students distinguish the pioneers from the Pilgrims and to cue a set of images about pioneer life and times that would be retrieved when the term was used in the future.

Her richly developed image of her own pickup truck became the prototype image of a pickup truck for her students, and her own wedding dress (which she showed in photos and discussed at some length in a lesson on special clothing) became the prototype symbol for cultural rules about clothing worn on special occasions. When a student mentioned a work van in the process of talking about her grandfather's job delivering food, Barbara shifted the terminology from work van to the more specific and lesson-functional delivery van, and subsequently the grandfather's vehicle became the prototype image of a delivery van.

After defining food gathering, Barbara gave several examples of gathering, both to distinguish it from hunting and to supply students with images to attach to this (for them) strange term. She also mimicked the process of picking berries off plants. To help her students appreciate the Native Americans' and pioneers' needs for food preservation methods, she used voice modulation and hand choreography to help them imagine a "huuuuuge" bison that would supply enough meat to feed a family for months if it could be kept from spoiling.

Planned Redundancy

Once she has provided a basic definition of a key term, Barbara reinforces and elaborates on this definition by repeatedly using the term in contexts and in ways that allow her to add synonyms, examples, or elaborations on its meaning. For example, during the lesson on wool, which is the first of several lessons on the land-to-hand steps involved in manufacturing different types of cloth, Barbara deliberately dropped the terms "fabric" and "fiber" five times each, repeating their definitions in varying language (see Chapter 4).

Planned redundancy of this kind typifies Barbara's vocabulary teaching, even during much briefer segments. In one lesson, she defined "moderate" as a "strange" word that means "kind of in the middle," and then used both terms (moderate and middle) frequently thereafter. In another lesson she used the terms "customs" and "culture" interchangeably, sometimes in the same sentence. These repetitions helped students remember the meaning of the new word by linking it to a more familiar word treated as synonymous. (Although distinctions can be made within each of these pairs of words, Barbara treated them as synonymous because this suited her instructional goals given the ages of the students and the big ideas of the lessons.)

Planned redundancy in the form of elaboration on the same repeated term can be seen in the following lesson excerpt, in which Barbara developed the meaning of the term "fleece":

T: [showing illustration] So here's the sheep and he's got this hair on his body and they cut his hair off. You can see how he has all of his hair cut off. There's a special name they give to the hair that's on the sheep. It's called fleece. "Fleece" is the name that they have for the hair that they cut off the sheep. So you start out and you've got a sheep and the sheep's all wooly and fluffy. Then they cut the wool off the sheep and they've got this big bundle of stuff. They call this stuff fleece. That's the stuff that they take off it. Now, where does the sheep live?

S: In the wild.

T: Maybe not in the wild, but outdoors. What's outdoors? Is there carpeting outside? [Asks a "no" question to cue students to the idea that sheep get dirty living outside, as a step toward eliciting recognition that the fleece needs cleaning.]

S: No.

T: What's outside?

S: Grass, trees, dirt.

T: Grass, trees, dirt, rocks, leaves. So what things do you suppose this sheep might have in its hair or in its fleece?

S: Dirt, grass, leaves.

T: So if you were a smart farmer, what do you think would be the first thing you're going to want to do with that fleece?

S: Clean it.

T: Clean it, wash it. So they take the sheep. They cut off all his hair. They have a bundle of fleece and the very next thing that they need to do is wash it. [Goes on with the story, continuing to use the term "fleece" frequently.]

In the following excerpt, Barbara used several techniques to develop the meaning of the term "convenient," which had been included in one family's explanation (on a home assignment) of where and why it might go out to eat:

T: Laurel's family likes to go out because it's convenient. What does "convenient" mean? Big voice, Laurel.

S: It means because it's easy.

T: "Convenient" means it's easy. You don't have to take time to cook, you don't have to get the ingredients, so "convenient" means easy. [Expands on this definition, using imagery-rich language.] It's easy to go out to a restaurant instead of having to make it at home. But what do you have to decide? If you go out to a restaurant, is it going to cost more money or less money?

Ss: More.

T: More. So if you want it to be easy, you've got to be willing to pay a little bit more . . . For Mikey's family, it's a tradition to go out every Saturday morning for breakfast. They say you can get good food and it's also fast and easy. That must be convenient. [When a related idea appears on another family's response, Barbara takes the opportunity to tie back to the term "convenient."]

Other Vocabulary Teaching Techniques

Barbara incorporates elements of playfulness or at least informality in her vocabulary teaching, to encourage her students to enjoy learning new words. She often tells them that there is a "special" or "fancy" name for something that they have described more colloquially (e.g., "plantation" is a fancy name for a banana farm). If the students' own language suits the instructional goals, she will stick with this more familiar language temporarily as she develops key ideas, only later "lifting" to more formal terminology. For example, she initially accepted and used the term "yucky" as a description of foods when they spoil, although she later shifted to the term "moldy" and added additional connotations (it dries out, gets germs, will make you sick if you eat it, etc.). Similarly, she stuck with the term "noodles" for a while before introducing the term "pasta."

If students use terms that are in the ballpark but not quite right, she will discreetly shift toward the preferred term in the process of responding to the students (in a way that focuses on developing understanding of the point under discussion, without making an issue of vocabulary). For example, when a student made reference to a sailing boat, Barbara accepted this as a correct answer to her question but shifted to the term "sailboat" when providing feedback. Similarly, when a student described a bus as a trolley, Barbara said that it looked like some trolleys but it was a bus, then repeated this desired term in a follow-up question.

These techniques observed in Barbara's teaching all follow the "gradual formalization" principle that has emerged consistently in studies of master teachers in action (Bransford *et al.*, 1999). Such teachers focus first on developing understandings of basic concepts and principles, building on prior knowledge and using existing vocabulary, before shifting to more formal terminology and definitions.

Barbara often makes reference to a term's etymological roots as part of her larger goal of helping students to realize that lesson content makes sense and can be used to understand their experiences. In teaching the term "pasta," she noted that it is the Italian word for paste and then connected paste and dough. In talking about the shipping of foods in modern times, she drew the connection to earlier times when goods were often transported on sailing ships. When teaching about pita bread she noted that it also is called pocket bread and demonstrated why. She commonly adds etymological explanations when there is a visual or sound connection to the root word (e.g., the spinnerets that silkworms use to spin silk fibers) or when the new term is a commonsense combination of other words and their meanings (undershirt, motor home, jet plane, horseless carriage). She also points out the connections between contractions or colloquialisms (TV, fridge, etc.) and the longer words that they stand for.

When there is high potential for confusion of two words, Barbara will introduce only one of them, or at least make sure that one is well established before introducing the other. If that is not possible, she will take steps to preempt the potential confusion by underscoring the differences in the process of teaching the words together. Thus, she took extra time in defining and explaining the terms "pickling" and "preserving" when talking about the pioneers' methods of food preservation, and also gave several familiar examples of pickled foods to distinguish pickling as a process from pickles as a food. When introducing the term "sari" in talking about clothing in India, she preempted confusion by distinguishing "sari" from "sorry." When talking about the wagons used by the pioneers, she took time to clarify their size and other characteristics, to make sure that her students didn't confuse them with modern children's wagons.

Barbara develops a tentative strategy for teaching a new term but is prepared to adjust it if necessary. For example, when introducing the concept of a nuclear family, she drew the connection to a nucleus as a piece to start with. However, her students lacked the background knowledge to make sense of this, so she dropped it and subsequently focused the definition of a nuclear family on a mom and dad living together with their children. However, in defining a blended family, it proved helpful to draw the analogy to a blender mixing things together.

Dropping in Definitions and Explanations on the Fly

Besides the terms that she introduces and defines in a planned way when they are needed, *Barbara sometimes "drops in" a definition "on the fly" because a term has come up and she recognizes that some of her students are not familiar with it.* Students often create such occasions when they ask or comment about some aspect of the topic that Barbara did not intend to introduce. These initiations often are stimulated by illustrations in books that Barbara is using as instructional resources. For example, a student used the term "planter" in reference to a photo in a book on farming. This led Barbara to say, "That's called a harrow. It kind of flattens things out and plants the seeds in." Barbara will delay or minimize her response to these situations if she knows that a better opportunity to teach the term will occur later in the lesson or in an upcoming lesson. For example, when the word "tram" came up in a transportation lesson, Barbara defined it briefly on the spot but said that they would talk more about it later (when looking through a book that included a picture of a tram).

Sometimes she will drop in a word without defining it, just as a way to expose students to its use in context. Typically these words are relevant to the topic but not central to the instructional goals. For example, in the process of explaining that large farms were not needed for certain purposes, she deliberately said, "they don't need acres and acres and acres." As another example, during the clothing unit, after she had carefully defined and developed use of the term "modesty," she deliberately dropped in the term "immodest" when an occasion for doing so arose, simply to expose her students to it.

Some circumstances dictate that Barbara insert not merely a definition but a more extended explanation. For example, one day she was reviewing responses to a home assignment that called for students to identify three forms of communication and say something about them. One student had written, "Long ago, printers made newspapers like on Dr. Quinn." Barbara knew that some of her students would not even pick up on the reference to *Dr. Quinn* in this response, let alone its implications about printing in the past. Consequently, she first explained about the television show for the benefit of students who were unfamiliar with it, then explained about early printing.

T: Darby said, "Long Ago, printers made newspapers like on *Dr. Quinn*." That's a TV show. Have any of you ever seen *Dr. Quinn, Medicine Woman*?

. . . It's like a western where they're pretending to be Long Ago, and did they just plug the machine into the wall?

S: No.

T: What did they have to do, Darby?

S: They had to put it in the printing press.

T: They put it in the printing press, and how did they make the printing press work?

S: By hand.

T: By hand. It takes a little longer that way, doesn't it?

In this chapter, we have described and illustrated the strategies that Barbara uses to establish a common base of information as she introduces topics about which her young students have only spotty and mostly tacit knowledge. In Chapter 12, we will describe and illustrate how she develops those knowledge bases through carefully structured discourse.

Chapter 12

Developing Knowledge Bases through Structured Discourse

Supporting Learning through Focused Content and Planned Redundancy

Our guidelines for focusing the information that we include in an initial content base (limiting its scope, structuring it around big ideas, establishing what is fundamental and prototypical before addressing complications or exceptions) reflect commonly emphasized instructional design principles based on studies of learning (Good & Brophy, 1995). The reason for this is that new learning proceeds most smoothly, especially in domains in which learners do not already possess a great deal of prior knowledge, when instruction helps them to establish a stable and well-connected knowledge base. Once such a base is in place, learners can develop it by assimilating relevant new information and can begin to accommodate anomalies and other complications. Learning new information is much more difficult, however, when students lack a stable knowledge base and must struggle to make sense of input that seems disconnected or even contradictory.

Another reason for carefully limiting and organizing the content base is that children in the early grades do not yet possess well-developed skills for learning through reading and writing, so their early progress in content areas such as social studies depends primarily on learning through listening and speaking. To support such learning, Barbara not only sticks close to the children's prior experiences and structures limited content around big ideas, but also takes care to be consistent in the vocabulary she uses to define and explain the big ideas.

She is thoughtful about terminology, choosing labels for concepts and processes that she believes her students will learn easily and be unlikely to confuse with other terms. Occasionally she will substitute for some of the terminology used in our lesson plans because the substitute term is more familiar, less likely to be confusing, better connected to other things that she has taught or intends to teach, or in some other way preferable for developing the lesson's big ideas with her particular students. In addition, she calls the students' attention to new terms as she introduces them, systematically repeats these terms in subsequent discourse, and in the case of the most important ones, records them on cards, features in them in co-constructed learning resources, or provides other graphic memory supports.

Occasionally, Barbara adopts language in order to set herself up to use terms that are familiar and comfortable to her, that "come easily to her lips." This will make it that much more likely that she will use this language consistently in her teaching, without even having to think about it.

Through these and other forms of planned redundancy, Barbara provides her students with a common vocabulary to use in communicating with her and with one another as they shift from primarily listening to increasingly talking about the lessons' big ideas. She supports this shift by initially providing basic definitions and examples, then modeling use of these terms to discuss concepts or principles in context, and subsequently asking questions that will engage the students in carrying out such applications themselves.

Barbara's teaching experience led her to an intuitive understanding of what Nuthall (2002) discovered in his research on learning in elementary classrooms: If we want students not only to learn a new idea but to retain it in a form that makes it accessible for subsequent application, we should make sure that their initial exposure to the idea is relatively complete and accurate and that they soon experience several repetitions that will help establish the idea firmly in their minds and model some of its applications. Otherwise, students may not retain the idea or may retain it in the incomplete or distorted form to which they were exposed initially rather than the more desired form taught subsequently.

There is an optimal level of redundancy. Too much is unnecessary and may lead to boredom, but an optimal amount helps students to remember key terms and ideas, make connections, and see applications. It also gives the teacher a chance to elaborate on things that were omitted or touched on only sketchily earlier, as well as to teach for the first time those students who were absent or poorly attentive earlier.

Sustaining Lesson Flow via Elaborations

Barbara is adept at what Jacob Kounin (1970) called overlapping: maintaining lesson flow without interruption while at the same time preparing or manipulating instructional resources or handling classroom housekeeping or management tasks. She often includes redundancies and elaborations on already introduced big ideas during these times, as when writing student responses on lists or making additions to a timeline or other graphic currently under construction. Rather than bring lesson flow to a halt as she performs these tasks, she repeats or elaborates on things that she has been teaching. Because her attention is split between what she is saying and what she is doing, she confines what she says during these times to repetition of or elaboration on what has already been introduced, rather than attempting to move on to the next big idea. However, this is not just a technique for maintaining student attention by sustaining the momentum of the lesson; students benefit from the redundancy and elaboration.

An ironic reminder of this occurred one day during a year in which she taught social studies to two combined classes as part of a team teaching arrangement. On that day, the lesson involved eliciting responses from students and recording them on cards. Ordinarily, Barbara would have done the recording herself while simultaneously sustaining the lesson, but her teaching partner was present and assisted by doing the recording, thus allowing Barbara to move at a quicker pace than usual. The transcript indicated that the students showed unexpected confusion during this lesson, apparently because they were not getting the extra layers of input that they ordinarily would have received during times when Barbara was recording their responses.

Recently, Barbara has sometimes used her laptop computer to develop lists that are displayed on a monitor, instead of writing them on chart paper or the board. This allows her to remain more interactive with her students (she does not have to turn her back to them as she writes). Later, she prints the list and blows it up to poster size for display and subsequent reference (and if relevant, makes copies for her students to take home).

Graduated Questioning

Once the initial knowledge base is established, primarily through explanations delivered in her narrative style, Barbara develops and extends the base by leading the students through several rounds of questioning. She begins with easier questions (calling only for yes/no or single-word responses) but gradually shifts to questions calling for extended explanations. These rounds of questioning are fewer and faster paced when most responses are confident and accurate, but are more numerous and slower paced when her students initially have difficulty responding or frequently respond incorrectly.

Once the knowledge base has been developed and the students are consistently responding to her satisfaction, Barbara may shift to an in-class activity calling for application of what they have been learning. More typically, however, she reviews aspects of the lesson that are most relevant to the day's home assignment, provides directions for the home assignment (typically including modeling or eliciting of approaches to take in responding to it), and then concludes with a "ticket out" activity in which she calls on students individually to state something that they learned during today's lesson before heading out to lunch or recess.

Scaffolding Learning and Retention

Working within the context of the limited and focused content base and the planned redundancy already described, *Barbara infuses additional learning and memory supports as she develops the content with her students. Many of these involve structuring the content to make it easier for students to follow and connect.* Big ideas provide the basic structuring elements, and she helps her students focus on these by calling attention to them as they are introduced, repeating them frequently thereafter using consistent vocabulary, adding rich imagery or multisensory elaboration of verbal content, modeling the use of big ideas for reasoning or other applications, and clarifying where to "file" them for future reference.

Examples of Barbara's rich imagery and multisensory elaboration of verbal content can be seen in most of the excerpts included in the book. A representative sampling would include noting that students who did not get enough to eat or had skipped meals would be "like cars running r-e-e-a-l-l-y s-l-o-o-w"; forming arches with her hands when talking about the McDonald's arches; calling attention to changes in the color of bananas as they ripen; making chopping motions and saying "Whack!" when describing use of a machete to chop bunches from banana plants; humming and singing several familiar jingles when talking about this form of advertising; and "quoting" the thinking or conversations that might have been produced by people in the past, as when generating the idea for an invention.

Establishing Prototype Images to Anchor Networks of Content

Barbara often consciously develops sets of prototype images that she wants her students to connect with key terms. This could be seen, for example, in the illustrations she produced and emphasized when introducing the terms "Long, Long Ago" (caves, hunting and gathering food, primitive clothing) and "Long Ago" (Pilgrims and pioneers depicted as dressed prototypically and engaged in farming, weaving their own clothes, building their own homes, etc.).

She makes similar use of the role play and simulation activities built into many of her lessons. For example, lessons in several units included references to increases in farm productivity, the proliferation of nonfarm occupations, or the shift from primarily rural to primarily urban and suburban living. Whenever these topics came up, she would remind students of the day she designated one of them as the farmer and had him call on twelve of his classmates to stand and represent the twelve people (besides himself and his own family) that a typical farmer could feed at that point in history. Here is part of the transcript from the day she introduced this role play:

T: [Concluding material on inventions that improved the productivity of farms] . . . They started figuring out how to make even better farms, and when they made these really great farms they were able to grow lots of food, so now instead of me having to grow food for me and Mikey having to get food for him and Joellen get food for her, and Gretchen get food for her and Haley get food for her, one person can grow enough food for twelve people. Mikey, will you pretend to be my farmer? [Barbara selects Mikey to be the farmer because in recent weeks he had shown interest in farms and farm machinery.] Come on up, Mr. Farmer. You keep picking kids until I say to stop. If Mikey was a farmer, here's how many people he could feed with the food from his farm. So Mikey's growing food for his family and for . . . these kids are going to buy your food from the store, so start picking them. Pick somebody. Sean. Just say his name. Stand up, Sean. He makes food for Sean and more. Another kid. [Has Mikey keep choosing classmates until twelve others are standing. Then she points to and names them all, then elaborates on big idea as follows.]

T: Look at this. He could grow enough food on his farm to feed all you people. So you know what? You guys don't have to work on a farm anymore. You don't have to spend your time hunting food or gathering food. Instead, because Mikey's going to grow all your food, you can do some other stuff. Instead of having to grow food, now T.J. could get a job building cars. Sean can now be a police officer because he could buy the food that Mikey grows.

Cory, you can be an auto mechanic working on the cars that Tim builds, and Arden can be a teacher. Darryl could choose to be a firefighter because, does he have to grow food?

Ss: No.

T: Who's growing his food?

Ss: Mikey.

T: So you [Darryl] can sit down. . . . [Barbara has each of the twelve students sit down in turn after establishing that they are free to pursue nonfarm careers because Mikey is growing their food. She suggests a career for the first few (based on what she knows of their interests) but then starts inviting them to declare themselves] . . . Gretchen, what can you do, now that you know someone else is going to grow your food? What would you like to be?

S: Truck driver.

T: She could choose to be a truck driver because . . .

Ss: Mikey.

T: . . . is growing her food. That's why if you'll look back here [early on the timeline], all their time was spent growing food and getting food. But now that we got better at farming and better at making food, now we can do other jobs instead. That's why the time when people started to invent things and make things and build things and find things, was when they didn't have to grow food anymore. It must have worked because somebody invented that thing that's great for food [points to illustration on timeline].

Ss: A refrigerator.

T: Mikey, the kids say thanks for being willing to grow the food so that they can pick other jobs. Come and have a seat. What was that thing that somebody had time to think of?

Ss: Refrigerator.

T: Yeah, people started having time to think of things like refrigerators, and if you have a refrigerator, you've got to have electricity, so somebody was able to think of electricity. If the guy who invented electricity—if he had to spend all of his time finding food and hunting . . .

S: He couldn't invent electricity.

T: He wouldn't have figured out how to do electricity and we'd all be sitting here with no lights.

S: Yeah, and no TV.

T: That's what happened. People started thinking about how to do things because they didn't have to spend all of their time hunting for food, but in fact, . . .

S: Like airplanes.

T: [Barbara is pleased that students have begun to volunteer relevant responses, but rather than stopping to gather more (and lose the intended flow), she incorporates the responses into her closing review/summary]. All of the things that people thought of, airplanes to fly food from one place to another, trucks to carry food from one place to another, refrigerators to keep food healthy and safe, electricity so it's easier to cook the food and easier to keep the food ready, stores . . . all of these things happened because we got better at making and growing and keeping food so that one person can get all the food for us and the rest of us can do other stuff. [Barbara concludes this segment with a summary designed to remind students "where to file" the information, connecting it to the big idea that technological advances enabled one farmer to feed twelve people. Then she shifts into a review of big ideas about developments in methods of obtaining/producing food.]

In addition to providing rich imagery for her students, Barbara encourages them to generate their own images and connect them with key terms. In talking about migration during the pioneer days, for example, she asked her students to "picture in your minds" the wagons making painstaking progress on rutted and muddy roads, frequently getting stuck or losing wheels.

Definitions of key terms are given at the points where the terms are introduced during the lesson, then reinforced several times during the next few minutes as Barbara uses the term in context and asks questions that will require the students to use it themselves. She may also write the word on a card, timeline, or graphic that will be used in subsequent review and application activities.

All of this is done within coherent development of a connected network of knowledge being taught with an eye toward application and an awareness of how the current lesson content fits within her larger curriculum. Frequently she will define a term or develop a big idea in a way that not only supports progress toward immediate lesson goals but facilitates connections with past or future lessons. For example, she sometimes will take pains to establish a key word or phrase as a trigger for accessing a package of connected knowledge and associated images, because she knows that she will want her students to retrieve this information package weeks or even months later during future lessons that relate to the current lesson in some important way.

Reviewing Earlier Lessons to Set Up the Current Day's Lesson

Barbara typically does a lot of reviewing in the early lessons of the unit, when much of the information is new to the students and not yet "cemented." In these early lessons, she works to establish and solidify a base of shared knowledge to build and draw upon subsequently. She monitors students' answers carefully to judge how much they have learned so far, whether they have mastered and begun to use key vocabulary, and so on.

Most reviews come toward the ends of lessons and focus on what was learned that day. However, Barbara sometimes reviews material learned the previous day or in earlier lessons as a way to set up the current day's lesson, especially if the new lesson will build on the earlier material. In the following example, Barbara begins a lesson with questions designed to assess understanding and retention of what has been taught about four functions of clothing (protection, modesty, communication, and decoration). This is preparation for today's lesson in which students will consider different forms of clothing (beginning with the clothing they are wearing but going on to consider different kinds of clothing designed for special purposes), with emphasis on the functions the clothing items serve. In the process, she also deals with certain anomalies (students might wear pajamas to school on special days) and acknowledges variation among families in clothing rules and expectations (using "safe" examples).

Because this is a review, she directs most of her questions to the weaker students and stays with them to try to elicit improved responses if their initial response has not been satisfactory. She focuses on cementing the shared knowledge base with those students who still need it, but at the same time adds new details to keep the other students interested.

T: Let's see if we can remember the four reasons why people wear clothes. There were four reasons. What's one of them, Tim?

S: Modesty.

T: What do you mean when you say "modesty," Tim?

S: Cover your body.

T: Cover your body parts. We have a rule at our school that says kids must have . . .

S: Must have clothes at school.

T: If you're going to the pool, is the rule a little bit different, Tim?

S: Yeah, because you only have a swimming suit.

T: Right, so are the rules the same here at our school as they are at the beach?

Ss: No.

T: No, so even rules for modesty change, and even from here at school to at your house. Is there anybody's house where it's OK that you go around without shoes on?

S: Yeah.

T: Is there anybody's house where it's OK if you go around in your pajamas?

S: We have to take off our shoes at our house.

T: Right, and so there are different rules at different places, but would it be OK for you to wear your pajamas and slippers here at this school?

Ss: No!!!

T: Maybe if there was a special celebration, but most days modesty means . . .

Ss: Cover all your body parts.

T: Cover all your body parts. What's another reason why people wear clothes? Why, Joellen?

S: Communication.

T: What might you be communicating if you're wearing clothes that communicate?

S: A sports jersey.

T: A sports jersey might communicate that you're on a . . .?

S: Team.

T: A team, you're part of a team. What else might clothing communicate?

S: A school shirt.

T: What would a school shirt communicate to somebody?

S: That you go to that school.

T: Sure, so clothing communicates. Two more things that clothing does. Howell, why do people wear coats?

S: So they don't get cold.

T: They don't get cold. So your coat pro . . .

S: Your coat keeps you from getting cold.

T: Right. What's the word that we used when we talked about not getting cold? We say that your coat pro . . .?

S: Protect.

T: Your coat protects you. So Howell, why do people wear clothes?

S: To protect you.

T: To protect you. It might keep you from getting cold. Clothes can sometimes keep you from getting what else, Howell? Clothes protect you from cold, clothes protect you from . . .?

S: Water.

T: From water, from being wet.

S: From getting rained on.

T: Yes, from getting rained on. You're absolutely right. There's one more reason why folks wear clothes. Gretchen, why else?

S: So in the winter they don't get frostbite.

T: So you're talking about protection again, aren't you? I'm thinking about one more reason why folks wear clothes. Pop your hands down. This is Gretchen's turn. Gretchen's the kid that I picked [protects Gretchen's response opportunity and helps her to generate an improved response]. There was one more reason, Gretchen. Can I give you some cues? This is the reason why the bride in the wedding doesn't just wear blue jeans and a T-shirt.

S: It's special.

T: Right, it's special, so sometimes we wear clothes for dec . . .?

S: Decoration.

T: [Continues with questioning mode, but shifts to having student talk about the clothes they are wearing that day.]

Reviewing to Consolidate before Moving Forward

In longer lessons, especially lessons that naturally divide into progressive segments, Barbara will often insert a brief review as she completes a segment, to help her students get oriented to the larger picture before she moves on to the next segment. She usually does this, for example, when teaching lists of categories (four functions of clothing; land, sea, and air transportation) or sequential steps (in growing corn or building a house).

Another common occasion for inserted reviews is when Barbara is leading the class through brainstorming a list of ideas or examples, especially when students start to repeat ideas or examples given earlier by one of their peers. For example, one day during a childhood lesson, she was eliciting examples of chores that her students performed at home. When the responses started to get repetitious, she suspended the elicitation to insert the following review:

T: Someone already said "vacuum." Let me read through the list and make sure that you have an idea different from the ones we've already got. I have wash windows, clean shoes, mop, vacuum, fold clothes, dusting, wash walls, sweep, wash clothes, help care for your brothers and sisters, take care of the animals, make beds, pick up toys, clean the bathroom, feed the animals, do the dishes, take out the trash, clean your room, and learn. Nolan, something different?

Modeling of Interior Dialogue

A powerful component of Barbara's teaching is her thinking aloud as a way to model the interior dialogue (self-talk) involved in reasoning, problem solving, and decision making. Such modeling of task-related strategic thinking is vital because most school tasks are primarily cognitive rather than physical, so that the processes used to accomplish them cannot be observed directly.

By thinking out loud to model use of a strategy, a teacher makes overt the otherwise covert thought processes that guide its implementation. Such modeling provides learners with first-person language (self-talk) that they can adapt directly when using the strategy themselves. This eliminates the need for translation that is created when instruction is presented in the impersonal third-person language of explanation or even the second-person language of coaching. Learners can focus directly on the processes to be learned, with minimum strain on their cognitive capacities (Brophy, 2004).

Barbara's systematic use of modeling as an instructional strategy includes three steps: (1) she models the reasoning and talks about it as she does it; (2) she provides opportunities for her students to begin using the reasoning strategies themselves (with her scaffolding and support); and (3) she requires her students to use the strategies independently (while she scaffolds as needed, but mostly assesses mastery). She uses this three-step sequence (modeling, shared use, independent use) across the curriculum.

For example, after teaching about food groups and balanced meals, Barbara leads her students through analyses of the food groups included in representative meals from the United States, Mexico, and China. She begins with the U.S. meal because it is the most familiar and allows her students to apply what they are learning within a familiar context. She asks questions that lead them to recognize that the meal of Salisbury steak, potatoes, and corn contains foods from several of the groups, then asks if the meal contains something from the milk group. When the students answer no, she says, "No, so I probably better have a nice big glass of milk with my meal." Later she asks if the meal includes representatives from the fruit group, again yielding a negative response. This time she says, "I only need to have two or three fruits in a day. Maybe I had a glass of orange juice for breakfast and an apple with my lunch, so I already had my two fruits for today. So there's my meal." After modeling task-relevant reasoning in this fashion as she led her students through the analysis of the U.S. meal, Barbara then shifted from primarily modeling to primarily attempting to elicit such reasoning from the students themselves as she led them through analyses of the Mexican and Chinese meals. Finally, the day's home assignment called for students to assess (and share with their families) the nutritional content of their meals that day.

In other lessons in the food unit, Barbara modeled reading the labels on food packages to get information about their ingredients that would allow her to draw inferences about the probable healthfulness of the food. She then modeled application of this information when making decisions about snacks. In the process, she modeled her own curiosity and surprise at times, such as noting that she was surprised to find that many fruit snacks contain so much sugar or corn syrup that they are better classified as junk foods than as healthy snacks. Other occasions for think-aloud modeling included the following: using the calendar (and thus connecting to calendar work in mathematics) to think about and illustrate the time that would elapse between harvesting of bananas in Guatemala and displaying them in food stores in Michigan; noticing details of the illustrations on the outside of a book and using these to draw inferences about whether the book is likely to be fiction or non-fiction; wondering or hypothesizing about the actions of people in the past; and observing the characteristics of people included in an illustration of a family and drawing inferences about which type of family the illustration represents.

Some of this modeling included attention to attitudes and dispositions along with cognitive processes. For example, whenever she is asked a question to which she does not know the answer but does have a hypothesis, she will state that she doesn't know but does have a "best guess," then model the reasoning involved in formulating it. She wants to encourage them to be willing to take intellectual risks—not by guessing wildly but by using what they know to develop reasoned hypotheses.

She also regularly reinforces the idea that what we learn is useful because it helps us to understand the world, or at least make well-informed guesses about it. When teaching about childhood in different societies, for example, she made a point of noting that she learned a lot of interesting things when reading about their lives, that their names were sometimes unfamiliar and hard to pronounce at first but it was important to learn to do so correctly, just as we would want them to pronounce our names correctly, and so on. This is part of her continuing emphasis on respecting individual and cultural differences.

When introducing the land-to-hand story of bananas, Barbara modeled the use of the globe as a tool for reasoning about climates suitable for banana growing. She traced the equator around the globe, describing it as a line around the middle of the earth. The lesson then continued as follows:

T: That's where it's warmest on the whole earth. So when you look at this globe, if you get closer to this line, you get . . .

Ss: Hotter.

T: Or warmer. If you go farther away, it gets . . .

Ss: Cooler.

T: Right. So look at Michigan. Here we are up here. Are we close to the line or far away from the line?

Ss: Far away.

T: So do you think this is a place where it's going to get hot enough for bananas to grow?

Ss: No.

T: [Goes on to show places in Central America where bananas are grown.]

Barbara is especially likely to use modeling when giving instructions for activities and assignments. For example, this is how she introduced an activity calling for students to classify pictures of vehicles as land, water, or air transportation:

T: I have a whole stack of pictures. Up at the top is a word that tells you what this picture is. If you have a hard time figuring out the word, turn to a great reader nearby and have them help you read the word. Your job is to look at the word, look at the picture, and be ready to tell me, "land," "air," or "water." It'll go just like this: "A raft. It goes in the water." And then you sit back down. If you have this one: "Stagecoach, it goes on the land." If you don't know what a stagecoach is, you can look at this picture and figure out if it's on the land, the air, or the water. I'd figure this one was land because there are wheels and it's rolling along the ground, so it must be land. [She then distributed the pictures and began the activity, scaffolding responses by first asking each student to name the vehicle shown on his or her picture and then asking for a land, air, or water classification.]

Barbara frequently includes modeling when presenting home assignments to her students. She verbalizes examples of things they might say to their parents that evening, in order to explain what they learned in social studies that day and what the home assignment calls for. She also models test-taking strategies by thinking out loud to demonstrate how she would approach representative test items. For example, to prepare her students for a multiple-choice test that required them to mark all answers that are correct, she would model first eliminating any of the choices that are clearly wrong, then considering each of the others.

Scaffolding Students' Thinking and Information Processing

Whenever Barbara is going to ask her students questions or present them with a task, she prepares them in advance by developing relevant concepts and principles and by explaining or modeling what to do. Once the children begin responding, she provides additional scaffolding, both to elaborate the content for the class as a whole and to help individuals improve their responses following initial failures. Ordinarily, she does not merely inform students that their answer is incorrect, but provides an explanation or asks a follow-up question designed to cue the student toward a more adequate response.

Students generally answer correctly when asked a question that requires them to consider only one criterion (e.g., name a form of transportation or name an animal). However, some have trouble when the question requires them to consider two criteria simultaneously (e.g., name a form of land transportation, name an animal used for transportation). They may even perseverate in generating answers that are incorrect because they meet one of the two criteria but not both. This problem emerged in the following excerpt:

T: Think of an animal that people use to transport something. Get ready . . . tell me now.

S: Dogs.
S: Camel.
S: Elephants.
T: Sure. Dogs, camels, elephants, . . .
S: Chickens.
T: Do we use chickens to transport things from one place to another?
S: A duck. [Instead of listening to and thinking about the question, the student blurted out a second response before Barbara had even finished asking it. So, Barbara slowed the pace and took time to insert a brief explanation before asking another question.]
T: You have to remember, when you're thinking, you've got to think of the whole thing, not just the animal part, but an animal that helps you transport. Tell me another animal that helps us get from one place to another.
S: A camel.
T: A camel. Yes, you're absolutely right.

While she is still in the process of establishing concepts or principles, Barbara frequently will shift from an explanation mode to a questioning mode, to stimulate students to actively construct and use the concepts or principles she is teaching. However, at this stage she will include a lot of relevant information in the question itself in order to scaffold thinking, as a way to match the response demand to the level that she believes her students are ready to handle. For example, the following exchange occurred as Barbara was in the process of establishing that different vehicles have different purposes.

T: We have a truck and a car at our house. We think about what we are going to do, and that helps us decide which one to drive. When we're going camping and we need to pull our trailer, do you think we take the truck or the car?
Ss: The truck.
T: If we're going on a long trip and we want to have plenty of room and be comfortable, what do you suppose we drive?
Ss: The car.
T: The car. If we were going to drive someplace and we wanted to take some people with us, do you think we'd take the car or the truck?
Ss: Car.
T: If we were going to go someplace where there might be a lot of snow or where we would need to drive off of the road, would we take the car or the truck?
Ss: The truck.

Later, the following exchange occurred as Barbara was teaching about personal vs. mass transportation:

T: What have you got, Krista?
S: A bike.
T: You have a bike. Who does it belong to?

S: Me.
T: It belongs to you personally. Who rides it?
S: Me.
T: So that bike is your . . .
S: Personal transportation.
T: It is. That bike is your personal transportation.

In the following example, Barbara was showing illustrations from a book about schooling in the pioneer days. She scaffolded her students' processing of these illustrations by first cueing attention to the larger or more salient aspects (woodburning stove, benches), before moving on to less salient objects (books, writing materials), and eventually to intangibles such as the curriculum. In the process, she took advantage of an opportunity to build appreciation for today's schools and reinforce some of the norms of the learning community she establishes in her classroom.

T: You know, they had things they used to count with. This strange contraption in this picture is called an abacus. It was used for helping folks count and add big numbers. One of the things that Jared said the other day during math was that you don't want to use your calculator to do your thinking for you, but it's great for checking problems. Right. They didn't have a calculator to check their problems. All of their math problems had to be done in their head or using this—the abacus—and there would be one for the whole school. See how there's a great big one in the corner—it's just one for the whole school.
S: Everyone had to use it?
T: Yeah, they'd have to take turns, and in fact that would very often happen with even things like books. They'd have to take turns. This is another picture of a student in school. He's using a slate. You see, he's copying right out of one book, but what do you think that is in his hand?
S: A feather.
T: Yeah, look at that pen. Sometimes they used quills, but look at this hand over here. What's he got?
Ss: A candle.
T: No lights, so all of their schoolwork would have to be done with candles or lamps that would burn.
S: Why did they have to make a fire?
T: Take a look. They did have to make fires. Look at this group of kids. Are there very many tables and chairs there?
Ss: No.
T: See the big stove in the middle? That's what they would have to use to keep warm. The school was often pretty cold in the winter time. Who's closest to the stove?
S: The teacher.
T: Folks thought about teaching differently then. I mean, we've learned a lot about how kids learn best and what everybody needs. They didn't think about stuff like teaching kids to be kind to each other and teaching kids to

be friends and teaching kids how to solve problems. When you went to school, it was so you would learn to read, so you could learn to write, and so you could learn math—adding and subtracting-type problems. That was it. And the teachers had no problems being tough and fussy and even mean . . .

The next day, Barbara leads her students through a review of similarities and differences between schooling in the pioneer days and schooling today. Then she begins teaching about schooling in other countries, pointing toward comparisons between the United States, Japan, and Tanzania. To scaffold these comparisons, she will have the students address a common set of questions: (1) How do kids get to school here? (2) What things do you see outside the school, and what does the outside of the school look like? (3) What does our classroom look like on the inside? (4) What is our schedule and what are all the things we learn during the day? (5) What things do we use for our learning and who helps us with our learning? (6) What happens at recess and at lunch time?

Because her students already are experts about their own school and classroom, she does not take time to lead the class through development of answers to these questions. Instead, after posing each question, she has the students pair-share their responses. She tells them that they will be co-constructing a chart showing answers to the questions as they apply to themselves (representing the United States) and to children in Japan and Tanzania (after she leads them through books on schooling in these two countries). Barbara commonly uses such questions or categories to scaffold students' information processing, then follows up with co-construction of a chart or other graphic to display the key ideas.

When reading stories to her students, she uses questions and comments both to provoke interest in the story and to make sure that students understand its key points as it unfolds. For example, when reading the story *Uncle Willie and the soup kitchen* (DiSalvo-Ryan, 1991), Barbara uses strategies to cue wonder ("Why do you think he doesn't want that man near him?" "He's looking in the garbage can. Do you usually see people digging through garbage?"), to foreshadow later developments ("When we talk at the end of the book, you're going to tell me what Uncle Willie meant when he said that people need him"), and to cue comprehension and reader response ("Why would somebody be sleeping on a park bench?" "Do they serve just soup at the soup kitchen?").

In another example, after Barbara introduced the food pyramid she showed pictures of different foods and called on students to say which groups they came from. If the students were not sure or answered incorrectly, she scaffolded their reasoning by posing questions that they could use to cue their thinking, as in the following exchange:

T: What do you suppose that might be?
S: A tomato.
T: A tomato is what? . . . [no response] . . . Does it come from a cow?
S: No.
T: Does it come from an animal?
S: No.

T: Does it grow on a plant?

S: Yes.

T: Ah ha! So it's gotta be either a vegetable or a fruit. What do you think?

S: Vegetable.

T: You're right. A tomato is a vegetable.

During subsequent exchanges with other students, she repeatedly posed the same kinds of questions (Does it come from a cow? Does it grow on a plant? etc.), to provide her students with a strategy they could use to process data for decision making.

In the following example, Barbara was preparing the class to develop an advertisement for an upcoming bake sale, using principles for good communication. After establishing that the announcement would be intended to advertise the bake sale to students and their parents, she used questioning to scaffold thinking about other information that might be included:

T: Why do we want to tell the kids about the bake sale?

S: So they come.

T: So they come and bring . . .?

S: Money.

T: Right, they need to raise enough money to pay for the field trip. Here's the next thing. What do we want to tell them?

S: That there's going to be a bake sale.

T: Thad, what else do we have to tell them?

S: To get some money.

T: To bring some money. What else, Heidi? . . . If I said to you, "Heidi, Miss R.'s room is having a bake sale. Bring some money," what are you going to ask me?

S: Why?

T: Sure, you've got to tell them why. Why are they having a bake sale? Everybody tell me.

Ss: For a field trip.

T: OK, what else should we tell them? . . . "Hey, Shane, there's a bake sale. Bring some money." Don't you want to know . . .?

S: When?

T: You want to know when to bring your money. We need to tell them when it is, right?

S: And where it is.

S: And how much it is.

Barbara includes extra scaffolding and elaboration when teaching content that her students will be expected to apply in activities or assignments. In teaching about peanut butter, for example, she used a role assignment strategy similar to the one she had used for the story of bananas. That is, one student was designated as the owner of the peanut farm, another as the trucker who would transport the peanuts to the peanut butter factory, and so on. She moved briskly through these stages until she reached the point where the shelled and skinned peanuts were going to be ground and mixed with other ingredients. Here, she slowed the pace considerably and developed each step in much more detail, because later that day the students were actually going to make peanut butter in class.

As another example, she concluded a lesson on clothing Long, Long Ago with her typical "ticket out" activity calling for students to state something that they had learned that day. She often models two or three examples of appropriate responses (or elicits them from some of her more reliable students) to help scaffold the thinking of students who may need such help. On this day, however, she went out of her way to review the big ideas in more detail than usual and to model more than just two or three possible answers. She did this because the last time she taught this lesson, her students did not provide a variety of good answers at this point. Consequently, she concluded as follows:

T: Now, before you leave to go outside for recess, you're going to tell me one thing about clothing Long, Long Ago. Let me tell you some things I might hear. I might hear that Long, Long Ago, people used fur for clothing. I might hear you say that they had to cut the fur with a stone knife. Maybe I'll hear you say that people used plants to make cloth or maybe they used plants to make clothing, or that very Long, Long Ago, people didn't have to have clothes because they had longer hair on their bodies. Maybe I would hear you say that people used plants to make long pieces to weave together. Maybe I'd hear you say that people made clothes out of big cloths that they wrapped around their body. Any one of those things, or maybe you have an idea that I didn't even come up with. As I start hearing things about clothes Long, Long Ago, you can pop out the back door and go out to play. Howell, tell me about clothes Long, Long Ago.

In conjunction with the transportation unit, Barbara gave a related language arts assignment calling for students to think about a form of transportation they would like to take, describe it using an appropriate adjective, then draw a picture to illustrate. She later gathered these productions into a class book that the students would take home (one at a time) to show and discuss with their parents. In the following excerpt, she modeled things that the students might say to their parents to describe what is in the book or start conversations about it:

T: I'm going to start with the book that you've written to get us warmed up and thinking about transportation. "I will go on a rocking elevated," said Laurel. An elevated is one of those trains that are moved up from the ground so that you can ride on them and cars can still drive around on the roads underneath [inserts definition on the fly]. "I will go on a quick motorcycle," said Arden. "I will go on a big submarine," said Renee. Wow! Look at how well her picture helped me figure out the words. That's what words and pictures do for each other. "I will go in a monster truck," said Sam. "I will go on a rocketing plane," said Tim. Look where the plane is getting off the ground. "I will go in a fast police car," said A.J. What did we learn about police cars and those lights and sirens? What does that mean?

S: Pull over.

T: Pull over, people, slow down. Stop and pull over. Give the police car the right . . .

Ss: Way.

T: Right of way. That's what it means. Give them the right of way [ties back to earlier lesson]. "I will go on a wild pogo stick," said Arden. [Continues in this vein for another few minutes, reading and commenting on the responses, then tells the students that each will have a chance to take the book home and talk about it with parents.]

From Transmission to Construction: A Gradual Shift

Traditional models of teaching call for carefully selecting, representing, and sequencing lesson content and then conveying it, using a transmission model that features initial instruction followed by testing for understanding, clarifying and reteaching as needed, and then shifting to application activities. In contrast, more recently developed constructivist models call for learning by engaging in discussion aimed at co-constructing negotiated understandings or by engaging in collaborative learning activities as members of small groups. In constructivist models, the teacher role involves much less transmission of information and much more scaffolding of discussion or small-group learning.

Constructivist methods tend to be problematic with young learners working from limited and often distorted knowledge bases, especially when the teacher is faced with developing an initial knowledge base rather than building on an already existing one. We find that this situation calls not only for beginning with the traditional model by emphasizing transmission in the initial teaching, but also for stretching the checking, clarifying and reteaching phases over several rounds of review and elaboration. Even after shifting to a questioning mode, the teacher continually needs to fill gaps and elaborate on the newly developing knowledge base when providing feedback to students.

That said, we also recognize the importance of providing students with opportunities to construct and apply new understandings. Consequently, we endorse the constructivist notion that *responsibility for managing learning should gradually shift from the teacher to the students as their expertise develops. In early social studies, this shift is not a one-time event or even a linear process.* There is always a tension between the desire to transmit new information and the desire to engage students in processing this information and constructing understandings. There may be a need to engage in several successive transmission–construction sequences, or to stretch out a given sequence so that some of the information is transmitted initially, more is added in teacher reactions to student responses to questions, and still more is added in periodic reviews.

At some point, Barbara will shift from a transmission to a construction mode in order to get the ball rolling, and, if things go well, will stay in a construction mode to keep it rolling in the right direction with appropriate scaffolding. However, she may need to revert to transmission if the students prove not to be ready or if "the well runs dry" after several successful answers to questions. Early questions mostly require only recall expressed through short answers, but subsequent questions call for more extensive construction and explanation. As students become able to handle them, Barbara provides more extensive construction opportunities through pair share, journal writing, and other communication activities at school as well as through the home assignments.

There are four basic instructional moves involved in accomplishing this sequence: establishing an initial content base, initiating a shift from transmission to construction, reverting to more transmission if this shift does not go well (there may be several repetitions of these second and third stages, although at successively higher levels of sophistication), and finally sustaining teaching in a primarily construction mode.

Shifting from Presenting to Eliciting Information

Typically, Barbara begins by presenting information and then shifts to the questioning mode, either when her initial presentation is completed or, if it is longer and needs to be divided into parts, when she wants to review and assess understanding of key ideas addressed so far. An example of the latter situation occurred when Barbara was reading the book *Uncle Willie and the soup kitchen* (DiSalvo-Ryan, 1991) toward the end of the food unit. After reading several pages, she interrupted the story reading in order to use a combination of elaborations and questions to call attention to some key understandings about soup kitchens. These understandings would be new and perhaps difficult for her students to absorb at first, yet they were crucial to following the story and appreciating its moral.

T: "Hello, Frank," says Uncle Willie, showing him the boxes of fruit and vegetables. "Help yourself. We have plenty today." [Stops reading.] That room was empty a few minutes ago and now it's filled up. All of these people are here because they are . . .?

Ss: Hungry.

T: Some of them don't have homes. Some of them might have homes and they paid for their home but now . . .

S: They don't have any more money.

T: They don't have enough money to buy food too. Did you see anyone paying to come in the door?

Ss: No.

T: At restaurants there's a cash register by the door and you pay . . . This food is for people that are hungry but don't have enough money to buy the food that they need.

S: Does that mean they can't buy food?

T: They can't buy it, so what happens? They can go there. No one that eats here has to pay, and the reason they can do that is because the stores gave them the food and the people like Uncle Willie work there for free. Now if you go to Cheddar's, the people at Cheddar's had to buy the food to give you and they have to pay the people that work there. But not at a soup kitchen. Remember Mr. Anthony from the meat market? He decided that he wanted to help other people so he gave them the chickens for free and the people that owned the market, they had some extra vegetables left over.

They knew that the vegetables would spoil, so they said, "Here, take them to the soup kitchen and give them to people that don't have money to buy food." Think for just a minute. What if Mr. Anthony and the market hadn't been kind and generous and thought about other people? What would all of these people be doing right now?

S: They would starve.

S: They would be hungry.

T: You know what generous is? Giving something even if it's important or it's worth something. What would have happened if Mr. Anthony and the people at the market hadn't given the food to the soup kitchen? What about all those people?

S: They would have to get food somewhere else.

T: They would have to try and get food somewhere else. Do they have money, Lionel, to get food somewhere else?

S: No, and if they don't have a home and stuff, they would die.

T: They might if no one was helping them out and being generous. [Deliberately repeats a word she has just injected and defined.] They might die or they might get sick. That's one of the things—we know that food keeps you . . .

Ss: Healthy.

T: Healthy. If you don't eat the right food, then you'll get . . .

S: Die. [Another reference to death that Barbara ignores.]

SS: Get sick.

T: Get sick. [Resumes reading the story.]

When introducing the contrast between mass transportation and personal transportation, Barbara talked about an upcoming trip in which she and her husband would fly to a distant city. After describing the airplane trip and talking about landing and getting their baggage, she asked her students about the choices that would be available to them for ground transportation in the city. One student mentioned taxis, and another mentioned rental cars. In each case, Barbara followed up with a brief explanation about each of these forms of transportation, what is involved in using them, and how they connect to the contrast between mass and personal transportation. Then a third student mentioned taking a bus. Barbara knew that her students were already familiar with this form of transportation, not only from riding the school bus regularly, but from discussions of the bus system run by the local transit authority (one of the students' fathers worked there). Consequently, instead of giving the kind of explanation she had previously given for taxis and rental cars, she used questioning to elicit the relevant information (that you pay for individual rides on this form of mass transportation, in this case for a ride from the airport to the hotel).

Reverting from Eliciting to Presenting

Sometimes Barbara initiates a line of questioning, pursues it for a while, but then reverts to an information transmission mode. Frequently such shifts are planned, as when she is reading a book and stops periodically to review its contents before resuming, or when the basic digest of information to be conveyed is sufficiently lengthy that she believes it needs to be divided into segments. Sometimes, however, she has to abandon a line of questioning earlier than she had intended because her students are not generating the kinds of responses that she had hoped to elicit.

On some such occasions, she finds that her students simply are not ready for the questions, so that most of them are unable to respond or are guessing in the absence of relevant knowledge. In the following example, she attempts but fails to elicit examples of beef products.

T: What kind of meat comes from cattle?
S: (no response)
T: Beef. Can you tell me some things that are beef?
S: Chicken.
T: Chicken is not from cattle.
S: Bouillon.
T: We did get bouillon from it, but I'm thinking of kinds of meat that you would buy at a store that are beef . . . [pauses for responses, but gets none] . . . Have any of you ever heard of steak?
Ss: Yeah!
T: That's beef. Have any of you ever heard of a roast?
Ss: Yeah.
Ss: No.
T: Mom might say, "I'm making a roast for dinner." She puts a big piece of meat in the oven and she bakes it for a long time [defines roast because some students did not know the term], Anybody ever heard of hamburger?
Ss: Yeah!
T: It comes from beef cattle. [Connects beef back to cattle.] Jeff, what were you thinking of?
S: Beef jerky.
T: Ooooh! Jerky. Yeah, we talked about that earlier this week, didn't we? So, a cattle farm. Let me find another farm for you.

Barbara knows her students well, so she rarely encounters situations like the previous example where she expects them to be able to respond successfully to a line of questions but finds that they are unable to do so. More common examples of reversion from an eliciting mode to a presenting mode occur when students initially answer successfully but then "the well runs dry," and she wants to provide additional examples before moving on. This can be seen in the following excerpt during a choice-making lesson on food in which she engaged her students in helping her plan a balanced meal to prepare for dinner that night.

T: Here's my problem. You said it was OK for me to pick potatoes for dinner, right?
Ss: Yeah.
T: So how do I do that?
Ss: Cook them.
S: Make mashed potatoes.

T: Well, now, wait a minute. We didn't decide what kind of potatoes we want. Let's see if we can list some of the kinds of potatoes we've got. Here we go. We've got mashed potatoes. Just shout it out at me. Just tell me any kind of potato. [Barbara wanted to quickly generate a list here, and each time she had taught this lesson in the past, her students had been able to do so easily. Unexpectedly, this class had difficulty.]

S: Raw. [This undesired but defensible answer compounds her problem; she has to take time to deal with it respectfully before resuming the flow.]

T: Do people eat raw potatoes for meals? I bet they did Long, Long Ago. But do we ever go to a restaurant and they just bring you a potato and just drop it down?

Ss: No.

T: Does your mom just say, "There. Here's dinner."

Ss: No.

T: No, we gotta do something with it. So far, baked and mashed are the only two I've got. Let's see if you guys have some other ways to make them. Alan.

S: My grandma puts them in a microwave and she cooks them with the skin on and then she takes them out and takes the skin off.

T: Yeah, it's called baked potatoes. When you put it in the microwave whole like that, it's called a baked potato. Mariah, what did you think of?

S: Sweet potatoes.

T: I could make sweet potatoes. What else, Laurel?

S: (no response) [Having failed to elicit further examples from even her most reliable students, Barbara determines that "the well is dry" and reverts to an explanation mode.]

T: Have you heard of hash browns? That's potatoes. What about French fries? Have you heard of scalloped potatoes? You take them and cut them into really thin slices and you put them in the oven with some flour and milk and butter and you bake them in the oven that way. OK, so mashed potatoes, baked potatoes, hash browns, French fries, scalloped potatoes. Fried potatoes where you just cut them up and put them in the frying pan with some butter. Are there other ways to make potatoes? Mikey? [At this point she tries again, eliciting one new response and a repetition of one that she supplied earlier.]

S: Potatoes where you put cheese on them.

T: Oooh, cheesy potatoes.

S: French fried potatoes.

T: OK, help me decide. Here are the choices of what we can have with our dinner tonight. All of these are potatoes. Some of these things are healthier than other things. A baked potato with just a little bit of butter on it is much healthier for my body than if I was to have cheesy potatoes because cheesy potatoes have a lot of butter and cheese and sour cream, and all of those things have fat in them—they have stuff from the fat group and that's not as healthy. [Ties back to earlier lesson on food groups.] I have to think about what's healthy.

Finally, Barbara sometimes reverts from asking questions to presenting information in situations where the lesson flow shifts from familiar to less familiar content. In these situations, when students do not have enough knowledge to enable them to supply desired answers to most questions, establishing a base of accurate information requires presenting it rather than attempting to elicit it. For example, Barbara's teaching about economic aspects of food includes a lesson segment that calls attention to the relative costs of eating at different kinds of restaurants. As a lead-in to this segment, Barbara invited her students to tell about their families' favorite restaurants. As they did so, she listed them on the board, but in three separate columns. After eliciting a list of about fifteen restaurants, she explained that while writing down the names of the restaurants, she also had been sorting them into three sets: least expensive, moderately expensive, and most expensive. She then explained that a family of four could eat for about $20.00 at the least expensive restaurants, but would have to pay $40.00 or $50.00 at the moderate ones and $80.00 or more at the expensive ones. After repeating and clarifying this information, she then went on to talk about how the cost of the meal would be one factor to take into account in making decisions about whether to eat out and, if so, where. She provided this information rather than trying to elicit it because she knew that few if any of her students had clear ideas about the relative costs of eating at the different restaurants on the list.

Opening to Student Questions and Comments

Once Barbara has introduced and developed the day's basic set of big ideas, she allows time for students to ask questions and make comments about what they have been learning. For example, near the end of the lesson excerpt shown on pages 43–46, she has just completed explaining how the pioneers created wool clothing by shearing sheep, pulling and twisting the fibers to create yarn, then weaving the yarn into cloth. At this point, she was going to elaborate on the basic explanation by showing and leading discussion of illustrations from a book. However, Cole is eager to talk about machines. Barbara initially makes a minimal response and attempts to move on, but Cole is persistent, so she adjusts her intended instruction to incorporate his interests and those expressed subsequently by several other students.

This chapter has focused on how Barbara develops an initially established knowledge base through carefully structured discourse, gradually shifting from primarily presenting information to primarily questioning her students as their familiarity with the knowledge base solidifies. In Chapter 13, we will continue our analysis of her classroom discourse, this time looking more closely at the questions she asks and how she uses them to scaffold her students' thinking.

Chapter 13

Using Questions to Develop Content with the Whole Class

Discourse structured around questioning is the time-honored method of developing content with students. *Effective teachers plan good sequences of questions that will help their students develop their understanding of big ideas and provide opportunities to apply them.* Constructivists place special importance on questioning, emphasizing that teachers ask questions not just to monitor comprehension but also to stimulate students to think about the content, connect it to their prior knowledge, and begin to explore its applications. As they do so, students process the content actively and "make it their own" by rephrasing it in their own words, elaborating its meaning, and building connections to prior knowledge.

Timing and Frequency of Questions

In general, Barbara emphasizes questioning her students more in lessons that occur later in units than in lessons that occur earlier, and, within lessons, more toward the ends of lessons than the beginnings. Thus, her questions focus on helping students develop and apply content bases established initially through narrative and explanation. Sometimes, however, Barbara discovers that she has omitted or underemphasized a big idea when establishing the initial content base. When this occurs, she will introduce and reinforce it during the subsequent questioning segment, either by briefly suspending questioning in order to insert an explanation or by building more information into her questions and her feedback to student responses.

Several other factors also affect the degree to which she emphasizes questioning, the nature and difficulty levels of the questions she asks, and the pace at which she leads students through these lesson segments. For example, first graders generally need more extensive establishment of the content base, whereas second graders generally can handle more construction stimulated through questioning. If she is running short of time or if the lesson has run long and students are beginning to fidget, she will take actions that allow her to finish the lesson quickly (by omitting less essential questions and making fewer sustained efforts to improve responses when students are unable to answer a question or answer it incorrectly). However, she will not omit or skip too lightly over content that she considers essential. Instead, she will slow the pace and if necessary carry the lesson over to the following day.

Barbara also will move more slowly and build in more redundancy when special circumstances dictate (such as when she knows that she will be absent the next day and her substitute will use a follow-up activity that requires the knowledge base being developed today, or when she wants to conclude the lesson with questions similar to those included in a follow-up home assignment, as a way to prepare the students for it). She will allow time for extensive questioning segments whenever the lesson will be the primary opportunity for the students to construct and communicate ideas about the topic, whereas she would feel less need for extensive questioning if the students would receive follow-up construction opportunities through a home assignment or a subsequent in-class activity such as writing about what they had learned (often with opportunities to inspect a book or manipulate a prop used during the lesson).

Types and Functions of Questions

Barbara uses many different types of questions, depending on how far she has progressed in developing particular content and what she is currently trying to accomplish. As students gain familiarity and expertise with a content network, her questions become progressively more demanding. Early questions often build a lot of information and cueing into the question itself and require students only to answer yes or no or to choose among provided alternatives. Later questions incorporate less scaffolding and demand more from the student, such as recalling information from memory or reasoning to draw a conclusion. Still later questions require students to engage in more elaborate forms of reasoning or to articulate rationales or explanations.

She has no standard sequence or formula for allocating particular question types (e.g., closed vs. open questions, fact vs. explanation questions). Instead, the point is to use questions in ways that help students to learn content networks with understanding, appreciation, and application to life outside of school.

As a way to introduce and get her students thinking about a new topic, Barbara will sometimes pose open questions that admit of a great many possible answers and engage the students in brainstorming to collect ideas, elicit examples, or construct some kind of list (e.g., "Our next unit is about food. Why is it important for us to talk about food?"). She also uses such questions at the ends of lessons or units to facilitate review, most notably during the "ticket out" activities that conclude the social studies period ("Tell me something that you learned today").

Open-ended questions also are used to get students personally involved with a topic or help them see connections or applications. This is most obvious in home assignment questions calling for students to tell the class about where the family likes to eat out and why, the kinds of vehicles it owns and what they are used for, or what clothing items family members own that were made in other countries.

Most of her questions, however, call for more specific answers. Many of them focus on processes and are designed to get students to notice and think about what is done, how and why it is done, or how this may connect with or have implications for something else.

Socializing Students' Attention and Participation

Because questioning is such a basic component of her teaching and because her questions are intended to stimulate her students to think about the content being developed, *Barbara establishes at the beginning of the school year (and reinforces consistently thereafter) that she expects her students to pay close attention to all of the question/answer/feedback exchanges that occur during lessons.* She elaborates on this expectation in several interesting ways.

First, to underscore the importance of listening carefully to the question, she makes it clear that her questions are genuine, not rhetorical, so her students will need to pay careful attention and think about the questions before seeking to respond to them. *To underscore this point, she frequently poses questions to which the correct answer is "no,"* often doing so using a voice tone and inflection likely to lead students to think that the expected answer is "yes" if they have not paid attention to the question's content. We call these *"no" questions* and have identified many of them as such in the commentary bracketed within the lesson excerpts. Note that if Barbara has asked several no questions in a row, she will shift to a yes question (again, to underscore the importance of paying attention to the question).

As a humorous alternative to more typical "no" questions, Barbara frequently poses *absurd questions*, such as asking if cave people would go to the supermarket to get a particular food. Absurd questions typically serve scaffolding functions along with motivational functions (in this example, by cueing students to remember that cave people had to rely on hunting and gathering to obtain food). They usually work well, but occasionally lead to flow interruption because students make humorous or fanciful responses to them.

Barbara has developed several "traffic control mechanisms" for regulating who has the floor during whole-class activities, and for what purpose. At the beginning of the year, as part of socializing students to listen carefully and respect the "turn" of whoever has the floor, she establishes that lessons include *"my turn" segments* (in which all students are expected to listen to her as she teaches) and *"your turn" segments* (in which students are invited to ask questions or make comments). She sometimes uses these terms as a way to signal transitions and cue expected behavior, as well as to remind students about expected behavior when necessary ("It's my turn now, so I want you to put your hands down and listen carefully while I teach").

This approach is a form of advance organizer that alerts students about what is to come and cues expected behavior, and it minimizes situations in which students find themselves being criticized for interruptions (unpredictably, from their point of view). Also, Barbara will get back to any student who she feels needs attention because of something that he or she wants to bring up.

Calling for Choral Responses

She frequently invites her students to respond as a group rather than raise their hands seeking to be called on as individuals, especially during reviews or on other occasions when she expects most if not all of them to know the answer. She still wants them to listen to the questions and respond thoughtfully, however, so she uses verbal directions ("Get ready . . . tell me now") or hand signals to ensure that all of the students withhold their response until she has concluded her question and allowed time for them to think about it.

Unpredictably, she will use playful variations on the technique, such as extending the pause longer than usual, asking for a response from just one student instead of the whole class, or asking for responses from just the boys, just the even-numbered students, etc. This is a positive way to accomplish an important group management objective: to preserve time for slower students to process and respond to her questions. If only a minority of the students respond to a choral question, she will note this and remind the class that all are expected to respond, then repeat the question.

When choral responses from the whole class yield more incorrect answers than she was expecting, she may call for responses by subgroups (e.g., first just the girls, then just the boys) in order to cut down on the number of students responding at one time so that she can zero in on who is saying what. She then will follow up with feedback and explanations that are meant to be heard by the entire class but directed in particular to the individual students who responded incorrectly.

Barbara also uses other mechanisms that allow all of her students to respond to a question simultaneously. For choice questions, she may ask them to respond nonverbally, such as by tugging on their left ear if they prefer one alternative but tugging on their right ear if they prefer the other. For questions likely to produce diverse or lengthy responses, she may invite her students to share their thinking with a partner (pair-share). As they do, she monitors to listen for content that she may want to follow up on when she reasserts "her turn" again (such as misconceptions that need to be addressed or ideas that support a smooth segue into the next point she wants to develop).

Protecting Individuals' Response Opportunities

Barbara also does several other things to encourage her students to listen carefully and respond thoughtfully to her questions. She makes it clear that once she has shifted from addressing the class as a whole to interacting with an individual student, that student "has the floor." Instead of waving their hands or calling out answers, the other students are expected to listen carefully to the exchange between Barbara and the student who has the floor, even if the student is having trouble generating a response and even if the exchange extends over several question/answer/feedback sequences. Onlookers who blurt out answers are encouraged to "Keep your answer in your head" until called on, and admonished that "You're keeping him from getting his own ideas."

By consistently protecting individual response opportunities, Barbara simultaneously (1) eliminates most of the ostentatious hand waving, calling out of answers, and exclamations of "I know!" and "Call on me!" that plague many primary classrooms; (2) eliminates most of the peer distractions and felt pressures to respond quickly that often undermine students' ability to concentrate and think in response to the teacher's cues or follow-up questions; and (3) makes it likely that other students whose knowledge of the point at issue is limited or confused will benefit from the exchange (more than they would if she elicited the answer from an eager responder and then quickly moved on).

The fact that Barbara protects individual response opportunities in this manner also makes students aware that they will need to listen to questions, think about them, and generate responses; if Barbara calls on them and they remain silent or just take a wild guess, she is not going to accept this and give the answer or move on to get it from someone else. Instead, she is going to stay with them and extend the response opportunity, typically by first providing some feedback or explanation but then by posing at least one additional question.

This combination of learning opportunities and accountability pressures applies to all of the students in the class, not just the eager responders and high achievers. However, it unfolds within a learning community that features mutual support and collaborative learning, and Barbara's follow-ups to initially inadequate or mistaken responses focus not only on building understanding, but on helping the student conclude the response opportunity on a positive note (i.e., by generating acceptable responses to one or more follow-up questions). Consequently, the emotional tone of these interactions is supportive, not threatening.

When students answer incorrectly and her cueing and scaffolding do not succeed in leading them to generate desired responses, Barbara will provide the correct information for them. However, she often will have them repeat it or will come back to them shortly afterwards to make sure that they have it. She also uses "no" and absurd questions to keep students on their toes in this regard, especially with respect to common misconceptions ("If I want a blue shirt, can I grow blue cotton?" or "Dinosaurs and people were together Long, Long Ago, right?").

Juggling Whole-Class and Individual-Student Agendas

It is challenging for teachers to keep young students on topic and sustain the intended flow when working primarily in a questioning mode. They need to keep the lesson's big ideas in mind as they make decisions about what to ignore or minimize vs. make salient or elaborate in questioning and responding to students, as well as when to stay in the questioning mode and when to revert to presentation.

In the process, they must address simultaneously (or rapidly move back and forth between) agendas at two levels (Kennedy, 2005). *Class-level agendas* focus on developing content with the class as a whole, ideally moving smoothly through the intended flow of big ideas and eliciting mostly correct answers. Questions at this level are designed to introduce and develop content networks, and, within that, to direct attention to big ideas and their connections.

Agendas for individual students focus on providing support to those who are unable to respond or have responded incorrectly, by scaffolding their thinking to help them generate good responses to follow-up questions. There is always tension between the class- and individual-level agendas, because attempts to move the whole class through a lesson segment quickly may leave several students with only partial or confused understandings, whereas too much time spent addressing individuals' confusions interrupts the intended flow and may impair the attention or learning of the class as a whole. There is no simple solution to this problem; it is an enduring dilemma that teachers have to manage as best they can.

Several planful aspects of Barbara's teaching are designed with this in mind. Some are strategies used routinely with the class as a whole (begin with easy questions but shift to more demanding questions as students develop expertise; begin with questions about the familiar before shifting to the unfamiliar; socialize students to respect one another's response opportunities by listening carefully to the discourse without waving their hands or calling out answers). Other strategies apply to specific situations (when students have been unable to respond or have responded incorrectly), or even to specific individuals (those who have chronic difficulties in public response opportunity situations, leading Barbara to formulate special yearlong improvement goals for them).

Barbara develops content with the class as a whole through a combination of storytelling, explanation, modeling, questioning, elaboration inserted into her feedback to students' responses, and periodic reviews. Her questions focus on big ideas and their applications. They are designed to scaffold students' thinking by helping them see connections in and draw inferences from what they are learning. This is usually the case not only with questions addressed to the class but with most initial questions addressed to individuals and even some follow-up questions addressed to those same individuals. Where an initial question has not produced an adequate response, however, Barbara's follow-up questions are usually addressed primarily to clearing up confusion and eliciting an improved response from the individual being questioned (see Chapter 14), and only secondarily to content development with the class as a whole.

Maintaining the Flow during Questioning Segments

During reviews or at other times when most of Barbara's questions elicit the desired responses, the lesson flows smoothly and quickly. She may even have time to insert material that she had not planned to include or to elaborate on the content by making connections: tying back to things discussed previously, underscoring applications to the students' lives outside of school, reinforcing connections with big ideas, or integrating with content that has been taught previously or will be taught subsequently in social studies or other subjects.

However, rather than run through a question sequence quickly and elaborate the content later, *Barbara typically elaborates as she goes, by expanding on students' responses in ways that introduce or reinforce connected content, review key ideas, or prepare them for upcoming questions. In the process, she frequently lifts their colloquial language to more formal terms or rephrases their answers to connect better to the intended flow.* Other researchers also have identified "reformulating" or "revoicing" as a way for teachers to acknowledge the significance of what a student says, expand the student's contribution, and underscore its connection to a big idea (Cobb *et al.*, 1998; Nuthall, 2002; O'Connor & Michaels, 1996; Varelas *et al.*, 1999). In the process, the teacher may "lift" from less formal or precise to more formal or precise language, expand a brief response to a more complete statement, or supply connecting links (so that, because, etc.) that call attention to reasons or explanations.

Another frequent purpose for expanding on students' responses is clarification, especially when students make reference to something that may not be familiar to all of their classmates, or when she suspects that some students have not understood a point made previously. For example, when she questioned students about products made from corn, the first two respondents mentioned corn on the cob and cornbread. Barbara accepted these answers without feeling any need to expand on them, because her students were familiar with both corn products. However, the third student mentioned corn syrup. Knowing that most of her students would not be familiar with either this term or the product to which it refers, Barbara elaborated as follows:

T: Corn syrup—absolutely. They take corn and they take the sugar that grows in corn, because there's sugar in fruits and vegetables . . .
S: My mom uses that in cookies. It's my favorite.
T: Yup, it's used for baking.

Increasing the Probability of Desired Responses

When questioning students about material that is relatively new or difficult, Barbara will take steps to make sure that her questions elicit the responses she desires often enough to allow her to maintain a reasonably coherent flow throughout the lesson. She may cue students' thinking through leading questions, break complex questions into simpler parts, or direct a question to a particular student who is likely to generate the response she is looking for (because the student is one of her more reliable responders or has a personal connection to the topic). For example, during a review segment of an early clothing lesson, she asked students to name one of the four functions of clothing. Students quickly named the other three but not modesty. To elicit "modesty," she called on a student who had raised the modesty issue earlier.

After students have been with Barbara for some time, at least some of them come to realize that if they have displayed a special interest in or knowledge about a particular idea, she may call on them when she wants that idea injected into the flow. Whether or not they are conscious of this fact, Barbara often gets the intended response because she knows her students' interests and response tendencies and keeps track of the questions, comments, and responses they make during lessons.

Barbara also will attempt to reduce flow breakdowns by indicating that she soon will be calling on a student who is currently distracted or who may be startled if called on unexpectedly. This gives the student time to focus and begin processing in preparation for the question, which reduces the likelihood that the question will produce no response or a far-fetched response that leads to a greater interruption of the flow than her brief forewarning does.

Another frequently used technique is to interrupt a questioning segment to introduce some key information that the students will need in order to understand and respond well to upcoming questions. For example, in teaching about wheat and corn, Barbara intended to ask for examples of foods derived from each of these plants. Before doing so, however, she explained how the material harvested from the plants is processed into flour and then asked about products made from wheat flour (and later, corn flour). Without these clarifications, most of her students would have been working from images of wheat or corn plants (rather than wheat or corn flour) when attempting to respond to her questions about food products, and thus would have struggled to answer them.

Embedding Scaffolding within Questions

As an alternative to interrupting a questioning segment by shifting from questioning to presenting information, *Barbara frequently will embed key information within the question itself as a way to cue students toward desired responses.* For example, the following excerpt is from a lesson on the land-to-hand story of peanut butter. At the time, Barbara was eliciting additions to a co-constructed list of jobs associated with work roles performed at each stage in the process. After establishing that crates of peanuts would be loaded onto a truck, she proceeded as follows.

T: How's the trailer full of peanuts going to go anywhere?
S: Somebody has to drive the truck.
T: Aha! They need a truck driver. Perhaps you would want to be the truck driver. They take the peanuts to the warehouse. Let me ask you a question about that truck. Maybe your company owns a whole bunch of trucks and they all take peanuts places. What happens if the truck carrying the peanuts breaks?
S: You couldn't get them there.
T: So is that a problem?
Ss: Yeah.
T: So what do you think you probably ought to have if you're in charge of that truck getting the peanuts to the warehouse? What, Alan?
S: Somebody to fix your truck.
T: Right. What do you call somebody who fixes trucks and cars?
S: Tow truck.
S: Mechanic.
T: Dad's job. Tell them, Cory.
S: A mechanic.

Having introduced the truck (and its driver), Barbara takes the opportunity to add the idea of vehicle maintenance staff, represented by the job of mechanic. She ordinarily would not include a mechanic in the story of peanut butter, but that year the father of one of her students (Cory) worked as a mechanic, so she included that job here as a way to make a personal connection.

Barbara frequently will precede a question with information or embed the information in the question itself as a way to calibrate difficulty of question to the students' current knowledge. After introducing the four basic functions of clothing, for example, she showed illustrations of clothing items and asked her students to identify the primary functions they illustrated and explain their reasoning. She began with the functions most familiar to the students (protection and modesty), which enabled them to handle more of the explaining and allowed her to focus more on eliciting than presenting information. In addition, rather than attempt to include the whole task within a single question, she scaffolded by first asking her students which function of clothing was emphasized in an illustration and then following up by asking "Why do you think so?" When she got to the function of communication, she shifted her follow-up question to "What is it communicating to us?" as a way to help students maintain focus on the key idea.

Barbara concluded her lesson on land, water, and air transportation by distributing a card to each child showing a cartoon version of a vehicle with the name printed at the top. When called on, they were supposed to name the vehicle shown on the card and state whether it travels on land, on water, or in the air. Before beginning, she added more structuring and modeling than usual because the cartoon versions of the vehicles were often fanciful in ways that might be distracting to her students. Also, the students needed to be clear about the three categories of transportation because they would be the basis for the next home assignment. Consequently, she first told the students that if they were unable to read the name of the vehicle shown on their card, they should consult with a neighbor. After allowing time for this, she modeled the thinking processes that might be used and the kinds of responses that might be given (e.g., if the vehicle has wheels, it probably rolls along the ground, so it probably is a form of land transportation).

In the following excerpt, Barbara is relying primarily on a questioning mode rather than a narrative mode, even though the interaction occurred very early in the childhood unit. To make it possible for most students to respond and thus to sustain a reasonably coherent flow, she scaffolds heavily by building a lot of content or vocabulary into the questions and frequently framing them as choice questions rather than open-ended questions.

T: What's new or different about them? [toddlers]. Different than an infant? Different than a baby? What do you think, Scott?
S: They can do more stuff.
T: What is it about their body that makes them able to do more stuff?
S: They're growing up.
T: By that do you mean they're getting bigger?
S: They're getting really big until they're all grown up.
T: What else do you notice about their bodies, Karla?
S: They start to walk.
T: Yes, they do start to walk; and man, do they get into stuff when they start walking. What else, Alan?
S: They grow more teeth.
T: More and more teeth, don't they? Even more teeth, and they start eating food. Here's something important for toddlers. How do they communicate with you?
S: Talk.

Another example of heavy scaffolding prior to and during questions occurred in a lesson in which the students were asked to classify features of schooling as representing schooling Long Ago, schooling Today, or both. In prior experiences with these kinds of classification questions, Barbara has found that if she begins with the item and asks whether it belongs with Group A, Group B, or both groups, students will tend to pick either Group A or B and then stop thinking, without considering the possibility of both groups. However, they do better if she calls attention to the "both" category and gives or elicits examples. In this lesson, before beginning questioning she is careful to define "both" and to clarify that Today responses will refer to the students' own school (not to schools that may exist today but in other parts of the world). She further scaffolds by drawing a Venn diagram showing overlapping Long Ago and Today circles, emphasizing that the area of overlap represents "both," repeating all three choices, and giving students time to think before responding (as another way to encourage them to consider the "both" option).

T: I'm going to call this circle Schools Long Ago, and I'm going to call this one Schools Today. Who's an expert about Schools Today?

Ss: All of us.

T: You guys are because you are in school! What do you suppose this space here in the middle is?

S: Both.

T: Both, so I'm going to write Both right here. Now, I have some cards that I wrote down some words on. Now, I know that these aren't the only things that you might remember from Thursday. In fact, one of your jobs was to go home and chat with mom and dad and maybe they have an idea that's not up here. Maybe you can remember something that I talked about or that I showed you a picture of. Maybe you can even think of some things about schools today that I can add in here, or maybe you'll even think of things that will go with both. So we'll go through these cards and pop them up there, and then if you have more ideas, you can add to them. The first one I have is a log school—a school made out of logs. Get ready to tell me—do you think that's Long Ago, Today, or both? What do you think? A log school. Get ready . . . Tell me . . . Now.

Ss: Long Ago.

T: It sounds like most of you are thinking that was Long Ago and you're absolutely right. If you look around now, the schools aren't made out of logs—they're made out of cement blocks. So a log school would definitely be Long Ago.

Sometimes Barbara will preface a question within information designed to cue students toward a desired response. For example, after completing the "Breads around the World" lesson, she segued into instructions for the home assignment via the following interchange:

T: Your job tonight will be talking with your moms and dads about the different kinds of bread that people have, what they make it out of, how some bread has . . .

S: Has different stuff in it.

T: Has different stuff in it, so the ingredients might be different.

The information that Barbara provided in the lead-in to the response slot here was sufficient to cue one of her students to supply the response she had hoped to elicit. She immediately repeated the response ("has different stuff in it") and then rephrased it using more precise language ("so the ingredients might be different"). She repeated the response because she wanted to make sure that all of her students heard it from her, and she elaborated so as to reemphasize and rephrase it because it was the first of a series of templates that her students could use to organize their thinking about the home assignment. She then went on to model other questions that might be asked (Did all the bread taste the same, look the same, feel the same, smell the same, etc.?).

Maintaining the Flow when Questions Do Not Elicit Desired Responses

Sometimes Barbara's students do not provide the response she was hoping for, but nevertheless respond in a way that allows her to sustain the intended flow. If a response is generally accurate but imprecise or not phrased in the most helpful way, she will treat it as correct but then revoice it to fit the intended flow better (especially if she is establishing a key term or concept that will be used repeatedly).

Similarly, if a response is correct as far as it goes but incomplete, she will ask a follow-up question to elicit the missing piece. For example, during a lesson on the food pyramid she had asked students to identify examples of common foods and identify the category in the food pyramid in which they would be classified. If students merely identified the food but did not name the category ("chickens"), she would follow up by saying, "Chickens, so this comes from an animal, so what group does it go in?"

When the technique is applicable, Barbara will cue a desired response by "suggesting" its opposite. For example, when teaching about mass versus personal transportation, she asked about buses, and a student said, "A bus transports people." Barbara responded, "One or two?", which caused the student to elaborate the original response by noting that a bus carries many people, so it is a form of mass transportation. Like its cousin the "no" question, this "opposite" question usually is effective because she uses it frequently and her students quickly learn to interpret and respond to it as desired.

When a student's response includes the desired idea but also adds extraneous elements, Barbara will preserve the flow by focusing on the relevant part. For example, in reviewing ways that children get clothes, she sought to elicit the concept of hand-me-downs, with the implicit expectation that the students would be working from images of getting clothing items handed down from older siblings or cousins. However, the student she called on talked about getting hand-me-downs through churches. Barbara acknowledged that this was correct but then went on to focus on the main idea that still-usable clothing can be passed on to younger children, without commenting on the church reference.

Undesired but Usable Responses

Sometimes students will generate responses that are unexpected but usable without breaking flow if Barbara is willing to rearrange her intended sequence of topics. For example, during the historical segment of the food unit, Barbara was eliciting ideas about foods and food-related things that exist in modern times that did not exist in the past. The cueing that she built into her questions and her previous experience teaching this lesson led her to expect her students to name particular foods or talk about food stores or restaurants. However, the student she called on said "farms." This led Barbara to make a quick decision to begin talking about developments in farming, a topic that she had planned to address later in the lesson.

Sometimes it even is possible to incorporate incorrect answers into the ongoing flow, especially "useful incorrect answers" that allow Barbara to clarify or emphasize an important point. For example, the "land-to-hand" lessons on clothing begin with the story of wool, then proceed to cotton, then silk. After teaching about the sequence of steps involved in creating silk clothing, she asked her students to name these steps as part of her review. One of the students said "combing," a response which would have been correct for wool or cotton but was incorrect for silk. Barbara responded as follows:

T: Combing helps to keep wool and cotton nice and straight, but do we have to comb these guys [silk fibers]?
Ss: No.
T: No, because look, it's not tangled, is it? We had to unravel it, but did we have to comb it?
Ss: No. [Barbara goes on to clarify that silk fibers are ready for weaving without requiring combing first.]

Barbara considers this kind of incorrect response useful not only because it allows her to clarify the point, but also because she assumes that if the respondent has this incorrect idea, other students probably do too. In reacting, she tries to convey to the respondent that his answer is useful (because sometimes incorrect answers help us learn).

Sometimes an answer is correct and Barbara will acknowledge this in her feedback to the student who provided it, but then take action to preempt further responses in the same category. This is especially likely to occur when she has posed a relatively open-ended question and would like her students to generate a variety of responses to it. For example, when she asked them to identify foods that people ate long, long ago, one of them said peanuts. Barbara immediately said that this was correct, that the people ate peanuts and other nuts, and gathering nuts was one of the ways they got food. One of her agendas in making this response was to generalize to all kinds of nuts, thus encouraging her students to think about kinds of foods other than nuts rather than continue to name specific kinds of nuts (walnuts, pecans, etc.).

Inability to Respond Correctly

When students cannot respond, or respond incorrectly, Barbara's basic policy is to provide a second response opportunity by following up the initial question (sometimes simply repeating it, but usually simplifying it or providing cues), *but then to shift to providing an explanation if the second opportunity does not elicit an acceptable response.* While this is occurring, the rest of the class is listening rather than calling out answers or seeking to be recognized (because this is what she has trained them to do).

Although she follows her basic policy most of the time, situational conditions sometimes lead her to do something else in addition or instead. If the student's initial response is a misconception or a statement that threatens to shift attention to something that Barbara would like to avoid, she is likely to forgo her usual attempt to elicit an improved response and instead go immediately to providing an explanation. In these situations, the idea is to "bury" the misconception or unwanted sidetrack by immediately refocusing the group's attention on the intended content, and keeping it there. She may even insert a bit of review or move into an explanation of the next idea at this point, to increase the likelihood that what the student said will be forgotten as attention reverts to her intended flow.

She also might forgo an attempt to elicit an acceptable response in situations where her first question yielded no response at all. This is especially likely if the question was asked relatively early in a sequence of teaching about a given topic, when students are still just developing their knowledge (as opposed to later during review), or if the student appears completely lost and unlikely to be able to respond to a follow-up question either. In these situations, the whole-class agenda takes precedence over the individual student agenda, so she provides a quick explanation and moves on.

If Barbara recognizes that an undesired answer reflects a line of thinking that may be shared by other students, she may provide extensive feedback designed to clarify the point and preempt the emergence of similar responses. When students begin to perseverate on the same type of response, she will indicate a need to shift to other types.

If a response is incorrect because it attends to only one of two criteria (e.g., naming a ship or an airplane when asked about forms of land transportation), she will note the problem and remind the class to pay careful attention to the question. The same is true for incorrect answers that appear because students are recalling responses that were correct earlier but not now or recalling information that "would be correct for a different question but has been filed in the wrong place in the child's mind."

If students have been responding well but run out of relevant or desired answers ("the well is dry"), Barbara will shift to a new type of question or a new topic. However, if she was seeking to elicit particular examples that it is important to include, she will supply them herself and underscore whatever it is about them that she wants her students to remember.

Sometimes Barbara uses a combination of techniques to improve the chances that question sequences go smoothly, especially at the beginning. For example, when teaching the land-to-hand story of peanut butter, she wrote on cards brief descriptions of each of the jobs involved. As a review, she told the class that she would shuffle the cards and then display them one at a time. As she did so, students were to determine whether the job depicted on the card occurred before the peanuts got to the factory, during processing at the factory, or after they left the factory. To further ensure understanding, she modeled the process herself by drawing a card, reading the job, and explaining that this job occurred after the peanuts left the factory. She then pulled another card and noted that it referred to "buying the peanuts." This description was meant to refer to the representative of the factory who bought the peanuts from the farmer. However, most of the students took it to refer to the person who bought the jar of peanut butter at the store, so they responded, "After the factory." Barbara sensed the problem and immediately shifted to an explanation mode, without attempting to elicit an improved response through questioning. Then she moved to another (easier) card, and for the next several cards called on some of her more reliable responders.

Her main agenda here was to get the questioning activity "up and rolling," so she focused on eliciting desired responses, both to establish a satisfactory flow and to provide models of good responses for her struggling students. In situations like this, Barbara often will "go to the bullpen" or "call on my heavy hitters" (i.e., call on the students most likely to respond correctly) to elicit model responses.

In any case, when students fail to respond or give poor responses and the situation dictates prioritizing maintaining the flow over working to get a good response from an individual student, Barbara will forgo her usual response improvement attempts and instead supply the answer along with any needed clarifications about knowledge gaps or misconceptions. If subsequent questions also fail to yield desired responses (even from her "go to" students), she will revert from a questioning mode to a more extensive explanation mode, by reviewing and expanding on content taught earlier until she thinks that her students are ready to begin to respond to questions more successfully.

As is explained in more detail in Chapter 14, *Barbara typically works for an improved response when she feels that the situation allows her to suspend the flow briefly in order to do so.* For example, when she asked about products that we get from a dairy farm, a student said, "Wheat." This answer is correct for the larger category (farm) but not for the subtype that the question addressed (dairy farm). She probably would have called the student's attention to this immediately if she had covered grain farms in previous lessons. However, the food unit calls for teaching about dairy farms before grain farms, so she did not introduce this point and instead focused on getting a better response. She first simply said, "Not wheat." When this did not yield any further response from the student, she noted that dairy farms give us milk and asked about things that are made from milk. This also failed to yield any further response, so she completed the exchange by saying, "If I had some milk, I could make some ch . . .?", which finally elicited "cheese."

Responding to Answers That Are Correct but Undesired in the Context

Unexpected student responses can disrupt the intended flow even when they are accurate (or at least, could be considered accurate). Several examples are shown in Table 13.1. Barbara's basic procedure in these situations is to acknowledge the accuracy of the student's response but then move quickly back to the planned agenda. For example, when she asked about "things that are beef," she expected to elicit prototypic examples of beef entrées (steak, roast beef, etc.). However, the first student to respond said "Bouillon." Barbara replied, "We do get bouillon from it, but I'm thinking of kinds of meat that you would buy at a store that are beef. Have you ever heard of steak? . . . Have you heard of a roast?" She frequently uses the phrase "but I'm thinking of . . ." in these situations as a way to signal to students that their answers are accurate but not what she is looking for at the moment.

Sometimes she will stay with the student and try to elicit the desired response by rephrasing the question or giving cues, as in the following example.

Table 13.1 Correct but undesired answers

Question	Desired Response	Obtained Response
1 What might you do with a carrot before you eat it?	Dip it in vegetable dip.	Wash it.
2 What do they add to cooked mushy apples when they make applesauce?	Sugar (Wanted to make the point that applesauce is not as good for you as plain apples).	Cinnamon.
3 What foods did they eat long, long ago?	Prototypical foods (meat, berries, etc.).	Bugs.
4 What will I need to use to get a plant into the ground?	A shovel. (Wanted to focus on the tools and labor involved in farming.)	Water.
5 Then when they have the big roll of dough, what do they do with it?	Cut it. (Wanted to go one step at a time.)	Make noodles out of it (collapsed the rest of the steps).
6 What kind of meat comes from cattle? . . . (no response) . . . beef. Can you tell me some things that are beef?	Steak, hamburger meat, etc.	Bouillon.
7 What is special about a subway?	It runs underground.	People ride on it.
8 After the plants have grown, what do you have to do if you want food?	Harvest—pick the food off the plant.	Needs sun. You have to get the seed out.

T: After the plants grow, you've weeded them, you've watered them, the plants grew. Now what do you have to do, if you want the food?

S: Needs sun.

T: It does. It had sun. It grew and here's this beautiful plant with the ripe food on it. What do I need to do if I want to eat that food?

S: You have to get the seeds out.

T: You have to pick it, don't you? You have to take the food right off the plant.

In this situation, her follow-up question yielded a second correct but undesired response, so at this point she gave the answer she was trying to elicit.

Occasionally one of these answers is so unexpected that Barbara treats it as incorrect, at least initially. When she asked about foods eaten Long, Long Ago and a student said "bugs," she initially responded as if the answer were incorrect. Although some people past and present do eat bugs, this was not something that she had mentioned or listed on the timeline as an example of food Long, Long Ago. After a moment's reflection, however, she acknowledged to the student that some people Long, Long Ago probably did eat bugs, then returned to her intended flow.

Responding to Unexpected Problems during Questioning Sequences

Because Barbara is so well prepared, her questions are usually well phrased and effective in supporting the content flow that she wants to develop. However, sometimes she will experience confusion, frustration, or dissonance because events do not unfold as planned and she has to diagnose and adjust to the problem in the moment, while at the same time continuing the lesson. *The most challenging situations occur when a student's response introduces an anomaly that she wanted to avoid or suggests that her development of a big idea has been ambiguous or misleading.*

Good questions focus on the most important elements of the content and guide students' thinking in ways that move them toward key understandings. They also are clear, in the sense that they specify the points to which students are to respond (Good & Brophy, 2007). If a question is phrased too broadly, vaguely, or ambiguously, students may interpret it differently than the teacher intended, and in effect answer a different question than the question the teacher intended to ask. This often leads to responses that are correct in the sense that the substance of the student's statement is accurate, but undesired because they do not support smooth progress through the intended content flow.

For example, the following excerpt is from a lesson in which Barbara had described and shown illustrations of advances in farming technology (initially incorporating animal power, then machine power). As the excerpt begins, she has just shifted into a questioning mode, intending to elicit understanding that the basic steps in farming remained the same (till the soil, plant the seeds, etc.), but improvements in technology allowed these steps to be done much more efficiently. However, her initial question was too broad and initiated a sequence in which the students repeatedly answered both correctly and incorrectly.

T: Tell me, did the jobs that you need to do change?
Ss: Yes.
Ss: No.
T: Which would it be? Did you have to dig up the ground?
Ss: Yes.
Ss: No.
T: Do you have to dig up the ground?
Ss: Yes.
T: Do you have to dig up the ground? [Barbara repeats the question to make sure that all of the students now understand this point.]
Ss: Yes.
T: Who does it over here [pointing to an illustration]?
Ss: People.
T: Who does it here?
Ss: Horses and ox.
T: Animals. Who does it here?
Ss: Machines.
T: The tractor. Did the job change?
Ss: Yes (a few).
Ss: No (most).
T: No. The only thing that changed is who does the job, who does the work. Here, it's people doing the work. Here, it's animals helping with the work. And here, it's tractors helping with the work.

This rough spot in the lesson occurred because students interpreted Barbara's initial, overly broad question differently. Those who answered "no" interpreted it similarly to the way that Barbara intended (Did the basic jobs—digging up the dirt, planting the seeds, etc.—remain the same?). However, other students said "yes" because they thought she was asking whether the tasks performed by farmers changed when animal power, and later machine power, was introduced. Such situations not only disrupt the intended flow, but sometimes leave Barbara temporarily confused, so she may initially treat an unexpected but accurate statement as if it were an incorrect response.

A similar situation developed during the transportation unit, when Barbara was teaching about motor homes. Intending to make the point that motor homes can be driven from place to place, she asked, "Who does the work [when you're in a motor home]?" She expected students to respond by mentioning engines or motors, but a student says, "Grown-ups." This required her to note that grown-ups do not make the motor home go, then ask the more specific question about what makes the motor home go.

Barbara's original question might have been successful if she had asked "What does the work?" rather than "Who does the work?" in the motor home. Her lessons on transportation consistently used the phrase "does the work" to refer to supplying the power to move vehicles. However, the term "who" cued her students toward persons rather than power sources. The same problem appeared later in the transportation unit when she asked "who" does the work on an airplane, and a student answered "the pilot" instead of "the engine."

Frequently, initially vague questions need to be clarified before students can respond to them successfully. For example, when reading and discussing a book about a soup kitchen, Barbara pointed to an illustration of a woman sleeping on a park bench and asked, "What do you know about her?" Finding her students unable to respond, she narrowed the question to "Why would a woman be sleeping on a park bench?" This led to responses supporting recognition that many of the people who came to eat at the soup kitchen were homeless.

A vague initial question contributed to the problems Barbara experienced during the lesson in which she enlisted her students in helping her plan the menu for her dinner that night (excerpted more fully in Chapter 12):

T: Here's my problem. You said it was OK for me to pick potatoes for dinner, right?

Ss: Yeah.

T: So how do I do that?

Ss: Cook them.

S: Make them mashed potatoes.

T: Well, now, wait a minute. We didn't decide what kind of potatoes we want, all right? Let's see if we can list some of the kinds of potatoes we've got. Here we go. We've got mashed potatoes. Just shout it out at me. Just tell me any kind of potato.

S: Raw.

T: Do people eat raw potatoes for meals? I bet they did Long, Long Ago, don't you think? But do we ever go to a restaurant and they just bring you a potato and just drop it down?

Ss: No.

T: Does your mom just say, "There. Here's dinner"?

Ss: No.

T: No, we gotta do something with it. So far, baked and mashed are the only two I've got. Let's see if you guys have some other ways to make them.

In this situation, Barbara's initial question ("So how do I do that?) was much less specific than the question she intended to ask ("So how do I choose what kind of potatoes to have for dinner?"). As a result, it elicited answers about the preparation of potatoes instead of criteria for choosing what kind of potatoes to select. This required her to scaffold by clarifying that she meant what kinds of potatoes to consider, and identifying mashed potatoes as an example. However, her problem immediately became compounded when a student mentioned raw potatoes, which led to a sidetrack in which she had to establish that we do not ordinarily eat potatoes raw.

Barbara was surprised and temporarily confused at this point because in two previous experiences teaching this lesson, she had gotten quick and easy answers along the lines she desired when she asked about types of potatoes to consider. Consequently, she treated the student's "raw" response as incorrect even though it can be seen as defensible given her immediately preceding request ("Just tell me any kind of potato"). She also took more time than she ordinarily would in responding to it, partly because she wanted to make sure to clarify the point, but also because she needed a moment to analyze the situation and decide how to proceed. Then, having determined that this class possessed less knowledge about food preparation than her previous classes had, she adjusted to include more explanation in the rest of this lesson segment than she had intended to.

Sometimes what seemed clear to Barbara proves to be vague or confusing to students, and she ends up shifting her plans instead of merely clarifying her intended questioning and pursuing the original plan. For example, she began a lesson on careers in communication by asking students if their parents worked in communication jobs, and, if so, to tell the class about these jobs. However, the flow did not develop as planned because the first few students who responded talked about jobs that involve some communication but would not ordinarily be classified as communication jobs (restaurant cashier, auto mechanic). Sensing that she had started down an unprofitable path, Barbara aborted this line of questioning and shifted to teaching from a book on communication used as a picture resource. Eventually, she realized that she needed to clarify a distinction between people who communicate as part of doing their jobs (almost everyone) and people whose jobs specifically involve facilitating communication.

These situations in which events do not unfold as planned can create confusion, frustration, or dissonance in Barbara and require her to think on her feet to diagnose and adjust to the problem in real time, all the while continuing the lesson. They are similar in many ways to what happens when students introduce anomalies, but more serious because they involve some problem in conveying the big idea itself, not merely a need to introduce a relatively minor qualification or elaboration on a basically sound initial presentation.

Monitoring student comprehension is vital. When only one or two students seem confused, it often is best to ignore or respond only minimally to incorrect statements and focus on repeating and elaborating correct ones. However, if many students are making responses that are either incorrect or valid but unexpected and undesired in the situation, there is reason to suspect that her teaching about the big idea has been misleading, or, more likely, that her questions have been ambiguous, vague, overly broad, or misleading. This will require her to clarify her questions and perhaps back up a bit to reorient her students before moving forward again.

Sometimes Barbara will sense that her students are likely to say something undesired in response to an upcoming question, especially if she is about to shift from one line of questioning to another or to ask a type of question that is unusual and thus unexpected. For example, when teaching about breads from around the world, she wanted to show examples and cue her students to notice and describe their physical characteristics (size, shape, color). As she showed the first example, however, she sensed that many of her students were primed to begin guessing its type (e.g., rye), instead of carefully listening and responding to the question she was about to ask. So, she preempted by saying, "Let's take a look and see. I'm not asking you what kind of bread it is. I'm asking you what you notice about this bread right away." This preemptive clarification was effective in that it led to the response "It's black."

Sometimes Barbara senses that a question is too difficult (either for the class as a whole or for the individual with whom she has been interacting), so she temporarily shifts from the questioning mode to the explanation mode. For example, as part of her line of questioning designed to scaffold thinking about what kinds of potatoes to have for dinner, she asked if French fries are healthy. Many of her students said "yes" and only one said "no." She was tempted to ask the latter student to explain, but decided to do so herself because she did not think that he would be able to explain effectively. An explanation was needed at this point because it was clear that many students did not understand the reasons why French fries would be a less healthy choice than most other potato alternatives. In this example, Barbara made an in-the-moment decision to delete a question that was likely to be too difficult. More typically, she would ask the question, realize from the nature of students' responses (or lack of responses) that it was too currently difficult for them, and temporarily revert from questioning to explaining.

Summary: Maintaining the Flow

During lesson segments in which they are questioning and responding to students, teachers must address two agendas: (1) a whole-class agenda focused on developing understanding of a content network, and (2) an individual student agenda focused on addressing confusions and scaffolding improved responses.

Interruptions and Shifts in Anticipated Lesson Flow

Lesson planning leads teachers to anticipate a lesson flow composed of segments built around selected big ideas addressed in sequence. Lesson flow develops most smoothly when (1) teachers are able to ask the questions they intended to ask in the order they intended to ask them; and (2) students' responses are not only accurate, but expected and desired because they allow the teacher to respond in ways that facilitate smooth transition into the next step in the anticipated flow. However, a brief loss of momentum or even a more serious interruption of lesson flow may occur if the student is unable to respond, generates an incorrect answer, or even generates an answer that is accurate but undesired because it requires the teacher to deal with some unanticipated complication before moving on.

Brief loss of momentum typically occurs when a student is unable to respond to a question or provides an incomplete or incorrect answer. These situations require Barbara to use scaffolding routines to help the student improve the response (and, ideally, end up giving the response that she was looking for in the first place). Sometimes she has to do a lot of this kind of scaffolding within a brief time frame (30–90 seconds), either because several students in succession have difficulty responding or because an individual student requires unusually extensive scaffolding. In these situations, Barbara may need to revert to information presentation temporarily by not only giving the answer, but backing up to explain a key idea that several students apparently have misunderstood or to reconnect with the larger flow by quickly reviewing the most recently developed points that led up to the present one.

More serious loss of flow can occur when certain kinds of undesired answers or interjected student questions or comments shift the discourse completely off-topic or at least down a side road into an aspect that Barbara wanted to omit. Barbara refers to these as potential *"bird walk" situations* and underscores the need for a clear focus on goals and big ideas to help her make good decisions about what questions to ask, what to emphasize in responding to students' answers, and how to respond to their comments and questions.

Bird walk situations occur much more frequently in social studies than in mathematics, because social studies embodies a much broader range of content that may trigger associations in her students' minds. Their comments and questions also create (in Barbara) a greater felt need to provide something more than a minimal response, even if this means temporary loss of lesson flow. Sometimes this is because the question or comment allows her to address an important social studies goal or big idea (albeit one not planned for inclusion in today's lesson). At other times, she judges that the student is expressing a genuine wonder, and she wants to encourage that. In summary, unanticipated events that interrupt the intended flow require Barbara to make in-the-moment adjustments to her plans. She usually acts so as to return to the flow quickly and move on, but she sometimes suspends the flow temporarily and occasionally even adjusts it (to expand it or deviate from the planned sequencing).

Adapting Scaffolding Routines to Students and Situations

When students are mostly answering smoothly and providing expected answers to her questions, Barbara focuses on repeating or rephrasing answers to reinforce the vocabulary and big ideas that she wants to emphasize, perhaps elaborating on explanations or adding new material in the process. If students' answers are good as far as they go but incomplete, she is likely to ask additional questions or provide cues to help them answer more completely (or, failing this, to give the desired answer and perhaps explain a bit). Examples of her expansion and clarifications of brief student responses are shown in Table 13.2.

Sometimes a student is unable to respond or offers a guess that is not even in the ballpark. This may occur because the student is confused or has been inattentive, or because the question was vague, misleading, or simply too difficult for that student at that time. When this occurs, Barbara employs her scaffolding routines. Initially, she attempts to elicit the desired answer (by offering cues or using two or more simpler questions to build toward it in stages). If this is not successful, she at least tries to enable the student to generate a successful response before concluding the interaction. In the latter case, she is likely to revert to information presentation briefly to explain the point she was intending to elicit, then move on.

If such response failures are widespread, it is likely that many of her students have missed or misunderstood some key point. In this case, she will make a more extensive reversion, backing up to the point in the flow where the students do understand and then providing extensive explanation to fill the gap or clear up the misunderstanding before moving forward again.

Sometimes a student generates an answer that would have been correct for a different question (especially one asked earlier) but is not for the current question. If Barbara believes that the mistake occurred because the student did not pay

Table 13.2 Barbara's expansions and clarifications of students' responses

Question	Answer	Expansion/Clarification
What is that?	Meat.	It is meat. It's a pork chop, and it's from the meat group.
What do they make cheese out of?	Milk.	That's right. It's from the milk group, and it comes from cows. That's actually Swiss cheese—the kind with the holes.
Which group is carrots from?	Vegetables.	Yes—vegetables have lots of vitamins and minerals to keep your body healthy.
What group is a waffle from?	Bread.	You're right—it is from the bread group, because it is made out of a grain. Waffles are made from wheat flour.
What food choices were available Long, Long Ago?	Pigs.	Yes, that would be like hunting for meat, like wild pigs or wild boars. Did they have farms with pigs? (No.) No, but they could hunt animals for meat.
What have you seen mom use that white powdery flour for?	Pizza.	Pizza dough—the bread or crust part of the pizza.
Why do you think my husband and I should have French fries for dinner tonight?	They don't take much time.	Right, as long as I get the kind from the freezer bag.
Why do you think we should have grilled cheese sandwiches at home?	It's not expensive.	Right—you can get a package of cheese and a whole lot of bread for just a few dollars, but eating out at a restaurant would cost $20.00 or more.
What does harvest mean?	Forage.	It's like forage, only when it's on a farm, it means you just go out to the fields and pick it—you don't have to look for it.
[Riddle] This one carried people, it had horses, and it was made long ago.	A covered wagon.	Yes, and in fact, a covered wagon not only carried people, but if you were a pioneer going to a new home, it would carry your family and everything you owned. So it would carry your stuff, too. Imagine trying to put everything you owned into a wagon.
[Barbara is showing an illustration from a book about an adopted child, when a student comments]	He looks like he's oriental.	He looks like part of his family came from China or Japan long ago—you're right.

close attention to the question and pick up on the ways in which it differed from earlier questions, she is likely to clarify this, attempt to elicit the right answer from that same student if possible, and then move on. However, if she believes that the problem occurred because this student (and probably others) "misfiled" key information, she will suspend the flow temporarily while she explains in a way that enables such students to file the information correctly.

Sometimes students provide "useful incorrect" answers that are not what Barbara was expecting but useful because they allow her to clarify and elaborate on key ideas or address common misconceptions. Conversely, sometimes students generate "correct but undesired" answers that are accurate in content but undesired in the moment because they focus on aspects of the topic that Barbara would like to avoid (because they are not relevant to the big ideas or may cause needless confusion). Typically, she acknowledges these responses briefly and then moves on quickly, refocusing on desired content and hoping that most students will quickly forget the undesired content (because it will not be repeated or developed). However, she may suspend the flow temporarily and deal with the undesired content at some length if she believes that the student has expressed a genuine wonder; that this student and perhaps others may perseverate on this content unless it is addressed; or that now that a misconception that she intended to avoid has been articulated, she needs to address it.

Correct but undesired content often is injected when students respond to details of photos or illustrations, when other adults in the room make well-intended but unwanted comments, or when students start to tell stories about personal or family experiences with the topic. Barbara ignores a lot of these comments, especially if they are made to no one in particular (e.g., "I did that once"). Alternatively, she may acknowledge the comment briefly and then move on quickly, perhaps incorporating some part of the comment that provides a reentry route to the intended flow.

Sometimes a student's answer is in the ballpark but too vague, too specific, or phrased in a way that highlights something other than the aspect she wants to emphasize before moving forward. In these situations, she will revoice or interpret the student's statement so as to make it clearer, more generalized, more specific, or rephrased in ways that use desired vocabulary or highlight big ideas.

More challenging are situations that lead to significant suspensions of the flow or even online adaptation of the flow to accommodate emerging events. One is the situation already described, where undesired answers or comments provide stimulus material that Barbara has to decide whether to ignore, briefly acknowledge, partially incorporate, or address at length. Other challenging situations involve mixed responses that convey the desired answer but embed it within longer comments that include undesired additional correct material and perhaps incorrect material as well. Unless such responses incorporate a misconception that Barbara feels the need to address directly, she is most likely to respond by ignoring the undesired portion and focusing on the desired portion, typically by restating it (as if the student had given only the desired answer) and moving on. If some of the undesired content is useful, she may also incorporate it into the flow as she proceeds.

Mixed responses in a different sense may occur when Barbara invites choral responses or asks students to share their ideas with a partner. In these situations, it often happens that most of the students make correct statements but one or a few do not. Here, she sometimes will repeat the correct answer and proceed as if everyone had given it, but sometimes will suspend the flow in order to address the incorrect responses (especially if they involve significant misconceptions).

Barbara typically sticks with her planned flow but occasionally moves on to the next topic earlier than she had intended, or even shifts the order of topics, in response to a question or comment from a student. More typically, though, if a student asks about an aspect of a topic that will be addressed later in the current or some other lesson, she makes a minimal response at the time but tells the student that the point will be addressed later.

In this chapter, we described and illustrated Barbara's use of questioning (and responding to students' answers) to scaffold her students' learning and application of big ideas. In doing so, we focused on how she directed the discourse so as to create an intended idea flow and support the progress of the class as a whole. In Chapter 14, we will examine Barbara's techniques for addressing the needs of individual students as she works within the whole-class format.

Chapter 14

Scaffolding for Individual Students within Whole-Class Lessons

Researchers (including teachers) who have examined the subtleties involved in successful teaching often speak of the dilemmas involved in trying to address several agendas simultaneously. During lessons, teachers must continuously negotiate tensions between the whole-class agenda (maintain a coherent flow through the intended lesson plan) and agendas for individual students (address their individual knowledge gaps and misconceptions, connect with their individual needs and interests). These issues arise routinely whenever the student who is called on to answer a question is unable to do so (either being unable to respond or responding incorrectly). Researchers who have written about these situations commonly recommend taking actions (rephrasing or simplifying the question, providing cues, scaffolding reasoning) designed to help the student generate an improved response and conclude the interaction on a positive note. However, they also recognize that time pressures or the need to maintain lesson coherence may cause the teacher just to give the answer and resume the flow (Brophy, 2002; Englert & Dunsmore, 2002; Kennedy, 2005; Okolo *et al.*, 2002; Roth, 2002; Schaffer, 1996; Stone, 1998).

Scaffolding to Elicit Improved Responses

Barbara holds similar views. Even though her students are children, whose reasoning and communication skills are still developing and whose prior knowledge of most topics is limited, *her preferred method of handling initially poor responses is to stay with the student and try to elicit an improved response. Her standard operating procedure includes three steps*: (1) following the initial failure to respond or incorrect response, provide scaffolding to try to elicit a better response; (2) if this does not yield an acceptable response, scaffold one more time (typically by providing a lot of help or simplifying the question considerably at this point); and (3) if this still does not yield an acceptable response, provide the answer (and any needed explanation) and move on.

Barbara tries to implement this approach routinely, and often does. However, she will shorten it or omit it entirely (i.e., simply give the desired answer and move on) if time is short or if circumstances dictate that the whole-class agenda take precedence over individual student agendas (see Chapter 13). In other situations, she may extend her typical pattern by staying with the original student through several additional response opportunities because this allows her to address a special agenda for the particular student involved or to exploit a teachable moment for the class as a whole.

Barbara's methods of addressing her agendas for individual students sometimes begin even before she asks the question, or at least before she calls on the student to respond to it. For example, she will pitch questions on certain topics toward students who have a special interest in or connection to those topics. When reviewing responses to homework assignments, she will pitch questions to students whose responses touched on the topic of the question. Also, she adjusts the difficulty level of questions and the degree of help included in follow-up scaffolding to her students' capabilities and needs. She will challenge her more assertive students but provide more support and encouragement to timid or struggling students.

For example, when teaching about mass transportation, Barbara had made the point that some form of taxi service exists in many parts of the world, especially cities, and she wanted to elicit the additional idea that people pay for taxi rides. She engaged in the following interaction with one of her struggling students.

T: Do they have taxis in Kenya?
S: Yes.
T: What do you have to do if you want to ride in a taxi—even the people in Kenya have to . . .?
S: Drive it.
T: Do you get to drive the taxi or do you pay the person driving?
S: Well, yes.
T: Yes? Which yes? Do you pay the person that drives the taxi?
S: Yes.
T: Yes, that's what let's you ride in it.

In this situation, Barbara's original attempt to cue some version of "you have to pay for your ride" elicited an undesired response (drive it). She responded with a follow-up clarification question that was intended to simplify the level of response demand, but this question elicited an ambiguous response (yes). At this point, Barbara realized that the unfolding sequence of events had created a level of response demand that was too complicated for this particular student to handle successfully, so she simplified to an easy yes/no question, then confirmed and elaborated the response.

In the following example, Barbara stayed with one of her more capable students across several response opportunities, adjusting her response demand to the developing situation. She had passed out illustrations of foods to her students and now was asking them to identify the foods and assign them to their appropriate food groups.

T: What do you have?
S: Some juice.
T: What kind of juice?
S: Orange.
T: Which group do you suppose orange juice is from?

S: Milk.

T: Orange juice doesn't come from a cow. Everything in the milk group comes from a cow. What does orange juice come from? . . . Orange juice comes from oranges. If it comes from oranges, which group is oranges? . . . Is it fruit or bread?

S: Fruit.

T: So orange juice is part of the fruit group.

When the student originally identified the illustrated food merely as juice, Barbara probed for the more complete "orange juice," confident that he could supply this answer without help. However, his next answer stated that orange juice belongs to the milk group. Barbara first explained why this is incorrect, then sought to elicit a better response by asking questions that embedded cues. She asked what orange juice comes from, but got no response, so she told the student that it comes from oranges. She then scaffolded again, asking, "If it comes from oranges, which group is oranges?" Ordinarily, the first or at least the second of these response improvement attempts would have been successful with this student, but in this case he was unable to generate a response. Consequently, to allow him to exit the sequence on a positive note, she reduced the response demand to an easy choice ("Is it fruit or bread?"). This excerpt is typical in that Barbara first scaffolded in ways that still challenged the student to reason through to the desired response, but concluded with a "giveaway" question when this was not successful.

With students who often do not respond or respond only minimally, Barbara sometimes will pursue improved responses across several exchanges, as a way to socialize them to begin to think and respond to her questions more actively. This can be seen in the following excerpt, in which Barbara has established that buying clothes or sewing them yourself are two ways that people commonly acquire clothing, and she is now seeking to elicit other ways.

T: Do you have a different one?

S: She could make one.

T: That's the same as sewing. Sewing and making. Have you ever gotten a new coat but mom didn't buy it and she didn't make it?

S: Yes.

T: Where did it come from? . . . Have you ever gotten any clothes that mom didn't buy or she didn't sew? Where did they come from?

S: A company.

T: She might have had to pay for it if it came from a company. Are there any clothes at your house that you've gotten that didn't come from a store?

S: Yes.

T: Where did they come from?

S: From my grandma.

T: Your grandma got it for you as a gift?

S: Yes.

Barbara worked to elicit an improved response at length here, partly because she was trying to socialize this particular student and partly because it was a brainstorming situation where many different answers would be acceptable (so the student was likely to come up with one if he put his mind to it). She tried personalizing and then restating the question several different ways until the student finally was able to answer. She refers to interchanges like these as "shaking the tree" (until a nut finally falls).

Attempts to scaffold improved responses can get complicated and include more than one student. The following excerpt occurred during a segment on food choices. Barbara had just read a brief scenario for which the likely choices were picking up fast food to take home or eating out at a restaurant.

T:	What do you think the family should do for dinner? What do you suppose, Gretchen?
Gretchen:	Home.
T:	You think they should eat at home so it won't cost so much money? What do you think, Haden?
Haden:	(No response)
T:	What should Mary and her mom and dad do for dinner? They live in the city. Both mom and dad work. What do you think they should do after a day of working and picking up Mary from the babysitter's? What do you suppose they should do for dinner?
Haden:	(No response)
T:	Should they eat at home or at a restaurant?
Haden:	Home.
T:	You think they should eat at home. Why do you think that Mary and her mom and dad should eat at home?
Haden:	So it will be hot.
T:	What will be hot?
Haden:	The food.
T:	So they could make food for themselves at home and it will be nice and hot.

In this situation, Gretchen's initial response was not what Barbara hoped to elicit, but she accepted it temporarily and then sought to elicit a more desired response from Haden. However, her interactions with Haden initially yielded no response, then a repetition of Gretchen's "home" response (probably because Barbara's initial acceptance of it made Haden think that it was correct), and finally a response (so the food will be hot) that threatened to derail the flow away from her intended focus on economics. To avoid that problem, Barbara called on one of her "heavy hitters," who supplied a more desirable response (go out to eat). She then probed his reasoning, making sure that what she elicited from him and what she added in the process of elaborating on his answer clarified the reasons why picking up fast food or eating out were likely choices in the depicted scenario. As the segment progressed, she never told either Gretchen or Haden that the "home" answer was incorrect, but instead "buried it" by shifting the focus to the family's reasoning for its decision to eat at a restaurant.

Sometimes Barbara will adjust her lesson plans to address an issue of concern to one or more of her students. For example, in talking about work roles and associated job titles at the factory manufacturing peanut butter, she always teaches about the foreman in charge of the workers and the different jobs that workers do in the process of manufacturing and packaging peanut butter. One year she added the job of personnel manager, because Anthony had mentioned the idea of people getting fired from their jobs several times in the previous weeks. She explained that the personnel manager's job involves mostly hiring but occasionally also firing workers. She elaborated with a scenario in which a worker continually fails to do his job properly, despite attempts by both the personnel manager and the foreman to explain the problem and how it needs to be corrected.

She thought that this addition was worth including not only to speak to Anthony's continuing concerns, but also as part of her more general socialization regarding future selves and self-efficacy. She wants to make her students aware that a great many options are open to them, but also that jobs and other social roles involve responsibilities as well as rewards, and there are penalties for people who do not fulfill their responsibilities.

Knowing what she does about her students' home backgrounds, Barbara sometimes makes home references as a way to cue improved responses. For example, one day she was asking students to name forms of transportation. Her initial question yielded several responses, but as the well began to dry up, she began to cue students to think of additional ideas. Intending to cue "bus," she called on a student whose father worked for the local transportation authority and asked:

T: If I wanted to get to someplace here in the city, I could go on a . . .?
S: Airplane.
T: Think about dad.
S: A CATA bus.
T: You could get on a CATA bus. A CATA bus helps you get from one place to another.

In this case, Barbara's cueing initially elicited the unexpected response "airplane." This was a perseveration from an earlier exchange with the same student, in which airplane was the correct response. She made an instant decision to "bury" this response because commenting on it would require dealing with complications she did not want to address (airplane is a correct response to the original call for examples of transportation, but not a correct response to the immediate question about local travel). Instead, her reference to the student's father enabled him to make the connection and produce the desired response (bus).

Barbara frequently calls attention to relevant information or evidence as a way to cue thinking following a response failure. For example, in one segment she was asking students to tell her what forms of transportation would be appropriate for particular trips. In the process of establishing that an airplane but not a car would be appropriate for a trip from the United States to Kenya, she pointed out on the globe that the trip required crossing the Atlantic Ocean. She then asked if you could take a boat to Kenya. The student she called on initially said no. Barbara's response was to show the globe again and say, "Take a look." This was sufficient to enable the student to realize that a boat would be appropriate.

Barbara often responds to incorrect answers with a comment or question that both indicates to the student that the response was incorrect and provides cues to the desired response. For example, in response to a question about the steps in making cloth, a student jumped to spinning without first mentioning combing. Barbara's response was "It's got tangles in it." A question about the communication function of clothing elicited the response that clothing might communicate something about work. Barbara responded, "Are you going to a job?" When she asked the class what might be a good symbol for Long Ago on the timeline, a student suggested that she draw a house "kind of like our houses." Barbara asked if they had houses like ours long ago, leading the student to say "no" and then go on to give a better answer. Her students understand that if she asks a question or makes a comment like this, it is a signal that they need to rethink their answer.

At times when she is asking for students' personal opinions or experiences (as opposed to times when she is asking questions about curriculum content, for which certain answers are correct and others are incorrect), Barbara sometimes will choose to accept rather than challenge responses that are probably not accurate. For example, one day she was talking about vehicles that might be used for racing. After giving a couple of examples, she asked students about vehicle races they had witnessed. She elicited a couple of expected responses (snowmobiles, monster trucks), but then a student said "airplane." Barbara immediately asked, "Have you seen airplanes racing?" The student said "yes." This struck Barbara as very unlikely, but she did not challenge him further because he was one of her lowest-functioning students who frequently got things confused. Instead, she resumed the flow by calling on other students to provide examples of vehicles used for racing.

Students' Questions and Comments

Besides answering Barbara's questions, students inject their own thinking into lessons by asking questions and making comments. Barbara encourages this because she wants her students to be active learners who think about what she is teaching and connect it to their life experiences. Responding to questions and comments automatically ensures that she is connecting with the interests of the students who make them, and it is likely that a question or idea voiced by one student will be shared by several others.

Students' questions and comments often advance Barbara's agenda by leading into points that she was intending to raise herself. Even when they raise other points, they often create teachable moments that Barbara exploits by departing from the intended flow temporarily. However, students' questions and comments also can create unwanted intrusions. In fact, they are more likely to do so than students' answers to Barbara's questions, because the students are initiating their own agendas, not just filling the response slots that Barbara creates as part of enacting the intended lesson flow.

Another potential problem with student questions and comments, especially with students as young as Barbara's, is that they may have little or nothing to do with the topic at hand. Worse, they may raise issues that Barbara would prefer to avoid altogether, or at least take up with the student privately later, but not at the time or not in front of the rest of the class. *In summary, Barbara encourages questions and comments as a way to connect with students' interests and promote active learning, but, depending on their timing and nature, such questions and comments can either enrich a lesson or distract from it.*

Barbara employs several strategies for managing this dilemma. Right from the beginning of the year, she displays willingness to listen to and follow up anything that a student wants to raise with her, but she emphasizes that during lessons, students are expected to pay close attention to the lesson as it develops, and respond accordingly. Questions and comments should be confined to issues directly related to the aspect of the topic being developed at the time. Requests for word definitions or clarifications of explanations are always welcome, as are brief comments that relate directly to the current topic. Questions or comments about other aspects of the topic usually are not desired (at least at this time), and off-topic bird walks are unwelcome (although Barbara will listen and respond with interest after the lesson).

She minimizes responses to student questions and comments and generally retains tight control over lesson flow during "my turn" segments of lessons, but welcomes questions and comments at other times. Most notably, she invites "wonders" before launching instruction on a new topic and invites students to ask questions or make comments during "your turn" segments. She also frequently includes pair-share segments that allow students to raise questions or express ideas with one another.

Barbara typically delays inviting student questions and comments (during "your turn" segments) until she has finished developing big ideas (during "my turn" segments). Waiting until she is confident that the basic network of big ideas is in place allows her to respond more coherently to unanticipated questions and comments by fitting them into the developed network (e.g., in response to a student's comment about President Lincoln, who was depicted in an illustration shown during a clothing unit lesson, she focused attention on Lincoln's clothing and connected it to points made earlier in the lesson).

In the rest of this chapter, we discuss and present examples of Barbara's reactions to students' questions and comments. We begin with situations in which relevant questions or comments created teachable moments that Barbara exploited as such, then turn to situations in which undesired questions or comments created problems for her.

Teachable Moments

Possibilities for teachable moments arise whenever a student says something that is relevant to the current topic but outside of Barbara's planned agenda. Some of these are triggered by unexpected responses to her questions, as described in Chapter 13 (useful incorrect answers). More are triggered by students' questions and comments that convey misconceptions, articulate unusual perspectives on the topic, or provide opportunities to make useful connections. Barbara is especially likely to exploit teachable moments that provide opportunities to reinforce main ideas, fill in gaps (add material that could or should have been included earlier), clear up confusions or misconceptions, personalize or apply big ideas, insert tiebacks or other connections, or elaborate on the content in useful ways.

For example, after introducing information about the food pyramid and about components of foods that affect their desirability from a health standpoint, Barbara shifted attention to "healthy snacks." She invited her students to speak about the snacks they had brought to consume during snack time at school. Then she commented on selected examples, describing healthy snacks as providing protein, vitamins, and minerals that would provide energy and "keep you going" between meals. She also characterized junk foods as full of sugar or fat and not providing much useful nutrition. In talking about potato chips, she elicited that they contain a lot of salt and grease. At this point, a student observed that he had eaten potato chips that did not contain salt. Barbara welcomed this comment because it gave her an opportunity to explain that many sugar- or salt-free snacks nevertheless are not healthy snacks because they contain a lot of corn syrup, fat, or other undesirable ingredients.

Later in the same lesson, Barbara noted that some foods that are developed from healthy ingredients become less healthful because of sugar or other substances added to them in the process. She gave fruit cocktail as an example. At this point, a student asked, "If fruit cocktail is unhealthy, why would they make it if you wouldn't eat it at all?" Barbara first clarified that she did not mean to imply that we never eat unhealthy foods, just that we should not eat them as often as healthier foods. Then she explained that one reason they make fruit cocktail is that "They can put it in a can and send it to places where that fruit doesn't grow, or so we can have it in the winter when there's no fruit growing on the trees."

Sometimes student questions or comments are so directly relevant to the ongoing flow that Barbara can incorporate them easily. In the following excerpt, Barbara was using pictures from the book *Sarah Morton's day* (Waters, 1989) to illustrate clothing worn by Pilgrim children, emphasizing that getting dressed was a more complicated process for them than it is for modern children. The students raised several questions and comments that Barbara incorporated into this agenda, as well as one that led to a brief connection to mathematics.

T: This was probably the only dress she had to wear every day, so she would put an apron on over the top. So she'd have her shirt, her waistcoat, a couple of petticoats, and then an apron over that.

S: She's got a lot of petticoats.

T: Right, she's got three petticoats and an apron over the top of that. The apron was to keep it clean because that's the only outfit she had. She had to wear it every day.

S: Didn't they have washers?

T: No. No such thing as washers or dryers, so she probably had to wait until she was in her pajamas at night to wash her clothes every once in a while, probably not more than once a week for sure . . . Look! She's tying her pocket on. Pockets are hard to put on, so instead of sewing pockets into their clothes, they made a pocket all by itself, like a little purse, and it was on strings and what would she do with the strings?

Ss: Tie it.

T: Tie them around her waist because that's how they wore them. That's how they hooked things on—by tying them up. So they'd tie them around their waist and then she would put on her shoes. Oh, my goodness, gracious. Can we write all those things down? Let's see if we can remember all the things she had to do to get herself dressed. Here we go. Girls. Before we even started, she had to put on her . . .

S: Petticoat.

T: Nope. Her shirt, and in fact, that was called an undershirt because they were underthings. She had to put on her undershirt. Then she would put on a petticoat. She'd put on her stockings. She'd tie them up with a garter. Then she'd put on another petticoat. It was considered if you went out without all this stuff on, it was very immodest. That means you weren't keeping yourself protected enough.

S: That would be showing your body.

T: And people would be upset and shocked. It would be just like one of us coming to school without a pair of pants on. Like everybody would go "Ugh!" and be really surprised. Just like that. Next was her waistcoat. She put on her coif. That was for her to have on her head. Babies wore something kind of like that to keep them protected. A waistcoat, a coif. She might tie on her pocket. She has her apron to wear, and her shoes. This wasn't even winter. This was just every old day. Like my birthday's in August, so in August these were all the clothes that she'd wear.

S: She'd be late for school.

T: Why would she be late for school, Laurel?

S: Because she'd have to put on eleven things.

T: She'd have eleven things to put on. Laurel counted and she said "eleven." Laurel, how many things do you have to put on to be ready for school?

S: Five.

T: A shirt, jeans, underwear, socks and shoes. We have five things. These girls had eleven things that they would have to put on.

S: They've got six more things to do than us.

T: Everything was either ties or buttons, so not only did she have eleven things to put on but even no zippers. No. So where we just pull and pants go up, they even had buttons on shoes, and if they had boots on, there would be buttons all the way up the boots. Sometimes they even had to have somebody help them to get dressed because there were so many things. Imagine all that.

S: How could you run?

T: How could you run? How are you going to play, Mikey?

S: You'd just have to walk.

T: Yeah. Wouldn't it be hard for her to play tag with her friends? Imagine if she tried to play soccer.

S: They couldn't—they had no soccer ball.

T: There were other games that they played, though. Kids have been play- ing tag since Long, Long Ago. But can you imagine how hard it would have been to play tag with all of those clothes on? There she is. You can see her in this picture. Same kind of stuff. She's got on her waistcoat, she even has something on called pantaloons. These were like underpants. They were long ones. Let's take a look and see if it would be any different for a boy . . .

The following excerpt illustrates a more typical teachable moment. Barbara had been teaching about foods eaten Long, Long Ago, establishing that cave people had to hunt for meat and gather foods such as berries and eggs. The mention of eggs triggered the following interaction.

Haley: Could they have cake?
T: Could they have their cake? What would they have to have for a cake?
S: Flour.
T: You gotta have flour, and milk, and eggs, and oil, and sugar. Did they have all those things?
Ss: No.
T: So, Haley, could they make a cake?
Haley: No.

Barbara welcomed this question because it referred to a food that had to be made from combined ingredients rather than eaten with minimal processing. Also, she interpreted this as a thoughtful "wonder" indicating that the student was actively thinking about the topic. Consequently, she suspended her intended flow in order to address the question beyond just saying "yes" or "no." In the process, she modeled the reasoning involved in developing not merely an answer but an explanation as well.

Two examples of fruitful student questions appear in the following excerpt. Barbara had just finished her basic teaching about developments over time in clothing manufacture, which included showing illustrations of pioneers spinning and weaving using eighteenth-century machines. She then invited questions.

T: A.J., what are you wondering?
A.J.: How did they like make the machines?
T: Hmmm. When people are inventing things, they might take a machine that is already around and then change some things to make it better. Or maybe they say, "Hmmm, this job of weaving is really hard. I wonder what I could do to make it easier?" And that's what happened all along. People came up with new ideas for clothing and weaving and sewing. They would say, "Here's this machine. How can I make it better?" Or, "Wow, I bet there's a way we could make a machine that could do this job." Then they came up with the idea. Sometimes you can find a book that will explain what the person was thinking and what they tried. We have some of those books about clothes. I'll put them in the maroon crate for you to read. Laurel, what are you wondering?
Laurel: When they make clothes, how do they make colors?
T: Hmmm. Colors are really interesting. They first started making colors long, long ago by putting different plants in water, which would change the color of the water, and then they'd put in the cloth. So if you made white cloth and you put some blueberries in, what do you suppose the cloth would turn?
Laurel: Blue.

T: Right, and they would use different plants and find out which plants would make the fabric turn different colors. Now today, people have figured out ways to put chemicals together to make like paints and dyes to make cloth different colors.

A.J.'s question about machines gave Barbara the opportunity to reinforce a big idea that she likes to emphasize frequently: inventions occur because people ask themselves how they can improve a process or product. Although she did not do so in this situation, she often adds that maybe some of her students will invent new ideas or technologies themselves. Then, Laurel's question gave Barbara an opportunity to expand on her clothing lesson by talking about dyeing the cloth. She viewed this as a worthwhile addition because she knew that colors are one aspect of clothing that is of special interest to children and because, as she stated, the story is interesting (her students were very taken with the idea that fruit juices can be, and were for a time, used as dyes).

Sometimes even students as young as Barbara's will raise questions to which she does not know the answer. For example, when she was teaching about transportation Long, Long Ago, a student asked if people rode wooly mammoths. Barbara was unsure about how to answer this, so she first stalled by asking students if they had heard the question and then repeating it for them (meanwhile formulating a response). Then she stated that she did not know for sure and would "look it up," but meanwhile she could give them her best guess. She explained that from what she knew about wooly mammoths, they were plenty big enough to ride but also aggressive and dangerous animals, so people probably did not attempt to ride them, just as they would not attempt to ride lions or tigers. Her response here was typical of the way that she consistently conveys that what we are learning is meaningful and is supposed to make sense, and that when we do not have an immediate answer for a question, we often can use our reasoning skills to develop the answer, or at least formulate a "best guess."

In general, *Barbara tries to remember her students' curriculum-relevant questions and comments, so she can connect back to them when opportunities arise in the future.* In some cases, she extends this to establish that certain students "own" certain questions, words, or special interests (so she can exploit those connections as extra memory cues for the class as a whole whenever these topics arise).

Responding to Unhelpful Student Questions and Comments

We have noted that some student questions and comments can be assimilated into the intended flow, and others create teachable moments that Barbara is willing to exploit even though it means suspending the flow temporarily. However, students also ask questions or make comments that are not helpful because they raise issues that are unrelated to the topic, are related to the topic but not to the big ideas that Barbara wants to develop, or are likely to create problems that she wishes to avoid. As with undesired responses to her own questions, *Barbara's handling of these undesired student questions and comments ranges from ignoring them to interrupting the flow in order to provide an extended explanation.*

Barbara ordinarily will not ignore a student's question, but she will ignore certain types of comments. Most of these are instantaneous personal reactions to something that she has said or shown in an illustration. Typically, they are voiced aloud but not addressed to anyone in particular. They include various "ooh" and "aah" reactions as well as comments such as "I've seen that before," "I know what that is," or "My grandpa has one of those on his farm."

She also ignores comments that are more substantive but do not carry much potential for profitable follow-up. For example, when she asked what farmers might do to nurture their crops once they have planted the seeds, several students gave expected and desired answers (water the plants, protect them from insects), but one suggested that the farmer might talk to the plants. This student appeared to be talking to himself rather than seeking to contribute to the lesson, and many of his classmates did not even hear what he said. Barbara did hear him but saw no pedagogical value in following up his comment, so she did not respond to it.

Instead of simply ignoring an unhelpful question or comment, Barbara typically will briefly acknowledge or respond to it and then resume the flow. For example, when she was teaching about how people Long, Long Ago relied on hunting and gathering to get food, Mariah commented that the people could get a lot of animals and keep them with them to use as needed (i.e., she anticipated herding as an advance over hunting). Barbara gave a brief acknowledgement ("That's right, that's what happened later on"), but then returned to hunting and gathering. Later, when she got to herding, she noted that Mariah had mentioned this earlier. This is her typical practice when students ask a question or make a comment about something that will be addressed later or in a subsequent lesson: make a brief acknowledgment at the time, note that the point will be taken up later, and when it is taken up, credit the student who mentioned it previously.

Early in a lesson about family composition, Barbara had defined and shown illustrations of the nuclear family and then went on to introduce the extended family, again using an illustration from a book.

T: This is an extended family. It also happens to have a mom and dad but it also has an uncle and a grandmother. An extended family doesn't have to have an uncle—it could be an aunt or maybe a cousin, but it's somebody other than just the people that are the mom and the dad and the kids that are at the house together.

S: Some families don't live together.

T: A family doesn't all have to live together, but they're still part of your family. Folks that don't live with you but are part of your family, we call those relatives. Relatives is just a fancy word that means the people in your family that you're related to.

Barbara provided only a brief response to this comment and then resumed the flow, for two reasons. First, she knew that she was going to get to different types of families (including separated and reconstituted families) as the lesson progressed, and she wanted to stick with her intended sequence. Second, the student who made this comment had a complicated family situation that Barbara did not want to get into at that moment.

During the part of a lesson about transportation around the world that focused on economic issues, Barbara showed a picture of a man in an undeveloped rural area taking plants he had grown to market. A student asked what the plants were. Barbara said that she was not sure and then quickly returned to the flow, talking about how he used a wagon to transport the plants.

In another transportation lesson, a student asked what a motor home is. Barbara knew that later in the lesson she was going to be using a book that showed a good illustration of a motor home, so she gave only a brief answer to the student's question at the time, but a more extensive one later. A parallel situation arose during her land-to-hand lesson on bananas, when a student asked why it is hottest near the equator. Wanting to maintain focus on the banana story, Barbara said that she would explain later. She did follow through on this promise subsequently, using the analogy that if you hold your hand near a hot light bulb, the part of your hand that is closest to the bulb gets the warmest.

Two typical examples of briefly responding and then moving on with the intended flow occur in the following excerpt. Barbara had been teaching about dairy farms, emphasizing that they produce milk and products made from milk. She added that dairy farms were the source of "all of the milk that we drink here at school and the milk that you buy from Quality Dairy." Then she asked her students why Quality Dairy stores were given the name "Quality Dairy."

S: Probably because they got the milk from a dairy farm.
T: Doesn't that make sense? Quality Dairy started out selling milk, cheese, and butter, and ice cream and yogurt.
S: They sell doughnuts.
T: Then they started selling doughnuts and other stuff, too, but they started out selling stuff from the dairy farm. The farmer would take his stuff right there and he would sell it to them.
S: There's a butter churn. (Reacting to a detail on an illustration.)
T: You were looking at a butter churn because those were some of the tools they used long ago to make butter and ice cream. Nowadays we use machines to even milk the cows. [Goes on to explain more about dairy farm operations.]

The students' comments about doughnuts and the butter churn were both accurate observations but undesired in this situation because Barbara wanted to focus on dairy farms and their products. Consequently, she responded directly to each comment, but then quickly resumed the intended flow.

In the following excerpt, Barbara's initial question elicited a desired response, but her expansion on that response triggered an undesired comment from one student, and, in addition, her response to that comment triggered an undesired question from another student.

T: What do they build bridges out of now that makes them better than when they were just a vine?

S: Steel.
T: Steel. Bridges are now made out of steel and cement.
S: Bricks.
T: There are some bridges built out of bricks, but the new bridges are usually made out of cement, but you might find a bridge that's made out of bricks.
S: What are bricks made out of?
T: Bricks are similar to cement. [Goes on, but shifts content from bridges to tunnels.]

In this situation, Barbara wanted to focus on inventions that made it easier for people to cross rivers, but the initial comment and especially the subsequent question about bricks threatened to derail the focus from crossing rivers to the composition of construction materials. Consequently, she made a very brief response to the question (not really answering it) and then moved on with the intended flow.

When students' questions or comments are clearly off-topic, Barbara may begin her response by noting this, both as a way to remind students to stay on-topic and as a way to provide a rationale for her unwillingness to deal with it at the moment. The following example is typical in this regard. Barbara had been teaching about assembly lines in the auto industry, and a student interrupted with a question about keys, a topic that had not been addressed earlier in the lesson and was not relevant now.

S: How come they didn't have keys back then?
T: Are you wondering about keys for cars?
S: Yes.
T: Is that something that we're talking about right now?
S: No.
T: That's a really great question. Will you remember to ask me at the end and I'll tell you about that? [Student nods, Barbara resumes intended flow.]

When Barbara Has to Stop and Regroup

Most of the time, Barbara is able to move through her intended flow relatively smoothly, accommodating unexpected content in students' answers, questions, or comments by assimilating the content into the ongoing flow or making a brief digression and then returning. Occasionally, however, events develop in such a way as to leave Barbara at least momentarily confused and uncertain, either about what the student is saying and where this idea is coming from, or about how she should respond. These situations may lead to loss of lesson momentum or even to a decision to change the planned agenda, as Barbara suspends the flow temporarily while she diagnoses the situation and decides what to do.

For example, one day she was reading to her students from an illustrated book about how the pioneers met their food, clothing, and shelter needs. Now, she typically uses such books only for their illustrations, supplying her own narrative to provide content rather than reading the book's text, but this was before she had attained this degree of confidence in her content knowledge. She tried reading from the text in this situation, but, sure enough, she encountered problems. The book was not organized around the big ideas that she wanted to emphasize, and it did not include any of the personal connections to her students that she commonly incorporates in her narratives. Worse, it did not define new terms when they were introduced, and in other ways it lacked the coherence and reader-friendliness features that make it easier for students to understand and remember what they read in informational texts (Beck and McKeown, 1988). As a result, too much information was coming at the students too quickly, so they picked up just bits and pieces of what they were hearing. They could not connect the pieces coherently, or, worse, connected them inappropriately.

One student said, "They had to spin the cows—get things off of the cows" (confusing spinning with shearing and sheep with cows). Other students made reference to spinning yarn (rather than spinning the raw material into yarn) and gathering syrup (rather than sap) from the trees. Recognizing the problem, Barbara stopped reading extensive passages from the text, backed up and went over some of what she had read, and subsequently read shorter passages before stopping to insert explanations or question the students to check their under-standing.

When she experiences such problems with books or other props, Barbara will omit or substitute for those props in future lessons, or else modify her use of them. For example, in telling the land-to-hand story of peanut butter, she uses a book on the topic that contains many useful illustrations. However, she does not read the text to her students, because it is not organized around the big ideas she plans to develop. The text is wordy but nevertheless sketchy because it omits some important information. Also, it can be distracting and potentially confusing because it incorporates several anomalies that she prefers to avoid (peanuts are legumes, not nuts; they might be considered vegetables because they grow on a plant but they are classified with the meat group because they have protein). These problems with the book's text led her to shift to her own narration as the primary vehicle for presenting content, using the book only for its illustrations.

Anything that Barbara reads or shows to students that includes details extraneous to her intended flow can stimulate questions or comments that require her to insert unplanned explanations. For example, when teaching about the manufacture of pasta, she showed an illustration of a pasta-making machine. She had focused on prototypical pasta (spaghetti noodles) and intended to maintain that focus, but the illustration included depictions of different types of pasta. A student noted this and asked about one of these types (tortellini), so Barbara felt it necessary to suspend the flow temporarily while she explained that tortellini are meat-filled pasta. She would not have included this content if the student had not asked about the tortellini illustration.

Sometimes the students are not satisfied when Barbara attempts to provide only a brief response to their question or comment. They pursue the point on the spot or bring it back again later in the lesson (or even later in the week), which indicates to Barbara that she needs to provide a more extensive explanation. For example, one day she was quickly reviewing main ideas from her lesson on silk. As she was repeating the reasons why silk is an expensive fabric ("it comes from far away, takes long to make, you have to feed a lot of silkworms to make it"), a student interjected the comment, "You've gotta find them." This wasn't exactly correct, because farmers grow silkworms rather than search for them. However, time was getting short, and this detail was not directly related to the points she wanted to make, so Barbara simply repeated the statement (as if it were an accurate addition to her list) and moved on. However, when she subsequently shifted into her "ticket out" activity requiring each student to state something learned in that day's lesson, the same student said, "They had to find the silkworms." At this point, Barbara took the time to explain that although the first people to realize that silk fibers could be collected from silkworms had to find the silkworms, later people realized that they could preserve silkworms' eggs to get more silkworms in the future.

Occasionally things do not go at all as expected, and Barbara has to stop and regroup. For example, she begins the first lesson on transportation by defining and giving examples of transportation and underscoring its importance by noting that everything in the room was transported there. Then she invites students to state their wonders about transportation. Ordinarily, this leads to questions that reflect or are easily assimilable to some of the main points she wants to develop (e.g., Did they have transportation Long, Long Ago?). One year, however, this segment unfolded as follows.

T: Tim, what are you wondering about?
Tim: If there are any plants that came here.
T: Plants. Where do plants get transported from? [Writes this on the wonders list.] What else are you wondering about? Mikey?
S: Plants came from a garden.
T: I don't want you to be thinking about a garden. I want you to be thinking about transportation.
S: How do they transport glass, like in windows?
T: How do they transport glass? I don't want you thinking about our room. I want you to be thinking about transportation. What do you wonder about transportation? What do you wonder about transportation, Derek?
S: How did God get transported here?
T: I want you to think about transportation. Tell me about something that transports things from one place to another. What do you wonder about trucks?
S: How do trucks get here?
T: How do trucks get here? The trucks do the transporting. How do the trucks get here? That's mighty curious. How do trucks get here? I never even thought about that before, Derek.
S: They make them at a factory.
T: We're not answering questions today. What are we doing, Mikey?
S: Asking.
T: Yeah, we're asking. How do trucks get transported? Laurel, what are you wondering about?
S: How do they transport plants?
T: That's what Tim was wondering about. Are you thinking about the same thing?

S: Yeah.
T: Cory, what are you wondering about?
S: How did they invent transportation?
T: What, are you thinking about transportation and inventions? Can I just write that down—inventions? Don't you wonder about a lot of stuff about inventions? Transporting. We just need to know about transportation inventions. A.J., what are you wondering about? What kind of transportation were you thinking about?
S: How do they take erasers to stores?
T: How do they take things to stores? Erasers are in stores. How do they transport things to stores? Not just erasers—don't you wonder about pencils and crayons and glue and shirts and shoes? How do things get to stores? Sam, what are you wondering about?
S: How do they make eggplants?
T: That's an interesting question about plants. What are we talking about today?
S: Transporting.
T: Transporting. So what do you suppose might go along with transporting?
S: How do they make kinds of transportation?

The students' initial questions baffled Barbara briefly because she didn't see their relevance to transportation until she realized that, as a carryover from the previous segment, some of her students were still focusing on objects in the room (plants, window glass). Once she made this realization, she reminded them to focus on transportation, but the very next question she elicited was not easily addressed ("How did God get transported here?"). Not wanting to go down that path, Barbara chose not to respond to the question and instead reemphasized that she wanted to elicit wonders about transportation. To make it easier, she then asked what the students wondered about trucks, expecting to elicit questions about what kinds of things are transported in trucks or where trucks pick up and unload their cargo.

However, the next question was "How do trucks get here?" This was relevant but potentially confusing because although trucks can be transported (e.g., on trains), they are prototypical vehicles for transporting other things. She complimented the questioner and then called on another student, hoping to move on to something closer to her planned agenda. However, one student commented that trucks are made at factories and another asked about transporting plants (repeating an earlier question). Then she got two more desirable questions and elaborated on them in her responses to underscore their connections to transportation and reformulate them to suit her agenda (e.g., shifting from how erasers get to stores to how things in general get to stores). However, the next student asked about how they make eggplants (another carryover from the earlier focus on plants), a question that had nothing to do with the topic at hand. Only after yet another reminder of the kinds of wonders she was seeking did the class begin to generate more desired responses consistently.

Students' difficulties in "getting into" voicing wonders about transportation were not completely unexpected. Even though children have many personal experiences with transportation and see it occurring around them every day, it is not as immediately salient to them as topics such as food, clothing, or family. Furthermore, their thinking about transportation focuses more on the transportation of people than the transportation of goods and raw materials. This is why Barbara defines transportation, gives examples, and develops some initial big ideas about it before inviting students' wonders. In most years, this is sufficient to enable her students to articulate wonders that are not only relevant to the topic but useful as lead-ins to upcoming lessons. That year, however, an unusual combination of unexpected events left her temporarily confused and required her to insert an unusual degree of structuring and scaffolding to get the intended flow up and running.

Even more rarely, a single event occurs that is so unexpected as to boggle Barbara's mind, as seen in the following excerpt. Jan and Jere believe that this event is in a class by itself as the funniest thing that happened throughout our long collaboration, although Barbara is less amused. As part of the story of peanut butter, she talked about how the factory not only produces and packages the peanut butter for shipment to stores, but advertises the product to make people aware of it. She defined commercials as messages telling us to buy certain products, then developed the idea as follows.

T: Have you seen commercials?
Ss: Yeah.
T: You know what commercials are, right?
Ss: Yeah. [Not all students were responding, so Barbara decided to give an example.]
T: You're watching *SpongeBob*, and all of a sudden it stops, and what happens?
S: A commercial comes on.
T: And maybe the commercial says, "We've got the peanut butter with the most peanuts in it. It tastes terrific." Have you heard them say something like that?"
Ss: Yeah.
T: "Our peanut butter is the peanut butteriest." That's called a commercial, and the owner is trying to talk you into buying his peanut butter. He pays somebody to make what we call an ad or a commercial. It's commercial advertising. Do you know what? Maybe you'd want to be the person that thinks of the idea. Maybe you'd want to be the actor that pretends to love the peanut butter. Maybe you'd want to be running the TV camera that tapes the commercial and puts it on our TV. Maybe you'd want to direct the commercial and tell the actors what to do. Look at all those jobs, just for making a commercial ... OK, while they're making a commercial and running it on *SpongeBob SquarePants* and talking you into buying this man's peanut butter, they're putting it in the jar at the factory. Now they're putting it in the boxes. Who puts it in the boxes? Tell me, everybody.
Ss: SpongeBob SquarePants!
T: ... [significant pause] SpongeBob SquarePants does *not* put the peanut butter in the boxes!
S: Factory workers.

This was a "when bad things happen to good teachers" moment. The lesson had been moving along smoothly, and when Barbara temporarily shifted attention from events at the factory to efforts to advertise the product, she gave an example that connected nicely with the students' experiences (the commercials that interrupt their favorite cartoon shows). In the process, she introduced some relevant vocabulary, clarified that commercial advertising is intended to persuade us to buy the sponsor's product, and mentioned several potential career options in the advertising industry. Then she attempted to shift attention back to events at the factory, wanting to focus on factory workers packing jars of peanut butter into boxes.

The enthusiastic answer that she elicited with her "Who puts it in the boxes?" question left her momentarily stunned, dismayed, and speechless. Under other circumstances, she probably would have said something like "You're thinking of the commercials, but now we're talking about what the workers are doing at the peanut butter factory." In this case, however, all she could come up when she recovered her senses was an emphatic negation of the "SpongeBob" response. Fortunately, one of her students then supplied the desired response, which enabled her to resume the intended flow.

This concludes a series of chapters on the discourse patterns that occur during Barbara's whole-class lessons. In Chapter 15, we shift attention from her lessons and discourse to her learning activities and assessments.

Chapter 15

Activities and Assessments

Activities include the full range of learning tasks, activities, and assignments—anything that students are expected to do in order to learn, apply, practice, evaluate, or any other way respond to curricular content. We do not make clear distinctions between activities and assessments (and we treat them together in this chapter) because any worthwhile activity can serve both learning and assessment functions. Activities may call for speech (answering questions, participating in discussion, debate, or role play), writing (short answers, longer compositions, research reports), or goal-directed action (conduct an inquiry, solve problems, construct models or displays). They may be done either in or out of the classroom (i.e., as homework); in whole-class, small-group, or individual settings; and under close and continuing supervision or largely independently (on one's own or in collaboration with peers).

Jere and Jan have studied fundamental questions about the nature and roles of learning activities: What are the intended functions of various types of activities? How do they perform these functions? What makes the best activities so good? What faults limit the value of less ideal activities? What principles might guide planning and implementation of activities (Alleman & Brophy, 1992; Brophy, 1992; Brophy & Alleman, 1991, 1992)? They emphasize that activities are not self-justifying ends in themselves but instead are means for helping students to accomplish major curricular goals.

Activities provide structured opportunities for students to interact with content, preferably by processing it actively, developing personal ownership and appreciation of it, and applying it to their lives outside of school. Different types of activities serve different functions, which evolve as units develop. When introducing new content, teachers might emphasize activities designed to stimulate interest, establish an initial learning set, or link the new learning to prior learning (such as by providing opportunities for students to compare and contrast, or make predictions from the old to the new). When developing content, teachers might stress activities that allow students to extend and apply their learning. When concluding the unit, teachers might plan activities that help students to appreciate connections or provide opportunities to synthesize their learning.

The key to the effectiveness of an activity is its cognitive engagement potential—the degree to which it gets students actively thinking about and applying content, preferably with conscious awareness of their goals and self-

Table 15.1 Barbara's use and adaptation of activities suggested in selected lesson plans from the Food Unit

Lesson 1: Functions of Food

Activities in the Lesson Plans	Barbara's Use or Adaptation
1 Give each student an illustration of a food item, then call out the names of each of the food groups. Students should be prepared to stand when you call the name of the food group that their item belongs to, and explain why the item belongs in that group.	1 Used as suggested.
2 Ask students to put their heads together at their tables and share the most interesting ideas they learned about food. Elicit two responses from each table, record them on newsprint, and have the class read them aloud.	2 Omitted: Barbara felt that her students would not yet have sufficient knowledge for this activity.
3 Assessment: Have the class complete a journal entry for a class book that focuses on the functions of food.	3 Incorporated this idea into a larger development of a class food book, beginning here with entries about each of the food groups.
4 Home assignment: Using the provided food pyramid worksheet, have students work with family members to tally the numbers of servings in each category that family members ate during a given day, then discuss whether the meals were balanced, then return the sheets to class for a discussion on "our eating habits."	4 Used as suggested.

Lesson 2: Choices: Snacks

Activities in the Lesson Plans	Barbara's Use or Adaptation
1 Have students work in pairs to identify nutritious snacks that obviously fall into the food pyramid's categories and develop posters representing nutritious snacks.	1 Omitted: Barbara preferred the optional activity suggestion.

Table 15.1 Continued

Activities in the Lesson Plans	Barbara's Use or Adaptation
2 Optional: Using provided recipes, make and sample a variety of nutritious snacks. In the process, bring out information such as the geographic origins of the ingredient products, whether they are eaten in their natural state or processed first, and how these factors contribute to their costs.	2 Used as suggested.
3 Assessment: Distribute copies of a provided list of snacks, read each item, and have students mark either N (nutritious) or J (junk food) on the line beside each word. Discuss responses, underscoring the importance of nutritious snacks, then have the class prepare a group journal entry describing what snacks are, why we need to select nutritious snacks most of the time, and how geography, climate, economics, culture, and personal preference influence our choices.	3 Barbara did a whole-group version of the N versus J classification task as a sponge activity at another time.
4 Home assignment: Have students discuss with their families their favorite nutritious snacks and bring a recipe for one of them to school, then compile a recipe book of nutritious snacks.	4 Implemented to the extent of compiling a list of nutritious snacks, but not a recipe book.

Lesson 3: Changes in Food over Time

Activities in the Lesson Plans	Barbara's Use or Adaptation
1 Have 12 students stand and line up in a row to illustrate how in the past it took 12 people to do farm work that today requires only one farmer, so the other 11 people can do other jobs.	1 Used as suggested.
2 Option: Have students work in pairs. Hold up a food item or picture, ask pairs to determine where it fits on the chart listing cave people's foods, pioneer foods, and our foods today, giving reasons for their answers.	2 Used as suggested.

Activities in the Lesson Plans	Barbara's Use or Adaptation
3 Optional: Divide the class into three groups (cave dwellers, pioneers, and people today). Show foods and have groups decide if their group had that food available. Call on spokespersons to give answers and reasons.	3 Omitted in favor of previous options.
4 Optional: Give each table group a blank timeline and an envelope of food cutouts. Have them place items in appropriate places on the timeline and then explain how the foods were secured during each time period.	4 Omitted in favor of other options.
5 Assessment: In collaboration with one or more students, role-play a family from each period. Talk about what foods were eaten, how they were secured, trade-offs that the family faced, and what they did to overcome challenges. Finally, brainstorm all of the ways of getting food (hunt, forage, grow crops, raise animals, shop, eat at restaurant) and have them decide which they prefer and why.	5 Omitted: Barbara did not think her students had enough information to enable them to role-play successfully. Instead, she asked them to choose a time they would like to live in and tell why.
6 Home Assignment: Have students explore with family members what foods at their evening meal are available to them only because of modern means of preserving or transporting foods. Students should bring their lists to class to share, and a master list will be compiled.	6 Used as suggested.

Lesson 7: The Story of Bananas

Activities in the Lesson Plans	Barbara's Use or Adaptation
1 Use the timeline, cut out pictures, and a blank calendar to retell what happens during the two weeks between the day that bananas are picked in Honduras and the day they reach our tables. Note the many workers on whom we depend to bring bananas to us.	1 Used as suggested.
2 If time permits, have each student draw a picture of the worker that he or she enacted during the lesson and then describe it to the class.	2 Omitted: Barbara's students could not yet draw such pictures accurately enough to make this activity worthwhile for them.

Table 15.1 Continued

Activities in the Lesson Plans	Barbara's Use or Adaptation
3 Ask students to take turns sharing the most interesting ideas they learned from the lesson.	3 Omitted: too time consuming.
4 Lead the class in developing a list of things learned about bananas and post the list for use as a reference when making journal entries. Then have students make individual entries in their journals describing things they learned.	4 Used as suggested.
5 Home assignment: have students take home their journal entries and use them as resources for retelling the story of bananas to family members. Then, have them list with family members the ways that bananas are used in their diets and bring their lists to class for group sharing.	5 Used as suggested.

Lesson 8: The Story of Peanut Butter

Activities in the Lesson Plans	Barbara's Use or Adaptation
1 Using the supplied recipe, lead the class in making your own version of peanut butter.	1 Used as suggested.
2 Write brief sentences on paper strips describing steps in the peanut butter story (e.g., "harvest peanuts," "grind peanuts."). Provide a set of strips to each table group and then have the groups collaborate to put them in order.	2 Used as suggested, except that the sentences were on cards rather than paper strips.
3 Assessment: Pose questions about key steps in the banana story, give small groups time to confer among themselves, then call on a spokesperson from each group to give the group's response.	3 Omitted because of time constraints.
4 Assessment: Provide students with sheets numbered 1–10. Read statements and have students decide whether it is correct (Y) or incorrect (N).	4 Omitted: Barbara did not think that her students were ready for this kind of test format yet.

5   Home Assignment: Send home the peanut butter recipe and encourage students to share the story about peanut butter with their families, then develop a list of possible nutritious snacks using peanut butter. They should bring the lists, and if possible, recipes for the snacks, to the next class session.

5   Used as suggested.

Lesson 9: The Story of Pasta

Activities in the Lesson Plans	Barbara's Use or Adaptation
1 Pass out sets of materials that illustrate and describe 12 steps in the pasta story, ordered randomly. Have students work in pairs to put these steps in the proper order.	1 Omitted: Barbara questioned the cost-effectiveness of this activity, especially given her first graders' limited reading skills.
2 Using 12 "helpers" who each receive one card, call on them to stand and interact with you as you review the 12 steps in the pasta story.	2 Used as suggested.
3 Assessment: Give each student 12 strips of paper with the steps for making pasta, have each individual place the steps in order, then check responses with a partner. Then as a class, prepare a group journal entry that focuses on the main ideas. Each student will take home a copy of the group journal entry.	3 Omitted the activity calling for placing the 12 steps in order (viewed as not cost effective) but did use the group journal entry activity as described.
4 Home Assignment: Have each student take home a copy of the group journal entry and read it to family members, then develop a list of ways that pasta is used in the family's meals, underlining their favorites. Bring list to school to share with class.	4 Used as suggested.

Instead of scheduling pair-sharing of newly learned ideas at the end of one day's lesson, Barbara may schedule it at the beginning of the next day's lesson, especially if the same lesson is stretched across two days or the second lesson builds directly on the first. In these situations, the pair-share activity functions not just as a review, but as a way to stimulate relevant prior knowledge in preparation for the new lesson. For example, one of the lessons in the food unit involved developing a chart listing foods eaten even Long, Long Ago; foods not available Long, Long Ago but available to the Pilgrims and pioneers (Long Ago); and foods not available until Modern Times. Because the next day's lesson was going to follow up on that lesson, Barbara began by displaying the chart, reminding the class of the previous day's activities, and then allowing time for pair-sharing about the food choices available at the three time periods (again, this allowed her to assess which big ideas from the previous day had stuck with her students and which needed cementing). Then she reverted to the whole-class lesson mode and shifted from reviewing the previous lesson to initiating the new lesson.

Barbara frequently uses pair-sharing as a way to help her students prepare for their home assignments. This is especially the case when the home assignment calls for first telling family members about big ideas learned in the day's lesson, then applying these ideas in an activity done jointly with the family members. In these situations, Barbara instructs her students to "talk with your partner about what you will share with your parents tonight when you tell them about today's lesson and work with them on your home assignment." One way or another (e.g., through her own modeling, calling on and interacting with individual students, or allowing time for pair-sharing), she always places special emphasis on any lesson content that will be used as the basis for the day's home assignment.

Barbara also uses pair-sharing as a way to respond to students' needs when they are eager to talk about something (right now!), but not necessarily in ways that will support the lesson's goals. When she introduces a topic that is especially interesting or important to her students, many of them may be eager to share personal experiences. This was the case, for example, after Barbara had introduced basic information about the six types of family configurations. Before continuing with the lesson, Barbara gave the class a few minutes to pair-share information about their own families. Similarly, on the day that students brought their completed food books from home, she gave her students a few minutes to talk with partners about their favorite pages before launching a more formal review in the whole-class lesson format.

Finally, Barbara sometimes will shift briefly into pair-share mode when her students have been perseverating on the same basic idea and she wants to broaden their focus. For example, to introduce the topic of functions of clothing she asked her students to give reasons why we wear clothing, hoping to elicit all, or at least most of, the four functions discussed in the lesson (modesty, protection, decoration, and communication). However, all of the answers she elicited were focused on protection from weather. Consequently, she introduced pair-sharing at this point to see if at least some of her students might move on to other functions. She monitored the conversations to listen for nonweather reasons that she could then bring out when she resumed the whole-class lesson.

Other Review Activities

Barbara has several formats that she uses when she wants to conduct more extensive reviews. One is blackboard baseball, in which table groups seek to score runs by accumulating hits (correct answers) before making three outs (incorrect answers). Individuals can choose whether they would like to try for a single, a double, a triple, or a home run (more difficult questions are worth more bases if answered correctly, but also are also more likely to lead to an out). Blackboard baseball is especially useful when time is short. It does not require writing and it causes students to listen carefully to peers because they are hoping for correct answers that will create runs for their team. With older students who have better writing skills, and especially if more time is available, she might use the carousel or cloze sentence format.

The cloze sentence (fill-in-the-blank) format involves displaying statements of big ideas from the unit but omitting a key word. Students are asked to read the sentence and supply the missing word. She might begin with a poster version of the cloze task, calling on individuals to respond to each item and then adding any necessary clarification or discussion. She then might follow up with paired or small-group versions in which students take turns reading and responding to the items.

The poster version is the kind of interactive (high-touch, low-tech) instructional resource that Barbara favors, and including it helps serve as a self-check for her to make sure that she has covered all the big ideas sufficiently. The follow-up paired or small-group version functions as foreshadowing, modeling, and practice for follow-up homework assignments based on copies of the poster. In the carousel format, students rotate to visit stations set up around the room and answer the questions or perform the activities presented there. Carousel activities are described in more detail later in this chapter.

Ticket-Out Activities

In addition to pair-sharing, other activities that occur almost daily are "ticket-out" activities and writing activities. Ticket-out activities provide review but more specifically require each individual student to make some kind of substantive response indicating comprehension of something taught in the day's lesson. Once students have responded satisfactorily to this accountability activity, they can move on to the next part of their day. Usually, the ticket-out activity only calls for the stating of something learned in the day's lesson. This can be challenging, however, because each student's statement must reflect something specifically taught that day (not something taught earlier or learned elsewhere), and it cannot repeat a statement already made by another student. Barbara will provide cues to help students who "freeze" in this situation, but, even so, it helps to hold them accountable for paying attention to and remembering the big ideas taught in her lessons (including paying attention to what is said by other students).

Sometimes the ticket-out activities are more conventional, involving processing and responding to instructional resources. For example, Barbara concluded one of the transportation lessons by giving each of her students a card showing a labeled illustration of a vehicle. As their ticket-out for the day, they would be required to tell her (when called upon individually) the name of the vehicle and whether it is used for land, water, or air transportation. To help prepare them, she told them to get help from a neighbor if they could not read the name of the vehicle, and she modeled the thinking processes that might be used to support responses (e.g., if the vehicle has wheels, it probably is intended to roll along the ground, so it probably is land transportation). She did more of this kind of structuring and modeling than usual because the illustrations of vehicles were cartoons that were often fanciful in ways that could be distracting (more authentic illustrations were not easily accessible). In addition, the same illustrations would be used in that day's home assignment, which also called for the classifying of vehicles within the same three categories of transportation. Another transportation lesson taught a few days later contained a similar ticket-out activity, this time built around distinctions between mass versus personal transportation.

Writing Activities

Another form of activity that occurs daily is writing. Barbara's students engage in many different kinds of writing, mostly during times allocated for literacy instruction. This includes keeping journals in which they record observations and big ideas about topics addressed in all subjects. In addition, at any given time, students usually are working on entries for a class book on the topic currently being addressed in science or social studies. So, even though Barbara typically devotes all or almost all of her science and social studies time to whole-class lessons (interrupted for brief pair-sharing or small-group activities), her students regularly write journal entries or material for class books in these subjects.

Other Common Activities

Review activities, home assignment preparation activities, pair-sharing, writing, and ticket-out activities occur daily. Less frequent, but still common, are sponge activities and activities that involve constructing lists or learning resources; sorting or categorizing; following sequences or steps; observing, describing, or comparing; or developing a class or group composition or product.

Sponge activities "soak up" unstructured or leftover time. Barbara does not need to rely on such activities nearly as much as most teachers do, and when she does, she emphasizes the reinforcing of big ideas rather than just keeping students busy with activities such as coloring. One form of sponge activity occurs when Barbara needs to interrupt her teaching temporarily in order to answer the phone or a knock at the door, get or prepare some instructional resource, or ask her students to move from one learning setting to another (e.g., leave their desks and gather on the rug in the social studies teaching area). Both to minimize potential disruptions and to help her students maintain a lesson focus during these times, she often will assign them some mental task to perform as they wait for her to return or make the needed transition.

For example, she might ask her students to think about what they have learned so far that they might want to restate during the ticket-out activity at the end of the class. Or she might assign a task that will prepare them for the next lesson segment (e.g., think of examples of concepts just introduced or wonders about a topic about to be introduced). At the conclusion of the interlude (when Barbara returns or when her students have completed the transition), she will follow up on this activity by calling on students to share their thinking.

Construction of lists or other learning resources occurs commonly. To introduce a map lesson, for example, she had table groups look at a selection of maps and develop lists of what they observed. In a lesson on childhood in the past, she had students look at the illustrations in books about family life among the Pilgrims and the pioneers, then develop lists of chores that children had to perform Long Ago. During lessons, Barbara frequently leads the class in constructing timelines, charts, graphs, or other learning resources.

Many activities involve categorizing, such as by assigning examples to types or noting steps in a sequence. During one of the food lessons, Barbara led her students in categorizing foods according to whether they were available to cave dwellers, not available to cave dwellers but eaten by pioneers, or eaten only in modern times. Various transportation lessons involved categorizing forms of transportation according to whether they are used on land, in water, or in the air; whether they are personal or mass transportation; or whether they are people powered, animal powered, or engine powered. One of the lessons in the communication unit involved looking at clips of television commercials and identifying which categories of persuasion techniques were used in them. Such classifying and sorting activities often involve co-construction of charts to provide visual representation of the groupings.

Sorting and classification tasks can be confusing if some of the examples can be included in more than one category. This occurs commonly during historical segments of units in which students are asked to classify examples of food (or clothing, transportation, etc.) with respect to the categories of Long, Long Ago, Long Ago, and Modern Times.

More generally, it often happens in social studies that some examples fit more than one category, because many social studies concepts have fuzzy boundaries or admit to exceptions (some things are mostly A but can be seen as B in certain respects). Barbara tries to anticipate these problems by phrasing definitions and examples in ways that minimize potential confusion and, where relevant, by emphasizing the possibility of the "both" category when examples could be classified as A only, B only, or both A and B.

Sequencing activities often occur with respect to timelines or to the land-to-hand sequences involved in developing products and bringing them to our stores. Sequences are likely to get special emphasis and review in class when they will be used as the bases for home assignments (as when students are expected to explain to family members what they have learned about steps in producing some product).

Barbara frequently asks her students to observe, describe, and make comparisons between objects or illustrations that she provides for them to examine. These activities allow her students to handle and satisfy their initial curiosity about instructional resources that will be used during a lesson, and the instructions to observe, describe, or compare establish a learning set to build upon later. Activities calling for application of these skills are frequently useful in social studies, although Barbara uses them even more than she might otherwise because the skills are emphasized in the science curriculum. This is one productive way for her to integrate across subjects.

For example, Barbara's experience in teaching about functions of clothing has taught her that her students usually already understand the protection and modesty functions, but are less familiar with the decoration and especially the communication functions. As a way to bring the latter functions home to them, she has them examine their own and their classmates' clothing, then engage in discussion of their observations. Her students' clothing typically includes many examples of the decoration and communication functions (e.g., T-shirts or sweatshirts with artistic decorations, team logos, and so on).

She also has her students observe and discuss cereal boxes and fruit snack packages to identify strategies being used to make the products appear attractive to potential purchasers (featuring ingredients/taste, healthfulness, cost, decorative packaging, premium offers, or celebrity endorsements). She includes potentially misleading examples such as packages showing attractive people doing impressive things that have nothing to do with consumption of the food product, as well as a box showing the cereal in a bowl with raspberries, when the box contains the cereal but not the raspberries.

In addition to journal writing and composing contributions to class books, Barbara's students also frequently engage in other forms of writing related to their social studies learning. As a follow-up to a lesson on advertising, for example, she engaged her class in composing a letter to another teacher, who was in charge of an upcoming bake sale to raise money for the school. This activity involved generating a list of ways that the bake sale might be advertised in the community, then composing a letter conveying this advice to the teacher in charge of the bake sale. This activity proved difficult for her students because it called for communicating in complete sentences. More typically, she involves them in contributing to posters composed of single words or short phrases.

Less Frequent Activities

Barbara's lessons occasionally incorporate role play, simulations, or skits. Some of these activities do not involve much more than role assignment, as when one student is designated as the owner of the banana plantation, another as the foreman, another as a truck driver, and so on. Occasionally, these role assignments involve sustained simulation or role enactment.

For example, Barbara organized her class into an assembly line to make sandwiches efficiently. In this simulation, each student actually carried out the task required at his or her step in the sequence. She also attempted a pretend simulation of an assembly line constructing school buses, although this proved difficult to implement cost-effectively. She found it easy to convey that each person does a different part of the total job, but difficult to show that this allows the group as a whole to make more units per hour than they could make if working on the task individually. Everyone is continuously busy in real assembly lines, but in the simulation, each individual did his or her piece, then stood watching. Also, it was difficult for her to keep track of the "jobs" that each individual had been assigned and to get the group lined up in the right order. One student never was clear about what he was supposed to do; another wanted to leave to wash glue off of her hands; and there were three "leftover" students who did not have assigned roles. Finally, students were focused much more on their personal roles than on the functioning of the assembly line as a whole. Barbara tried to keep them involved by assigning them to act as storytellers who would verbalize and record what was happening, but this did not work very well because of the frequent interruptions and logistical confusions involved in implementing the activity itself.

Barbara has used this simulation effectively with other classes, but on this day, a combination of practical difficulties undermined its effectiveness. Our discussion led us to wonder if it might be better to use something else as the basis for illustrating an assembly line, arranging to show a video of a working assembly line in the auto industry, or using a smaller assembly line and allowing more students to observe.

As a variation on more conventional matching or classification tasks, Barbara sometimes uses riddles. In one example, she gave clues based on the common functions of particular forms of transportation (e.g., it carries food products from warehouses to food stores) and asked her students to identify the type of transportation described (e.g., trucks).

As a way to apply the concepts she has been developing, Barbara sometimes will engage her students in problem solving or decision making based on those concepts. For example, after teaching about forms of transportation and use of maps, she engaged her students in helping her plan travel arrangements for a (fictional but realistic) family reunion to be held in the Lansing area. The students were asked to discuss and reach agreement on how relatives located in various places should travel to Lansing (fly or drive, and if drive, following what route?).

Barbara sometimes incorporates students' illustrations, especially when she can use the products as instructional resources. For example, as a follow-up to a lesson on how childhood talents and interests can become the basis for lifelong avocations or even careers, she asked her students to draw illustrations of themselves doing things they were good at. She then questioned the students about and led discussions of the talents illustrated in the pictures, bringing out potential paths to careers. Later, as a conclusion to the childhood unit, she had her students draw, on small fabric squares, pictures of something they had learned about childhood. She then sewed these together into a quilt that was displayed in the classroom as a remembrance of the unit.

A rare but significant form of activity is the field trip. Barbara plans field trips as integral parts of, not interruptions in, her social studies teaching. For a trip to a local museum, for example, she divided her class into small groups led by parent volunteers. Each group was supplied with a camera and data sheet and asked to photograph and describe two things in each square of a four-by-four matrix: items relating to clothing, food, transportation, or families, situated either Long, Long Ago, Long Ago, Today, or in the Future.

Her transportation unit included a visit to a car dealership. As preparation, she engaged her students in brainstorming about what kinds of jobs they might see performed during the visit. She led them quickly through a number of books on transportation, focusing on their illustrations to identify jobs that they might encounter the next day, either during the visit to the dealership or in transit to and from it (e.g., emergency workers transporting people in an ambulance or police car). As students identified car dealership workers they might encounter the next day, she elicited questions they might ask these people (e.g., about their uniforms or about the nature of their work and how they felt about it).

She had arranged with the car dealership to make sure that her students saw and heard a lot about the jobs carried out there by different employees. The next day, the class traveled to the dealership by bus. On the way, she and the parent volunteers led small groups of students in noticing and recording forms of transportation and transportation-related occupations they observed during the trip. Later, during the visit itself, the small groups filled out forms summarizing what each of the observed jobs involved, what tools were used to perform it, and so on. During and after the trip, Barbara took every opportunity to draw parallels between the things that her students were learning about in class and things that the dealership staff mentioned as important in doing their jobs (not only skills and tools involved in working on cars, but problem solving, people skills, etc.).

Barbara finds field trips valuable and likes to schedule as many as she can, although transportation costs and access difficulties limit her opportunities. She wanted to schedule a visit to a supermarket during the food unit, for example, but was unable to do so because she could not work out compatible time schedules with the supermarket manager, even though he had approved initial plans.

Home Assignments

Most home assignments involve at least two of three common activities: (1) telling family members about big ideas learned in the day's lesson (often supported by copies of a co-constructed list or graphic), (2) talking with family members about some application of those big ideas to the family's functioning or about aspects of a new topic to be developed the next day, and (3) filling out a form briefly communicating the results of the discussion to be used as data for the next day's lesson.

Some of these discussions with family members involve simply talking about past or potential future activities (how the family came to live where it does, reasons for purchases and other economic decisions, ideas from other cultures that might be incorporated into the child's next birthday party). Others involve taking actions as a basis for filling out a data sheet (inspecting and discussing the house's heating system, going to a closet to inspect clothing labels to find out where the clothing items were manufactured, filling out a home safety inventory, using maps and other resources to plan a possible family vacation). The information recorded on the data sheets from these home assignments is then discussed the next day, sometimes with construction of graphs or other visuals that summarize and preserve the data.

A few home assignments are more demanding, such as those calling for the interviewing of people who work in sectors of the economy related to the cultural universals (food industry, transportation industry, etc.). In these cases, Barbara provides considerable structuring and scaffolding, preparing students for the assignments through thorough in-class directions and providing them with interview guidelines and questions. She encourages the students to engage in lengthy discussions with their interviewees, but only requires them to report a few highlights on the data sheet to be returned to class.

For many home assignments, she provides lists that can be used as a basis for discussing and then checking what the students or their families have done or would like to do, then adding information at the bottom (such as identifying and explaining the reasons for their favorite things or their plans for the future). Although the home assignments regularly call for students to interact with family members, she prefers assignments that the students can handle completely or at least mostly on their own, and avoids assignments that end up being done entirely or mostly by the parents.

Assessment

Jere and Jan view assessment as an integral component of curriculum and instruction, not just an add-on used mostly to provide a basis for assigning grades. The assessment component should reflect the same goal orientation and focus on development and application of big ideas that is emphasized in the curriculum as a whole (Brophy & Alleman, 2007; Newmann, 1997; Parker, 1991; Wiggins, 1989a, b).

Recognizing the need for accountability but concerned about high-stakes testing's narrowing effect on the curriculum, the National Council for the Social Studies (1990) has called for forms of assessment that are well aligned to major social studies goals, more complete in the range of objectives addressed, and more authentic in the kinds of tasks included. The NCSS guidelines call for assessment that (1) bases the criteria for effectiveness primarily on the school's own statement of objectives; (2) assesses progress not only in knowledge but in thinking skills, valuing, and social participation; (3) includes data from many sources, not just paper-and-pencil tests; and (4) is used for assessing student progress in learning and for planning curriculum improvements, not just for grading.

Conventional test formats (true–false, multiple choice, essays) can be used appropriately to measure progress toward certain instructional goals. However, a comprehensive assessment that attends to all of the major goals will also include other formats such as observation checklists, self-assessment checklists, open-ended "I learned" statements, reflective journal entries, performance assessments, or portfolios. Also, many instructional activities generate information about student progress and thus can be used as assessment tools.

Assessments are opportunities to take readings on student progress toward important goals. It is most critical that the assessment tools match the goals. Other considerations include their level of difficulty, their cost-effectiveness in terms of time and trouble, and their feasibility for use in the classroom with the students involved.

Assessments can be characterized as preliminary, formative, or summative, depending on whether they occur before, during, or at the end of a unit. Preliminary assessments focus on eliciting students' prior knowledge, including both valid ideas and misconceptions. They may be as simple as a TWL exercise (listing what I *Think* I know and what I *Want* to learn, with later attention to what I *Learned*), collection of "wonders" (students tell what they wonder about the content of the upcoming unit), or group or individual interviews focused on the unit's big ideas. With older students, a more formal pretest might be given. Whatever its form, the preliminary assessment should focus on the upcoming unit's goals and big ideas, and its results should be used to inform unit planning. These results can be revisited at the conclusion of the unit to document student learning.

Teachers should conduct ongoing formative assessment as the unit progresses, checking for student understanding of each new cluster of knowledge or skills. These assessments provide information about whether the class as a whole is ready to move on or needs further review, as well as identifying specific misunderstandings or other learning problems that will require follow-up with targeted individuals.

Summative assessments focus on students' understanding of and ability to apply big ideas emphasized in the unit as a whole. Each of Jan and Jere's units culminates with a review lesson designed to provide summative assessment information. Most of the tasks included in these assessments are relatively conventional, although some follow the laboratory or the carousel model.

For the laboratory model, stations are distributed around the classroom at desks, bulletin boards, whiteboards, wall charts, computer screens, or other appropriate places. Each station displays material from the unit, such as a chart, artifact, student product, or open book with a marked passage. Students visit the stations with clipboards, answer sheets, and pencils in hand. They follow the instructions posted there, record their answers, then move to the next station. If necessary, students are helped to read questions or understand the tasks called for at each station, but then required to respond on their own.

The carousel model is implemented most effectively if a parent volunteer or upper-grade mentor is available to serve as a reader/recorder for each group. If not, one student at each table is named scribe for the group. Each scribe receives a different-colored marker. When using the carousel model, Barbara sets up stations that each contain a question about the unit topic and chart paper for recording responses. There are as many stations as there are small groups in the class. Each group begins at the station where the question written at the top of the chart paper matches the color of its marker. The group has five minutes to discuss and record its response to the question. Then it moves to the next station to the left, keeping its own marker. The groups progress through all of the stations in this fashion, reading and discussing the questions and then recording their responses. As they proceed, they place a question mark beside any part of a response written previously by another group that they disagree with or are unclear about. This continues until all of the groups have responded to all of the questions and returned to their original stations. At this point, each group reviews all of the responses to the question at its station and prepares to expand on the question during a large-group discussion. For the unit on communication, for example, the carousel questions might include:

- What is communication?
- Why is communication so important to all of us?

- How has communication changed over time?
- What are examples of communication types?
- Why is mass communication so interesting?
- What can you tell us about signs, symbols, and signals—all important means of communication in our lives?
- What are things we need to consider when making decisions about how we spend our time, especially television viewing time?

Jan and Jere also recommend time-consuming but richly rewarding forms of evaluation such as portfolio assessment and student-led parent conferences. These formats enable both students themselves and their families to appreciate the progress that the students are making as the school year progresses.

Portfolio assessments might be scheduled two to four times per year. To prepare for them, students would develop a collection of artifacts representing their work across the quarter or semester. This portfolio might include research projects, essays, charts, graphs, maps, correspondence with pen pals, interview data and analysis, tests, notes from home assignments, or any other artifacts that reflect their progress in social studies. During reviews of these portfolios, the teacher might ask students to talk about each included artifact (i.e., explaining why it was included and what it shows about the student's learning). The teacher also might ask questions such as "Which pieces of work are you most proud of and why?" "What would you add or do differently the next time?" or "Which social studies unit was most meaningful to you and why?"

Once or twice during the year, portfolios also might be used during a student-led parent conference. Here, students explain and demonstrate their work not only to their teacher but to their parents or guardians. We have witnessed primary students conduct conferences with their parents regarding their social studies goals, showing work samples to represent where they are in their development, what aspects they need to work on more diligently, and what types of assistance and support they need from the family. These student-led parent conferences provide extraordinary opportunities for students to develop self-efficacy in the social education domain and for the teacher to establish or reinforce collaborative relationships with family members.

Other, less formal, options that Barbara uses include family night and learning celebrations. On family nights, family members come to an open house at the school. During the hour spent in her classroom, each of her students individually demonstrates to family members what he or she learned during the unit. To prepare for family night, Barbara and her students co-construct a list of learning opportunities experienced during the unit that can be shared with family members. For example, the following list was co-constructed for the family unit:

- Families are different: poster and graph in project area on blended, extended, single-parent, nuclear, foster, and adopted families.
- Families come from different countries: ancestor map in project area.
- Families have changed from Long, Long Ago to Long Ago to Today: timeline in project area.
- Families celebrate different holidays: poster and book in project area.

- All families have relatives: family tree and book in an adjoining room; "everybody says" poster in hallway.
- Your family teaches you: learning poster in project area.
- Some families speak different languages: poster on immigrants coming from other countries in project area.
- Sometimes families change: word cards and books in adjoining room.
- Families make choices about clothes, food, houses, jobs, and recreation (fun). They think about climate, available things, geography, and choices: poster in project area.
- All families are special: posters displayed in hallway (take home at end of evening).
- Families help each other: poster in adjoining room.
- Families get help in their community: map and poster in adjoining room.
- Families eat different foods: treats in cafeteria.
- Find Mrs. Knighton and tell her one interesting thing about tonight (in cafeteria, later).

Learning celebrations typically occur at the ends of units or the school year. Each student shares some significant understandings associated with one or more lessons. The audiences for these celebrations can include families, students from other classrooms, school administrators, or invited guests.

Both family nights and learning celebrations make use of co-constructed learning resources, children's books, and other artifacts. The activities expected of the students are kept simple to encourage them to focus on communicating what they have learned rather than on performing.

Barbara's Approach to Assessment

Barbara also views assessment as integral to curriculum and instruction rather than an add-on that provides a basis for grading. In fact, none of her assessments are designed specifically to provide input to report card grades, because her district's report card for the primary grades call for characterizing students' progress only in very general terms (e.g., progressing satisfactorily, needs improvement).

Nevertheless, Barbara maintains an ambitious assessment agenda, monitoring her students' conceptual understandings and skill development on a daily basis (not just at the ends of units). She uses the information she gleans from these assessments to adjust her lesson plans as units progress, to alter or elaborate each day's lesson plan in response to information about student needs that she acquires during the lesson, and to provide special input or scaffolding during her inter-actions with individual students.

In addition to tracking her students' attainment of intended outcomes (know-ledge and skill mastery), Barbara tracks their participation habits and learning strategies (how they take in new information, connect it to other information, use it in application situations, use learning resources, develop information through their own inquiry, and so on). This allows her to introduce a degree of individualization into her general structuring and scaffolding of her students

learning, taking into account personal characteristics and general learning-to-learn skills in addition to needs for assistance with specific learning objectives. Just as informing herself about her students and their families enables her to incorporate a lot of curricular personalization into her lessons, her attempts to keep abreast of all of her students' learning progress enable her to incorporate special adjustments targeted to individual needs. Most of this assessment is ongoing and occurs during daily lessons and activities rather than during tests or other formal assessments.

Barbara routinely begins units and lessons with stories drawn from her own life and the lives of her students, so her students are much less likely to be lost or confused than they might be if she launched into unfamiliar content more directly. Consequently, she does not use pretests. Also, although she usually invites her students to tell what they are wondering about the content of an upcoming unit, she ordinarily does not use KWL, TWL, or other techniques that call for asking students to tell what they know or think they know about this content. In part, this is because, after teaching the units for several years, she now has a good knowledge of which information her students are likely to know already and which is likely to need special emphasis.

Also, her students are very young and typically lacking in well-articulated and connected knowledge about the big ideas introduced in social studies, so inviting them to tell what they know or think they know about the topic typically yields not only a great many misconceptions, but a great many comments that have little or no relevance to the big ideas she wants to develop. Consequently, relatively formal preliminary assessment is less useful for her than it is for teachers working at higher grade levels.

Even so, she monitors her students carefully during these introductory parts of lessons, noting signs of recognition and interest but looking in particular for signs of confusion. Frequently, she will ask the students to raise their hands or signal thumbs up if they have had experiences like the one she is describing. If she is only concerned about one or two students, she will direct questions to those students and respond accordingly (providing extra structuring and scaffolding if needed).

Once she is confident that her students are ready for the day's basic content presentation, she delivers that presentation, using the narrative style described in previous chapters. Then, much of the rest of the lesson is devoted to review and elaboration built around assessment questions. She usually begins with expectant pauses that invite the whole group to supply a word that will complete a sentence (usually, one of the big ideas being developed that day). Then she begins directing questions to individuals, beginning with questions that require only the recalling of a word or two but progressing to questions that call for more thoughtful and elaborated answers.

Even when asking choral questions that call for group responses, she tries to keep track of individual students. Which ones are responding confidently and correctly? Which are unsure, incorrect, or unresponsive? She will target elaboration and follow-up to students who are not yet confident in their knowledge or are struggling with misconceptions, and she will question individuals who have not been responding overtly.

Barbara does a lot of this kind of reviewing early in the unit, as part of her effort to solidify a knowledge base to build on in subsequent lessons. She monitors students' answers to judge how much they have learned to date, whether they understand key vocabulary, and so on. As she develops the knowledge base, she begins asking more substantive questions that call for students not merely to recall but to connect and apply big ideas.

Often, she decides that she needs to do some prompting and scaffolding halfway through the lesson, because she has inferred that the big ideas did not stick very well with many of her students. She will work with the group as a whole and with targeted individuals until all of the students are 100 percent successful at some level. Then she will push them for more substantive responses.

Most lessons conclude with a "ticket-out" activity in which students are asked to share something they learned. She wants to determine what the group as a whole has acquired, including what is solid and what is still shaky. If many students mention aspects of the same idea, she can be confident that it is cemented. If something important is not mentioned by anyone, however, this tells her that the group did not connect to the information. If the day's lesson included a lot of ideas, she will ask each student to share a different idea.

In reviews held toward the ends of lessons or units, Barbara will include questions that go beyond the current content by asking students to connect it to lessons or experiences from the past or to what they are learning in other areas of the curriculum. She also will test for lingering misconceptions and if necessary provide additional clarification about points of confusion.

Barbara gleans most of her assessment information from questioning her students during lessons. However, she also assesses progress through follow-up activities and home assignments, and through writing activities included in her literacy program. Many of her in-class activities are forms of assessment, especially the cloze (fill-in-the-blank) exercises and tasks calling for students to sort stimulus objects into groups (e.g., food groups, types of transportation) or place them in serial order (e.g., historical events or steps in a manufacturing process).

When these activities expose limitations in her students' understandings, she responds accordingly. For example, the cloze item "Clothing is something that every person _____" produced the response "wears" instead of the expected "needs." This made her realize that although she had developed knowledge about the functions of clothing in detail, she had not placed much emphasis on clothing as a basic need. Consequently, she injected an explanation about this (as well as a brief review of the concepts of needs and wants) into one of the later lessons in the clothing unit.

The writing activities that Barbara includes in her literacy curriculum often double as opportunities for application and assessment of social studies content. Her students write about what they are learning in response journals, and she often invites or assigns them to compose journal entries about what they are learning in social studies. Also, many of the poems and stories that she includes in her literacy curriculum are chosen because they connect with social studies content. Discussion and writing assignments relating to these stories provide additional opportunities for her to assess her students' thinking about the social studies topics.

Formal and Informal Assessment

In planning for and talking about assessment, Barbara distinguishes between formal assessments conducted with the class as a whole and less formal assessments conducted with individual students (mostly during lessons). *Formal assessments* tend to focus on specific ideas from a particular lesson. For example, to assess her students' understanding of the categories in the food pyramid, she followed two days of teaching about the food pyramid with an assessment exercise calling for students to sort food pictures into their respective food groups. To help prepare them for the exercise, she modeled questions they might ask themselves about the foods to provide input into their decision making (Is it from a plant or an animal?) and assess their tentative conclusions (How do I know it belongs in the fruit and vegetable group?).

Informal assessments tend to be more holistic and pulled from material taught across several lessons. Many occur during conversations at lunch, during recess, or in other informal situations in which Barbara will pick up information that leads to adjustments in her plans for the following day. However, sometimes she will plan oral or even written (but nevertheless still informal) assessments, especially following a connected sequence of lessons.

In the food unit, for example, she might present illustrations of selected food items and ask her students to tell her as much as they can (or write as many sentences as they can) about each food item. A broad range of potential responses would be accurate and acceptable in this situation, although Barbara would be looking for connections to ideas taught in her lessons (concerning lettuce, for example, her students might identify it as a vegetable, state that it is part of a plant, or note that it is a healthy food if you do not put too much dressing on it).

Barbara frequently conducts informal assessments when going over her students' responses to home assignments. She usually asks each student to elaborate on what the student or family member wrote on the feedback sheet. This provides more information about where students are in their understanding of recently developed big ideas, and it also functions as an accountability mechanism (underscoring that her students are supposed to remember and think about the curriculum-related substance of the conversations with family members that occur as they carry out home assignments). She also will ask follow-up questions to engage her students in elaborating and applying what they are learning. For example, while reviewing responses to the home assignment calling for tallying food consumption on a particular day, she encouraged students to use the data as a basis for responding to questions such as: Are you a healthy eater? How do you know? Do you see ways to improve? What would a scientist say in response to your data?

In summary, assessment is integral to Barbara's teaching. She assesses continually, in ways that give her information about the progress of the class as a whole and each individual within it. They generate information about points that she has taught successfully (her students not only remember the content accurately, but show personal connections to it and can connect it to other content), as well as aspects of learning that are fragile or distorted (indicating the need to cement the new learning, cycle back and elaborate, or initiate other remedial instruction). Assessments also illuminate gaps or confusions in the progress of individual students, helping Barbara to determine what forms of additional support they will need in order to be successful.

She also views assessments as useful to her students, providing them with opportunities to talk or write about their learning, make connections, or explore applications. She emphasizes that activities and assessments are opportunities for them to test out what they know. This is part of her larger and continuing emphasis on self-regulation of learning, and the development of self-efficacy perceptions with respect to each of the school subjects.

Conclusion

This chapter brings to a close our substantive portrayal of Barbara's social studies teaching (see Brophy *et al.*, in press, for our portrayal of more generic aspects of her teaching). The book concludes with a brief Afterword, and then an Appendix designed to support reflection on and application of the big ideas about teaching that we have emphasized.

Afterword

This book has offered detailed explication of Barbara's social studies teaching, backed by detailed analysis of the rationales for her planning decisions and in-the-moment adjustments. It illustrates how teaching at a high level requires detailed knowledge of both the curriculum and the students' learning trajectories and home backgrounds; goal-oriented planning focused around powerful ideas; adjustment of even basically sound unit plans to fit local circumstances; fleshing out of a plan by assembling needed instructional resources and adding personal connections to students; making adjustments "on the fly" to take advantage of teachable moments or address issues raised by students' comments or questions; continuous monitoring and assessment of individual and group progress; and reflection with an eye toward adjusting plans for the future.

We have presented many aspects of Barbara's teaching in enough detail to allow you to imitate them. Barbara is an exemplary model, so imitating her teaching is appropriate, up to a point. She would be the first to tell you, however, that rather than simply replicating what she does, you should follow the same reflective approach that she follows: think carefully about the degree of fit between what she does and what would work best in your particular teaching situation, and adjust accordingly.

To facilitate this kind of adaptation, she finds it useful to anticipate and rehearse the intended lesson flow. She generates detailed images of anticipated narrative explanations and teacher–student discourse, making adjustments to the initial versions whenever it appears that they would not support progress toward the major goals or would not work well with her students. She also monitors carefully during instruction and reflects on it afterwards to take note of any needed adjustments in her plans, either short term (e.g., beginning the next day with extra review of content that her students struggled with in this day's lesson) or long term (e.g., changing plans for how this lesson or section of the unit will be handled in the future).

If you are a relatively new teacher, it will take time for you to acquire and integrate the many forms of professional knowledge that enable Barbara to teach at such a high level of sophistication. You cannot expect to reach that level quickly, but you can expect to do so eventually if you work at it persistently.

If you have not been using the Appendix all along as you read through the book, now would be a good time to do so. To solidify your learning and help you begin to adapt to your particular teaching situation, reread each chapter and then address the reflection questions and complete the application activities suggested in the corresponding section of the Appendix. If feasible, you might consider doing this in collaboration with fellow preservice teachers or inservice teacher colleagues.

For information about working with colleagues to support one another's professional development, see Good and Brophy (2008). For the detailed lesson plans and instructional resource suggestions that Barbara was working from in developing the instruction featured in this book, see Alleman and Brophy (2001a, 2002, 2003c). For detailed description and analysis of the more generic aspects of Barbara's teaching (learning community, classroom management, student motivation, and so on), see the forthcoming companion volume to this book (Brophy *et al.*, in press).

Appendix

This Appendix offers an array of tools to assist you in processing the information found in Chapters 1–15. Whether you are reading this book on your own, engaging in a school- or district-wide professional development initiative, or using it in a college class, you will need to process the information.

There are multiple ways to do this (speaking, listening, writing, mapping, drawing, charting, graphing, etc.), and many challenges involved in attempting to incorporate new practices into existing ones (or replace habits that are not effective). Our hope is that getting to know Barbara through the reading will lead you to examine your practice to find connections and disconnections with hers. Using the tools in this Appendix (or modifying them to fit your needs) should make it easier for you to self-audit, make changes, share your struggles and successes, and document your growth.

Chapter 1: Introduction

Reflective Questions

1   What are your views of social studies textbooks and teachers' manuals?
2   Typically there are few state or local mandates for social studies in the early grades. Do you view this as a problem or an opportunity? Explain.
3   Currently there is a major emphasis on literacy in the early grades. Do you view this as an advantage or disadvantage for teaching social studies? Explain.
4   What questions do you have regarding the Brophy, Alleman, and Knighton collaboration?

Activities

1   Examine several early elementary social studies textbooks and teachers' manuals. What do you notice about these materials? What questions do you have regarding their design or implementation?
2   Familiarize yourself with Volumes 1, 2, and 3 of *Social studies excursions, K–3*, published by Heinemann. What do you notice about these materials? What questions do you have regarding their design and/or implementation?
3   Reflect on your current social studies curriculum for level of powerfulness. What evidence is there that its content is based on coherent goals and big

ideas? What evidence is there that the instructional activities reflect such goals and enhance the development of big ideas? How can you assess students' abilities to apply what they have learned?

Check Out Your Practice

1 Review your lesson plans for the current social studies unit. What evidence is there that they are goal oriented with an eye toward the development of big ideas? What sections could be enhanced to make your teaching more powerful?
2 Select one of your social studies lessons for audiotaping. Listen for evidence of goals and the development of big ideas. What new information did your students acquire? How did the activity enhance their understanding of big ideas?

Chapter 2: Prior Research on Primary Social Studies

Reflective Questions

1 What has been your experience with early elementary social studies textbooks and other commercially produced instructional materials?
2 How would you prioritize the three major goals of early elementary social studies and why? (The three goals are: (1) socializing students concerning prosocial attitudes and behavior as members of the classroom community, (2) introducing them to map concepts and skills, and (3) introducing them to basic social knowledge drawn mostly from history, geography, and the social sciences.)
3 Do you agree that the difficulty level of content resides primarily in the manner and depth with which it is approached? Why, or why not?
4 What are your overall reactions to the Expanding Communities approach? Lace your response with concrete examples that illustrate your view.
5 What are your overall reactions to using cultural universals as unit topics in the early grades? Explain.
6 What surprises you about the authors' position on the teaching and learning of early elementary social studies? Explain.
7 Do you agree or disagree with Brophy, Alleman, and Knighton in their approach for addressing prior knowledge and misconceptions? Explain.
8 What do you envision as potential roadblocks for using cultural universals as your curricular emphasis?

Activity

The need for an emphasis on understanding, appreciation, and life application is underscored by the research on social studies teaching. Using a select unit that is teacher made or commercially produced along with other instructional materials such as the textbook, look for examples that promote these higher-order goals.

Check Out Your Practice

Select a lesson in your upcoming unit and tape it. Then listen to it for evidence of promoting understanding, appreciation, and life application. If the lesson is void of these robust goals, rethink your instruction, and in subsequent lessons provide enhancements accordingly. Audiotape subsequent lessons. Listen for improvement. Pay particular attention to students' responses.

Chapter 3: Generic Aspects of Our Instructional Units

Reflective Questions

1   How does the Brophy–Alleman approach compare to how you teach social studies? Where are their intersections? Major differences?
2   What do you see as the potential advantages of cultural universals? Why? Potential challenges? Why?
3   What questions do you have about the Brophy–Alleman unit development and pilot testing? If you were to engage in a similar initiative, what would you add? Delete? Approach differently? Why?
4   What have been your experiences with Socratic teaching of young children? What guiding principles do you consider when using this approach in social studies?
5   Of the seven key characteristics of Brophy and Alleman's unit development, which do you view as most compelling? Least compelling? Why?

Activity

Imagine that you are going to teach a unit on shelter. Revisit the seven key characteristics of Brophy and Alleman's unit development; the big ideas for the lessons as well as ideas presented that were associated with Socratic teaching, children's literature, etc. In pairs or triads, develop at least one robust lesson that you could teach to your peers. Enact the lesson. Be prepared to explain the whys of what you do.

Check out Your Practice

Select one of the social studies units that either you feel quite satisfied with or you know needs revising. Study it carefully, looking for the use of big ideas, the use of children's literature, opportunities for students to learn about and be able to explain human life, and opportunities for connecting what is learned to out-of-school situations. Design any needed enhancements, and when you enact the unit, be mindful of what happens. How do the students respond? How does social studies instruction become more powerful?

Chapter 4: Using Narrative to Build a Content Base

Reflective Questions

1   Imagine an observer was in your classroom to determine how your students develop social studies understandings. Describe what will be occurring.
2   Imagine you are planning one of the early lessons for your next social studies unit. How will it look? Describe one of the final lessons. Compare the two.
3   Reflect on your last social studies unit. Describe how the phenomenon of conceptual change unfolded.
4   Reflect on a recent or current social studies unit. What does it take to seriously build a content base with your students? Make sure you consider your students with special needs.
5   How can the narrative format serve the students from diverse backgrounds?
6   What aspects of your social studies curriculum are amenable to representation within narrative structures? Explain.

Activity

Bring to the session a lesson that lends itself well to the narrative format because it has a robust body of new content to be shared with the students. In small groups, present mini-lessons emphasizing the "story" and focusing on a few big ideas. What do you observe? What are the challenges associated with this approach? What are the payoffs?

Check Out Your Practice

Audiotape a lesson in your current social studies unit that needs modeling or explanations from you to provide grounding for subsequent discussion. As you listen to it, what do you notice? Do your explanations feature informed narrative (storytelling) rather than formal lecturing? Does the narrative illustrate networks of connected ideas? Substantive coherence? Continuity? Other? How and why will the content be memorable?

Chapter 5: Structuring the Curriculum around Big Ideas

Reflective Questions

1   What is your overall reaction to the importance of focusing on big ideas?
2   Which of the layers of big ideas is most challenging for you? What do you think you might do to overcome the issues associated with it?
3   Assuming that you, too, believe that teachers go through four stages in developing expertise in structuring their teaching around big ideas, what stage are you in? What evidence can you show?
4   What is your reaction to Barbara's use of big ideas as a basis for deciding which children's literature to include in a unit and for planning how to present and use the books?

5   Typically, Barbara uses four elements in lesson segments that introduce big ideas. Which one are you most comfortable with? Least comfortable with? What might you consider doing to increase your comfort level as well as your actual enactment of all four elements?

6   Barbara feels strongly about maintaining focus on big ideas without getting sidetracked. Are you equally determined to make sure the big ideas remain center stage? Why, or why not?

7   Barbara has developed several techniques for focusing students' attention on big ideas. Which of the techniques are new to you? Which will you begin incorporating into your lessons immediately?

8   Which of the techniques that Barbara has perfected for focusing students' attention on big ideas will you attempt to investigate further—and then probably incorporate into your practice?

Activity

Carefully examine one or more sections of the lesson transcripts provided in this chapter with an eye toward the development of big ideas. What specific "strategic moves" does Barbara make to keep her students focused? What are your overall reactions to her approach?

Check Out Your Practice

Take a careful look at your current social studies unit or an upcoming one. List the three levels of big ideas associated with the unit. We encourage you to make a concerted effort to consciously incorporate these big ideas throughout the unit or lessons as appropriate. Use some of Barbara's techniques to focus on the ideas. Audiotape one or more lessons. As you listen to them (in the car on the way to school, perhaps), ask yourself, "What do I notice?" "Do the lessons have more direction?" "What happens to the discourse?" "How do I feel at the end of the lesson?" "What happens for the students?"

Chapter 6: Developing Big Ideas about History

Reflective Questions

1   Why should history be taught in the early grades?

2   Which of the principles for teaching history do you find most challenging to follow? Why?

3   Do you envision using narratives in the teaching of history lessons? What advantages do they have over other pedagogical approaches? What challenges do they present?

4   Imagine yourself observing one of Barbara's history lessons. What do you think you would see? Hear? How would the students be responding? Why? What patterns will emerge? How is Barbara's approach using time-lines different from one using a textbook or other commercially prepared sources?

Activity

Revisit the transcript section of the chapter. As a group, create a profile of Barbara and her teaching. Establish the setting. Look for examples that illustrate why Barbara's students always seem to be excited about lessons associated with timelines. How does Barbara unlock the mysteries of the past with her students? What do you notice about her narrative? What does she say in order to foster empathy? Avoid presentism? Foster learner engagement? Promote memorable learning?

Check Out Your Practice

Select a lesson in your current or an upcoming social studies unit that has a history focus. Audiotape it, and as you listen to it, ask yourself: Does my narrative focus on networks of connected ideas? What do I say to avoid presentism? To foster empathy? If I use a timeline, how do I engage students in its development? How does it help students to focus on key information about the time periods? What else do I notice?

Chapter 7: Developing Big Ideas about Geography

Reflective Questions

1   How do you think about the intersection of history and geography as you plan your social studies lessons and units? Why? Provide an example to illustrate your approach.
2   What do you notice about Barbara's geography teaching? What elements of her practice would you consider expanding in your instruction?
3   From the description of Barbara's teaching, what can you infer about her approach to standards and benchmarks? What are you left wondering about?
4   What is your reaction to giving early elementary students multiple opportunities to construct maps?
5   What are your views regarding the teaching of maps and globes as a separate unit as against naturally integrating them into each unit of instruction?

Activity

Select a robust unit topic that is part of your current social studies curriculum or a cultural universal that will become a part of your enhanced curriculum. Using the Five Themes of Geography, identify at least one major understanding associated with each theme that brings specific meaning to the content. Prepare explanations of these big ideas. Design one or more activities that process or apply the information and bring the big ideas to life.

Check Out Your Practice

You will note that Barbara takes an active role in students' acquiring geographical content. Select a social studies lesson to tape that provides rich opportunities for the development of geographic content or skills. As you listen to your lesson, ask yourself, "How successful was I at incorporating meaningful geography? What should I do more of or less of the next time? What will I want to make sure I attend to in my upcoming lessons?"

Chapter 8: Developing Big Ideas about the Social Sciences

Reflective Questions

1   What is your reaction to the statement "Tendencies toward chauvinism and noticing the bizarre or exotic suggest that it is important to help students see each culture through the eyes of its own people rather than through outsiders' stereotypes"? Think of examples to illustrate your views.
2   As you reflect on the teaching of culture—the importance of avoiding chauvinism and not holding on to the exotic—think about how this connects to your decisions about using children's literature as enhancements to social studies. What should be your guiding principles when making selections and when using the resources as integral parts of lessons?
3   What is your reaction to the authors' focus on human similarities rather than differences? How might that emphasis modify your practice?
4   Where and how can cultural differences be addressed successfully?
5   Economics traditionally has been minimized in the early elementary grades. Why? What can you do to overcome this mindset in your social studies instruction?
6   Revisit the NCSS and state standards associated with economics. What new ideas do you have for bringing these to life for your students?
7   Barbara frequently builds choice into conversations about culture, economics, etc. What are ways that you can incorporate this idea into class discussions to enhance meaningfulness?
8   What is your reaction to the personalizing of government for early elementary students? After reading the section in this chapter that describes how Barbara teaches about government and civics, think of ways you might expand your curriculum and instruction to engage students in meaningful learning about these topics.

Activity

National and state standards should be viewed as tools for planning curriculum more than testing. Using standards focusing on anthropology/culture, economics, and political science/government/citizenship, along with new insights you acquired from this chapter, identify big ideas associated with each standard and powerful instructional practices you could use to foster memorable and meaningful learning.

or

Select the one social science addressed in this chapter that you think is most underdeveloped in the early grades. Brainstorm a list of goals and big ideas that could be added to the curriculum. Identify the grade level and theme for each designated level (family, neighborhoods, communities, cities, etc.) Add content and activities that promote meaningfulness relative to anthropology, economics, or political science for each of the early grades.

Check Out Your Practice

Review your current social studies unit and/or an upcoming one. Find one or more natural places to add selected big ideas associated with culture, economics, and/or government/citizenship. Design and implement the instruction and tape one or more of these new lessons. As you listen, ask yourself, "What did I notice? How did the new section enhance the unit? Will I retain this section for future enactments? If so, what modifications should I make? Why? If not, why not?"

Chapter 9: Using Instructional Resources

Reflective Questions

1   What is your overall reaction to Barbara's thinking and practices associated with her use of instructional resources? What points were raised that you simply had not considered? What are your reactions to those?
2   Given the push for integration as a way to eke out more social studies instructional time, the points the authors make about the use of books often get lost. What are your reactions to Barbara's practices? What are related issues you need to consider personally?
3   Often the use of video and other technological advances is encouraged as means of enriching social studies in the early grades. How would Barbara respond to this? Do you agree or disagree with her? Why?
4   Barbara considers charts, lists, word webs, and graphs as powerful co-constructed learning resources to be used when they match the goals. What are your experiences with these resources? What new insights have you acquired? What are you still wondering about?

Activity

Review Barbara's list of principles that underlie her development and use of co-constructed learning resources. Prioritize them in terms of your desire to discuss them (e.g., because they include elements you had not considered before, or they seem especially challenging). Lace the discussion with examples illustrating the principles.

Check Out Your Practice

We hope that as the result of reading and discussing this chapter, you have added new considerations for developing and using instructional resources and realized that you do not need to spend hours preparing or shopping for these resources. They can be far more effective when developed with your students.

In planning an upcoming social studies unit, select one (or more) of the nine principles Barbara provided and apply it as you strategically co-construct materials with your students. Pay particular attention to their level of engagement and involvement, interest, and use of the resources during review.

Chapter 10: Making Connections and Avoiding Undesired Content

1   How do you think individuals obsessed with mandated achievement tests would react to the pedagogical principles addressed in this chapter? Why?

2   How do you think middle and upper elementary teachers would react to these pedagogical principles?

3   When considering anomalies or potential misconceptions, the authors are convinced that it is essential that the big idea be established first by defining it carefully and exploring several of its protypical examples or applications, maintaining sufficient lesson coherence to sustain forward momentum without getting sidetracked. What experiences have you had that convince you of this or cause you to question it? What challenges are associated with this approach?

4   How does your philosophical stance regarding integration compare to Barbara's? Explain using examples.

5   As you know, families often are viewed by children as their most reliable informants. How do you handle students' questionable statements that obviously reflect family input? What is your overall reaction to Barbara's approach? Why?

6   What is your reaction to Barbara's unwillingness to let a wrong statement stand?

7   Barbara focuses on similarities and explains differences between cultures as understandable and rational. What challenges do you face with this approach?

8   What are the most difficult aspects of controlling students' exposure to undesired content, and how can these be overcome? Which of the tactics that Barbara uses is most challenging? Why?

9   What are your reactions to Barbara's approach to economic disparities? Taboo topics? Negative emotions? Magic words? Which of these areas do you find particularly difficult? Why?

Activity

By now you have developed images of what Barbara's social studies teaching looks and sounds like as well as her philosophical stance regarding early elementary social studies. As a class, describe and illustrate this stance, with special emphasis on making connections and avoiding undesirable content. What new insights have you acquired from Barbara? What aspects would you challenge and why?

or

Barbara provides a host of insights and strategic moves associated with making connections and avoiding undesired content: making connections, foreshadowing, tiebacks, integrating across subjects, anomalies, misconceptions, controlling students' exposure to undesirable content, economic disparities, taboo topics, negative emotions, and magic words. As a class, prioritize them in order of challenge, difficulty, or some other classification. In groups, examine the select categories by reviewing the transcripts included, discussing your past experiences and how you would handle those in the future after learning how Barbara addresses them, considerations you would entertain, and new questions that are raised for you.

Check Out Your Practice

Allocate some additional planning time for reflecting on your current social studies unit. List the strategic moves you have made to establish connections and/or avoid undesired content. What principles, if any, do you now realize you have violated? As you look ahead, what areas addressed in this chapter do you want to work on? Select from the following list:

- making connections
- foreshadowing
- tiebacks
- integrating across subjects
- anomalies
- misconceptions
- controlling students' exposure to undesirable content
- taboo topics
- negative emotions
- magic words.

Mark areas in your unit that strike you as naturals for intervention.

Chapter 11: Introducing New Knowledge Bases

Reflective Questions

1   Overall, what were the most powerful insights you acquired regarding the introduction of new knowledge bases for social studies?
2   What are your reactions to the emphasis placed on planning the physical setting for teaching social studies?
3   What are your reactions to the emphasis placed on choosing instructional resources? What new insights did you acquire that you will apply as you prepare future instructional units?
4   How does Barbara's approach for eliciting prior knowledge and introducing new content compare to yours? What aspects of her practice might you consider incorporating into your social studies teaching?
5   Making connections is emphasized in Barbara's approach to fostering memorable learning. What are your reactions to this practice? Why?
6   What are your overall reactions to the proposed guidelines for introducing and controlling vocabulary?

7   What is your reaction to the idea of planned redundancy? Explain.
8   What is your reaction to the gradual formulation principle? Why?

Activity

Select one or more transcription sections from this chapter that seem particularly compelling. Then, as a group, analyze and discuss what they entail—for example, making connections, alternative topic introductions, building on previous lessons, starting with a question, addressing strong interest first, and tailoring definitions to instructional goals. Finally, as a group, using a unit selected from Volume 1, 2, or 3 of *Social studies excursions*, develop examples of what you could do to increase your application of these very important pedagogical considerations. Use the outline shown in Table A.1 to guide your analysis.

Check Out Your Practice

Using your current social studies unit or one that you will be teaching in the very near future, complete the matrix (shown in Table A.2) provided as a means of auditing your attention to the practices put forth in this chapter.

Chapter 12: Developing Knowledge Bases through Structured Discourse

Reflective Questions

1   What is your reaction to the statement "If we want students not only to learn a new idea, but to retain it in a form that makes it accessible for subsequent application, we should make sure that their initial exposure to the idea is relatively complete and accurate and that they soon experience several repetitions that will help establish the idea firmly in their minds and model some of its application"? If you agree with it, find places in your current plans where you attend to this. If you challenge this idea, what are your concerns?
2   What do you see as the major challenges associated with overlapping?
3   Barbara works within the context of a limited and focused content base, uses lots of planned redundancy, and infuses many additional learning and memory supports as she develops content with her students and at the same time meets her district's social studies standards as well as those proposed by the state. Does that surprise you? Why, or why not? What questions would you like to ask her about this?
4   There is always a tension between making accommodations for struggling learners and at the same time insuring that the more academically able remain "minds on" throughout the discourse. How does Barbara address this challenge, and what are your reactions? What other strategies have you used or observed others using to address this matter?
5   Modeling interior dialogue is one of Barbara's notable strengths, but one that many teachers find difficult to master. What can you do to incorporate more of it into your practice?

Table A.1 Outline for recording enhancements to a social studies excursions unit

Planning and Teaching Strategies	Examples of What I Do	Enhancements I Can Make
Building on previous lessons		
Starting with a question		
Addressing strong interests first		
Introducing and controlling vocabulary		
Deciding which terms and distinctions to teach		
Tailoring definitions to instructional goals		
Enriching understanding		
Planned redundancy		
Other vocabulary teaching techniques		
Dropping in definitions and explanations on the fly		

Table A.2 Outline for recording enhancements to one of my own units

Planning and Teaching Strategies	Examples of What I Do	Enhancements I Can Make
Adapting and elaborating lesson plans		
Choosing physical settings		
Choosing instructional resources		
Developing skills		
Starting by eliciting "I wonders"		
Establishing the initial content base		
Starting with the prototypical		
Building on prior knowledge		
Making connections		
Alternative topic introductions		

6   Barbara is very planful in how she gradually moves from transmission to construction. What are your reactions to this approach, and how does it map on to how you teach?

Activity

Multiple considerations for developing knowledge bases through structured discourse are illustrated by transcriptions in this chapter. These include (a) establishing prototype images to anchor networks of content, (b) reviewing earlier lessons to set up the current one, (c) modeling of interior dialogue, (d) scaffolding students' thinking and information processing, (e) shifting from presenting to eliciting information, (f) reverting from eliciting to presenting, and (g) opening to student questions and comments. Select one or more of these considerations and study an appropriate transcription. What do you notice? How does it align with your current practice? What accommodations do you need to make in your practice?

Check Out Your Practice

Select one or more lessons to tape. Then, as you listen to the discourse, use colored pens (one color for transmission and another for construction) to create a graphic that depicts your patterns. What did you learn? (This strategy takes time, but it can serve you well as you develop even better practice.)

Note: The shift from transmission to construction is gradual and creates reverberations among multiple variables. There are, however, four basic instructional moves involved in accomplishing this sequence: establishing an initial content base, initiating a shift from transmission to construction, reverting back to more transmission if this shift does not go well (there may be several repetitions of these second and third stages, although at successively higher levels of sophistication), and, finally, sustaining teaching in a primarily construction mode.

Chapter 13: Using Questions to Develop Content with the Whole Class

Reflective Questions

1   What did you learn or have reaffirmed for you as you read about Barbara's use of questioning in developing the content base with the whole class?
2   What is your reaction to Barbara's use of planned redundancy? What specific challenges do you associate with this strategic move?
3   What is your reaction to the statement "There is no standard sequence or formula for allocating particular questions types—for example, closed versus open or fact versus explanation questions. Instead, the point is to use questions in ways that help students to learn content networks with understanding, appreciation, and application to life out of school"?
4   Picture in your head Barbara's strategies for socializing students' attention and participation. How does your approach mirror or differ from hers? What will you do to extend or enrich your approach?

5   Some might regard Barbara's position on accountability as a bit strict or rigid. What is your reaction to her stance?
6   Minds-on learning is vitally important. What strategies does Barbara use during her questioning to insure that the whole class is "with her"? Would these strategies be effective with your class? Why, or why not?
7   What is your response to the tension associated with balancing whole-class and individual-student agendas when using questions to develop content?
8   How closely do the glitches you experience when using questions to develop content parallel Barbara's? Do you typically handle those glitches in similar ways? Explain.

Activity

Review the list of considerations Barbara addresses as she plans and enacts lessons that emphasize structured discourse. Select one or more that you think would be most challenging to implement in your practice. Discuss ways of shifting to make this one of your strengths.

or

Select one or more of the transcription sections found in this chapter. Create a mental image of what is happening. Reflect on the interaction. Cite similar examples from your practice. What are the challenges associated with becoming more anticipatory? What questions would you pose to Barbara as the result of reflecting on the transcription(s)?

Check Out Your Practice

Audiotape a social studies lesson that will be using questions to develop content with the whole class. Use the matrix shown in Table A.3 to examine your current practices associated with questioning. Prepare ways of making revisions and/or enhancements in future lessons.

Chapter 14: Scaffolding for Individual Students within Whole-Class Lessons

Reflective Questions

1   What comes to mind when you read the title of this chapter?
2   What do you view as the most challenging aspects of scaffolding for individual students during whole-class lessons? Why?
3   What are your reactions to Barbara's approach that calls for minimizing responses to student questions and comments and generally retaining tight control over lesson flow during "my turn" segments of lessons, but welcoming questions and comments at other times?
4   How effective do you think you are in capturing teachable moments during your social studies instruction? Explain.
5   What does Barbara's use of student questions to formulate teachable moments tell you about her practice?

Table A.3 Outline for recording enhancements to my current questioning practices

Student Responses	Strategic Moves I Make	✓ if satisfactory. If revision would be more effective, what do you propose to do next time?
• Students begin to fidget		
• Students need to become more personally involved with a topic		
• When students seem not to be paying attention		
• When students automatically think the answer is either yes or no		
• When students immediately raise their hands and want either to blurt out an answer or to tell a story		
• When an individual student is having trouble generating a response		
• When students wave their arms, exclaim "I know," etc.		
• When an individual student is confused		
• When most of the students are unable to produce an adequate response to an initial question		
• When a particular student has a personal connection with the content under discussion		
• When most of the students give an undesired response to a question		
• When only a few students respond to a cue for a specific response		
• When a student's response introduces an anomaly that you want to avoid or suggests that the development of a big idea has been ambiguous or misleading		
• When students repeatedly answer both correctly and incorrectly		
• When the students are confused by the question		
• When only one or two students seem confused by the question		
• When many students are making responses that are either incorrect or valid but undesired in the situation		
• When students are unable to respond because the question is too difficult		

Activity

Bring to class a collection of teaching experiences you have had that relate to scaffolding for individual students within whole-class lessons. Discuss what you would consider doing differently as a result of reading this chapter. Imagine that Barbara was there to chat with you. What might she say? Why?

Check Out Your Practice

Audiotape one of your social studies lessons that involves the whole class. As you replay the tape, focus on issues associated with scaffolding for individual students within whole-class lessons. Use the self-auditing tool shown in Table A.4 to judge your level of effectiveness.

This chapter provides a host of considerations associated with scaffolding for individual students within whole-class discussions. Select from the following list which one you want to focus on:

- scaffolding to elicit improved responses
- responding to students' helpful questions and comments
- exploiting teachable moments
- responding to students' unhelpful questions and comments
- stopping and regrouping.

Converse with another teacher about its usefulness and what you can do to embrace it more fully within your practice.

Chapter 15: Activities and Assessments

Reflective Questions

1   This chapter offered many insights about instructional activities for students in the early grades. What was a real "aha" for you?
2   Which of the guiding principles for selecting or implementing social studies instructional activities do you think is most challenging? Why?
3   What is your reaction to Barbara's approach of spending more time in teacher-led whole-class lessons and activities than most other primary teachers?
4   Picture in your head the pair-share activities in Barbara's classroom. What unique features would these have?
5   Picture in your head Barbara's approach to review activities. What unique features would these activities have?
6   If you were to observe Barbara teach, what sorts of writing activities would you expect to see? What guiding principles would she be using for making the decisions?
7   Home assignments are a feature of Barbara's social studies units. What do you think parents' responses to these assignments would be? Why?
8   In Barbara's classroom, activities and assessments are inseparable. Do you view that as a good or bad thing? Explain.

Table A.4 Outline for recording enhancements to my scaffolding for individual students within whole-class lessons

Scaffolding to Elicit Improved Responses

Steps to follow:	Your Examples	What I Will Attempt to Do Next Time
Following an initial failure to respond or incorrect response, provide scaffolding to elicit a better response.		
If an acceptable response is not given, scaffold one more time.		
If an acceptable response is not given, provide an answer and explanation, then move on.		

Students' Questions and Comments

Steps to follow:	Your Examples	What I Will Attempt to Modify Next Time
Students answer your questions.		
Students answer questions and inject their own thinking.		
Accepting student questions that relate directly to the aspect of the topics being developed at the time.		
Minimizing responses to student questions that are off topic.		

Students' Questions and Comments

Teachable moments: (made available whenever a student says something that is relevant to the topic but outside of the teacher's planned agenda)	Your Examples	What I Will Attempt to Do Next Time
Triggered by questions and comments that convey misconceptions.		
Articulate unusual perspectives on the topic.		
Provide opportunities to make useful connections.		

Stopping and Regrouping

Reasons I Need to Stop and Regroup	Your Examples	Plan for Next Time
Students fail to connect the ideas expressed within a piece of literature being used to provide content.		
Students are stimulated to ask questions by extraneous details presented in the illustrations.		
Students are not tracking your questions and instead are thinking about a previous lesson—or simply are confused.		

Activity

Select a two to three-lesson sequence from one of the three volumes of *Social studies excursions*. Pay close attention to the goals and big ideas. In small groups, create mind movies that describe the range of learning tasks, activities, and assignments that Barbara likely would use to foster learning, practice, and assessment.

Check Out Your Practice

Identify an upcoming social studies unit that needs better learning activity/ assessment components. Using the matrix shown in Table A.5, expand the range of learning activities and assignments to foster practice and assessment.

Table A.5 Planning Guide for Expanding Learning Activities

| Unit Title | _____ |
| Unit Goals | _____ |

Activities	Learning Activities and Assessments I Will Implement
Whole-class learning	
Pair-share	
Review	
Ticket-out	
Writing	
Home assignments	
Sponge	
Unique (given unit content)	

Keep a journal documenting how students react to the activity enhancements. How do these enhancements inform your practice? How does this shift address accountability? How has it affected your assessment concerns?

Co-Constructed Portfolio/Journal

We hope that as a result of reading *Inside the social studies classroom*, you will develop a deepened understanding and appreciation for powerful social studies teaching as exemplified by Barbara. Because of the "up close" approach and the inclusion of fine-grained analysis, it is our intent that you will become personally connected to the content, carefully examine where you are in your development as a social studies teacher, and chart your course for expanding your practice using the principles and insights shared in this text (see Table A6).

Table A.6 Outline for summarizing results of portfolio/journal assessments of my own teaching*

Facets of Powerful Teaching	Principles of Good Teaching	Barbara's Thoughts and Techniques	My Current Thoughts/Practices	My Plans for the Future
Chapter 1: Introduction				
Chapter 2: Prior Research on Primary Social Studies				
Chapter 3: Generic Aspects of Our Instructional Units				
Chapter 4: Using Narrative to Build a Content Base				
Chapter 5: Structuring the Curriculum around Big Ideas				
Chapter 6: Developing Big Ideas about History				
Chapter 7: Developing Big Ideas about Geography				
Chapter 8: Developing Big Ideas about the Social Sciences				
Chapter 9: Using Instructional Resources				
Chapter 10: Making Connections and Avoiding Undesired Content				
Chapter 11: Introducing New Knowledge Bases				
Chapter 12: Developing Knowledge Bases through Structured Discourse				
Chapter 13: Using Questions to Develop Content with the Whole Class				
Chapter 14: Scaffolding for Individual Students within Whole-Class Lessons				
Chapter 15: Activities and Assessments				

* One page per chapter.
Note: We encourage you to co-construct this journey using a portfolio/journal to document what you learn from Barbara, what you currently do, and what changes you will enact in the future. Adding evidentiary materials (student work, classroom photos, unit ideas, supportive articles, etc.) can result in a personalized and growth producing social studies experience.

References

Alleman, J., & Brophy, J. (1992). Analysis of activities in a social studies curriculum. In J. Brophy (Ed.), *Advances in research on teaching. Volume 3, Planning and managing learning tasks and activities* (pp. 47–80). Greenwich, CT: JAI Press.

Alleman, J., & Brophy, J. (1993). Is curriculum integration a boon or a threat to social studies? *Social Education*, 57, 287–291.

Alleman, J., & Brophy, J. (1994a). Taking advantage of out-of-school opportunities for meaningful social studies learning. *Social Studies*, 85, 262–267.

Alleman, J., & Brophy, J. (1994b). Trade-offs embedded in the literary approach to early elementary social studies. *Social Studies and the Young Learner*, 6(3), 6–8.

Alleman, J., & Brophy, J. (1998a). Assessment in a social constructivist classroom. *Social Education*, 62(1), 32–34.

Alleman, J., & Brophy, J. (1998b). Strategic learning opportunities during out-of-school hours. *Social Studies and the Young Learner*, 10(4), 10–13.

Alleman, J., & Brophy, J. (1999a). Current trends and practices in social studies assessment in the early grades. *Social Studies and the Young Learner*, 11(4), 15–17.

Alleman, J., & Brophy, J. (1999b). The changing nature and purposes of assessment in the social studies classroom. *Social Education*, 65, 334–337.

Alleman, J., & Brophy, J. (2000). On the menu: The growth of self-efficacy. *Social Studies and the Young Learner*, 12(3), 15–19.

Alleman, J., & Brophy, J. (2001a). Assessment in the early grades. *Social Studies and the Young Learner*, 14(1), 13–19.

Alleman, J., & Brophy, J. (2001b). *Social studies excursions, K–3. Book 1, Powerful units on food, clothing, and shelter*. Portsmouth, NH: Heinemann.

Alleman, J., & Brophy, J. (2002). *Social studies excursions, K–3. Book 2, Powerful units on communication, transportation, and family living*. Portsmouth, NH: Heinemann.

Alleman, J., & Brophy, J. (2003a). Comparing transportation units published in 1931 and 2002: What have we learned? *Journal of Curriculum and Supervision*, 19, 5–28.

Alleman, J., & Brophy, J. (2003b). History is alive: Teaching young children about changes over time. *The Social Studies*, 94, 107–110.

Alleman, J., & Brophy, J. (2003c). *Social studies excursions, K–3. Book 3, Powerful units on childhood, money, and government*. Portsmouth, NH: Heinemann.

Alleman, J., & Brophy, J. (2004). Building a learning community and studying childhood. *Social Studies and the Young Learner*, 17(2), 16–18.

Alleman, J., & Brophy, J. (2006). Introducing children to democratic government. *Social Studies and the Young Learner*, 19(1), 17–19.

Alleman, J., Brophy, J., & O'Mahony, C. (1999). Renewing social studies: Standards in context. In J. Block, S. Everson, & T. Guskey (Eds.), *School improvement programs* (pp. 337–354). Dubuque, IA: Kendall-Hunt.

Alleman, J., Brophy, J., & Knighton, B. (2003). Co-constructing classroom resources. *Social Studies and the Young Learner*, 16(2), 5–8.

Alleman, J., Knighton, B., & Brophy, J. (2007). Incorporating all children using community and cultural universals as the centerpiece. *Journal of Learning Disabilities*, 40, 166–173.

Alter, G. (1995). Transforming elementary social studies: The emergence of a curriculum focused on diverse, caring communities. *Theory and Research in Social Education*, 23, 355–374.

Barrett, M. (2005). Children's understanding of, and feelings about, countries and national groups. In M. Barrett & E. Buchanan-Barrow (Eds.), *Children's understanding of society* (pp. 251–285). Hove, England: Psychology Press.

Barton, K. & Levstik, L. (2004). *Teaching history for the common good*. Mahwah, NJ: Erlbaum.

Beck, I., & McKeown, M. (1988). Toward meaningful accounts in history texts for young learners. *Educational Researcher*, 17(6), 31–39.

Beck, I., McKeown, M., & Gromoll, E. (1989). Learning from social studies texts. *Cognition and Instruction*, 6, 99–158.

Berti, A., & Bombi, A. (1988). *The child's construction of economics*. Cambridge: Cambridge University Press.

Boehm, R., & Petersen, J. (1994). An elaboration of the fundamental themes in geography. *Social Education*, 58, 211–218.

Booth, M. (1993). Students' historical thinking and the national history curriculum in England. *Theory and Research in Social Education*, 21, 105–127.

Bransford, J., Brown, A., & Cocking, R. (Eds.) (1999). *How people learn: Brain, mind, experience, and school*. Washington, DC: National Academy Press.

Brophy, J. (1992). The de facto national curriculum in U.S. elementary social studies: Critique of a representative example. *Journal of Curriculum Studies*, 24, 401–447.

Brophy, J. (2002). Discussion. In J. Brophy (Ed.), *Social constructivist teaching: Affordances and constraints* (pp. 333–358). Boston: Elsevier.

Brophy, J. (2004) *Motivating students to learn* (2nd ed.). Mahwah, NJ: Erlbaum.

Brophy, J., & Alleman, J. (1991). Activities as instructional tools: A framework for analysis and evaluation. *Educational Researcher*, 20(4), 9–23.

Brophy, J., & Alleman, J. (1992). Planning and managing learning activities: Basic principles. In J. Brophy (Ed.), *Advances in research on teaching*. Volume 3, *Planning and managing learning tasks and activities* (pp. 1–45). Greenwich, CT: JAI Press.

Brophy, J., & Alleman, J. (1993). Elementary social studies should be driven by major social education goals. *Social Education*, 57, 27–32.

Brophy, J., & Alleman, J. (1996). *Powerful social studies for elementary students*. Fort Worth, TX: Harcourt Brace.

Brophy, J., & Alleman, J. (1998). Classroom management in a social studies learning community. *Social Education*, 62(1), 56–58.

Brophy, J., & Alleman, J. (2006). *Children's thinking about cultural universals*. Mahwah, NJ: Erlbaum.

Brophy, J., & Alleman, J. (2007). *Powerful social studies for elementary students* (2nd edn), Belmont, CA: Thomson Wadsworth.

Brophy, J., & VanSledright, B. (1997) *Teaching and learning history in elementary schools*. New York: Teachers College Press.

Brophy, J., McMahon, S., & Prawat, R. (1991a). Elementary social studies series: Critique of a representative example by six experts. *Social Education*, 55, 155–160.

Brophy, J., Prawat, R., & McMahon, S. (1991b). Social education professors and elementary teachers: Two purviews on elementary social studies. *Theory and Research in Social Education*, 19, 173–188.

Brophy, J., Alleman, J., & O'Mahony, C. (2000). Elementary school social studies: Yesterday, today, and tomorrow. In T. Good (Ed.), *American education: Yesterday, today, and tomorrow*. Ninety-ninth Yearbook of the National Society for the Study of Education, Part II (pp. 256–312). Chicago: University of Chicago Press.

Brophy, J., Alleman, J., & Knighton, B. (in press). *Inside the primary-grade classroom*. New York: Routledge.

Bruner, J. (1990). *Acts of meaning*. Cambridge, MA: Harvard University Press.

Cobb, P., Perlewitz, M., & Underwood-Gregg, D. (1998). Individual construction, mathematical acculturation, and the classroom community. In M. Larochelle, N. Bednarz, & J. Garrison (Eds.), *Construction and education* (pp. 63–80). New York: Cambridge University Press.

Core Knowledge Foundation (1999). *The Core Knowledge sequence*. Charlottesville, VA: Core Knowledge Foundation. www.coreknowledge.org.

Crabtree, C. (1989). History is for children. *American Educator*, 13(4), 34–39.

Cuban, L. (1991). History of teaching in social studies. In J. Shaver (Ed.), *Handbook of research on social studies teaching and learning* (pp. 197–209). New York: Macmillan.

Cutting, B., & Cutting, J. (1996). *The map book*. Bothell, WA: The Wright Group.

Davis, O. L., Jr., Yeager, E., & Foster, S. (Eds.) (2001). *Historical empathy and perspective taking in the social studies*. New York: Rowman & Littlefield.

dePaola, T. (1973). *Charlie needs a cloak*. New York: Simon & Schuster.

Dewey, J. (1902). *The child and the curriculum*. Chicago: University of Chicago Press.

Dewey, J. (1938). *Experience and education*. New York: Collier Books.

DiSalvo-Ryan, D. (1991). *Uncle Willie and the soup kitchen*. New York: Demco Media.

Downey, M., & Levstik, L. (1991) Teaching and learning history. In J. Shaver (Ed.), *Handbook of research on social studies teaching and learning* (pp. 400–410). New York: Macmillan.

Duke, N., & Bennett-Armistead, S. (2003). *Reading and writing informational text in the primary grades: Research-based practices*. New York: Scholastic.

Egan, K. (1988). *Primary understanding: Education in early childhood*. New York: Routledge.

Egan, K. (1990). *Romantic understanding: The development of rationality and imagination, ages 8–15*. New York: Routledge.

Englert, C., and Dunsmore, K. (2002). A diversity of teaching and learning paths: teaching writing in situated activity. In J. Brophy (Ed.), *Social constructivist teaching: Affordances and constraints* (pp. 81–130). Boston: Elsevier.

Evans, R., & Saxe, D. (Eds.) (1996). *Handbook on teaching social issues*. Washington, DC: National Council for the Social Studies.

Fair, J. (1977). Skills in thinking. In D. Kurfman (Ed.), *Developing decision-making skills*. Forty-seventh NCSS Yearbook (pp. 29–68). Arlington, VA: National Council for the Social Studies.

Ferretti, R., MacArthur, C., & Okolo, C. (2001). Teaching for historical understanding in inclusive classrooms. *Learning Disability Quarterly*, 24, 59–71.

Fertig, G. (2005). Teaching elementary students how to interpret the past. *Social Studies*, 96, 2–8.

Gardner, H., & Boix Mansilla, V. (1994). Teaching for understanding—within and across the disciplines. *Educational Leadership*, 51(5), 14–18.

Geography Education National Implementation Project (GENIP/NGS). (1986). *Maps, the landscape, and the fundamental themes in geography*. Washington, DC: National Geographic Society.

Geography Education National Implementation Project (GENIP/NGS). (1987). *K–6 geography: Themes, key ideas, and learning opportunities*. Washington, DC: Author.

Girod, M., & Wong, D. (2002). An aesthetic (Deweyan) perspective on science learning: Case studies of three fourth graders. *Elementary School Journal*, 102, 199–224.

Good, T., & Brophy, J. (1995). *Contemporary educational psychology*. White Plains, NY: Longman.

Good, T., & Brophy, J. (2008). *Looking in classrooms* (10th ed.). Boston: Allyn and Bacon.

Goodlad, J. (1984). *A place called school*. New York: McGraw-Hill.

Harms, J., & Lettow, L. (1994). Criteria for selecting picture books with historical settings. *Social Education*, 58, 152–154.

Hinitz, B. (1992). *Teaching social studies to the young child: A research and resource guide*. Boston: Garland.

Hirsch, E. D., Jr. (1987). *Cultural literacy: What every American needs to know*. Boston: Houghton Mifflin.

Hoberman, M. (1978). *A house is a house for me*. New York: Viking Press.

Houser, N. (1995). Social studies on the back burner: Views from the field. *Theory and Research in Social Education*, 23, 147–168.

Howard, R. (2003). The shrinking of social studies. *Social Education*, 67, 285–288.

Joint Committee on Geographic Education (1984). *Guidelines for geographic education: Elementary and secondary schools*. Washington, DC: Association of American Geographers and the National Council for Geographic Education.

Kennedy, M. (2005). *Inside teaching: Classroom conditions that frustrate reform*. Cambridge, MA: Harvard University Press.

Kliebard, H. (2004). *The struggle for the American curriculum, 1893–1958* (3rd Ed.). New York: Routledge.

Knight, P. (1993). *Primary geography, primary history*. London: David Fulton.

Kounin, J. (1970). *Discipline and group management in classrooms*. New York: Holt, Rinehart & Winston.

Lamme, L. (1994). Stories from our past: Making history come alive for children. *Social Education*, 58, 159–164.

Larkins, G., Hawkins, M., & Gilmore, A. (1987). Trivial and noninformative content of elementary social studies: A review of primary texts in four series. *Theory and Research in Social Education*, 15, 299–311.

Leming, J. (1989). The two cultures of social education. *Social Education*, 53, 404–408.

Levstik, L. (1986). The relationship between historical response and narrative in the classroom. *Theory and Research in Social Education*, 14, 1–15.

Levstik, L. (1993). Building a sense of history in a first-grade classroom. In J. Brophy (Ed.), *Advances in research on teaching: Case studies of teaching and learning in social studies* (Vol. 4, pp. 1–31). Greenwich, CT: JAI Press.

Levstik, L., & Barton, K. (2005). *Doing history: Investigating with children in elementary and middle schools* (3rd ed.). Mahwah, NJ: Erlbaum.

Levstik, L., & Pappas, C. (1992). New directions for studying historical understanding. *Theory and Research in Social Education*, 20, 369–385.

Libbee, M., & Stoltman, J. (1988). Geography within the social studies curriculum. In S. Natoli (Ed.), *Strengthening geography in the social studies*. Bulletin No. 81 (pp. 22–41). Washington, DC: National Council for the Social Studies.

London, T. (1992). *Froggy gets dressed*. New York: Viking.

Ludwig, G., Backler, A., Bednarz, S., *et al.* (1991). *Directions in geography: A guide for teachers*. Washington, DC: National Geographic Society.

Marker, G. & Mehlinger, H. (1992). Social studies. In P. Jackson (Ed.), *Handbook of research on curriculum* (pp. 830–851). New York: Macmillan.

Marzollo, J. (1998). *How kids grow*. St. Paul, MN: Cartwheel Books (Scholastic).

Morin, K., & Bernheim, R. (2005). Who can be a hero? Helen Keller, Annie Sullivan, and discovering strength of character. *Social Studies and the Young Learner*, 17(4), pp. 17–30.

National Council for the Social Studies (NCSS) (1990). *Social studies curriculum planning resources*. Dubuque, IA: Kendall/Hunt.

National Council for the Social Studies (NCSS) (1993). A vision of powerful teaching and learning in the social studies: Building social understanding and civic efficacy. *Social Education*, 57, 213–223.

National Council for the Social Studies (1994). *Expectations of excellence: Curriculum standards for social studies*. Washington, DC: NCSS.

Newmann, F. (1990). Qualities of thoughtful social studies classes: An empirical profile. *Journal of Curriculum Studies*, 22, 253–275.

Newmann, F. (1997). Authentic assessment in social studies: Standards and examples. In G. Phye (Ed.), *Handbook of classroom assessment* (pp. 359–80). San Diego, CA: Academic Press.

Nuthall, G. (2002). Social constructivist teaching and the shaping of students' knowledge and thinking. In J. Brophy (Ed.), *Social constructivist teaching: Affordances and constraints* (pp. 43–79). Boston: Elsevier.

O'Connor, M. & Michaels, S. (1996) Shifting participant frameworks: Orchestrating thinking practices in group discussion. In D. Hicks (Ed.), *Discourse, learning and schooling* (pp. 63–103). New York: Cambridge University Press.

Ogle, D. (1986). K-W-L: A teaching model that develops active reading of expository text. *Reading Teacher*, 39, 564–570.

Okolo, C., Ferretti, R., & MacArthur, C. (2002). Westward expansion in the ten-year old mind: Teaching for historical understanding in a diverse classroom. In J. Brophy (Ed.), *Social constructivist teaching: Affordances and constraints* (pp. 299–331). Boston: Elsevier.

Onosko, J. (1990). Comparing teachers' instruction to promote students' thinking. *Journal of Curriculum Studies*, 22, 443–461.

Palmer, J. (1994). *Geography in the early years*. New York: Routledge.

Parker, W. (1991). *Renewing the social studies curriculum*. Alexandria, VA: Association for Supervision and Curriculum Development.

Pascopella, A. (2005). Staying alive: Social studies in elementary schools. *Social Studies and the Young Learner*, 17(3), 30–32.

Petersen, J., Natoli, S., & Boehm, R. (1994). The guidelines for geographic education: A 10-year retrospective. *Social Education*, 58, 206–210.

Priceman, M. (1994) *How to make an apple pie and see the world*. New York: Alfred P. Knopf.

Pugh, K. (2002). Teaching for transformative experiences in science: An investigation of the effectiveness of two instructional elements. *Teachers College Record*, 104, 1101–1137.

Ravitch, D. (1987). Tot sociology or what happened to history in the grade schools. *American Scholar*, 56, 343–353.

Roth, K. (1996). Making learners and concepts central: A conceptual change approach to learner-centered, fifth-grade American history planning and teaching. In J. Brophy (Ed.), *Advances in research on teaching*. Volume 6, *Teaching and learning history* (pp. 115–182). Greenwich, CT: JAI Press.

Roth, K. (2002). Talking to understand science. In J. Brophy (Ed.), *Social constructivist teaching: Affordances and constraints* (pp. 197–262). Boston: Elsevier.

Schaffer, H. (1996). Joint involvement episodes as context for development. In H. Daniels (Ed.), *An introduction to Vygotsky* (pp. 251–280). New York: Routledge.

Scoffham, S. (1998). Young geographers. In R. Carter (Ed.), Handbook of primary geography (pp. 19–28). Sheffield, England: Geographical Association.

Shaver, J. (1987). What should be taught in social studies? In V. Richardson-Koehler (Ed.), Educators' handbook: A research perspective (pp. 112–138). New York: Longman.

Smith, J., & Girod, M. (2003). John Dewey and psychologizing the subject-matter: Big ideas, ambitious teaching, and teacher education. Teaching and Teacher Education, 19, 295–307.

Spiro, R., Collins, B., Thota, J., & Feltovich, P. (2003). Cognitive flexibility theory: Hypermedia for complex learning, adaptive knowledge application, and experience acceleration. Educational Technology, 43, 5–10.

Stanley, W. (1985). Recent research in the foundations of social education: 1976–1983. In W. Stanley (Ed.), Review of research in social studies education, 1976–1983 (pp. 309–399). Washington, DC: National Council for the Social Studies.

Stevenson, R. (1990). Engagement and cognitive challenge in thoughtful social studies classes: A study of student perspectives. Journal of Curriculum Studies, 22, 329–341.

Stodolsky, S. (1988). The subject matters: Classroom activity in math and social studies. Chicago: University of Chicago Press.

Stoltman, J. (1990). Geography education for citizenship. Bloomington, IN: ERIC Clearinghouse for Social Studies/Social Science Education. ED 322 081.

Stone, C. (1998). The metaphor of scaffolding: Its utility for the field of learning disabilities. Journal of Learning Disabilities, 31, 344–364.

Sunal, C., & Haas, M. (1993). Social studies and the elementary/middle school student. Fort Worth, TX: Harcourt Brace Jovanovich.

Thornton, S. (1991). Teacher as curricular-instructional gatekeeper in social studies. In J. Shaver (Ed.), Handbook of research on social studies teaching and learning (pp. 237–248). New York: Macmillan.

Thornton, S. (2005). Teaching social studies that matters: Curriculum for active teaching. New York: Teachers College Press.

Thornton, S., & Vukelich, R. (1988). Effects of children's understanding of time concepts on historical understanding. Theory and Research in Social Education, 16, 69–82.

Thornton, S., & Wenger, N. (1990). Geography curriculum and instruction in three fourth-grade classrooms. Elementary School Journal, 90, 515–531.

VanFossen, P. (2005). "Reading and math take so much of the time . . .": An overview of social studies instruction in elementary classrooms in Indiana. Theory and Research in Social Education, 33, 376–403.

Varelas, M., Luster, B., & Wenzel, S. (1999). Making meaning in a community of learners: Struggles and possibilities in an urban science class. Research in Science Education, 29(2), 227–245.

Waters, K. (1989). Sarah Morton's day: A day in the life of a Pilgrim girl. New York: Scholastic.

Westcott, N. (1992). Peanut butter and jelly: A play rhyme. New York: Penguin.

White, J. (1993). Teaching for understanding in a third-grade geography lesson. In J. Brophy (Ed.), Advances in research on teaching: Case studies of teaching and learning in social studies (Vol. 4, pp. 33–69). Greenwich, CT: JAI Press.

Wiegand, P. (1993). Children and primary geography. New York: Cassell.

Wiggins, A. (1989a). A true test: Toward more authentic and equitable achievement. Phi Delta Kappan, 70, 203–213.

Wiggins, A. (1989b). Assessing student performance: Exploring the purpose and limits of testing. San Francisco: Jossey-Bass.

Willig, J. (1990). *Children's concepts and the primary curriculum*. London: Paul Chapman.

Woodward, A. (1987). Textbooks: Less than meets the eye. *Journal of Curriculum Studies*, 19, 511–526.

Zhao, Y., & Hoge, J. (2005). What elementary students and teachers say about social studies. *Social Studies*, 96, 216–221.

Index